ST. THOMAS AND INDIA

ST. THOMAS AND INDIA
RECENT RESEARCH

EDITED BY

K.S. MATHEW

JOSEPH CHACKO CHENNATTUSERRY, CMI

ANTONY BUNGALOWPARAMBIL, CMI

FORTRESS PRESS

MINNEAPOLIS

ST. THOMAS AND INDIA
Recent Research

Cover image: The Incredulity of Saint Thomas 1601–1602 by Caravaggio; Wikimedia Commons

Cover design: Tory Herman

Paperback ISBN: 978-1-5064-6136-6

eBook ISBN: 978-1-5064-6137-3

CONTENTS

About the Editors   vii

Preface   ix

1. Introduction   1
   K.S. Mathew

2. Historiography of the Apostolate of St. Thomas in India:
   A Critical Review   35
   Francis Thonippara, CMI

3. Mission of St. Thomas the Apostle in India:
   Archaeological, Epigraphic, and Numismatic Evidences   55
   James Kurikilamkatt, MST

4. Significance and Role of Tradition in the Historiography
   on St. Thomas Christians   69
   Benedict Vadakkekara, OFM Cap

5. St. Thomas Traditions in Ancient Christian Folk Songs   89
   Byju Mathew Mukalel

6. Thomistic Apostolate and Knanaya Community   115
   Mathew Kochadampallil

7. Acts of Thomas versus Ramban Pattu   131
   Thomas Koonammakkal

8. The Tradition of Seven Churches   149
   James Puliurumpil

9. Patristic Evidence on the Apostolate of St. Thomas with
    Special Reference to St. Ephrem   161

    Johns Abraham Konat

10. Guidelines for Rebuilding Missions of Apostle Thomas
    and a Reassessment of Acts of Thomas   175

    Pierre C. Perrier

11. Historical, Apocryphal, and Theological Sources from
    the Armenian Church about Apostle Thomas and India 225

    Maxime K. Yevadian

    Index   271

ABOUT THE EDITORS

K.S. Mathew obtained his MPhil and PhD degrees and a post-graduate diploma in Portuguese language from the Jawaharlal Nehru University, New Delhi. He has served as professor and head of the department of history at the Hyderabad Central University, and Pondicherry Central Universities respectively. He had also been a visiting professor/fellow at University of Wisconsin (USA), University of Bordeau (France), University of Ottawa (Canada), Heidelberg University (Germany), and was honored as an Eminent Professor in History by the UGC. His tenure as a member of the UGC panel for history and archaeology for two terms; as a member of the Indian Council of Historical Research, Ministry of Human Resources Development for one term, and as a member of the Kerala Council of Historical Research has shaped his approach towards education and research. He has successfully guided and supervised nineteen candidates for doctoral degrees in history and has published and edited twenty-six books of international standard. He is the founding director of the Institute for Research in Social Sciences and Humanities.

Joseph Chacko Chennattuserry, CMI had completed his post-graduate degree in history, followed by a MEd and a PhD. His research areas include maritime history, Indo-Portuguese history, and organizational culture and work values. His publications are in the field of organizational culture and work values; traditional and indigenous shipbuilding practices, and navigation in the sixteenth century Malabar Coast; Chinese maritime relations with the Malabar Coast; and a historical understanding of St. Kuriakose Elias Chavara: a Christian humanist. He served as the principal of Christ Junior College, Bengaluru for ten years. At present, he is working as a professor in the department of international studies and history, and director of student affairs, CHRIST (Deemed to be University), Bengaluru. He took leadership in the restoration of the St. Kuriakose Elias Chavara Archives and Research Centre from 2014 to 2017.

Antony Bungalowparambil, CMI is serving at present as the director of the St. Kuriakose Elias Chavara Archives and Research Centre, Mannanam. He has taken the initiative to make the resources of the archives accessible to researchers and academicians. His knowledge of Syriac language has facilitated his motivation for research, conservation, and preservation of the Syriac documents in a systematic way. Fr. Antony has post-graduate degrees in Syriac and English. He translated the book *Holy Qurbana: a Pictorial Journey*. He is also engaged in teaching the Syriac language in schools and seminaries.

PREFACE

Encroachment upon and unfounded statements on areas not falling within one's own field of expertise have become the order of the day, attracting the attention of gullible readers who are easily liable to be carried away by controversies and novelties. People backed by their own preconceived ideas, hidden agendas, and bias come out in print and electronic media with utterances of random and scathing attacks on certain historical facts supported by evidences of diverse nature and create confusion in the minds of the public.

One such topic is the apostolic heritage of the St. Thomas Christians of India. Therefore, the authorities of the recently established St. Kuriakose Elias Chavara Archives and Research Centre at Mannanam, Kerala took the initiative to delve deeper into the details of the heritage of the St. Thomas Christians of Kerala by organizing an international seminar, wherein the scholars from various educational institutions in India, France, Italy, and Portugal were invited to share the output of their research with themselves and the public.

The Kuriakose Elias Chavara Research Centre, Christ (Deemed to be University), Bangalore, St. Joseph's Monastery, Mannanam, and the Association of the Catholic Historians of India (ACHI) joined hands in realizing the long-cherished plan. The authorities of Chavara Kuriakose Elias Higher Secondary School, Mannanam came out with open arms to provide the required wherewithal to make it a memorable event. Thirty-seven research papers related to various aspects of the heritage of the St. Thomas Christians were presented by the scholars from far and wide.

Taking into account the ongoing wayward discussions on the apostolate of St. Thomas in India and the urgency to apprise the readers of the source-based and well-documented studies conducted by the scholars all over the world, it was decided to make a selection of the papers dealing exclusively with the arrival and activities of St. Thomas in India.

The editorial committee referred the shortlisted papers to experts in the respective fields and obtained their comments for publications. This explains the background of the publication of the eleven articles in the book in your hands. Attempts are afoot to bring out the entire proceedings of the seminar. Your valuable suggestions and comments shall be highly appreciated.

K.S. Mathew
Joseph Chacko Chennattuserry, CMI
Antony Bungalowparambil, CMI
(For the editorial committee)

1

INTRODUCTION

K.S. Mathew

Jesus Christ during His public ministry chose St. Thomas, known also as Judas Thomas, to be one among the twelve apostles who were commissioned to preach his Good News, as mentioned by the evangelists St. Mathew,[1] St. Mark,[2] and St. Luke.[3] St. Mark, the evangelist, clearly mentions that they were given the title as apostles by Jesus. According to the narratives of St. Mark and St. Luke, this appointment took place on a mountain to which he called them. This means that this was an important matter, as many other serious events during the public ministry of Jesus took place on mountains.

When Jesus came down from the mountain, in training the newly appointed apostles in their mission, he gave them an example by preaching to the multitude of people hailing from Judea, Jerusalem, and the coast of Tyre and Sidon.[4] Further, he took them along with him when he preached in public and worked miracles.

On sending the apostles charged with the mission, Jesus Christ restricted their activities first to the lost sheep of the house of Israel keeping them away from the gentiles (non-Jewish people) and Samaritans as mentioned by St. Matthew, the evangelist.[5] The mission entrusted to the twelve apostles consisted in proclaiming that the kingdom of heaven has come near. The work of curing the sick, raising the dead, cleansing the lepers, and casting out demons without any remuneration was enjoined upon them.[6] We learn from the Gospel of St. Matthew that the mission given to them was the same for which Jesus was sent. For, when the messengers of St. John, the Baptist asked Jesus about his identity and mission, he told them very succinctly that the works done by him such as the restoring of sight to the blind, giving the ability to walk to the lame, cleansing of the lepers, giving the power of hearing to the deaf, raising of the dead, and proclamation of the good news bore testimony to his identity.[7] The

1

Apostles were asked to do their services *gratis* since they received the power to do these works free of charge.[8] They were, however, allowed to accept hospitality from the people of the town or village where in they worked.[9]

The apostles themselves worked among the sick and the possessed as they were sent by Jesus. As and when they encountered difficulties in their activities, they turned to Jesus for solutions and necessary instructions. When St. Peter started walking on the water as suggested by Jesus, he was about to sink. Then Jesus came to his help and rebuked him for the lack of faith in Jesus who asked him to do it.[10] We see the apostles seeking clarification from Jesus when they failed in their attempt to exorcise a possessed person. Jesus told the apostles that only with deep faith and prayer demons could be driven away.[11]

The works of Jesus witnessed by the apostles prompted them to continue the mission entrusted to them with great enthusiasm. St. Thomas, being convinced of the divinity and other aspects of the life and activities of Jesus Christ, exhorted his colleagues to go and die with him.[12] This shows the intensity of the commitment of St. Thomas to the mission of Jesus.

After his resurrection, Jesus appeared to his apostles and disciples several times with a view to confirming them in faith in him. St. John, the evangelist gives a lively report about the apparition of Jesus to the disciples and adds that "Thomas (who was called the twin), one of the twelve was not with them when Jesus came."[13] St. Thomas stated that he would insist on a personal experience of the resurrected Jesus rather than believing the report of his colleagues. Jesus condescended to pay heed to his demand and appeared after a week to the group of disciples in which Thomas too was present. He asked Thomas to have close experience of his resurrected person that St. Thomas did and declared with full conviction of his belief in the risen Jesus.[14]

Again when St. Thomas, the twin gathered with St Simon Peter, Nathanael of Cana in Galilee, the sons of Zebedee and two others from among the disciples of Jesus by the sea of Tiberias, he got another opportunity to meet the risen Lord and experience his divine power, which also enabled the apostles to have a miraculous catch of fish from Tiberius against all the odds of the time. He further witnessed Jesus handing over to St. Peter the supreme authority of shepherding his flock.[15]

The mission entrusted to the apostles, as we have seen above, initially was restricted to the lost sheep of the house of Israel. This lasted only till his death and it was further extended to embrace the entire world, even to the ends of the earth, only after the resurrection of Jesus. At the time of his ascension to Heaven, Jesus directed his eleven Apostles including St. Thomas to a mountain (Mount Olivet near Jerusalem) where they all gathered together. Having appeared to them, he instructed them to preach the Good News to all nations beginning with Jerusalem[16] and further on to Judea and Samaria[17] and even to the ends of the earth.[18] But they were asked to stay in the city (Jerusalem) until they received the power from the Holy Spirit promised by the Eternal Father.[19] After receiving the instruction from Jesus at the Mount Olivet, they returned to Jerusalem and all of them including St. Thomas spent the time in prayer in the company of Blessed Virgin Mary and a few brothers and sisters.[20]

The Holy Spirit, promised by Jesus as well as His Father descended upon them on the day of Pentecost.[21] Having received the power, St. Peter, who was given authority to shepherd the flock, addressed the crowd gathered on the day of Pentecost and converted a number of Israelites to faith in Jesus Christ and baptized 3000 of them.[22] Peter took the lead in healing the sick too.[23] After making arrangements for dispensing charity and looking after affairs other than preaching the good news, the apostles concentrated on proclaiming the good news.[24] It is reasonably assumed that St. Thomas, one among the apostles, preached the Good News initially in Jerusalem. Gradually, the apostles extended their activities to non-Israelites (gentiles).[25] St. Peter took the lead after having a vision in Joppa and baptized a large number of them to the great dissatisfaction of the Jews.[26]

With the widening of the mission, the apostles left for various places to preach the Good News beyond Jerusalem. Chosen by Jesus as one among the twelve apostles, trained by Jesus during the period of the public life of his Master, empowered through the apparition of the resurrected Jesus and finally inspired by the promised Holy Spirit on the day of Pentecost, St. Thomas, known to the world of the Edessan tradition as Judas Thomas, commenced his mission entrusted by Jesus and preached the good news in India.

Here it seems opportune to say a word about the nomenclature. The name "Thomas" pointing to one of the apostles is derived from the Aramaic term "toma" meaning twin. The Greek writers transcribed it as Thomas and translated as Didymos. The ancient Christian texts of the Church of Edessa called the twin apostle as Judas Thomas. The Gospel according to St. John refers three times to the name "Thomas" followed by the Greek term Didymos.[27] Both Aramaic and Hebrew texts use the term "Thomas" as an epithet indicating "twin", not a personal name.[28] It is further held that the Church of Edessa always considered Judas as the personal name of the apostle while the term "Thomas" or Didymos was only an epithet. St. John, the evangelist, while reporting the conversation of Jesus with his apostles on the way to his Father makes mention of a

3

query put forward by Thomas regarding the way to the place Jesus was going to. Here the evangelist uses the epithet "Thomas."[29] Later, when Jesus was giving the promise of sending the Holy Spirit upon the apostles, one of them by name Judas asked him why Jesus was revealing himself to them and not to the world. Here, St. John the evangelist distinguishes this apostle from Judas Iscariot.[30] This would mean that there were more persons than one among the apostles with the personal name Judas; one was Judas Thomas (twin or Didymos) and the other Judas Iscariot and the third was Judas, the son of James.[31]

A few of the scholars raise doubt about the identity of India where St. Thomas preached the Good News. This prompts us to add a few words about India and its inter-continental relations in the past. The subcontinent of India was known to the West for centuries together before the birth of Jesus Christ. Homer (born c. 750 B.C.E.), the legendary author of the *Iliad* and the *Odyssey*, two epic poems, the central works of ancient Greek literature, makes mention of India in his works.[32] Herodotus (484–424 B.C.E.), a Greek writer, known as the father of History refers to the conquest of parts of India by Darius I (55–486 B.C.E.), the fourth king of the Persian Achaemenid Empire.[33]

Alexander III of Macedonia known as Alexander, the Great (356–323 B.C.E.) founded the port town of Alexandria in 331 B.C.E. and laid the foundation for maritime contacts between the port of Alexandria and India. Later in 326 B.C.E., he invaded India and defeated the former Achaemenid satrapy of Gandhara, including the city of Taxila. He advanced further into Punjab. The Battle of the Hydaspes river against a regional Indian King, Porus, is considered by many as the costliest battle fought by Alexander and his armies. Subsequently, his army refused to cross the Beas River, fearful of the powerful Nanda Empire that lay to the East along the banks of the Ganges. Therefore, Alexander turned to the South, advancing through southern Punjab and Sindh, along the way conquering more tribes on the lower Indus River, before returning to the West.[34] Alexander died in Babylonia in 323. In 321 B.C., two years after Alexander's death, Chandragupta Maurya of Magadha founded the Maurya Empire in India.

Megasthenes (350–290 B.C.E.), the Greek historian and ambassador of Seleukos I Nikator (358–281), the ruler of Seleukid Empire to the Mauryan Empire, collected a lot of details on India during his sojourn for several years at Pataliputra, the capital of the Mauryans and brought out his famous work *Indika*. This served as an authoritative and exhaustive source of knowledge about India for the Greeks especially during the period when contact with India was totally interrupted on account of the defeat of the Greek Seleukid king by the Parthians, nomadic tribes from

Northeast Iran in 248 B.C.E.. The Parthian rulers (248 B.C.E.–226 A.D.) obstructed the trans-Asiatic traffic via land route.

Later, Alexandria became the seat of the Ptolemaic Kingdom, and quickly grew to be one of the greatest cities of the Hellenistic world. Ptolemy I, Soter, one of the body guards of Alexander the Great founded the Ptolemaic dynasty in 305 B.C.E. and it lasted till the death of Cleopatra VII and the Roman conquest of Egypt in 30 B.C.E.[35] Commercial relations with India that remained rather weak during the Ptolemaic period of Egypt became stronger. The most remarkable and visible effect of *Pax Romana*[36] was the spurt in external trade especially with India.[37] Octavian, later known as Augustus (27 B.C.E.–14 C.E.), the first Emperor of the Roman Empire promoted trade with India. It was reported by Strabo[38] that during the reign of Augustus as the Roman Emperor, up to 120 ships set sail every year from the Egyptian ports of the Red sea regions to India.[39] The constant contacts of the merchants from the Roman Empire with India, prompted the well-known Roman poet Quintus Horatius Flaccus (65 to 27 B.C.E.), known to the English as Horace, to write that the "diligent merchant with a view to fleeing from poverty travels through sea to remote India."[40] Pliny the Elder (c. 23–79 C.E.) qualifies Muziris on the Malabar coast situated in the vicinity of Cranganore, the haven of the Roman merchants with the epithet *"primum emporium Indiae"* (premier emporium of India). He writes:

> They sail with the wind Hippalus in forty days to the first emporium of India, Muziris. Besides, the station for ships is at a great distance from the shore and cargoes have to be landed and shipped to little boats. There reigned there, when I wrote this, Calabotras.[41]

The Greco-Roman merchants started their voyage to India from Alexandria in Egypt that was one of the four or five largest cities in the Roman Empire. It housed the body of Alexander the Great embalmed in honey inside a transparent glass sarcophagus. It was connected with Muziris on coastal Malabar through a long-distance international trade route.

Small Egyptian boats known as *feluccas* hoisted with two lateen sails carried cargo, crew, and passengers from Alexandria through the Nile with the help of north winds to the Nile port of Koptos. The traffic from Koptos was arranged with the help of caravans moving through the desert to Berenike, on the Red Sea coast, about 380 kilometers to the southeast of Koptos. Often the caravan consisted of twenty-two or so camels and the distance from Koptos to Berenike was covered in twelve days.[42]

This port town of Berenike was established in 275 B.C.E. Spices brought from the East to Berenike were carried to Coptos on Nile by caravans and from there to Alexandria. It turned out to be the principal point of communication between Europe and India. Among the unexpected discoveries at Berenike were a range of ancient Indian goods, including a large quantity of teak wood, black pepper, coconuts, beads made of precious and semi-precious stones, cameo blanks, a Tamil Brahmi graffito, etc. A holding of 7.55 kgs of black pepper corns was stored in one of the containers devoid of wooden lid, suggesting widespread use of pepper in the city throughout the early to late Roman periods as well as the shipment of pepper to the Roman Empire through Berenike.[43] There were several forts (*praesidia*) manned by soldiers along the route providing accommodation for a few dozens of people.[44] These forts were designed to control the desert routes and their precious water supplies. The passengers travelling with their goods through the desert with the help of camels after reaching Berenike, situated on the coast of the Red Sea, had to look for ships bound for Qana in southern Arabia, a peninsula jetting out into the Indian Ocean, since there was no non-stop sailing between Egypt and India during the period of the Romans.[45]

Besides Berenike, Myos Hormos, north of Berenike, a Red Sea port constructed by the Ptolemies around the third century B.C.E. also served as an important port from where ships left for India. This port according to the findings from the excavations conducted by David Peacock and Lucy Blue of the University of Southampton, was located on the present-day site of Quseir al-Quadim, eight kms north of the modern town of Al-Qusayr in Egypt. A large number of ships bound to India during the time of Emperor Augustus is reported to have left for India according to Strabo.[46]

There were a few stops along the African coast in between Berenike and Qana. The first of the stops was at Ptolemaic Epitheron, the next Adulis, the major Red Sea port of the kingdom of Axum[47] and Ocelis.[48]

There were two harbors at Qana. Ships plying the routes between India and Berenike, between Qana and the Persian Gulf and between Indian Ocean coast of Africa and southern India touched Qana from where valuable products like frankincense could be obtained. The consignments were unloaded from the vessels coming from Berenike and re-loaded on the vessel proceeding to Muziris or Broach (Barygaza), a great port town on coastal Gujarat described as a great center of trade by the anonymous author of *Periplus of Eritrean Sea* (written probably in 60 C.E.) or Muziris on the Malabar coast. The voyage from Qana to Muziris took forty days.[49] Vessels bound for Puduke (Pondicherry, precisely Areekamedu on the bank of Aryankuppam River on the Bay of Bengal) proceeded around Taprobane.[50]

Evidently the propulsion of the ships to and from India in those days was done by harnessing the force of winds, especially seasonal and intercontinental ones known as monsoons, namely southwest monsoon and northeast monsoon. The writer of the *Periplus of the Eritrean Sea* credited Hippalus, a Greek navigator and merchant who probably lived in the first century B.C.E. with discovering the direct route from the Red Sea to India over the Indian Ocean by plotting the scheme of the sea and the correct location of the trade ports along the Indian coast. Pliny the Elder (23–79 C.E.), the author of *Historia Naturalis*, claimed that Hippalus, discovered not the route but the monsoon wind also called *Hippalus* (the south-west monsoon) wind. This trade route allowed sailing vessels to run before the wind from the mouth of the Arabian Sea to the southern ports of India during the summer, and return with the winter monsoon during the first century. His stature as a skillful navigator is associated with the riches of this discovery brought to Rome and the western world at the time.

It was to this India, connected with the Mediterranean regions chiefly through water ways and known all over the world for years together before the birth of Jesus Christ, that St. Thomas the apostle planned to reach and preach the Good News as commanded by his Master. As mentioned elsewhere in this study, the Parthian rulers (284 B.C.E.–A.D. 226) blocked the trans-Asiatic traffic via land route from Jerusalem and the Mediterranean world especially Alexandria to India and so the passage was chiefly and most probably through the sea route alone during this period. This helps us emphasize the maritime passage from the Mediterranean ports to India whether north-western or south-western coast. So, St. Thomas at the command from Jesus Christ to preach the Good News even to the ends of the Earth had to opt for the sea route to India commencing from Alexandria that was frequented by merchants trading between Broach and Muziris on the western coast of India on one side and Alexandria on the other.

Alexandria had another attraction for St. Thomas. Besides being a great center of knowledge, it was also home to the largest Jewish community in the ancient world. The *Septuagint*, a Greek translation of the Hebrew Bible (the *Torah* and other writings), was produced here. Jews occupied two of the city's five quarters and worshipped at synagogues. In view of the practice followed by the apostles right from the beginning, he would get an opportunity to preach the Good News to the Jews first and then proceed to India through the sea route traversed by the Greco-Roman merchants.

Reiterating and reconfirming the basic fact that history is reconstructed by making use of various sources or historical facts, a number of historians have proved indubitably that St. Thomas preached the Good News to people of India and brought them to Christian faith in the first century C.E., much before the developed countries of the West received it. They reaffirmed that Christianity is an Asian religion originated in Asia and spread to various parts of Europe and the wider world. Their arguments rest on a number of historical evidences.

We do not have any historical documents of the first century C.E. regarding the Indian apostolate of St. Thomas. The absence of contemporary sources is compensated by a host of other evidences in the light of which historians can fill up the gap as they are reasonably entitled to. Right from the beginning of the twentieth century, a few historians based on archaeological and near-contemporary literary sources, numismatic as well as epigraphic evidences proved that St. Thomas the apostle started his mission first in the north-western parts of India currently falling in the political region of Pakistan and secondly in South India.

APOSTOLATE OF SAINT THOMAS IN NORTHWEST OF ANCIENT INDIA

There are a few literary and archaeological sources that help us throw considerable light on the apostolate of St. Thomas in the Northwestern India that now falls in Pakistan. Recent research fix the period of the visit to and activities of St. Thomas in the kingdom of Gondaphares, the Indo-Parthian king with his headquarters at Taxila between 44 and 45 C.E. before the invasion of Kushans.[51] J.N. Farquhar is of the opinion that St. Thomas reached Taxila probably around 48 or 49 C.E.[52]

Literary sources

Acts of Thomas

The most widely known literary source used by scholars writing on the apostolate of St. Thomas in India and especially South India is *Acts of Thomas,*[53] known also as the *Acts of Judas Thomas (AJT)*. The contents of this work can be compared with those in the other four ancient *Acts* viz, those of Paul, John, Peter, and Andrew. According to the opinion of most of the scholars, it was originally written in Syriac language in the third century C.E. and the complete version is found in Greek and Syriac. Recent research place its origin in the period between 225/230 and 250 C.E. written in Syriac in a Syriac milieu at Edessa, a city in Northern Mesopotamia well before the origin of Manichaeism.[54] The researchers on *AJT* have come to the conclusion that *AJT* in its original form was written as a manual of instructions for visitors to the shrine of St. Thomas in Edessa. It is further held that the remains of the apostle were taken to Edessa from India by a Jewish Christian of Edessa during the third

8

century C.E. in a wooden case.[55] St. Ephrem (347–420 C.E.) the famous historian and theologian writing from Edessa attests clearly that the body of the apostle was taken from India to Edessa. The *Acts of Judas Thomas* in its present form consists of 12 acts related to the apostolic activities of St. Thomas in Barukacha, Taxila, and South India starting with the assignment of different countries to different apostles and ending with his martyrdom in south India.

Apostolate of St. Thomas in North India was brought to the notice of the public in 1905 by Adolf E. Medlycott, Anglo-Indian Catholic Bishop of Trichur (1887–1896) who derived his conclusion from the apocryphal work, *Acts of Judas Thomas,* and the coins of Gudnaphar discovered from Kabul, Kandahar, Seistan, and Western and Southern Punjab since 1834.[56] This opinion was shared by Joseph Dahlmann.[57] The name of King Gondophares appears in the Syriac text of *AJT* as *Gudnaphar* while in the Greek version as *Goundaforos.* Archaeological, numismatic, and epigraphic evidences have identified Gondophares as the king of Northwestern part of ancient India now in the political segment known as Pakistan. He was an Indo-Parthian ruler with an Iranian name having his capital at Taxila during the period from 21 to 51 C.E. Taxila at that time had an international fame being the seat of the Buddhist University and Jain centers of learning. Different international trade routes met at Taxila. Well-travelled caravan routes connected Taxila with the central Asiatic markets from Kashagar to Kandahar. It was further linked to Mathura and Pataliputra by the grand route first noticed by Megasthenes. A network of roads connected Pataliputra with cities like Savvatthi, Kosambi, Champa, Tamralipti, Varanasi, Mathura, and Vidisha. Another important route connected Mathura with Ujjain. The great royal highway connecting Taxila and Pataliputra, two great centers of trade and civilization in India had a branch to Barygaza from Mathura via Ujjain. The anonymous author of *Periplus* makes mention of the sea route connecting these regions.[58]

Alphonse Mingana (1878–1937), of the John Rylands Library argued that "the main Christian penetration of India seems to have been by sea towards the west and north-west, and it is that side of Indian Christianity that withstood in later generations the many vicissitudes which, from the tenth century downwards, have completely destroyed its less fortunate sister Church in the North."[59]

J.N. Farquhar,[60] in his lecture delivered in the John Rylands Library, University of Manchester in October 1925, speaks of the *Acts of Judas Thomas*, qualified by him as a clear piece of fiction. But, in the light of other corroborative evidences he sifted the historical facts found in the *Acts of Judas Thomas* and affirmed the North Indian apostolate of St. Thomas. In other words, he rightly used the literary work as an auxiliary source for the reconstruction of history. He indicates the route from Alexandria to Taxila most probably taken by St. Thomas. The passage from Alexandria though the Nile to Koptos took eleven days and from there by land route to Myos Hormos for seven days. The voyage by sea from Myos Hormos in early May ends at Okelis, the last part on the eastern side of the Red Sea early June. After a few days' sailing, the vessel would come out of the Gulf of Aden exposing the passengers to the seasonal wind from southwest (Southwest Monsoon) in those days. By the middle of July, the vessel would reach Pattala (Thatta) at the mouth of the Indus River in modern Pakistan. The passage from there continues by suitable boats through the Indus River for about 1300 miles to Attock, where the railway to Peshawar crosses the Indus. The next leg of the passage to the southeast for some forty miles would end in Taxila about the middle of August.[61]

In other words, the names of the places found in *AJT* were corroborated by the archaeological evidences. In the recent past, scholarly investigation has been conducted in the history of the arrival of St. Thomas in Northwest India making use of the Acts *of Judas Thomas*, the coins bearing the legend of Gundaphares, and the lithic (stone) inscription discovered in Takht-i-Bahi against the backdrop of the history of ancient India. Historical importance of *Acts of Judas Thomas* is brought out by using archaeological, numismatic, and epigraphic evidences.

Archaeological evidences

Archaeological excavations were conducted by Hergrew from 1912 to 1930 in Sirkap, which is known in history as Taxila, situated 36 kms away from Rawalpindi in Pakistan under the supervision of Sir John Marshall. Mortimer Wheeler and his colleagues excavated further parts of Taxila in 1944 and 1945. The findings brought out a lot of information confirming the fact that it was the headquarters of the Indo-Parthian king Gundaphares during his reign from 21 to 51 C.E.. The name of the king is found in *AJT*.[62] Taxila was known to the wider world as the city of India. Internal evidences in the text of *AJT* also show that Taxila must have been the city meant by the author.[63] "There are many circumstantial internal and external evidences in the *AJT* itself to assume that the author had Taxila in his mind when he wrote about the kingdom of Gudnaphar. The apostle met the king in the royal palace, which according to the *AJT* was well inside the city walls."[64] J.N. Farquhar who visited the archaeological site of Taxila gives a vivid narration of the place.[65]

Numismatic evidences

It was reported by General Alexander Cunningham in 1854 that in the preceding twenty-five years no less than thirty thousand coins bearing

Greek and Indian legends had been found in Afghanistan and Punjab.[66] A portion of the horde belonged to the reign of Scythian conquerors and of Parthian kings like those of Gondophares who had become masters of these territories.[67]

The name of Gundaphares found in the *AJT as* a historical person who ruled from Taxila has been clearly and convincingly proved by the study of the coins discovered from Punjab, which further confirms the historical nature of *AJT*. Coins bearing the name of Gondophares from the Kabul Province in 1834 were discovered by Charles Masson alias James Lewis (1800–1853). The inscription on one side of the coin was in Greek and in *Karoshti* on the other side. *Karoshti* was the form of writing in the Northwest India. This could be Prakrit, the ancient form of Sanskrit or something having its origin from Aramaic. The name of the king in Greek on the obverses of the coins appears as Gondophares, Gondaphares, and Undophares, The legend on the reverse side in *Karoshti* script gives the name as Gudaphara, Gadaphara, or Gudaphana.[68]

More coins were found in successive years from Kabul, Kandahar, Seistan, and Western and Southern Punjab. The coins are preserved in different museums and libraries like the British Museum, Bibliotheque National de Paris, Berlin Museum, Lahore Museum, and National Museum, Kolkata. Some of these coins besides his name bear the names of his family members too. The scientific analysis revealed that these coins were minted in the first half of the first century C.E. at the behest of the then ruler Gondophares. They can be dated to the period between 10 and 40 C.E. The discovery makes it clear that Gondaphares was the ruler of the area and references to him in the *AJT* renders its historical value stronger.[69]

M. Reinaud for the first time in 1848 drew the attention of the scholars to the connection between the coins of Gondophares and *AJT*.[70] This discovery proves the historicity of Gondophares and his family members. Medlycottt supports the North Indian Apostolate of St. Thomas. The king Gondophares of the *AJT* could be none other than the Gondophares of the Indian coins. So, there is nothing legendary and mythical in the story of the *AJT* as far as the name of the king is concerned, argues Kurikilamkattt.[71]

Epigraphic evidences

Takht-i-Bahi inscription

A piece of stone with inscriptions was discovered at Takht-i-Bahi village a little northeast of Peshawar in 1864/1872 by H.W. Bellow. It was kept in Lahore museum. Cunningham who studied the inscription gave the following reading. "In the twenty-sixth year of the great king Guduphara, in the *samvat* year three and one hundred (repeated in figures 100+3 = 103)) in the month of *Vaisakh,* on the fourth day for his own religious interest and the religious merit of his mother and father."[72] Those who made serious studies on the inscription agree that the twenty-sixth year of the reign of Gondophares and the 103rd year of the *Samvat* is one and the same and 103rd year of Samvat is 46 C.E., which was the twenty-sixth year of the reign of Gondophares. This calculation helps us conclude that Gondaphares became the king in 21 C.E. After examining the comments of General Cunningham, Dowson, M. Senart, member of the Institut de France, Rapson and Vincent A. Smith on the inscription, Medlycott concludes that the Takht-i-Bahi inscription is of 46 C.E. and the beginning of the reign of Gondophares falls in 21 C.E.[73] Medlycott concludes: "We maintain there is every reason to conclude that the apostle Thomas had entered King Gondophares' dominion in the course of his apostolic career."[74] According to the recent studies on the North Indian Apostolate of St. Thomas, the apostle Thomas visited the kingdom of Gondophares sometime around 44–45 C.E. and the King died in 51 C.E.[75] The Kushan dynasty, the famous ruler of which was Kanishka began to rule the area held under the sway of Gondaphares from 51 C.E.[76]

Udaipur temple inscription

There is an inscription in one of the Udaipur temples in the Madhya Pradesh now in the catholic diocese of Sagar. Scientific analysis of the inscription on the wall of the temple placed the date of original church in Udaipur as 78 C.E. that would prove the existence of a Christian community there by 78 C.E.[77] The origin of the community is traced back to the preaching of St. Thomas in India.

Other material evidences for the North Indian Apostolate of St. Thomas

Taxila Cross

A cross was discovered in 1935 from the ancient city of Sirkap where the palace of the King Gondaphares once stood. This provides evidence for the presence of Christianity at the archaeological site in ancient times. Farquhar using the data collected from the excavations conducted in ancient Taxila under the supervision of Sir John Marshall affirmed in 1926 that there is some reason to believe that the apostle Thomas sailed from Alexandria with Habban, the merchant of King Gudnaphar, to the Indus and reached the king's Indian capital, Taxila probably A.D. 48 or 49.[78]

Ancient Christian communities in Tatta and Islamabad

i) Christian communities in Tatta

Remnants of Christian communities are found in Tatta and its environs in Sind in Pakistan as proved by Kurikilamkattt. Some Fakirs both in northern and southern parts of Sind with their headquarters at Tatta claim to be the followers of St. Thomas, *Thum Bhagat i.e.,* of Thomas the Saint. They are reported to be practicing Christian rites and claim to possess a book that they call Gospel of Matthew.[79] The investigations conducted by Rev. A. Trotter, suggest that they call themselves *Bar Thoma.*

ii) Descendants of the converts of St. Thomas near Taxila

Attempting to establish the fact that there are descendants of the converts of St. Thomas, in Northwest India, Kurikilamkattt, refers to a village near Taxila in the district of Islamabad, which is called *Gar Thoma.* Some Christians and Muslims in this village are devotees of St. Thomas.[80]

Christianity in Barygaza

The Syriac version of *AJT* makes mention of Sandruck Mahosa as the port of disembarkation of St. Thomas who left Alexandria for India while the Greek version names it Andrapolis. Based on a serious study on *AJT* and the details provided in the anonymous work of *Periplus of the Erithrean Sea,* a scholar asserts that it was Barygaza on the Gujarat coast where the apostle disembarked.[81] He contends that the Andrapolis meant the city of Andhra, Barygaza being the royal city and port of the Andhra dynasty of the Satkarni kings. The term Satkarni, according to him, must have been the root from where the expression Sandruck or Sandruck Mahosa comes. *Periplus,* moreover, makes mention of only Barygaza where girls of Jewish origin were brought to the kings as gifts. *AJT* refers to the Jewish girl dancing at the banquet organized by the king. The Andhra dynasty came to an end in 225 C.E. around which the *AJT* was composed. Therefore, the author of *AJT* must have this city of the Satkarni kings in mind while he wrote of Sandruck or Andrapolis.[82] Barygaza is situated at the banks of Narbada from where there was accessibility by sea to the river Indus and then to Taxila. There was also a land route connecting Barygaza with the capital of Gondophares. The great royal highway connecting Taxila and Pataliputra (modern Patna) situated on the banks of the river Ganges had a branch stretching from Mathura via Ujjain to Barygaza located on the banks of the river Narbada.

St. Thomas on his arrival at Barygaza established contacts with the king as mentioned in Act I of the *AJT.* He met a Jewish flute-girl entertaining the guests at the residence of the local ruler who organized a grand party in connection with the wedding of his only daughter. The cupbearer of the king smote the apostle on his cheek probably since he did not take part in the banquet and remained unaffected by, and indifferent to, the celebrations. A lion rent the cupbearer and tore him limb from limb when he went out to fetch water. His right hand was dragged off by a black dog as pronounced by the apostle while he was smitten. The news about the miraculous event spread to many people. Convinced of the divine power in the apostle, the flute-girl, the newlywed couple, the royal household, and a few people accepted the apostle as the envoy of Christ though the *AJT* does not give any indication about direct conversion to Christianity. However, it can be reasonably assumed that the apostle commissioned to preach the Good News took the first opportunity on entering into the Barygaza, the gateway to India, to bring a few people in Barygaza to Christ, his master. Therefore recent researchers identify the few Christians found in Barygaza by Jordanus of Severac in 1321 as the followers of those converted to Christianity by St. Thomas, the apostle.[83]

George Nedungatt, while dealing with the mission of St. Thomas in Northwest India, says that there are a number of coincidences that compel one to accept the mission of St. Thomas to Taxila or the kingdom of Gondophares. The reign of the King Gondophares corresponded precisely to the period of the post-Pentecostal mission of the apostles so that the visit of St. Thomas to the king clicks into place chronologically. Besides, according to the tradition in vogue in Kerala, St. Thomas landed in Kodungalloor (Muziris) in 52 C.E., a year after the death of Gondophares in 51 C.E. This chronological sequence could not have been invented by any fake tradition. Further, this period coincides with the invasion of Kushans causing wide-spread devastation that must have compelled St. Thomas to move out. Finally, the Council of Jerusalem (Acts 15:6,22) took place about 50 C.E. in which all the apostles participated. According to the tradition, St. Thomas too was present at the council.[84] Thus, Nedungatt is in full agreement with the opinion about the North Indian mission of St. Thomas.

Benedict Vadakkekkara furnishes a host of quotations supporting the North Indian mission of St. Thomas based on the *AJT*, coins bearing the names of Gondophares, Gad, his brother and successor, and the Takht-i-Bahi inscription.[85] He seems to endorse the opinion about the North Indian apostolate of St. Thomas and says that the *AJT* makes it clear that St. Thomas moved from there to the South probably after the death of Gundaphares. He makes reference to the apocryphal work, *De Transitu Mariae*, a very ancient Christian writing, where it is mentioned that Apostle Thomas from his mission at Taxila was summoned to be present at the bedside of Blessed Virgin in her last moments.[86] He concludes:

"Hence the acceptance of a mission of Apostle Thomas to Northwest India, instead of undermining in any way the tradition of the Indian Christians, actually endorses it."[87]

Benedict Vadakkekara writes:

> Until recent times, it was objected that the name of the King Gondaphares could not be Indian, and that it was urged that no historian had ever spoken of a king of that name. In fact, up to the middle of the nineteenth century, the name was to be found nowhere outside the legend. Thus, the discovery of coins minted in Gondopharnes's name provides further credibility to at least some of the circumstances in the *Acta Thomae*.[88]

St. Thomas is said to have directed his attention to Gondopharnes's kingdom on account of the Jewish presence there.[89] Jewish influence was so great there that even a special script originated in those districts, denominated *Karoshti* script, which is derived from the Hebrew script. The script was officially used during the whole of the first century C.E. The coins of the Greek, Scythian, and Parthian kings bear inscriptions in Greek and *Karoshti* scripts, the language of the later inscriptions being nevertheless in Sanskrit.

George Mark Moraes based on *AJT*, epigraphic and numismatic evidences deal with the mission of St. Thomas in Punjab, the region under Gondophares. He goes to the extent of establishing the possibility of the conversion of the king to Christianity. But he says that the port of disembarkation namely, Sandaruk—Andranopolis cannot be identified.[90] Similarly, T.K. Joseph, who devoted fifty years of his life for the investigation of the history of the St. Thomas Christians while decrying his mission to Malabar and the South, supports strongly the north Indian apostolate of St. Thomas. A.M. Mundadan cursorily states: "In support of the early Christianization of North India, we do not have any actual vestiges as we do for South India."[91]

Kurikilamkattt concludes: "All these elements enable us to establish the mission of the apostle Thomas in North India as an event that has tangible historical results in the country. So now the *AJT* can also be considered a book having a historical nucleus, a fact that really adds weight to our findings. The *AJT* is historical in the sense that it was composed during a certain period and in a historical place and had based its story on historical places, persons and events."[92] Finally it is concluded that the "North Indian tradition about the mission of Thomas in India is both valid and historical."

The Kushans started attacking the king of Gondophares somewhere near 50 C.E. though the exact date is not available to the students of history. But it is clear from inscriptions that Gondaphares was reigning the kingdom in 45 C.E. and that the Kushan rulers were supreme in this region in 64 C.E.[93] So, it is assumed that St. Thomas left the kingdom of Gondophares ca. 50 C.E. and took part in the synod of Jerusalem held in 50 C.E.[94]

APOSTOLATE OF ST. THOMAS IN SOUTH INDIA

A short discussion on the relation between the Mediterranean world and the Malabar coast before the Christian or Common era is considered to be an appropriate step to set the backdrop for the study of the apostolate of St. Thomas in South India.

Muziris on the Malabar coast was closely connected to the Mediterranean regions especially through Alexandria. This became all the more important after the annexation of Egypt to the Roman Empire in 30 B.C.E. consequent upon the battle of Actium on September 2, 31 B.C.E. The ongoing trade in spices available on the western coast of India was augmented by leaps and bounds. The fact that Roman merchants used to come to India for trade fleeing the poverty they experienced in their land even before the Christian era was acknowledged by a well-known Roman poet, Quintus Horatius Flaccus (65 B.C.E.–27 B.C.E.) as seen above. Barbaricum (Barbarikon, a port near Karachi) and Barygaza (Broach) on the northwestern coast of India and Naura, Tyndis, Muziris, Nelcynda, and Becare on the Malabar coast were some of the ports with which the merchants from the Roman Empire had vibrant commercial relations.

As Pliny the Elder (c. 23–79 C.E.) qualifies, Muziris was the premier emporium of India (*Primum emporium Indiae*).[95] It was a haven of vessels from various parts of the world as reported by the anonymous author of *Periplus of the Erithrean Sea*.[96] Some historians making use of the classical works of Strabo, Pliny, Tacitus, Ptolemy and sources like *Periplus of the Erithrean Sea* and the Peutingerian table related to the Roman Empire in Greek and Latin brought to light the details of trade between Imperial Rome and India. The study of the Vienna Papyrus or *Papyrus Vindobenensis* G.40822 brings to light the details of commercial contacts between Muziris and the Mediterranean regions. This papyrus contains a commercial contract regarding the transport of goods from Muziris to the Red Sea, then on to Coptos and across the Nile to Alexandria.[97] Warmington worked on the commerce between the Roman Empire and India from a western point of view covering the period from the victory of Augustus Octavian (ruling from 29 B.C.E. to 14 C.E.) up to the death of Marcus Aurelius (16–80 C.E.).[98] Strabo, writing during the time of Augustus states that 120 ships left for the East every year from the Egyptian port of Myos Hormos.[99] Wheeler in his *Rome Beyond the*

Imperial Frontiers speaks of Indian merchants going to Egypt occasionally and Greek merchants from there coming to India now and then for carrying pepper and other spices, especially pepper to Egypt in the second century B.C.E. and affirms that pepper from South India reached the Mediterranean in considerable volume in the early part of the first century B.C.E.[100] He used references in the *Sangam* literature to speak of the import of gold to Muziris and export of pepper in exchange.[101] H.G. Rawlinson underlines the favorable milieu in the Roman Empire for development of international maritime trade after the annexation of Egypt to the Roman Empire in 30 C.E.. Piracy was put down and the trade routes were made safe as a result of *Pax Romana* on account of which demand for oriental luxuries increased in a hitherto unprecedented manner. Based on the writings of Pliny, he highlights the great demand in the Roman Empire for pepper that was sold at the astounding price of 15 *denarii* a pound even in the days of Pliny.[102] He refers to Pliny again on the grievance of the Romans for the drain of gold to India, China and Arabia.[103] Muziris of the classical writers is located in the lower Periyar basin not far from the Arabian Sea, as indicated in the Latin, Greek, and Tamil sources. According to them Muziris is situated on the bank of River Periyar, slightly away from the seashore. It is further added that the cargoes for the import had to be unloaded from the Ocean-going ships onto smaller vessels that could carry the goods through the river to Muziris and commodities of export also had to be loaded into such vessels for transfer to the big vessel anchored in the sea. As in the case of Arikamedu, the well-known Roman settlement in ancient times, Muziris was not on the seashore, but on the banks of a river opening into the sea. The fourth-century Peutingerian table also points out the location of Muziris. Excavations conducted under the auspices of Kerala Council of Historical Research under the Muziris project have thrown open the working hypothesis that Pattanam, situated 2 km north of Parur in Vadakkekara village in the district of Ernakulam, Kerala, 8 kms south of Kodungalloor, could be the lost Muziris of international fame. These excavations were done on a regular basis during the period from 2007, to 2013 annually. Large number of artifacts that support the contact with the Mediterranean regions were collected from the site. The fact that this site, as well as Maliankara, is located in the same land mass surrounded by the branches of River Periyar falling into the Arabian Sea could buttress the local tradition regarding the landing of St. Thomas at Maliankara in 52 C.E.

A host of references to the apostolate of St. Thomas in South India are available to the inquisitive and unbiased minds such as archaeological evidence, near contemporary literary sources, ballads in circulation in Kerala, and long-standing tradition.

Archaeological evidences

Archaeological evidences are profusely employed by historians for the reconstruction of history and so the scholars like George Nedungatt lay great emphasis on the existence of the tomb of St. Thomas in Mylapore, Madras to prove his apostolate in South India.

i) It is remarkable that the tomb in Mylapore is the only one the world over which is claimed and venerated as the tomb of St. Thomas. Another important point to be underlined is that the St. Thomas Christians of Malabar (Kerala) have never ventured to claim the tomb in their own land. This adds strength to the argument based on the existence of the tomb.

ii) St. Ephrem (306–373), born in Nisibis in Turkey and died in Edessa, very clearly mentions that St. Thomas worked, died, and was buried in India from where his relics were shifted by a merchant in a casket to Edessa, known in modern times as Urfa, located in Sanliurfa Province in the Southeast Anatolia Region of Turkey.[104] St. Jerome (ca 345–419/420) makes mention of his death in Calaminain, India.[106]

A number of the Fathers of Eastern and Western or Latin Churches make mention of the burial of the body of St. Thomas in India and the subsequent transfer of the relics from here to Edessa. Gregory of Tours (538–594) makes it very clear that St. Thomas was buried in India and later the relics were shifted to Edessa.[107]

iii) Several pilgrims from various parts of the world flocked to Mylapore to obtain blessings from the Saint interred there. Bishop Ambrose of Milan (337–397) makes mention of the pilgrimage of Museus, Bishop of Doleni, while St. Gregory of Tours refers to a certain Theodore who went on pilgrimage to the tomb of St. Thomas in India.[108] Anglo-Saxon Chronicles recorded in 883 C.E. that King Alfred the Great of England sent Swithhelm, the future bishop of Sherbone and Aethelstan with votive offerings to St. Thomas at his tomb in India.[109] The pilgrimage of the foreigners to Mylapore continued through the centuries and we have the names of widely known visitors like Marco Polo (1293), Franciscan Friar John of Monte Corvini (1292–1293), Bishop John de Marignoli (1349), and Nicolo di Conti (1430).

The Portuguese who established their headquarters of the Asiatic possessions in Cochin in 1505 and heard about the importance of Malacca as far as the international sea-borne trade was concerned extended their interest to the Southeast Asian regions and also the Coromandel coast. In the course of their activities in this region, they came to know about the existence of the tomb of St. Thomas and the house in his name in Mylapore. On the way back from Malacca, Diogo Fernandes, Bastião

Fernandes, and other Portuguese officers got the information in 1517 about the tomb of St. Thomas from the Armenians residing in Pulicatt, near Mylapore, namely Coje Escander and his companions. These Portuguese persons at the invitation extended by the Armenians visited the tomb.[110] Portuguese king Dom Manuel I (1495–1521) after obtaining the details about the tomb in Mylapore instructed his officials in India to make detailed inquiries about the tomb. A few of the Portuguese after detailed information regarding the place visited the tomb in 1521, knelt before the tomb, made confessions, prayed, and participated in the holy mass celebrated in the chapel containing the tomb of St. Thomas on the feast of the Corpus Christi. Gaspar Correa who was in the service of the Portuguese in India for over half a century or so and authored the *Lendas da India*, was one among those who made a pilgrimage to the tomb along with Pero Lopes de Sampayo.[111]

King John III (1521–1557), the son of Dom Manuel I followed up the instruction of his father. He collected more details from Dom Duarte de Meneses who later became the governor in India (1522–1524). St. Thomas was adopted as the patron of the Portuguese possessions in India. The Portuguese Governor Dom Duarte de Meneses (1522–1524) at the instruction of the king, appointed in 1522 Manuel de Frias as the captain and factor of the Coromandel coast along with Father Alvaro Penteado and asked them to repair the house of St. Thomas in Mylapore with a view to celebrating holy mass there. But Penteado returned to Portugal without accomplishing the work entrusted to him. So, a certain cleric Pero Fernandes was appointed by the captain as the chaplain of the house. Later a priest by name Antonio Gil was appointed to take up the work of renovation of the house. While doing the excavation, they came across the relics of the saint along with an iron lance. At the request of Antonio Gil, Manuel de Frias made a casket available to keep the relics that were with great care placed in it. It was kept under the altar. A solemn procession with great devotion was organized. Further enquires were made by the Portuguese governor Nuno da Cunha (1529–1538) and few more attempts were made to confirm their findings. The Portuguese authorities being convinced of the genuineness of the tomb of St. Thomas in Mylapore, and his apostolate in India, besides declaring him as the patron of the Portuguese possessions in India, named fortresses after his name,[112] christened a vessel *Santhome* and issued a gold coin *Santhome*.

In course of time further excavations were conducted in Mylapore like those in 1523, 1524, 1729, 1893–1896, 1903 and 1970. While Nedungatt after resolving the Calamina riddle[113] and at the same time, being aware of the absence of modern and technical sophistications of archaeological excavations in the sixteenth century, attaches great emphasis to the unrivaled tomb of St. Thomas in Mylapore as strong evidence for proving the apostolate of St. Thomas in India[114] Benedict Vadakkekara, a historian from Kerala itself sets aside its importance and discredits the efforts of the Portuguese.[115]

Another strong archaeological evidence for the genuineness of the tomb is the use of bricks baked in the first century C.E. for the lowest strata of the tomb at Mylapore. They are of the same quality and size (15.5 inches of length, 8 inches of breadth, and 3 inches of height) as those used in the construction of the Roman establishments in Arikamedu during the second half of the first century C.E. owing their origin to Italian manufacture as revealed through the archaeological excavation scientifically conducted by Mortimer Wheeler and his associates. The merchant vessels from the Roman Empire used to carry bricks as ballast. So, it is assumed by the scholars that the tomb at Mylapore was constructed almost during the same period, i.e., first century C.E. and this is confirmed by the tradition regarding the martyrdom of St. Thomas in 72 C.E.

Nedungatt, basing his arguments also on the validity of positive, uniform, and constant tradition for the reconstruction of history as held by Benedict Vadakkekara, strongly affirms that the existence of the tomb of St. Thomas in Mylapore is a proof for the apostolate of St. Thomas in South India. The conclusion regarding the tomb put forward by Nedungatt seems to be convincing.[116] Nedungatt adds:

> The relics of the Apostle Thomas were venerated at Edessa in the fourth century. This is historically certain. And Edessa itself proclaimed through its mouthpiece, Ephrem, the Harp of the Spirit "that those relics were brought there from India. If so, the quest for the historical Thomas, the Apostle of India, can be terminated here, giving the true value to the Indian tradition that the Apostle died a martyr's death at Mylapore and was buried there in a tomb that has not ceased to attract pilgrims from antiquity down the centuries.[117]

He suggests that Calamina could be a variant of *Cholamannu,* a Tamil-Malayalam word indicating the land of the Cholas where the tomb of the apostle was known to be located.[118]

In the West, from the time of the *Acts of Judas Thomas* there has been a tradition locating the apostle's tomb in India. But it was Mar Solomon (Metropolitan of Perath-Maishan ca. 1222 C.E.) who first cited this tradition pinpointing Mylapore in India as the place of the tomb.

> Habban, the merchant, brought his body, and laid it in Edessa, the blessed city of Our Lord. If ever the tomb's genuineness had been suspected or if the community's unanimous consensus had been wanting, there would have cropped up "rival tombs" or rival traditions. It does not otherwise

make sense why a people who have always been natives of Malabar should consider a spot in a remote and alien land as their hallowed place.[119]

A.C. Perumalil refers to the removal of the relics of the apostle from Mylapore by the ruler of Vijayanagar in 1559 and the return of the same to Mylapore after some time. He writes that half of the relics and the spear-head were taken away by Fr. Lopo d'Almeida who gave them to Dom Jorge Temudo, bishop of Cochin. Later on Bishop Dom Frei Andre de Santa Maria gave the relics to the church of St. Thomas in Goa.[120]

> Georg Schurhammer SJ summarizes the findings conveniently. "The main building in Arikamedu was built in the second half of the first century A.D. ... but it was abandoned before the end of that century because of flooding. A close study of the measurements of the bricks of this building has shown that they are identical with those of the apostle's tomb at Mylapore. ... According to the tradition of the Thomas Christians the martyrdom of the Apostle Thomas took place in the year 72. This coincides with the dating of the bricks of the tomb and of the Roman warehouse at Arikamedu in the second half of the first century.[121]

> Against the opinion that the tomb in Mylapore was forged, Adolph Medlycottt writes: "If the claim of Mylapore to be the place of the martyrdom and of the burial of the apostle was not based on undeniable fact, the Christians of Malabar would never have acknowledged their neighbour's claim to hold the tomb of the apostle, neither would they ever be induced to frequent it by way of pilgrimage. Had this been a case of a fictitious claim put forth to secure public notoriety and importance, they would as probably have, anyway, set up one for themselves, and would have certainly ignored the claim of the former"

The cross with Pahlavi inscription in the tomb of St. Thomas also points to the antiquity of the site as a Christian shrine. Pahlavi was the official language of Persia during the Sassanian dynasty (227–651 A.D.) and, thereafter it went out of use. Hence, this cross with its inscription could have been made only when Pahlavi was still a current language, i.e., before the middle of the seventh century. It is noteworthy that when the *Acta Thomae* situates St. Thomas's mission field in the kingdom of Gondopharnes in North-west India, it does not attempt to locate his tomb there.

Bishop Gregory of Tours (A.D. 538–594) in his work, Gloria Martyrum writes: Thomas the apostle, according to the narrative of his martyrdom, is stated to have suffered in India. His holy Remains (corpus), after a long interval of time, were removed to the city of Edessa in Syria and there interred. In that part of India where they first rested, stand a monastery and a church of striking dimensions, elaborately adorned and designed. This, Theodore, who had been to that place, narrated to us.[122] According to Medlycott, Theodore was a travelled Syrian Christian who visited the Indian shrine and venerated the Relics at Edessa as well.

Ethnic evidences

Groups of people claiming their descent from those who were originally brought to the Christian faith by the apostle St. Thomas and preserving their endogamous identity are found in seven important localities all of which are accessible through water ways, either backwaters or rivers opening themselves into lakes and eventually connected to the Arabian Sea and the Indian Ocean. They are, from the north to south, Palayur, Maliankara (Kodungalloor), Kottakkavu, Kokkamangalam, Niranam, Nilackal, and Quilon. The existence of these basic Christian communities strongly affirms the apostolate of St. Thomas in South India.

It is a strange coincidence that the seven churches founded by St. Thomas in South India are situated in or near these Jewish colonies. In the close proximity of the ancient Church of Palayur, there is a spot still marked off as "Jewish Hill." It was normative for the St. Thomas Christians to have biblical names. Names of ancestors are automatically handed down with the result that one and the same name is perpetuated from one generation to another.[123]

Vadakkekara adds:

> The Apostles addressed the Good News first to their own kith and kin. It had been for preaching to the Jews that Apostle Thomas reached the Malabar Coast. Some socio-cultural elements and practices common to the Jews and the St. Thomas Christians are highlighted to show that the Jewish settlements drew Apostle Thomas to India and that the Christian community he established was made up of Jewish converts also.[124]

Literary evidences

Acts of Judas Thomas (AJT)

As it has been discussed above, the *Acts of Judas Thomas* composed in Edessa sometime between 230 and 250 C.E. in Syriac language deals with the apostolate of St. Thomas in India in general and the section from Act seven to the end is devoted to his work and martyrdom in South India. The historical value has been convincingly proved by recent research especially by those who use literary works as a source for the reconstruction of history.[125]

Folk songs in circulation among the Christians of Kerala

Some of the scholars working on the apostolate St. Thomas in South India have made use of a couple of folk songs in circulation among the

Christians of Kerala especially the members of the Knanaya community. Among them, *Margamkalippattu*, Rampanpattu, and *Thomaparvam* have St. Thomas apostolate in South India as the main content. There are a few others that have reference to the apostolate of St. Thomas such as *Pananpattu, or Veeradiyan pattu, Marthommanpattu* and so on. Bernard Thoma in his work *Marthoma Christianikal* speaks of the importance of *Rampanpattu* in the study of the apostolate St. Thomas in South India by reproducing the entire song in 448 lines.[126] Both *Margamkalippattu* and *Rampanpattu* refer to the landing of St. Thomas in Maliankara. But *Rampanpattu* gives the date of landing of St. Thomas as 50 C.E.[127]

Numismatic evidence and the Palayur tradition

On October 29, 1945, a hoard of gold and silver coins bearing the images of Augustus, the first Roman Emperor (27 B.C.E.–14 C.E.), Tiberius (14–37 C.E.), Claudius (41–54 C.E.), and Nero (37–68 C.E.) was discovered from Eyyal, in the vicinity of Palayur, which was linked with Cranganore through a canal. This shows that Palayur had commercial contacts with the Roman Empire during the first century C.E. that facilitates the visit of St. Thomas to Palayur.

According to Palayur tradition, St. Thomas worked miracle in Palayur and baptized thirty-four Brahmin families out of forty and others except one left the place after cursing it (*sapakad*-Chowgatt). Today it is a flourishing town of which Palayur is in the periphery. One *Nambudiri* family by name Orumana remained there without being converted to Christianity. Some of the Nambudiri families like Kalathur Mana are said to have guarded a document *Nagaragranthavari* that contains the following notice. "Kali year 3153 (= A.D. 52) a foreign *Sanyasi* called Thomas came to our village, preached there causing pollution. Therefore, we came away from that village."[128] Though the Palayur tradition is damaging to the self-esteem of the Hindus, they do not disown it, thus arguing for its credibility. According to *Rampanpattu*, the apostle Thomas preached the gospel at Palayur for an entire year and baptized 1,050 persons.[129] The number need not be exact.

The Brahmins who became Christians continued to use the temple at Palayur for their worship. Thus, the temple became Church. Close by is the water tank. On the ruins of that temple-church, the present church was constructed in 1600–1607 by the Jesuit priest James Fenicio. In the following century, it was set on fire by the invading Muslim army of Tippu Sultan of Mysore who burned many churches and forced people into Islam. After Tippu's retreat, the roof of the church was renovated and more recently new structures were added. Brahmin families of Kalli,

Kalikavu, and Pakalomattam were originally situated near the Palayur temple. Palayur tradition is shared both by Hindus and Christians.

The four Chaldean bishops who arrived in Malabar in 1504 wrote to their Patriarch Elias that Palayur ranked second among the three most important Christians centers along with Kodungalloor and Quilon.[130]

Palayur affords singular support for the Thomas Christian tradition regarding the apostle Thomas. Since it is a tradition shared by Christians and Hindus alike, it can be regarded as above suspicion. It explodes the Western theory that the apostolic origin of Indian Christianity was a fraud of the Indian Christians or one hoisted upon them by the Syrians. Since the Palayur tradition is attested by a written Hindu document, it is of singular historical value for Thomasology in its search for historical Thomas. Those writers, who regard the Indian tradition regarding the apostle Thomas as merely oral, legendary, based essentially on the *Acts of Thomas* or devoid of historical value for the lack of contemporary documents, have here something to unsettle their certainties and make them pause and reflect.[131]

This tradition is particularly significant because it is both Christian and Hindu at the same time. It involves Brahmins who recognize that their ancestors were converted to Christianity by the apostle Thomas, while several dispersed families trace their first Christian origins to the ministry of this Apostle at Palayur. This confluence of complementary traditions cannot be attributed to any collusion of the two communities of Christians and Hindus since the former stands to gain and the latter to lose. After an on-the-spot study of the Palayur story, the Belgian Jesuit Albert Gille expressed himself fully convinced of the genuineness.[132]

Consistent tradition among the St. Thomas Christians of Kerala

On the one hand, there is the fact of Apostle Thomas being sent out to preach, and on the other, there is a community of Christians that avers with persistence that it had been to its own ancestors that Thomas had preached. No other Christian community anywhere in the world has made a rival claim that would invalidate the tradition of the Indian Christians. Under these circumstances, the existence of an ancient Christian community in India professing that it was established by Apostle Thomas is itself indicative of the genuineness of the tradition.[133]

Vadakkekara has this to say:

> This uniqueness of the tradition finds tacit consonance with the other churches of antiquity, as no other Christian community in the world has a rival tradition e.g. of possessing the tomb of Apostle Thomas. . . . Given the fact that the apostle was a person known to all the Churches, the

absence of rival traditions is in itself a clear vindication of the authenticity of the tradition of Indian Christians.[134]

> Benedict Vadakkekkara, being fully aware of the disdain the western scholars maintained towards the *AJT*, proposes to highlight the Indian tradition independent of AJT and to affirm the South Indian apostolate of St. Thomas. He attempts to make tradition yield history.[135] He writes: The tradition of the Indian Christians is inseparably bound to precise dates, existing families, and places. All through the documented period of the history of Christianity in India, the contents of the tradition have remained constant and fixed. The unanimous and express consensus within the community regarding the particulars of the tradition has all the requisites of a contemporary historical document. All these specifics have been irremovably wedded to definite fixed points. These moorings have not undergone translocations or replacements. It is this constancy in the concreteness of the tradition that has made it function as history for the community.[136]

He holds the view that the traditions of the Indian Christians, the *AJT* and the ecclesiastical writings converge at the apostle's empty tomb in Mylapore.[137]

Down through the centuries, the new entrants into the community have accepted the communal tradition with the result that all the members have come to identify themselves personally with the descendants of those whom Apostle Thomas had won for Christ. The Suthists alone have a different tradition according to which they are not members of the community founded by Apostle Thomas but are the progeny of the settlers from West Asia who had come to offer logistic support to the Indian church.[140] It may be noted that Nedungatt, another scholar from Kerala, has his own reservations about the validity of tradition as a source for history.[141]

Patristic testimonies about the Apostolate of St. Thomas in India

Pantaenus, a stoic philosopher hailing from Sicily and a convert to Christianity as well as a teacher in Alexandria is believed to have been to India as missionary in 189–190. He was the teacher of famous Clement of Alexandria. Eusebius of Caesarea, the father of Church history makes mention of the missionary visit of Pantaenus to India[142] where, according to Eusebius, he found Christian communities using the Gospel of Matthew written in "Hebrew letters."

St. Jerome (c. 347–420)[143] apparently relying entirely on Eusebius' evidence from *Historia Ecclesiastica*, wrote that Pantaenus visited India, "to preach Christ to the Brahmans and philosophers there. According to Origen (184–253)[144] non-Aryan India was already evangelized."[145]

The Edessene author of *Doctrine of the Apostles* (*Didascalia Apostolorm* composed ca. A.D. 230) who flourished not later than A.D. 250 was aware of the existence of a Christian community in India ministered by St. Thomas the apostle.[146] Historians, poets, liturgical texts, and writers of all sorts in the Eastern Church firmly hold that the apostle Thomas evangelized India.[147]

Other patristic texts like those of Clement of Rome (third century), *Doctrine of the Apostles* (third century), Gregory Nazianzen (329–390), Cyrillona (d 396), Ambrose (333–397), Ephrem (+373), John Chrysostom (347–407), Gregory of Tours (538–594), Gregory the Great (590–604), Isadora of Seville (560–636), Codex of Fulda (eighth century), and so on testify that St. Thomas preached the Good News in India and brought many Indians to Christ.

It becomes clear from the discussions above that the apostolate of St. Thomas in India, is a historical fact supported by host of evidences. The tomb of St. Thomas in Mylapore and the transfer of the mortal remains from there to Edessa as testified by the witnesses of the second, third and fourth centuries confirm the tradition. The writings of St. Ephrem constitute a very important testimony to the existence of a tomb in India and necessarily the mission of St. Thomas in India. It is therefore historically correct to state that St. Thomas is the apostle of India and Pakistan. There are a host of historians who told this view though a few on account of their bias find it difficult accept the Indian apostolate St. Thomas. One has to examine their expertise in the field and their intentions.

ENDNOTES

1   Matt 10:1–4; Luke 12:16
2   Mark 3:13–19
3   Luke 6:12–16
4   Luke 6:17–20
5   Matt 10:5
6   Matt 10:7–8
7   Matt 11:2–6; Luke 7:18–23
8   Matt 10:8.
9   Matt 10:10
10   Matt 14:28–31
11   Matt 17:19–20; Mark 9:18–20, 28–29
12   John 11:16
13   John 20:24
14   John 20:26–29
15   John 21:1–17
16   Matt 28:16–20
17   Acts
18   Acts 1:8
19   Luke 24:49
20   Acts 1:12–14
21   Acts 2:1–4
22   Acts 2:14–41
23   Acts 3:1–10
24   Acts 6:1–8
25   Acts 10:34–48
26   Acts. 11:1–18
27   John 11:16, 20:24, 21:2
28   James Kuruikilamkattt, *First Voyage of the Apostle Thomas to India*, Bangalore: Asian Trading Company, 2005, 21.
29   John 14:5
30   John 14.22
31   Luke 6:12–16
32   Ref. K. Mazumdar, *Early Hindu India*, New Delhi, 1981, 30.
33   Herodotus, *Histories*, 4.44.
34   V.A Smith, *Early History of India*, OUP, 3rd edition, 1914, 88–113.
35   Roman Empire came into existence as an autocratic form of government on the ruins of Roman Republic. The appointment of Julius Caesar as the perpetual dictator in 44 B.C.E. marked the transition from being a Republic to Empire besides the battle of Actium in 31 B.C.E.. Shortly after wards, the Roman province of Egypt was established in 30 B.C.E. after Octavian(the future Emperor Augustus) defeated his rival Mark Antony, deposed his lover

Cleopatra VII and annexed the Ptolemaic kingdom to the Roman Empire. The Roman province of Egypt encompassed most of modern-day Egypt except for Sinai Peninsular that was later conquered by the Roman Emperor Trajan. Ref. K.S. Mathew, *Kerala and the Spice Routes*, Trivandrum, Stark World Publishing, 2014, 29–30.

36   The Roman Empire encompassed large territorial holdings around the Mediterranean in Europe, Africa, and Asia enjoying unprecedented prosperity for the first two centuries. The dissensions of the civil war ended at Actium. This period was known as the *Pax Romana* (Roman Peace).

37   H.G. Rawlinson, *Intercourse between India and the Western World from the Earliest Time to the Fall of Rome*, New Delhi: AES reprints, 2001, 101.

38   Strabo (64/63 B.C.E.–24 C.E.) was a Greek Geographer, philosopher and Historian who lived in Asia Minor during the transition period of the Roman Republic into the Roman Empire. His famous work having reference to India is *Geographica (Geography)* It first appeared in Western Europe in Rome as a Latin translation issued around 1469. The first Greek edition was published in 1516 in Venice. Isaac Casaubon, classical scholar and editor of Greek texts, provided the first critical edition in 1587. For more details ref. James Puliurumpil, *Classic India: Western Account before Christ,* Kottayam: OIRSI No. 407, 2016, 289–365.

39   Strabo, *Geography* II, 5.12.

40   "Impiger extremos currit mercator ad Indos per mare pauperiem fugiens" Horace, Ep.1.1.45.

41   Pliny, ref. W.H.S. Jones (tr & ed) *Pliny's Natural History*, London, 1969, 101. Pliny the elder was a Roman writer and was the author of the famous work *Historia Naturalis.*

42   Steven E. Sidebotham, "From the Mediterranean to South Asia: The Odyssey of an Indian Merchant in Roman Times" in K.S. Mathew, ed., *Imperial Rome, Indian Ocean and Muziris; New Perspectives on Maritime Trade*, Delhi: Manohar, 2015, 77.

43   Sidebotham and Wendrich, "Roman Emporium at Berenike: Archaeological Evidence of a Subsistence Trade in the Eastern Desert of Egypt," Los Angeles: Cotsen Institute of Archaeology, 114–119.

44   Steven E. Sidebotham, "From the Mediterranean to South Asia: The Odyssey of an Indian Merchant in Roman Times" in K.S. Mathew, ed., *Imperial Rome, Indian Ocean Regions and Muziris: New Perspectives on Maritime Trade*, Delhi: Manohar, 2015, 75–81.

45   For a graphic description of the voyage from Alexandria to Taxila ref. J.N. Farquhar, *The Apostle Thomas North India*, Manchester, 1926, 97–98.

46   Strabo, *Geography.*

47   Ref. K.S. Mathew, *Kerala and the Spice Routes,* Trivandrum, 2014, 30–33.

48   Ocelis (Greek: Okêlis) is an ancient port on the Red Sea, on the Arabian side near or at Bab al-Mandeb, the strait separating the Red Sea from the Gulf of Aden. Ocelis belonged to the South Arabian kingdom of Saba-Himyar and is known as a stop on the maritime route from Egypt to India in the

first centuries C.E. In the first century, *Periplus Maris Erythraei* describes it as "not so much a port of trade as harbour, watering station, and the first place to put in for those sailing on." Pliny the Elder reports their destination and describes Ocelis as the first stop on the sea journey from Egypt to India. Ocelis was visited by traders coming over from the African side on rafts with aromatics, myrrh, ivory, and tortoise shell, this being the only report of African navigation in this work.

49   Recent research on Roman trade with India proved that a voyage from Ocelis to Muziris with the help of South-west monsoon could be completed in twenty days instead of forty days of Pliny. In this case the ships start from Ocelis by late August, when the fury of monsoon subsides and it could then reach Muziris by mid-September. The return voyage should be scheduled from Muziris to the Red sea with the help of the north-east monsoon winds that starts blowing from October to February. Ref. K.S. Mathew, *Kerala and the Spice Routes,* 39–40.

50   Steven E. Sidebotham, 81.

51   Kurikilamkatt, 88.

52   J.N. Farquhar, "The Apostle Thomas in North India," 97.

53   A.F.J. Klijn, *The Acts of Thomaa: Introduction, Text and Commentary,* Leiden, Brill, 2003.

54   James Kurikilamkatt, *First Voyage of the Apostle Thomas to India. Ancient Christianity in Bharuch and Taxila,* Bangalore, 2005, 10–11.

55   St Gregory of Tours, *Libri Miraculorum,* I, 32 (PL LXXI) Col. 733 ref. also Kurikilamkatt, 14.

56   Adolf E. Medlycottt, *India and the Apostle Thomas,* London, David Nutt, 1905. Medlycottt supports the North Indian Apostolate of St. Thomas. Inscriptions were found in Greek on one side and in *Karoshti* on the other side of the coins. *Karoshti* was the form of writing in the Northwest India. The coins are preserved in different museums and libraries like British Museum, Bibliotheque Nationale de Paris, Berlin Museum, Lahore Museum and National Museum, Kolkata. Some of these coins bear the names of his family members too. The scientific analysis made reveals that these coins were minted in the first half of the first century A.D. Those who oppose the conclusions of Medlycottt say that he has not done a critical study of his sources of information.

57   Joseph Dahlmann, *Die Thomaslegende und die ä ltesten historischen Beziehungen des Christentums zum fernen Osten im Lichte der indischen Altertumskunde,* Freiburg im Breisgau, Herder, 1912. Richard Garbe of Tü bingen rejected the thesis of Dahlmann in his work relegating it to mythology, Richard Garbe, *Indien und das Christentum, Eine Untersuchumg der Religionsgeschichtlichen Zusammenhange,* Tübingen, Mohr, 1914.

58   Kurikilamkatt, 47–56.

59   A. Mingana, "The Early Spread of Christianity in India," *Bulletin of the John Rylands Library,* University of Manchester, 10/2, 438–439.

60   John Nicole Farquhar was born at Aberdeen in 1861. He was educated at Aberdeen Grammar School and Aberdeen University and finished his studies at Oxford University. With no prior ordination, he was recruited by London Missionary Society as a lay educational missionary and sent to India in 1891. He worked in India till 1923. He died in Manchester in 1929·

61   J.N. Farquhar, 97–98.

62   George Nedungatt is of the opinion that Gundaphares, the governor of Arachosia conquered the neighboring regions and ruled from 19 to 45/46 A.D. as the founder of Indo-Parthian kingdom. ref. Nedungatt, 115. Sirkap was built by Greco-Bactrian king Demetrius after he invaded ancient India around 180 B.C.E. He founded the Indo-Greek kingdom in the Northern and Northwestern parts of modern Pakistan. It lasted till 10 B.C.E.

63   Taxila was the city of India's first grammarian Panini. Aramaic was the *lingua franca* of the region from the time Darius I conquered in the fifth century B.C. It was a great center of Buddhist learning and a meeting place of three great trade routes, i.e. one from Eastern India described by the Greek writer, Megasthenes, as the royal High way. The second from Western Asia, and the third from Kashmir and Central Asia. At the time of Macedonian invasion under Alexander, the Great, in 326 B.C. it was a very rich and flourishing city ruled by Ambi who is generally called by his Dynastic title Taxiles. He surrendered himself and his kingdom to Alexander. About eighty years after the breakup of Alexander's empire Taxila was taken over by Great Asoka (273–232 B.C.) who made it his residence in the capacity of the viceroy of the Punjab in the Mauryan empire. Indo Greeks succeeded the Mauryas in the second century B.C and later the area with Taxila was wrested by the Indo-Scythians of whom Gondaphares was the greatest.

64   Kurikilamkatt, 84–85. He makes references to the reports of excavations conducted by ASI. Sir John Marshall, *Excavations at Taxila, Annual Report*, 1912–13 & A. Cunningham, *The Ancient Geography* of India, 111.

65   J.N. Farquhar, *The Apostle Thomas in North India, Manchester*, 1925, pp. 98–102

66   Alexander Cunningham, *Journal of the Asiatic Society of Bengal*, vol. xxiii, pp.679–712

67   A.E. Medlycott, *India and the Apostle Thomas: An Inquiry with Critical Analysis of the Acta Thomae*, Trissur, 2017, ç.3

68   Medlycott, 9–10.

69   For more details, ref. Kurikilamkatt, 69–74.

70   Reinaud, "Mémoire geographique, historique et scientifiquesur lÍnde", *Mémoires de l'Institute National de France*, Vol xviii, II, 1849.

71   Reinaud, 90.

72   Quoted by Kurukilamkattt, 75.

73   Medlycott, 15.

74   Meclycott, 16.

75   Kurikilamkatt, 88.

76 The exact date of the foundation of Kushan dynasty in India cannot be fixed though some of the writers place it in 50 C.E. by Kadphises I.

77 Kurikilamkattt, 143–144.

78 J.N. Farquhar, "The Apostle Thomas in North India", *Bulletin of John Ryland's Library* 10 (1926), 80–111; J.N. Farquhar & G.Garitte, *The Apostle Thomas in India according to the Acts of Thomas*, edited by Jacob Vellian, Kottayam, 1972, 40.

79 Kurikilamkattt, 114, quoting J. Rooney.

80 Kurikilamkatt, 116. The author has established the historical importance of AJT and therefore his opinion regarding the spread of Christianity in Barygaza presupposes the consideration of AJT as a source for the recon-struction of history. Ref. Kurikilamkatt, 158.

81 Kurikilamkatt, 44–46.

82 Kurikilamkatt, 55.

83 Kurikilamkatt, 108–113. Jordanus of Severac was a Dominican preacher, ap-pointed as the first Latin Bishop of India, sent by the Pope then residing in Avignon in 1321. He was nominated as the Bishop of Quilon.

84 Nedungatt, 275.

85 Benedict Vadakkekara, *Origin of Christianity in India: A Historical Critique*, Delhi, 2007, 137–146.

86 Vadakkekara, 146. In fact, Moraes underlining the exit of St. Thomas from the kingdom of Gundaphar, refers to this apocryphal document. Ref. George Moraes, *History of Christianity in India*, 34. It is interesting here to make a reference to a mural painting in a Church in Kalkar, Germany where the pic-ture of Blessed Virgin Mary, in her sickbed is presented. Nearby, St. Thomas was being brought in by an Angel. The Apocryphal work is reported to be of the fifth century A.D. Therefore, it is possible that the tradition of St. Thomas Apostolate in India was widespread in Europe in a very early period.

87 Vadakkekara, 146.

88 Vadakkekara, 138.

89 Henry Heras, *Two Apostles of India*, Trichinopoly, 1944, 8.

90 George Mark Moraes, *A History of Christianity in India from Early times to St. Francis Xavier:A.D 52-1542*, Bombay, 1964, 25–33.

91 A.M. Mundadan, *History of Christianity in India Vol. I, From the Beginning up to the Middle of the Sixteenth Century*, Bangalore, 1989, 61.

92 Mundadan, 218.

93 J.N. Farquhar, "The Apostle Thomas in South India" *John Rylands Library Bulletin*, Manchester, 1926, 21.

94 Acts 15:6, 22

95 Quoted in K.S. Mathew, ed., *Imperial Rome, Indian Ocean Regions and Muziris: New Perspectives on Maritime Trade*, New Delhi: Manohar, 2015, 9–10.

96 Wilfred H. Schoff, *The Periplus of Erythraean Sea*, Delhi, 1974, 44.

[97] L. Casson, "P. Vindob, G 40822 and the Shipping of Goods from India" *BASP*, 23 (1986),73–79; Federico de Romanis, A Muziris Export: Schidai or Ivory Trimmings" in K.S. Mathew, ed., *Imperial Rome, Indian Ocean and Muziris*, New Delhi: Manohar, 2015, 369–380.

[98] E.H. Warmington, *The Commerce between the Roman Empire and India*, Delhi, Munshiram Manoharlal,1995.

[99] Sir Mortimer Wheeler, *Rome Beyond the Imperial Frontiers*, Pelican Books, 1955, 156–157. Based on the statement of Strabo, Wheeler concludes that the monsoon winds known as Hippalus was in use certainly before 14 C.E. and declines to accept 40/1 C.E. as the date to which the discovery of Hippalus is ascribed by Warmington.

[100] Wheeler, 157

[101] "Thus agitating the white foams of the Periyaru, the beautifully built ships of the Yavanas came with gold and returned with pepper and Muziris resounded with the noise," Wheeler, 160.

[102] Pliny, *Natural History*, xii.14; H.G. Rawlinson, *Intercourse between India and the Western World from the Earliest Times to the Fall of Rome*, Delhi, AES Reprints, 2001, 106.

[103] H.G. Rawlinson, 103.

[104] Ephrem, Carmina Nizibena,42, quoted by George Nedungatt, *Quest for Historical Thomas*, 189.

[106] Jerome, *De Viris Illutribus*, Appendix. *De Vitis Apostolorum*, 5 (PL 23, 721 B); Nedungatt, 196.

[107] Gregory of Tours, *Miraculorum Libri, I, De Gloria martyrum in Monumenta Germaniae Historica,* Hanover, 1885, tom 1, 507–508; Nedungatt, 200.

[108] Gregory of Tours, Miraculorum Libri I, 32; Nedungatt, 307.

[109] *Anglo-Saxon Chronicle*, trans. and ed., G.N. Garmonsway, London, 1953, 79; Nedungatt, 307–308.

[110] João de Barros, *Da Asia, Decada* II, Parte 2, Lisboa, 1777, 222–238.

[111] João de Barros, 725–726

[112] Governor Nuno da Cunha laid the foundation stone of the fortress of Diu on December 21, 1535 the feast day of St. Thomas and on completion of the work it was named St. Thomas Fortress ref. João de Barros, *Da Asia*, Decada iv, parte 2, Lisboa, 1778, 85.

[113] Nedungatt, 157–173.

[114] George Nedungatt, *Quest for the Historical Thomas Apostle of India*, Bangalore: TPI, 2008, 308–313.

[115] Benedict Vadakkekara, *Origin of Christianity in India: A Historiographical Critique*, Delhi: Media House, 2007, 176–186.

[116] Nedungatt, 317–318: The Tradition, Western as well as Indian, is positive, uniform, and constant that the tomb of the apostle Thomas is in India. The Mylapore tomb is the only tomb of the apostle Thomas ever known to history, a tomb without a rival, like that of Peter in Rome. The archaeological evidence that this tomb was built with the first century Roman bricks may not by itself be a clinching argument; but within the whole setting of the

Mylapore tradition, it poses a question to those who demand contemporary documentary evidence about the mission of the apostle Thomas to India. The fact that this tomb is situated on the Coromandel Coast, and not in Malabar, has effectively the value of a *lectio difficilior* that adds up to the probability of its genuineness. The Mylapore tomb is free of the usual marks of a forged tomb. The foreign voice about "Calamina" constitutes no real alibi nor is there a riddle without solution. The nearly bimillennial tradition of pilgrimage, both foreign and Indian enhances the credibility of the tomb traditionally venerated at Mylapore as that of the apostle Thomas.

117 Nedungatt, 410.

118 Nedungatt, 172.

119 Vadakkekara, 131–132.

120 A.C. Perumalil, 87.

121 George Schurhammer, "gesammelte Studien, III, ed. Laslo szilas, Rome-Lisbon, 1964, 260. See also, "New Light about the Tomb of Mylaur," Festschrift Placid J. Podipara, ed. Jacob Vellian, Rome: Pontifical Oriental Institute, 1970, 99–101.

122 Adolph Medlycottt, *India and the Apostle Thomas,* 134.

123 Medlycottt, 72.

124 Medlycottt, 72.

125 Vadakkekara, 117.

126 Kurikilamkatt, 158.

127 Bernard Thoma, *Mar Thoma Christianikal,* Kottayam, Pellissery Publications, 1992,98–109.

128 Lines 22–24 Ref. Bernard Thoma, 99.

129 E.R. Hambye, "Saint Thomas and India", the *Clergy Monthly,* 16 (1952), 363–375.

129 Bernard Thoma, 101.

130 Simon Assemanus, *Bibiliotheca Orientalis,* III. Pars I, *De Scriptoribus Syris Nestorianis,* Rome, 1725, 594.

131 Nedungatt, 342.

132 Nedungatt, 335.

133 Vadakkekara, 113.

134 Vadakkekara, 121.

135 "And it is the task of today's historian to make their tradition yield a history that can be both historically coherent and scientifically verifiable," Vadakkekara, 28.

136 Vadakkekara, 339–340.

137 Vadakkekara, 343.

138 Vadekkekara, 113.

139 Vadakkekara, 347–48.

140 Vadakkekara, 123–24.

141 "Truth is consistent, but not all that is consistent and constant is truth. Error also can be consistent with itself from the beginning till the end."

[142] Eccl. Hist., lib .v., cap.x.

[143] Pat. Lat., "ut in Indiam quoque rogatus ab illius gentis, a Demetrio Alexandriae episcopo, mitteretur," xxiii, 651.

[144] Origen of Alexandria (184–253), also known as Origen Adamantius, was an early Christian scholar, ascetic, and theologian who was born and spent the first half of his career in Alexandria.

[145] Nedungatt, 410.

[146] "India and all its own countries, and those bordering on it, even to the farthest sea, received the apostle's hand of priesthood from Judas Thomas, who was guide and ruler in the church that he built there, and ministered there" Cureton, *Ancient Syriac Documents*, 33; From a Manuscript of about the fifth century, "It is the constant tradition of the Eastern Church that the apostle Thomas evangelized India, and there is no historian, no poet, no breviary, no liturgy, and no writer of any kind who, having the opportunity of speaking of Thomas, does not associate his name with India."

[148] F. Ferrão Vaz, 82–85.

[149] Gaspar Correa, tomo VI, part I, 432–434.

[150] Francisco da Costa, "Relatorio sobre o trato da Pimenta," in *Documentação Utramarina Portguuesa*, vol. III, Lisboa, 1963, 323.

2

HISTORIOGRAPHY OF THE APOSTOLATE OF ST. THOMAS IN INDIA: A CRITICAL REVIEW

Francis Thonippara, CMI

INTRODUCTION

The presence of the Christian religion in India was as old as Christianity itself, and it is a point of discussion for scholars from all over the globe. The amount of literature produced on this topic is immeasurable, and lot of literature in different languages are available to the general public today. The writings vary from apocryphal testimonies of the Fathers of the church to the contemporary authors. There are writers who support, doubt, or deny the apostolate of St. Thomas in India. Again, India itself is another topic of dispute, whether modern India or greater India of ancient times, including Parthia or Socortta. The results of modern archaeological excavations are at our help to identify the disputed persons and places. Once we accept the apostolate of St. Thomas in India, there arises the question regarding the geographical precision, South India or North India as some argue that St. Thomas had two missionary journeys, one to North India and another to South India. The scope of the present paper is to have a critical evaluation of the writings of a few selected authors on the topic of the apostolate of St. Thomas in India.

George Nedungatt, in his recent study the Quest for the Historical Thomas Apostle of India, approaches the whole debate in a different perspective, making use of the traditional Thomistic methodology. He divides the views of the scholars on the apostolate of St. Thomas in India into five categories:

I.   Unprovable: Vincent Smith (1908, but see also under section III), Frank Ernest Keay (1960), A.F.J. Klijn (1962), Ronald G. Roberson (1995).

35

II. Unhistorical, Legendary: Jean Daille (1664), Samuel Basnages de Beauval (1692), Louis-Sebastian Tillemont (1637–1698), Maturin Vessieres La Croze (1758), F. Wrede (1805), James Hough (1859), Sir John Kaye (1859), Alfred von Gutschmid (1864), G.Milne-Rae (1892), George Smith (1903), W.R. Philips (1903–1904), Richard Garbe (1914), Herbert Thurston (1912/1920), Christelle and Florence Jullien (2002).

III. Not Proven but Possible, not Unlikely: Wiihelm Germann (1877), Otto Wecker (1910), Vincent A. Smith (1924), Alfonse Mingana (1926), John Nicole Farquhar (1926/1927), Eugene Tisserant (1941), Kenneth Scott Latourette (1953), Nikolaus Zernov (1956), Leslie W. Brown (1956), Karl Staab (1965), Cyril B. Firth (1960/1974/2000 ed.), F.E. Keay (1960), Josef Wicki (1967), Stephen Neill (1984), Ian Gillman and Hans Joachim Klimkeit (1999), Cristiano Dognini and Ilarai Ramelli (2001).

IV. Probable or very Probable: Tisserant-Hambye (1957), Edward Hambye (1963), Samuel Moffett (1992/1998).

V. Historical and Certain: John P. Maffeus (1605), Joseph Simon Assemani (1728), Johannes F. Raulin (1745), Claudius Buchanan (1814), Matthias H. Hohlenberg (1822), E.C. Kenneth (1877), Sylvain Levi (1897), Alphonse E. Medlycott (1905), Karl Heck (1911), Joseph Dahlmann (1912), Ladislaus Zaleski (1915), Alfons Vaeth (1918/1925), Albert Gille (1924), John Stewart (1928) Henry Hosten (1936), Georg Schurhammer 1934; 1955–1973), P.J. Thomas (1920/1924), K.N. Daniel (1950), E.M. Philip (1950), A.C. Perumalil (1952/1971), Mark G. Moraes (1964), Placid Podipara (1966/1970), Thomas J. Navakatesh (1967), V.C. George (1969), Giuseppe Sorge (1983), A. Mathias Mundadan (1984), Martin Gielen (1990), Joseph Kolengaden (1993), Benedict Vadakkekara (1995/2007), Xavier Koodapuzha (1998), James J. Kurikilamkatt (2005), etc.[2]

There may be slight variations in the above division and one cannot make absolute categorization. The present writer may not fully agree with this division. However, one should appreciate the efforts made by George Nedungatt in categorizing the authors on the apostolate of St. Thomas in India.

CRITICAL REVIEW

Most Western scholars consider the Acts of Thomas as unreliable and some even argue that the patristic literature too is unreliable as the Fathers of the church depended too much on the Acts of Thomas. For them India mentioned in the Acts may not be the India of today. Different explanations are given to the tradition itself like a tradition wandered from North to South, South Indian tradition wandered in from Edessa, Thomas of Cana who migrated to South India in the fourth century or later, was confused with the apostle Thomas.[3]

We cannot put the Western scholars in one category as we have seen above in the differences of opinion. A.F.J. Klijn categorically denies the apostolate of St. Thomas in India. "It is impossible to prove that Thomas visited India. The traditions referring to this tradition were based on the apocryphal Acts of Thomas only. Before the composition of these Acts no traditions are available according to which Thomas went to India."[4]

One cannot make absolute statements of this type regarding the apostolate of St. Thomas in India. There is still scope for further studies and on the spot study of the living tradition of the St. Thomas Christian Community and the places associated with the life activities of Apostle Thomas surely will change the Western demand for contemporary documents to prove the authenticity of the tradition. Albert-Gille, a Belgian Jesuit, who paid a visit to Palayur, near Trichur in Kerala, a place associated with Apostle Thomas, made the following comment:

> This is a perfectly consistent tradition, and it is not enough to read it in books, one must go to the spot and feel the whole force of it. . . . I went to Palayur and saw the Catholic Church standing in the midst of old Hindu tanks... Even today no Brahman traveller passing through Palayur accepts or gathers any food in the locality which every Hindu knows by the name of "The–Cursed–Place."[5]

A new enthusiasm is noticed from the beginning of the twentieth century in the study of the apostolate of St. Thomas in India. They include both Indian and Western scholars and several writers have dedicated a whole book for the topic. Mention may be made of Ladislaus M. Zaleski, *The Apostle St. Thomas in India: History, Tradition and Legend*; Adolph E. Medlycott, *India and the Apostle Thomas*; Mathias Mundadan, *History of Christianity in India*, Vol. I; Benedict Vadakkekara, *Origin of Christianity in India: A Historiographical Critique*. A pioneer in the search for the historical Thomas and the Indian apostolate of St. Thomas from among the St. Thomas Christians was Bernard Alencherry, popularly known as the Eusebius of St. Thomas Christians. His monumental work in two volumes spare sufficient pages to deal with the question of the apostolicity of the St. Thomas Christians. In six chapters, around one hundred and fifty pages, the author puts forward various arguments to prove the apostolic origin of St. Thomas Christians in South India. His arguments consist of seven points including the local tradition, tomb of the apostle in Mylapore, seven churches founded by the apostle, the families that received the priestly ordination, the feast on July 3rd, the folk song called Veeradian Pattu, and the very name of the Community Nazrani. Then he counteracts the arguments of the Westerners and proves that St. Thomas preached the Gospel in South India. The author further makes use of the liturgical books and documents to prove the apostolate of St. Thomas in India.[6]

Bernard of St. Thomas[7] through his *A Brief Sketch of the History of the St. Thomas Christians* has brought out for the English-speaking world the results of his fifty years of research and studies on the history, traditions, and orthodoxy of the St. Thomas Christians. Bernard's work remains monumental with all the advances in research and studies on the history and traditions of the St. Thomas Christians made during the last one hundred years. The book has eight chapters with appendix. The first chapter deals with local sources and traditions, traditions about the seven churches and pilgrimage to Mylapore, etc.

Placid Podipara, one of the luminaries of the St. Thomas Christian Community, a pioneer among the St. Thomas Christians, dedicated his whole life for the cause of the promotion of the research in the area of the history of the St. Thomas Christians. Through his vast writings and deep research, always argue for the apostolic origin of St. Thomas Christians. In his book, *The South Indian Apostolate of St. Thomas*, originally published in Orientalia Christiana Periodica 18 (1952), pages 229–245, he substantiates his position by various evidences and testimonies of different people. The added strength to prove the apostolic origin, according to him, is the presence of the tomb of the apostle Thomas in Mylapore. Quoting from the Doctrine of the apostles, a Syriac work written most probably not later than 260 C.E., he states that "India and all its own countries and those bordering even to the farthest sea received the apostle's hand of priesthood from Judas Thomas who was guide and ruler of the church he built and ministered to there."[8] In the collected works of Placid, we come across the same topic in many places, especially in *A Short History of the Malabar Church*,[9] *The Thomas Christians*[10] and *The Hierarchy of the Syro-Malabar Church*.[11] The positive part of his presentation of the theme is the sharing of the first-hand knowledge of the tradition lived by the Community of the St. Thomas Christians.

Benedict Vadakkekara in his doctoral thesis presented the Indian tradition as consistent, living, well-rooted in the life and customs of the people, independent of the Acts of Thomas in origin and therefore historically true.[12]

George Moraes is for the traditions of Apostles Thomas and Bartholomew. He follows Acts of Thomas and concludes that there is an inner core of truth. The author is for the two missionary journeys of Apostle Thomas, one to North and another to South India. He argues that St. Thomas must have come to Muziris attracted by the existence of the well-established Jewish colony. On the question of the seven churches founded by Apostle Thomas, he is of the opinion that this number cannot be dismissed as symbolical, as some of these churches "have accounts of their foundation that are far from being mere imaginary fictions."[13] The Apostle proceeded to the Eastern or Coromandel Coast where he continued his preaching and finally he was martyred. He was buried in Mylapore and later his relics were transferred to Edessa. However, relying on the testimony of St. Ephrem, Moraes states that only a part of the head of the apostle was taken to Edessa.[14]

Leslie Brown,[15] an Anglican missionary and Principal in a theological Seminary in Malabar, begins his book with story of the St. Thomas Christians with the arrival of the Portuguese in the sixteenth century. He questions the traditional way of writing the history of the St. Thomas Christians, starting with an examination of the tradition of St. Thomas mission to South India. But according to Leslie Brown, such method is unsatisfactory because the sources for our knowledge of the first fifteen centuries are of very different degrees of historical worth, and the reader cannot easily get an unconfused picture of the events that certainly happened because of the entanglement of legendary, or only doubtfully probable, incident.[16] After presenting the life of the St. Thomas Christians at the arrival of the Portuguese, in the second chapter he deals with the St. Thomas tradition. He questions the historical reliability of the Acts of Thomas and says that the church fathers too had relied on Acts of Thomas to substantiate the apostolate of St. Thomas in India. For him, the very name India is confusing and there is no specific mention of South India or North India. He concludes that probably this must be the Parthian India of North-West. He analyzes the local tradition, Mar Thoma Parvam, Margam Kali, and a letter written in 1721 by Mar Thoma IV, etc. However, he was not convinced of the historical actuality of the apostolate of St. Thomas in India. But the following statement by the author is thought-provoking:

But, even if we cannot accept the claims made for the Mylapore tomb, the tradition of St. Thomas's death in South India is not entirely disproved, and no other place in the world claims the event. We cannot prove that the apostle worked in South India any more than we can disprove it; but the presence of Christians of undoubtedly ancient origin holding firmly to the tradition, the proof of very considerable commercial contact between the western world and the Malabar coast in the first century of our era, and the probable presence of Jewish colonies at the same time, may for some incline the balance to belief that the truth of the tradition is a reasonable probability. The evidence we have cannot do more than this.[17]

He continues that there is no doubt about the possibility of the apostolic mission in the first century, whether or not actually happened, was perfectly possible from a physical point of view. He concludes with recent excavations and Roman coins and the Jewish colony in Malabar, to add additional strength to the physical possibility. There is the physical possibility of the apostolate of St. Thomas.

James Hough[18] is for the improbability of any apostles having preached the Gospel in India. "There is satisfactory evidence indeed that it was carried to India at a very early period; but, considering the tedious mode of communication with that country, and the ancient's limited knowledge of its inhabitants until towards the close of the first century, it is not probable that any of the apostles of our Lord embarked on such a voyage."[19]

For James Hough, the story of St. Thomas associated with India is unworthy of credit as Eusebius, the historian of the church does not mention. Hough relied very much on Michael Geddes[20] and La Croze[21] who were anti-Catholics and highly polemical and indulged in many negative comments on Roman Catholic behavior. La Croze concludes by saying, "I shall not lose time in refuting this narration of the death of the holy apostle, (killed at Mylapore by Brahmins) that is not apparently less fabulous than the coming of St. Thomas into India."[22] La Croze was the first one to write the first general history of Christianity in India. He was a French Protestant and was the librarian of the King of Prussia. His anti-Catholic history focused on the St. Thomas Christians and the Udayamperur Synod was seen as a forced attempt by the Portuguese colonial power to bring the St. Thomas Christians under the papal authority.[23]

James Hough thinks it most improbable and holds the view that there would be much less probability in the tradition if supposed to refer to the Northern provinces bordering on the banks of the Indus.[24]

The Syrian Christians of Malabar[25] by Philipines Edavalikal was to my knowledge the first history in English written by a Syrian Christian. It was a short work in which he asserts the apostolic origin of the St. Thomas Christians. There was no scientific exposition of the topic.

George Milne Rae[26] was the first one to write the full-length history of the St. Thomas Christians. He was a former professor at Madras Christian College and his aim of writing this book was to inform the Western readers about the Indian Christians of St. Thomas. He argued, "on the basis of Acts of Thomas, that St. Thomas did not come personally to South India. However, since Thomas was the founder and patron saint of the Church of Edessa, when members of that Church migrated to South India, Thomas became by extension the founder of the church there, too. This, Rae called the "migration of tradition."[27] The Anglican biased historian argues that the emergence of Jacobites in Malabar was a switch of allegiance from Nestorian Edessa and Babylon to Jacobite Antioch and thus from the tradition of St. Thomas to a heretical tradition of St. Peter.[28]

E.M. Philip[29] in his book *The Indian Church of St. Thomas*, upholds "the tradition that St. Thomas himself came to India in A.D. 52, citing indirect evidence in its favor and arguing that, while it could not be proven, Rae had failed to disprove it with his conjectures."[30] He rejected Rae's "neat division of the church history into Nestorian, Roman and Jacobite periods, largely because he was not convinced that the Syrian church to which the Kerala Christians were ecclesiastically linked had been consistently Nestorian prior to 1500; he saw it as a mix of Jacobite and Nestorian, with the Jacobite being the stronger part of the mix."[31]

P. Thomas,[32] a Syrian Christian, authored *Christians and Christianity in India and Pakistan*. This book was written in order to give a connected account of Christianity in India from the time of Apostle Thomas, who preached the Gospel in India, to the present day. He tries to give due importance to the Indian traditions, especially of Kerala, on the apostolic origin of the church. In dealing with the arrival of St. Thomas to India and the early history of the Malabar Church, the author relies on the Western sources and the Kerala tradition, which according to him, are completely reliable.[33]

Cyril Bruce Firth,[34] through his *An Introduction to Indian Church History*, brought out a text book for the students of the history of Christianity in India. He makes an attempt to trace the outline of the Indian church history from the beginning down to the present time. "Firth was both critical and fair in his treatment of his sources, especially of the first eighteen centuries. His discussion of the St. Thomas tradition is still one of the most lucid and perceptive available."[35]

The apocryphal Acts of St. Thomas (possibly composed in the middle of the third century in Edessa) says that Thomas came first to the land of Gondophorus, a Parthian who, according to numismatic and archaeological evidence, ruled over parts of modern-day north-west India and Pakistan. From there he went to Mazday, interpreted as Mylai or Mylapore. The stronger tradition of Kerala, however, affirms that following the maritime trade route he came to Kodungalloor. Kerala was at the time a commercial center in contact with West Asia and the Mediterranean world. Thomas would first have preached to the Jews settled in Kerala and then to the indigenous population.

Whatever the traditions, we know that historically it is in Kerala that a Christian community has existed from very ancient times to our days. This community keeps the memory of St. Thomas as their apostle and identify themselves with legitimate pride as St. Thomas Christians.[36] Thus goes the statement in the book Christianity In India, by Leonard Fernando and G. Gispert-Sauch.

Rev. Dr. N.A. Thomas Nangachiveettil, in his two volumes of Asiayile Marthoma Sabhakal, Malayalam, (St. Thomas Churches of Asia), narrates the presence of the St. Thomas Christians in Asia and through convincing arguments he put forward evidences to prove that St. Thomas preached the Gospel in South India, especially in the Malabar Coast.[37]

Mathias Mundadan, one of the pioneers from among the St. Thomas Christians to undertake serious research on the question of the apostolate of St. Thomas in South India, presents his findings in the History of Christianity in India, Vol. I. Almost sixty pages of the five hundred and sixty pages of the volume are for the discussion on the apostolic origin of the St. Thomas Christians. "It is true that Christians of India came into the full limelight of history with the arrival of the Portuguese. One has to unearth the scanty and fragmentary material that is available and reconstruct the whole story that lies shrouded in legends, fables, fictions and confusing details."[38] The earliest record about the apostolate of St. Thomas in India is the apocryphal Acts of Judas Thomas, written in Syriac in the Edessan circle about the turn of the third century. Mundadan is of the opinion that there is a nucleus of truth in Acts of Judas Thomas, although it is an apocryphal writing with romantic style. He concludes the findings in the following words:

The investigation made above into the Western tradition (Acts) and different aspects of the Indian tradition give me the impression that the central content stands out in clear relief, namely St. Thomas, the apostle preached, died, and was buried in South India. None of the arguments so far advanced seem to be strong enough to erode the validity of this central content. Nor do I foresee the possibility, as things stand, of some positive evidence being suddenly unearthed that would impair its value. The argument of convergence mentioned above, therefore appears reasonable enough to be accepted.[39]

One weak point here may be the too much dependence on the Acts of Thomas.

K.S. Mathew, in one of his articles,[40] evaluates the Portuguese authors on the apostolate of St. Thomas in South India. They were well aware of the South India apostolate of St. Thomas. "The Portuguese came in contact with the St. Thomas Christians in 1500 when Pedro Alvarez Cabral with his men went to Cranganore for the purchase of pepper, ginger and other spices. They were the descendants of those who received the 'good news' preached by St. Thomas who constructed a church there."[41] In the local testimonies recorded by the Portuguese, there are references to St. Thomas Christians in Kodungallur and the tomb of the apostle in Mylapore. The Portuguese met the St. Thomas Christians in Quilon and Kayamkulam. The Portuguese Viceroy Francisco de Almeida (1505–1509) was told by the people of Malabar that their ancestors were converted by the apostle St. Thomas whose "house was found in the Coromandel Coast."[42] Eventually the Viceroy verified the fact and sent the information to the King of Portugal. Dom Alfonso de Albuquerque had discussions with the King of Kochi and the former was told that St. Thomas came to southern part of India and converted a number of people to Christian faith. Duarte Barbosa, another Portuguese wrote in 1518 about Christians who trace their origin to the apostle Thomas. Alvaro Penteado, the Portuguese priest who was doing the divine service in Mylapore conducted inquiries among the elders of that region and collected the details about the apostolate and martyrdom of St. Thomas. The people testified to the conversion of the Hindus of the locality by the apostle. "In fact, the Portuguese became convinced of the South Indian apostolate of St. Thomas and considered him patron of the Portuguese India."[43] The Portuguese started christening their ships also St. Thomas. They issued coins of gold in the name of St. Thomas. From the information we gather from the Portuguese writings, we could easily presume that they had some idea about this event even before they reached India. K.S. Mathew concludes thus:

> Thus, it may be concluded that the Portuguese writers of the sixteenth century did a great service to establish the historicity of the South Indian apostolate of St. Thomas. Though the people of India for various reasons did not question or did not make any serious studies till then in this field, the Portuguese trying to understand the people and their traditions took great interest in this matter and rendered to writing whatever they, in their investigations and inquiries, came through. The perusal of their findings bears out the truth of the said apostolate.[44]

Let us now analyze an article by E.R. Hambye in *The Clergy Monthly*.[45] During the last one hundred and fifty years, so many contradictory views have been expressed on the topic of the apostolate of St. Thomas, especially in South India. Authors like Fr. Peeters, S.J. (Bollandist), Harnack, Garbe, Winternitz, etc., started questioning the historical credibility of the Acts of Thomas. Some authors like Dahlmann, W.R. Philips, Dr. Carpentier, etc., favored the North Indian apostolate of St. Thomas. T.K. Joseph, a native Syrian Christian, has followed them. There came another group of scholars including Sir Richard Temple and Fleet who stand for the Northern tradition without denying the possibility of a Southern tradition. Yet another group of scholars are those who give more importance to the Southern tradition, combining the both traditions. These scholars include mainly Syrian Christians like Bernard of St. Thomas, J.C. Panjikaran, Placid Podipara, etc., and Msgr. Medlycott, J.N. Farquhar, partly Mingana, Hosten, Eugene Cardinal Tisserant, etc.

Western scholars discuss mainly the value of Acts of St. Thomas and for them it is an apocryphal book and there is little documentary evidence of a strong Christianity in India. The Southern tradition has many songs including Ramban Pattu, Margam Kali Pattu, Veeradian Pattu, and a Hindu account of the history of Kerala, Keralolpathi, etc. The Southern tradition is also supported by the liturgical books.

Various attempts have been made to combine the Northern tradition with the Southern tradition, even the Acts of Thomas with the Malabar tradition. But it is always liable to be corrected by fresh evidence and it deals with hypothetical explanations. It must be possible that St. Thomas moved from North to South. However, one must not depend solely on Acts as a historical document. Hambye concludes the article thus:

> All the materials we have mentioned above can be summed up in one single affirmation: since early times, at least since the fourth century, there is general agreement in the West and in India as to the coming of St. Thomas to this country. Still, a gap should be bridged, the first three centuries of the Christian era. For this we must look forward to a careful study of the South Indian tradition and to new excavations and archaeological finds in Kerala and at Mylapore.[46]

Medlycott A.E.,[47] in the preface of his work makes his stand clear, the apostolate of St. Thomas in India. The additional reasons to substantiate his arguments include the tomb of Mylapore and the transfer of relics to Edessa. He is of the opinion that after long research and study many apocryphal writings are recognized as reliable and historical documents. According to him:

> Acts of Thomas at an early date, were extensively interpolated and adapted for doctrinal purposes by certain sects; and that this manipulation of the text was carried out according to the system employed in the case of an earlier writing, the Acts of the Virgin–Proto–Martyr, Tecla, tending to prove that the Acts of Thomas had an early and independent position.[48]

So, Acts cannot be considered as merely legendary. The book has six chapters in the first part, and in the appendix, there are three sections. The first chapter deals with Apostle Thomas and the connection with Gondophorus, the Indian King. He concludes the first chapter thus: "But the name of Gondophorus is only to be found in a certain class of coins;

and the Acts of Thomas are the sole written document that reproduces it. Are we then not authorized to believe that here we are really dealing with the apostle Thomas, and with an Indo-Scythian prince, his contemporary?"[49] The second chapter is an attempt to prove the apostolate of St. Thomas with the support of the liturgical writings and writings of the Fathers of the church. The third chapter presents the tomb of the apostle and the testimonies of the visitors of the tomb through the centuries. The fourth chapter is on the analysis of further historical documents, including the transfer of the relics to Edessa. In the fifth chapter, there is a reference to the alleged apostolate of St. Bartholomew, St. Pantaeunus, Theophilus, etc. In the sixth chapter, the author refutes the argument that one of the disciples of Manes (Manichaeism) (Mani was born in Babylon in 216) went to India, and that this gave rise to the supposition that the apostle Thomas had not preached the gospel there.

The appendix is a critical analysis of the Acts of Thomas the apostle. The Acts had different versions in Syriac, Greek, Latin, and in other languages. The interpolations are possible.

In his book *The Apostles of India,* A.C. Perumalil[50] argues for the apostolate of St. Thomas in South India. At the same he is a great champion of the apostolate of St. Bartholomew in Western India, precisely in Kalyan. He begins his argument by saying that there is no confusion among the Western authors regarding India with Ethiopia and Saudi Arabia. The second apostolic journey of the apostle landed him in Muziris. A.C. Perumalil depends very much on the Acts of Thomas and concludes that St. Thomas had come to the Chola kingdom of South India. He relies also on the teachings of the Fathers of the church, local oral tradition, the folk songs, and the very name Nazrani. Again, he speaks about the tomb at Mylapore and the regular pilgrimage to Mylapore.

Paulinus of St. Bartholomew in his India Orientalis Christiana[51] strongly argues that whatever difference of opinions are forwarded by historians, one cannot deny the fact that Christianity was introduced in India in the first century itself.

Ladislas-Michel Zaleski[52] convincingly argues for the apostolate of St. Thomas in South India. Robert Eric Frikenberg[53] holds the view that questions about the antiquity of India's Thomas Christians, along with questions about the historicity of their origins, are not easy to answer. Indeed, it is impossible to this antiquity with any more scientific validity than any events of ancient history that are accepted without much question.[54] Again he says that "the historicity of apostolic origins rests upon conjectural or uncertain evidence. Yet, large measures of circumstantial and corroborative evidences are such that the plausibility, if not possibility, of historicity cannot be entirely or lightly dismissed."[55] The tradition that Thomas the apostle came and worked and died in India is as old as and as deeply rooted in India as many of the earliest Christian traditions. That this tradition is accepted as canonical cannot be denied.

In the introductory part Antiquities from San Thome and Mylapore,[56] Dr. P.J. Thomas mentions the following:

> On the one hand, we have unequivocal evidence of the early Fathers that St. Thomas preached and died in India; on the other, we have in India itself a local tradition which receives more and more support as historical research advances... and in Malabar itself we have a Christian community that claims Thomas as their founder and whose existence could be traced back to the early centuries of the Christian era. Considering the cumulative weight of all these different lines of evidence, it might seem that the mission of St. Thomas in India is as satisfactorily proved as the great majority of events in India's ancient history.[57]

There are a few Carmelite missionaries who in their writings presume the apostolic origin of the St. Thomas Christians and instead of going for further discussions on the topic they straight away go to their subject by passingly mentioning the question of the apostolic origin.[58] These authors had not made serious study on the subject as their interest was to bring back the rebel group among the St. Thomas Christians to the Catholic communion after the Coonan Cross Oath.

In Mirabilia Descripta Jordan Catalani of Severac, O.P. mentions the presence of scattered Christians in India and he has the following description: "In this part of the country there are scattered persons, one here, one there, who call themselves Christians, although they are not, nor do they have baptism nor know anything about the faith. Indeed, they believe St. Thomas the Greater to be the Christ."[59]

Antonio de Gouvea in his Jornada mentions that St. Thomas was allotted the remotest part of Eastern India and he landed in Cranganore.

After having built up and ordained the Christian Community of Cranganore, the apostle went across the entire coast of Malabar up to Quilon where also he halted because it was a noble and principal city, making many Christians therein; and proceeding further he went on to the city of Maliapor (Mylapore) the greater, the richest and most powerful at that time in the whole of India and that today, having changed its name, is inhabited by the Portuguese who call it San Thome, in reverence to the holy Apostle who died there.[60]

Alphonse Mingana wrote the article Early Spread Christianity in India[61] in the context of the reaction of the Western scholars to the writings of J.N. Farquhar's The Apostle Thomas in South India,[62] Adolf Medlycott's

India and the apostle Thomas,[63] Dahlmann's Die Thomas Legende.[64] All the three authors strongly hold the South Indian mission of St. Thomas that was denied by almost all the scholars of Europe in the latter part of the nineteenth century. In this context, the contents of the three books mentioned above, especially the last two books, caught the attention of the Western scholars, especially those of the Tuebingen School, and they were not convinced of the arguments put forward by Medlycott and Dahlmann. Tuebingen scholars represented by Robert Grabe argued that there were no traces of Christianity in India before the fourth century. He associated the origin of the Indian Christianity with the Persian migration in 345 and concluded that Persia would be the country of origin of the religious movement of India. Mingnana frankly states that it was not his intention to prove the historicity of the mission of St. Thomas in India. "It may or it may not be, true that Thomas evangelized the Indians, although we should find it difficult to reverse with a single stroke the constant tradition of the church to this effect, from the second century down to our days."[65] He is of the opinion that the history of the Christianity in India can be written only in an imperfect way mainly because of the remoteness of the followers of Jesus of Nazareth living far away from the centers of Christianity. Although the author refers to many documents and testimonies, he is not committed to hold the view that there is no hundred per cent historicity of the apostolate of St. Thomas in India.

Farquhar J.N.[66] concludes his study by saying that: "Thirty years ago the balance of the possibility stood absolutely against the story of the Apostolate of Thomas in India: we suggest that today the balance of probability is distinctly on the side of historicity. . . .Thus, the history of the Church of Travancore bears witness to the courage and endurance that the Apostolic Founder breathed into her spirit. In her case the word of Christ is fulfilled, "The gates of hell shall not prevail against it."[67]

Mackenzie G.T.[68] in his Christianity in Travancore gives great importance to the Malabar tradition and he finds nothing improbable in the tradition as it has been accepted as true by many writers of repute. There were trade routes in those days and "the tradition is supported by numerous passages in which early writers allude to the work of St. Thomas in India or mention the existence of Christians in India. Several old liturgies and martyrologies speak of St. Thomas in India and this shows that the tradition had spread throughout the various Christian Churches."[69]

Stephen Neil, an Anglican missionary who worked in Malabar for many years has written the two volumes of the History of Christianity in India. The first volume covers the period from the beginnings to A.D. 1707. After analyzing the sources, he has the following conclusion:

The story of the ancient church of the Thomas Christians is of great significance for the whole history of Christianity in India. It is to be regretted that, when all the evidence has been collected and sifted, much remains uncertain and conjectural.

For the first three centuries of the Christian era we have nothing that could be called clear historical evidence—references to India may relate to countries that would not today be called India.

It is possible that in this dark period the apostle Thomas came to India and that the foundation of the Indian church goes back to him; we can only regret the absence of any sure historical evidence to support this view.

Millions of Christians of South India are certain that the founder of their Church was none other than the apostle Thomas himself. The historian cannot prove to them that they are mistaken in their belief. He may feel it right to warn them that historical research cannot pronounce on the matter with a confidence equal to that which they entertain by faith.[70]

Among those who accept a dual ministry for Thomas in India include: Adolf Medlycott, J.N. Farquhar, and George Moraes.

Samuel Hugh Moffett through his two volumes, History of Christianity in Asia, laid a new path in the study of the history of Asian Christianity. He referred large number of primary and secondary sources to substantiate his arguments. After analyzing the mission of St. Thomas in India he has the following conclusion:

> The consensus of the majority is that both theories (North Indian Mission and South Indian Mission) are reasonable and, far from being mutually exclusive, can be interpreted as strengthening each other. It is not impossible to believe that after preaching in Gundaphar's kingdom in the north, Thomas moved as all traditions affirm, to preach the gospel to other kingdoms as well, the kingdoms of south-western and south-eastern India, until at last he was put to death, perhaps near Madras. If, as seems quite possible, he was the apostle to India at all, it is satisfying to believe with considerable reason that he was the apostle to all India.[71]

When we make a serious reference to some of the books or manuals on general church history, we come across only passing references to the apostolate of St. Thomas, especially the mission of St. Thomas in South India. The ten volume History of the Church, edited by Hubert Jedin[72] deals in a detailed with way the history of the church, especially of the Catholic Church. It is a collective work of different authors who are experts in the respective fields. Surprisingly there is no one from Asia among the sectional editors. First volume speaks about the mission of Apostle Thomas in India in the following way:

In view of the strength of that Christianity, it would be quite within the realm of possibility for east Syrian or Persian missionaries to have penetrated into western India at this time. The St. Thomas Christians of southwest India, of course, regard the apostle Thomas as their first missionary, but the apocryphal Acts of Thomas, on which they have to base this belief, is not a very sound source. When Origen mentions India on one occasion, he still regards it as a pagan country. Arnobius the elder, however, clearly assumes the existence of individual Christians about the year 300 and the well-organized Christian communities attested by Cosmas Indicopeustes about the year 525 in Malabar, in the region of present-day Bombay, and in Ceylon, oblige us to assume a fairly long missionary development with its beginnings in the fourth or fifth century. That again suggests the possibility of evangelization by Persian Christians who had fled east from Persia under persecution and this conjecture is supported by the later dependence of the Indian Christians on Seleucia-Ctesiphon.[73]

Another three-volume Church History by Karl Bihlmeyer and Hermann Tuechle[74] too has only very little space for the St. Thomas Christians. Quoting Origen St. Thomas is given to Parthia. Again, as a further discussion on the topic, we have the following:

> According to the apocryphal Acts of Thomas of the third century, and according to Ephraem, Ambrose, Jerome and others, the Apostle Thomas preached the Gospel in India. After wandering eastwards as far as Kalamina (near Mailapur?) he was put to death with a lance by order of King Masdai (Mzdai). His remains are said to have been brought back to Edessa. The so-called Thomas Christians of the Malabar Coast in the southwest India take their name from him and hold to the tradition that they received the faith from him. This tradition has recently received some support from the discovery that King Gundaphor whose name constantly recurs in the Acts was an historical person. It has further been proved that lively trade relations existed between Syria and India in the first Christian century, and that the sea route from Egypt to India was known as early as the second century. But, at best, this merely proves the possibility of a mission to India in apostolic times; it does not prove that there actually was one. Probably Christianity found its way into India in the third century by way of Syria (Edessa) and into the southern part (Malabar) in the fourth century through travelers from Persia or Armenia.[75]

The Christian Centuries by Jean Danielou—Henri Marrou[76] with the subtitle A New History of the Catholic Church, is a five-volume project with the original text in French. In the general introduction it is said "The series of volumes, of which this is the first, will endeavor to present the history of the church in a form, and on a scale, suited to the needs of the interested reader of today."[77] Here we have the typical example where international scholarship gives minimum details about the history of

Christianity in India, that too in a prejudiced way. Here too the focus is on the church in the Roman Empire and in the chapter on the church outside the Empire we read the following entry: "The Syro-Malabar Church, which still flourishes today in Kerala (South India), perhaps owes its origin to Nestorian missionaries; or to groups of emigrants driven out by persecution. The tradition that links this Church to the memory of the apostle Thomas may simply express its distant descent from the Church of Edessa."[78] Norman Tanner in his New Short History of the Catholic Church[79] notes that "There is the long tradition that the apostle Thomas reached India, or at least the Indus valley, and was martyred there."

Dale T. Irvin and Scott W. Sunquist[80] present a new approach in the study of the history of the church. They conclude the discussion on the mission of Apostle Thomas in India with the following observation:

> Providing an adequate historical assessment of these traditions is difficult. The sheer weight of their abundance in several variant streams commands our respect. An enormous body of legendary material concerning Thomas accrued in the early centuries of the Christian Church. Surprisingly, none disagrees that Thomas journeyed to the east; where and how far he went are what are in question. In the end we are left with a fascinating body of tradition, found in apocryphal sources, abundant later accounts, and a rich body of oral traditions and folk songs. The safest historical stance that we can take is to say that the evidence is compelling without yet being historically decisive.[81]

CONCLUSION

A humble attempt is made here to bring to light the various views of different great scholars on the topic of the mission of St. Thomas, the apostle in India. I do not claim that it is an exhaustive study. I could not deal with the literature on the apostolate of St. Thomas in India in the languages like French, Latin, German, Spanish, Portuguese, etc. I focused mainly on the writings in the English language. I also did not deal with the scientific studies done by Benedict Vadakkekara and James Kurikilamkatt on the apostolate of St. Thomas in India. These studies are worth discussing. It is not an easy task to deal with such a vast topic like the apostolate of St. Thomas in India. One has to admire and appreciate the seriousness with which the scholars undertook this painstaking study, although they differ in their findings. Except a few authors who have prejudiced judgments, all the other scholars have done a praiseworthy work for the academia. It is quite natural that St. Thomas Christians always stand for their apostolic origin.

One area where further study could be undertaken is the critical study of the Acts of Judas Thomas. The Church authorities should make use of the expertise in archaeological and numismatic sciences and encourage the critical study of the writings on the origin of Christianity in India.

ENDNOTES

1   George Nedungatt, S.J, *Quest for the Historical Thomas Apostle of India: A Re-reading of the Evidence*, Bangalore: Theological Publications in India, 2008.

2   Nedungatt, *Quest for the Historical Thomas*, XXII- XXXI.

3   Nedungatt, XXI.

4   A.F.J. Klijn, *The Acts of Thomas*, Leiden, 1962, 27.

5   Albert Gille, *Christianity at Home*, Calcutta, 1924, 15; See also, Nedungatt George, *Quest for the Historical Thomas*, XXIX.

6   Bernard Thoma, *Mar Thoma Christianikal* (Malayalam, reprint in volume), Kochi: CMI Publications, 1992, 49–207.

7   Prof. George Menachery, (Editor) *The Nazranies*, 293–312; Bernard of St. Thomas, A Brief Sketch of the History of the St. Thomas Christians.

8   Placid J. Podipara, CMI, *Collected Works of Rev. Dr. Placid J. Podipara, CMI*, Volume I, Editor Dr. Thomas Kalayil, CMI, Sanjos Publications, Mannanam, 2007, 203–214.

9   Podipara, 251–295.

10 Podipara, 313–419.

11 Podipara, 649–756.

12 George Nedungatt, *Quest for the Historical Thomas*, XXXI.

13 George Mark Moraes, *A History of Christianity in India From Early times to St Francis Xavier: 52 -1542*, Bombay, 1964, 39.

14 Moraes, 43.

15 Leslie Brown, *The Indian Christians of St. Thomas*, Cambridge University Press, London (revised), 1982.

16 Brown, 11.

17 Brown, 59.

18 James Hough, *The History of Christianity in India*, Vol. I, London, 1839.

19 Hough, 30.

20 Michael Geddes, *History of the Church of Malabar*, London, 1694.

21 La Croze V., *Histoire du Christianisme des Indes*, La Haye, 1724.

22 La Croze, *Histoire*, 39–40.

23 John Webster C.B., *Historiography of Christianity in India*, New Delhi: Oxford University Press, 2012, 15.

24 James Hough, *The History of Christianity*, 40.

25 Philipos Edavalikel, *The Syrian Christians of Malabar: Otherwise Called the Christians of St. Thomas*, London, 1869.

26 George Milne Rae, *The Syrian Church in India*, London, 1892.

27 George Milne Rae, *The Syrian Church in India*, 128; Cf. also, Webster, *Historiography*, 39.

28 Webster, *Historiography*, 39.

29 E.M. Philip, *The Indian Church of St. Thomas*, Nagercoil, 1950.

30 Webster, *Historiography*, 41; Cf. Philip, *The Indian Church of St. Thomas*, 47.

31 Webster, 41.

32 P. Thomas, *Christians and Christianity in India and Pakistan: A General Survey of the Progress of Christianity in India from Apostolic times to the Present Day*, London, 1954.

33 Webster, *Historiography*, 47.

34 Cyril Bruce Firth, *An Introduction to Indian Church History*, Madras, 1961.

35 Webster, *Historiography*, 49.

36 Leonard Fernando and G. Gispert-Sauch, *Christianity in India*, Penguin-Viking, New Delhi, 2004, 60.

37 Thomas Nangachiveettil, *Asiayile Marthoma Christianikal*, Trivandrum, 1982, 302–389.

38 A.M. Mundadan, *History of Christianity in India*, Vol. I, Church History Association of India, Bangalore, 2001 (revised edition), 2.

39 Mundadan, 61.

40 Mathew K.S. The South Indian Apostolate of St. Thomas and the Portuguese in the Sixteenth Century, *Christian Orient*, March 1985, Vol.VI. I, 5–12.

41 Mathew, 6.

42 Mathew, 7.

43 Mathew, 9.

44 Mathew, 12. Cf. also Mathew K.S., The South Indian Apostolate of St. Thomas: Some Reflections, St Joseph's Minor Seminary, Thalassery, 1957–2007, *Suvarna Jubilee Smaranika*, 38–41.

45 Hambye, E.R., Saint Thomas and India, The Clergy Monthly, Vol. XVI, November 1952, 10, 363–375.

46 Hambye, 374–375.

47 Medlycott A.E., *India and the Apostle Thomas: An Inquiry, with a Critical Analysis of the Acta Thomae*, London, 1905.

48 Medlycott, X–XI.

49 Medlycott, 18.

50 A.C. Perumalil, *The Apostles of India*, Patna, 1952/ 1971 (revised edition).

51 Paulinus of St Barthuloew, *India Orientalis Christiana*, Roma, 1794, p.1.

52 Ladslas-Michel Zaleski, *The Apostle St. Thomas in India*, Mangalore, 1912.

53 Robert Eric Frykenberg, *Oxford History of the Christian Church: Christianity in India from the Beginnings to the Present*, Oxford University Press, New York, 2008.

54 Frykenberg, 91.

55 Frykenberg, 114.

56 H. Hosten S.J., *Antiquities from San Thome and Mylapore*, published by the diocese of Mylapore, 1936.

57 Hosten, XIV.

58 Vincenzo Maria di S. Caterina da Siena, *Il Viaggio all Indie Orientali*, Roma, 1672, 1; Giuseppe di Santa Maria, *Prima Speditione All'Indie Orientali*, Roma, M.DC.LXVI, 1.

59 Jordan of Severac, O.P., *Mirabilia Descripta: The Wonders of the East* (Edited by Peter B. Lobo, O.P), Dominican Publications, Nagpur, 1993, 37. The editor gives an introduction and the original Latin text is given together with the English translation.

60 Antonio de Gouvea, *Jornada do Arcebispo Dom Alexis de Menezes*, Coimbra, 1606; the English translation with a detailed historical introduction was done by Dr. Pius Malekandathil, LRC Publcations, Kochi, 2003, 6.

61 Alphonse Mingana, "The Early Spread of Christianity in India," *Bulletin of the John Ryland's Library*, 10 (1926), 435–514. Reprint by Kraus Reprint Limited, Nendeln/Liechtenstein, 1967.

62 J.N. Farquhar, "The Apostle Thomas in South India," *Bulletin of John Ryland's Library*, 11 (1927), 20–50.

63 A.E. Medlycott, *India and the Apostle Thomas*, London, David Nutt, 1905.

64 J.S.J. Dahlmann, *Die Thomas-Legende und die aeltesten historischen Beziehungen des Christentums zum fernen Osten in Lichte der indischen Altertumskunde*, Freiburg i. B., 1912.

65 Alphonse Mingana, *The Early Spread of Chritianity in India*, 436.

66 J.N. Farquhar, "The Apostle Thomas in South India," *Bulletin of John Ryland's Library*, 11 (1927), 20–50.

67 Farquhar, 20–50; Cf., George Menachery (Editor), *The Nazranies*, The Indian Church History Classics, Thrissur, 1998, 329–330.

68 Cf. Geroge Menachery (Editor), *The Nazranies*, 113–114; Mackenzie G.T., *Christianity in Travancore*.

69 Menachery, 113.

70 Stephen Neil, *A History of Christianity in India The Beginnings to A.D. 1707*, Cambridge University Press, London, 1984, 48–49.

71 Samuel Hugh Moffett, *A History of Christianity in Asia*, Volume I, Beginnings to 1500, Theological Publications in India, Bangalore, 2006, 36.

72 Hubert Jedin, *History of the Church, Vol. I, From the Apostolic Community to Constantine*, Crossroad, New York, 1965.

73 Jedin, 373–374.

74 Karl Bihlmeyer and Hermann Tuechle, *Church History*, Vol. I, The Newman Press, Westminster, 1968.

75 Bihlmeyer, 64 & 71–72.

76 Jean Danielou and Henri Marrou, *The Christian Centuries, Volume One, The First Six Hundred Years*, Darton, Longman and Todd, London, 1983.

77 Danielou, V.

78 Danielou, 371.

79 Norman Tanner, *New Short History of the Catholic Church*, Burns & Oates, London, 2011, 35.

80 Dale T. Irvin and Scott W. Sunquist, *History of the World Christian Movement*, Orbis Books, New York, 2001.

81 Irvin, 94.

3

MISSION OF ST. THOMAS THE APOSTLE IN INDIA: ARCHAEOLOGICAL, EPIGRAPHIC, AND NUMISMATIC EVIDENCES

James Kurikilamkatt, MST

INTRODUCTION

St. Thomas has always been honored as the apostle of India. He probably made two journeys to India. The first journey (A.D. 40–50) was to the northwestern regions of ancient India that also included the present Afghanistan and Pakistan. In his second mission to India (A.D. 52–72) he established Christian communities in South India. He is also said to have made a journey to China (A.D. 67–69) from South India. The historicity of both these journeys has been sufficiently discussed by historians and is now held to be an established historical fact. Still, it is true that there are skeptics who consider the Thomas element in Indian church history as a pious fraud. They accept that traditional stories and pious legends exist in abundance both in India and outside about the mission of Thomas in India. But, are they substantiated by historical records? Do there exist contemporary archaeological, epigraphic, and numismatic records to prove the mission of Thomas in India? These are questions that they often ask. To satisfy their curiosity, we are making an attempt in this paper to bring together all the historical proofs from archaeology, numismatics, and epigraphy for the establishment of Christian communities in India by St. Thomas, the apostle.

TWO JOURNEYS OF THE APOSTLE THOMAS TO INDIA

St. Thomas is said to have made two missionary journeys to India. The first voyage led Thomas from Alexandria to Bharuch, the most important port in India in the first half of the first century C.E. From there, he travelled via Mathura to Taxila, the capital city of King Gondophares of the Indo-Parthian Dynasty. He travelled freely in the Indo-Parthian Kingdom of Gondophares and preached his way. After the destruction of the city of Taxila and the subsequent defeat of the Indo-Parthians by the Kushan dynasty who were hostile to Christianity, Thomas seemed to have crossed over to the Persian Empire and travelled back to Jerusalem.[1]

According to traditions, Thomas went back to Jerusalem to take part in the funeral service of the Mother of Jesus. He is also said to have participated in the Jerusalem council.[2] On a second journey to India, he reached Muziris in Kerala via Socotra in 52 C.E. After having established Christian communities in seven places in Kerala, he crossed over to the Coromandel Coast. There at Mylapore in 72 C.E., he was martyred for the glory of God. From Mylapore, he probably made a journey to China between the years 67 and 69 C.E.

NUMISMATIC AND EPIGRAPHIC DOCUMENTS

To substantiate this probable theory, we have in our possession certain proofs from several parts of India. First of these was the discovery of the coins bearing the name of King Gondophares. Gondophares was the name of the King mentioned in the *Acts of Thomas* in connection with St. Thomas, the apostle. The inscription of Takt-i-Bahi that also speaks about Gondophares is another document. The mural inscriptions of Udaipur temple also speak about the mission of Thomas in India. The St. Thomas Crosses discovered in several areas of India also are valid documents.

Coins of Gondopahres

A great discovery that was to change our understanding of the history of India was made in the nineteenth century. This was the discovery of the coins of King Gondophares. Hoards of coins were discovered all bearing the name of Gondophares, but in varied forms. In one side of the coins there were inscriptions in Greek and on the reverse side they were in *kharoshti*.[3] It all began in 1834 when some coins were unearthed from Kabul province by Masson.[4] The credit of first drawing attention of scholars to the connection between the coins of Gondophares and the *Acts of Thomas* is due to Reinaud in 1848.[5] It is assumed from the special characteristics of the Greek letters of the legends on the coins that they belonged to the first half of the first century C.E. These coins have been found in successive years from a large area such as Kabul, Kandahar, Seistan, and Western and Southern Punjab. Coins not only of Gondophares but of his family members were also discovered.[6] Different specimens of these coins are kept in the different museums and libraries of the world, such as

British Museum, Bibliotheque Nationale de Paris, Berlin Museum, Lahore Museum, and National Museum, Calcutta.

All coins speak clearly of a historical person who held different titles and who considered himself worthy and powerful enough to issue coins in his name. They speak of a king Gondophares or names similar to it, who was known to be or who claimed the title *autocrat* or the king of king as the *kharoshti* inscription means.

Various conclusions may be derived from an analysis of these titles of the king as we see them on the coins.

i) These coins belong to a wide range of time, as we think that these titles cannot be adopted by the same person in a short period of time.

ii) They belong to the same person who assumed different titles in different occasions of his reign.

iii) The king named in the coins had made numerous conquests and these titles were assumed after those conquests that he considered made him worthy of them.

iv) The coins were put into circulation to commemorate the victories of the king.

All these make Gondophares a great king who had made extensive conquests and established a great empire of his own in the Northwest India that included modern Punjab, Pakistan, and Afghanistan.

These coins unmistakably reveal a hidden history of India. When they are studied together with other coins of the same type, we are enabled to construct the early history of India in a better and more comprehensible manner. And what is more important to us is the fact that Gondophares, the hero of the *Acts of Thomas*, so far known only through the story of the apostle Thomas, is learned to have really existed in history. His reign becomes a historical reality uncovering the mist of doubts and curiosities of centuries. In what epoch of the time might have he ruled these parts of India? The study of the coins shows that he might have ruled in the first half of the first century after Christ. This is calculated from different criteria. First is the peculiar type of Greek characters used on the coins, especially sigma, omicron, epsilon, and omega. The particularities of the coins help us date them between the years 10 and 40 C.E..[7] They were minted during the first half of the first century C.E.. And the title *autocratos* also helps us date the coins around this period. This was a title adopted by the Roman emperor Augustus, but is first seen on the Indo-Persian coins in 76 B.C. The "contention is that the Augustan title took its origin in India and the cultural route by which it reached Rome was through the

Indo-Bactrian kingdoms."[8] We may note also that all the Indian kings of the time and after it always preferred to use these titles. About these titles being taken by the Indo-Parthians, see the following observation.

"The Western Punjab seems to have formed an integral part of the Parthian dominion for a few years. But during the trouble that ensured upon the death of Mithridates I, about 136 B.C.E., a chieftain named Maues made himself king of Taxila (120 B.C.E) and enjoyed practical, if not nominal, independence and assumed the title 'Great king of Kings' (*Basileosbasileonmegalon*)."[9]

Thus, these coins bring to light the life of the king who was described, by popular traditions, in connection with the mission of the apostle Thomas. The evidence is entirely numismatic and its bearing may be summarized as follows: The numerous varieties of coins of this monarch, copied as they are from so many previous issues, show that he ruled over a very extensive dominion; and the fact that these varieties are imitated from the currencies both of the family of Vonones and the family of Maues, leads us to the conclusion that he ruled over both the earlier kingdoms of the Pahlavas and the Sakas.[10]

Thus, the argument so far is clear. There was mentioned the name of an Indian king in the narrative of the story of the apostle Thomas in all its versions and this king was known only in connection with the apostle till the discovery of the coins bearing his name in 1834 and the subsequent findings in the northwestern parts of India. Now we know that there existed a king named Gondophares in India and he was an Indo-Parthian, which explains his Iranian name, who had his capital at Taxila and who ruled over a vast domain from 21–51 C.E.

Takt-i-Bahi inscription

The inscription of Takht-i-Bahi is yet another important document connected with Gondophares that was discovered by archaeologists. It was discovered at a place called Takht-i-Bahi, a little northeast from Peshwar, in 1872 by Dr. Bellow and was donated to the Lahore museum. The discovery of the inscription is detailed in the Trubner's Records of June, 1873:

> The inscription if not the stone, was discovered by Dr. Leitner, who after many useless attempts, finally and after much labor succeeded in restoring the whole of the inscription. Dr. Bellow had discovered the stone on which only IX was visible, and had abandoned it at Hoti Murdan, in Dr. Johnson's compound. Several years afterwards, in 1870, he authorized Dr. Leitner to take away anything he might have left at Hoti Murdan. Dr. Leitner, after personal inspection, got the stone carried down to Lahore by bullock-cart, and there got the inscription both lithographed and

photographed. . . . The discovery of the stone therefore belongs to Dr. Bellow and that of the inscription to Dr. Leitner.[11]

It is thought to be a memorial stone used perhaps as corner stone for some buildings. The following chart gives three translations made of the inscription of Takt-i-Bahi.

Senart	Cunningham	Dawson
L'an 26 du grand roi Gudupharas, 103 du comput continu, le cinquième jour du mois Vaiçakha … en l'honneur de … en l'honneur de ses père et mère.	In the twenty-sixth year of the great king Guduphara, in the samvat year three and one hundred 100+3, in the month of Vaisakh, on the fourth day.	In the twenty-sixth year of the great king Gudupharasa, on the 7, seventh day of the month of vaisakha.

A comparative study of these readings makes one thing clear: in spite of the apparent differences in the renderings, all of them agree on the basics. This agreement is more on the dates inscribed on the stone. The inscription speaks of two dates: one, the reigning year of the king and the other the actual year of the then era (*Samvat*). All agree that twenty-sixth year of Gondophares's reign and the 103rd year of the *Samvat* is one and the same. This stone might have been erected as a sign of thanksgiving for some favors received, by a pious Buddhist.[12] The date in which he wrote was the 103rd year of the *samvat,* and it was the twenty-sixth year of reign of the great king Gondophares. This showed that the king Gondophares really had a long tenure and at the time of writing this inscription he had been ruling for twenty-six years. This *Samvat* is the *Vikrama era*[13] that began in 57 B.C.E.. Cunningham writes,

> I have already assumed that the *samvat* of Kanishka, Huvishka and Vasu-Deva, is the same as the present *Vikramasamvat* of India, as the dates of their inscriptions, if referred to this era, corresponds exactly with the known dates which have been ascertained from other sources.[14]

The *samvat* 103 is 46 C.E. and according to the inscription 46 C.E. was the twenty-sixth year of the reign of Gondophares and accordingly he might have begun to rule in 21 C.E.

Inscription of Udayapur

At Udayapur in Madhya Pradesh state, in the present Syro-Malabar diocese of Sagar, there is a famous temple recognized as a national monument. It is said to be of the eleventh century C.E. A particularly interesting Sanskrit inscription was found in this Hindu temple. The inscription is incised on the stone jambs (doorposts) of the main entrance of this temple. It was translated and interpreted by a French missionary Bernard Burthey SJ of Madura mission. Mr. Baron Textor of Ravisi, member of Royal Asiatic Society of Paris and former governor of Karaikal presented it before the XXII International Congress of the Orientalists in Rome in 1899. English translations of it were given in Catholic Register of Madras of October 1, 1915 and in The Examiner, November 27 and December 4, 1915. Here is an excerpt from it.

Nine centuries had rolled by since the glory and mercy of the Uncreated, the Divine Orient, the man God, Christ, descended on the earth and also that, after having laid down the weight of his mortality he entered upon the possession of his glory, and after his holy Apostle (St. Thomas = Nadanigam Buddha) arrived among us, we should say, according to the era of Emperor Vikrama, 1,116 years, the new era, which ought to be given here together with the one that marks the nine centuries.

But after this time, he who carried upon his shoulders the cross, the conqueror of his enemies became our peace, one records 981 years. It was during this time that, all darkness being dispelled, and the sovereign power of the divine conqueror making art and virtue flourish, the Divine Orient (Udayadithya) was recognized as the master of all the sciences and the King of kings.

But in course of time the souls began to incline towards the earth and thus so great splendor of science and virtue disappeared. Heresies sprang up and men given to the use of the Kanja having prevailed, the whole empire was filled with trouble. A period of 446 years has elapsed since the commencement of these evils.[15]

Now, let us speak about the inscription. As Nedungatt writes, the Udayapur inscription is an extensive document like the rock inscriptions of Emperor Asoka, which were long edicts of imperial magisterium or Buddhist moral catechesis. The translation given above conveys an idea of its length. It is engraved on stone jambs of the principal porch of the temple facing east. Their measurements vary: most vertical stones measure 114 cm x 37 cm, while several horizontal pieces measure 79 cm x 37 cm. Others are smaller. The inscription fills the surface of the jambs on the right side and on the left side and extends to the doorway on the right. Most of the inscription is quite readable, but some portions have been worn out at the uncaring hands of visitors and devotees.[16] According to Burthey, this temple was a church. The inscription was done at the time of the rededication of the church in 1060. It speaks about the arrival of the apostle Thomas and the building of the first church in this place.

The date 1116 is of the Vikrama era that began, according to historians, in 57 B.C.E. Therefore, the inscription was done in 1059 (1116-57) C.E. The church of Udayapur was reconstructed and rededicated in 1059 C.E. There was a great celebration and 9000 people took part in it. According to the inscription it is 981 years since the Divine Orient was recognized as King of Kings. Here the author of the inscription seems to speak about the first construction of the church. It is 1059-981 = 78 C.E. Thus, it seems that the first church here was built by the disciples of St. Thomas.

It is quite probable that this region in Central India was included in the itinerary of St. Thomas the apostle. In his first journey to India, aiming to reach Taxila, Thomas had passed through Vidisa to gain the Taxila-Pataliputra highway at Mathura.[17]

St. Thomas crosses

The cross known as St. Thomas cross discovered by the Portuguese during excavations at Chinnamala is yet another important historical monument. Though it has no direct connection with the apostle, it is a clear evidence for the presence of strong Christian communities in Southern India.

Mylapore had been for centuries considered as the place where the tomb of St. Thomas was situated. When the first Portuguese arrived at Mylapore, there was no building, only foundation walls that rose above the ground about 1 cubit, stretching east to west. First, the Portuguese missionaries built a small oratory on this foundation in C.E. 1523. Later, in 1547, they decided to build a larger church and on Tuesday, March 23, 1547, when they dug around the old foundation, found another foundation deep, also east to west, which was unknown until then. They continued digging down and at 3 cubic, they found the "Holy Stone." This stone was of the size of a mile stone with the cross engraved on it, facing down with fresh blood stains on it. The granite tablet on which the cross is engraved, has raised edges and is round on the top. The Pahlavi inscriptions are on this round edge with a small cross in between two parts of the inscriptions. The cross inside is surrounded by two pillars and an arch surrounding it. The arch originates from the open mouth of something like an aquatic creature.

The cross has three steps on the bottom, three downward facing petals and upward facing floral petals look like a lotus on which the cross is erected. The cross shows the arms ends in a bud pattern. The bottom arm is a bit longer than the rest. A dove is seen facing downwards on the top arm. The entire structure is like a niche in which the cross and pillars are carved. What is of interest to us is the inscription on it. The letters, according to all who studied the inscription, are from Pahlavi. There were several attempts to decipher and translate this inscription. We are giving a few of them. The first translation was by local people who were commissioned by the Portuguese to do it. However, it seems to be a fabrication by the Portuguese.

First Translation by the Brahmins	Modern Translations
During the reign of the son of Sagad, who had protected this region during 30 years, the true, unique God came to the world taking flesh from a virgin and he destroyed the glory of the Jews. He lived in this world for thirty-three years and taught the doctrines that he was speaking to his twelve disciples, and then he suffered at the hands of the Jews the chastisement for the sins of man. One of his disciples came with a staff on his hands at Mylapore. He there constructed a church with the tree that he had brought from the seashore. Everybody was pleased with it. As the Law of Thomas was true, a king with three crowns, as well as Keralakon, Indialakon, Kuspardiad, the count of Ertinabad etc. have voluntarily accepted this Law. He gave the sign of the holy cross so that they may adore it. Then he was attacked by a lance by a Brahmin at Antinodore. He embraced this cross. It was soaked with his blood. His disciples brought him to Mailpuri. He was buried in the church that he had built. We the kings named above have seen all these and we have written this for eternity.	By the cross, as punishment, suffered the unique, who was the true Christ God above and guide always pure. (Bruenelle)

That which has liberated the true Christ from suffering is not the deliverance nor the punishment, but the death on the cross. (E.W. West)

He who believes in Christ and the Supreme God and the Holy Spirit remain in the grace of him who has suffered the punishment of the cross. (Haugue)

My Lord Christ, have mercy upon Afras son of Chaharbukht the Syrian, who cut this (or, who caused this to be cut). (C.P.T. Winkworth) |

The first translation connects the cross with the St. Thomas the apostle. But it cannot be historically proven that St. Thomas himself carved this cross on the cross. Similar crosses are seen in several parts of Central Asia, India, and China. Christians in Kerala and Mylapore sincerely believed that this cross was made by Thomas himself and that he died embracing it. This belief was all the more strengthened by the miracle that took place on the cross for consecutive years on 18th December.

The translation given by Winkworth seems to be the most probable one. He interpreted the inscriptions in the following way:

(a) "My Lord Christ, have mercy upon Afras, son of Chaharbukht, the Syrian who cut this.

(b) My Lord Christ, have mercy upon Afras, son of Chahrbukht, the Syrian who preserved this.

(c) My Lord Christ, have mercy upon Afras, son of chahrbukht, the Syrian who put this around." On analyzing the inscription itself, we can assume that these inscriptions were entered by Afras, son of Chaharbukht, the Syrian. It also says, Afras has preserved this/ put it around. That means, the cross without any inscriptions was already there, and Afras found it and preserved it–put it up. Putting an inscription around a cross is not a meritorious act, but setting up a cross or preserving a neglected cross is definitely a meritorious act. This raises the possibility that the Mount cross was found by Afras and he preserved it in 650 C.E. period.[18]

Famous Malabar Historian T.K. Joseph argues that "it may justify the supposition that the cross without inscriptions had been in existence on the Coromandel coast prior to the time of Mar Sabour Afroath who arrived in 825 C.E. We may also presume that on his visit from Quilon to the Mailapore tomb of Saint Thomas and the mount church or its ruins, Afras found the cross in a neglected condition and preserved it."[19] According to him, the Christians of Malabar made copies of it in Malabar and that became the tradition from C.E. 825 onwards until the Portuguese found and witnessed the "Cross of saint Thomas" in the churches of Malabar.

CONCLUSION

In the preceding pages, we presented a few historical documents, obtained through archaeological excavations, which shed light on the history of the time when St. Thomas the apostle reached India with the Gospel message. Though they do not directly describe the mission of Thomas in India, they do help us to situate this mission in the history of India. There are indeed a few more minor objects obtained after excavation in and around

Mylapore. Barring a small wooden statue of Thomas, none of them is directly related to Thomas. We did not also speak about the Pattanam excavations as nothing concrete that would directly connect Kerala with St. Thomas is obtained from the site. The artefacts recovered from the site suggest that Pattanam, with a hinterland port and multicultural settlement, may have had links with the Mediterranean, Red Sea, and the Arabian Sea and the South China Sea rime since the early historic period of South India. They just prove that all the historic details described in the Thomas story are true.

ENDNOTES

1 For a detailed discussion of the first journey of Thomas in India, see James Kurikilamkatt, *First Voyage of Apostle Thomas to India, Ancient Christianity in Bharuch and Taxila*, Asian Trading Corporation, Banglalore, 2005.

2 There are apocryphal stories about Thomas reaching Jerusalem from India. In them Thomas is seen as describing to the other Apostles his heroics in India. He tells them how he converted a King and his brother to Christianity. He also narrates to them how he was carried to Jerusalem by the angels.

3 "Eine Münze mit parthischem Königstzpus trägt nur eine griechische Inschrift mit dem Namen Undopheres (der erste Buchstabe wohl wie asperiertes Ypsilon auszusprechen); die übrigen tragen auf der Bildseite eine griechische Legende (Undopherres, Undopherros, Gondophares, Gondopharos, Dondophares, Gondoapharos), auf der Rückseite eine indische in Karoschti-Schrift (die Genetiv-Form von Guduphara, Gudapharna, Gundaphara, Gundapharna). A. Vaeth, *Der Hl. Thomas der Apostel indiens, Eine Untersuchung über den historischen Gehalt der Thomas-Legende*, Abhandlungen aus Missionskunde und Missionsgeschichte 4. Aachen: Xaverius, 1925, 25. Kharoshti was the form of writing in the Northwest India. It could be the Prakrit, the ancient form of Sanskrit. For more details, see A.L. Basham, *The Wonder that was India*, Rupa, Delhi, 1998 (New edition), 397. This work deals extensively with the ancient Indian culture, civilization, languages and kingdoms.

4 Many useful accounts regarding these excavations can be found. Here are a few of them. H.H. Wilson, *Ariana Antiqua, Antiquities and Coins of Afghanistan*, East India Company, London, 1871. C.J. Rodrigues, *Coin Collecting in Northern India*, Asian Educational Services, Allahabad, 1894; E. Thomas, *Essays on Indian Antiquities of late Sir James Prinsep*, John Murray, London, 1858; For a detailed study of the coins the following books are useful. V.A. Smith, *Catalogue of Coins of Indian Museum*, Published for the trustees of Indian Museum, Oxford, 1906; E.J. Rapson, *Indian Coins*, Bombay Education Society Press, Strassburg, 1897; *Catalogue of Coins of Andhra Dynasty*, British Museum, London, 1908; A. Cunningham, *Coins of Indo-Scythians, Sakas and Keshenas*, Royal Numismatic Society, London, 1888; P. Gardner, *Catalogue of the Coins of Greek and Scythian kings of India*, Trustees of the British Museum, London, 1886.

5 M. Reinaud, *Mémoire géographique, historique et scientifique sur l 'Inde (Mémoires de l'Institut National de France)*, vol. XVIII, II, 1849. "Now the Acts of the life of St. Thomas that are extant both in Greek and Latin mentioned a king named Gondophares. According to these Acts, St. Thomas, being at Jerusalem, embarked at the nearest port, and arrived at the coast of the Peninsula of Hindostan. Thence he travelled into the interior, and visited a king named Gondaphores who embraced Christianity; and after that he went to another province of India and received the crown of martyrdom. It will be seen that this narrative is in no way compatible with that transmitted by tradition, and indicated also by archaeological monuments." This

translation of the French text is from E. Kennet, *St. Thomas the Apostle of India*, Addison, Madras, 1882, 20.

6 "There were other types all much worn out and very poor, showing that they enjoyed extensive circulation. The name of the King is Gondophares. His nephew was Abdagases. A relative of his was Sasan and another relative was Orthagnes. Others who were probably related to him were Sanabares and Pakores." C.J. RODRIGUES, *Coins collecting in North India*, Asian Educational Services, Allahabad, 1894, 27.

7 L. Bachhoffer, "On Greeks and Sakas in India," *JAOS*, 1941, 223. "From a study of the coins themselves it was inferred that they were struck about A.D. 40 or 50. ... What so probable than as Thomas, in obedience to the Saviour's last parting words, should come to India by that route? The coins of Gondophares are found in the Northern Punjab, but there is one type that seems to be found only near Kandahar. They are very numerous, and this argues that Gondophares reigned a long time. If the king of this name who reigned in Kandahar is the same as the one who reigned in Peshawar valley, his kingdom was extensive... Here we have a group, with not only a family likeness, but with a monogram of unvarying form on the coins of the different kings, all telling us something about the king who murdered an apostle of Jesus Christ." C.J. RODRIGUES, *Coin collecting in Northern India*, Asian Educational Service, Allahabad, 1894, 27. Here the last part of the citation is born out of the ignorance or the misunderstanding of the *Acts of Thomas*. Because, according to *Ath*, it was not Gondophares but Mazdai who murdered the apostle.

8 J. Rooney, *Shadows in the dark*, Christian Study Center, Rawalpindi, 1984, 36. For more detailed study on this topic see, S. LEVY, "Indo-Scythians," *Journal Asiatique*, vol. 9, 1897; A.L. Medleycott, *India and the Apostle Thomas*, An Inquiry with a critical analysis of the Acta Thomae, Ballantine, Hanson, London, 1905.

9 G.N. Banerjee, *Hellenism in Ancient India*, Mittal Publications, New Delhi, 1995, 140.

10 E.J. Rapson, *Ancient India, from the Earliest Times to the First Century A.D.*, University Press, Cambridge, 1914, 145.

11 *Indian Antiquary*, vol. II, 1873, 242.

12 A. Cunningham, *Archaeological Survey of India Report*, Calcutta, 60.

13 The late Prinsep writes about the vikrama era, "The principal era to which the luni-solar system is exclusively adapted is that of Vikramaditya, called Samvat, or vulgarly sambat. The prince from whom it is named was of the Tuas dynasty, and is supposed to have reigned at Ujjain 135 years before Salivahana, the rival founder of the Saka era, south of the Narbada river. The samvat era commenced when 3044 years of the Kali-yug had expired; i.e., 57 years B.C., so that if any year, say 4925, of the Kali-yug be proposed, and the last expired year of Vikramaditya be required, subtract 3044 there from, and the result, 1881, is the year sought. To convert Samvat into Christian years, subtract 57; unless they are less than 58, in which case, deduct the amount from 58 and the result will be the date B.C." THOMAS, *Essays on Indian*

Antiquities of the late James Prinsep, vol. II, John Murray, London, 1858, 157. "The Vikrama-Samvat era was started in 57-56 B.C. to denote an important historical landmark in India of the first century B.C. and it came to be latterly called also "Vikrama-Sakabdam," while the Saka era proper of A.D. 78 was particularized as the "Salivahana-Sakabdam." The *Christusamhita*, a Sanskrit epic composed by Mill and Vidyabushan in 1834, has the following verses where the Vikrama era has been used to date a biblical pre-Christian event – the appearance of Gabriel to Mary. *When fifty years of Vikrama Saka (era) had passed, Gabriel, the divine messenger, who had been sent by God appeared to Mary and said."* A.S.R. Ayyar, "Martyrdom of St. Thomas the Apostle," *Journal of the Proceedings of the Asiatic Society of Bengal*, New Series, vol. XXI, 1926, 521–522.

[14] A. Cunningham, *Archaeological Survey of India Reports, 1872-1873*, vol. V, Calcutta, 1875, 60.

[15] Burthey, "The Udaipur Tablet", in *Examiner*, November 27, 1915, 477. It is reproduced in A.D. Mattam, *The Church of St. Thomas Christians, Missionary Enterprises before the Sixteenth Century*, OIRSI, Kottayam, 2004, 49–50 and G. Nedungatt, *Quest for Historical Thomas*, TPI, Bangalore, 2008, 286.

[16] G. Nedungatt, *Quest for Historical Thomas*, 287. There are three contemporary authors who made personal on the site studies about the inscription. Their experience and impressions can be read in the accounts that they have written. A.D. Mattam, *The Church of St. Thomas Christians, Missionary Enterprises before the Sixteenth Century*, OIRSI, Kottayam, 2004 (revised edition), 48–53; Abraham Kunnatholy, *St. Thomas Christians in Madhya Pradesh*, Bangalore, 2007, 72–80; G. Nedungatt, *Quest for Historical Thomas*, 281–304.

[17] As we have told in the beginning of this article, St. Thomas started his journey from Alexandria and disembarked at Bharuch. From Bharuch following the river Narmada for a while he gained the road to Mathura through Vidisa and Ujjain. At Mathrua he gained the royal high way built by Chandragupta Maurya between Taxila and Pataliputra (Patna) and reached Taxila. For a detailed discussion on the topic see James Kurikilamkatt, *First Voyage of Apostle Thomas to India*, Asian Trading Corporation, Bangalore, 2005.

[18] M. Thomas Antony, "Saint Thomas Cross: A Religio-Cultural Symbol of Saint Thomas Christians," https://www.nasrani.net/2010/10/09/saint-thomas-cross-a-religio-cultural-logo-of-saint-thomas-christians, accessed on October 1, 2017.

[19] T. K. Joseph, "The Malabar Christians and their Ancient Documents": in *Kerala Society Papers Series* 5, Gazetteers Department, Government of Kerala, Trivandrum, 1997, 269–270.

4

SIGNIFICANCE AND ROLE OF TRADITION IN THE HISTORIOGRAPHY ON ST. THOMAS CHRISTIANS

Benedict Vadakkekara, OFM Cap

In ecclesiastical historiography, the first monograph on the mission and spread of Christianity during the early three centuries of Church history is *Die Mission und Ausbreitung des Christentums in den ersten drei Jahrhunderten,* by the German Lutheran scholar Adolf von Harnack, first published in 1902. It was certainly a trail-blazing work and was destined to wield much influence on historians across the denominational barrier. Its English translation by James Moffatt appeared as a two-volume edition in 1904–1905, bearing the title, *The Expansion of Christianity in the first three Centuries.* In this scholarly work, Harnack attempts a critical appraisal of early Church history, and makes the sweeping statement: "The primitive history of the church's missions lies buried among legends; or rather, it has been replaced by a history (that is strongly marked by tendency) of what is said to have been enacted in the course of a few decades throughout every country on the face of the earth." In the same vein, he observes that "the formation of legends in connection with the apostolic mission, which commenced as early as the first century, was still thriving in the Middle Ages; it thrives, in fact, down to the present day." He unceremoniously dismisses such narratives as being of "worthless character" and observes, "Whatever item from the apocryphal Acts, the local and provincial legends of the church, the episcopal lists, and the Acts of the martyrs, has *not* been inserted or noticed in these pages has been deliberately omitted as useless."[1]

His rigorous "critical investigation of the sources" notwithstanding, Harnack seems to be somewhat soft on the time-honored tradition that associates Apostle Thomas with India. Without categorically excluding an earlier origin, he affirms that Christians were known to exist in India "by the first half of the third century," and adds that "the India where the early (third century) *Acts of Thomas* locate that apostle's work, is the N.W. territory of our modern India."[2] By making this explicit reference to "the N.W. territory," the German Lutheran historian seems also to advance a suggestive allusion to the tradition of the St. Thomas Christians in S.W. India.[3] One presumes that the discovery in 1834 of the coins bearing the name of Gondophernes in northwest India (Kabul Valley of Afghanistan) did accord some credibility to the tradition represented by *The Acts of Thomas*.[4] Be that as it may, the theories built around the apocryphal work *The Acts of Thomas*[5] find no resonance in the tradition of the St. Thomas Christians about the origin of their community and are, therefore, alien to the unearthing of the coins of Gondophernes.[6] In fact, the tradition of the Indian Christians has an origin that is independent of the stories built around this king who ruled in North-West India, a protagonist of *The Acts of Thomas*.[7]

All along, India's St. Thomas Christians have been persistently clinging on to their communal tradition, despite the "critical investigations" by historians like Harnack. Whether one approves of it or not, the tradition is there for all to see and it refuses to be swept under the rug.[8] Rightfully, historians feel called upon to explain it and pronounce on it. Since the middle of the twentieth century, the general tendency in historiography has been to recognize positively the long-drawn-out existence of the tradition of the St. Thomas Christians and openly admit the physical possibility of such a mission of Apostle Thomas to India.[9] However, in the same breath, some of them add that, nothing further can be said about it, since no indisputable historical sources are forthcoming by way of corroborating the tradition of the St. Thomas Christians. The present paper seeks to revisit the reality of the tradition of the Indian Christians regarding the origin of their community vis-à-vis historiography.

UNWRITTEN TRADITION AS SOURCE FOR WRITTEN HISTORY

Etymologically, the term "tradition" is retraceable to the Latin verb *tradere* literally signifying "to transmit, to hand over, to entrust for safekeeping." The object of the transmission may be a belief, a narrative of an event, or a way of conduct that is handed down within a particular group or society, attaching to it a symbolic meaning or special significance going back to the primordial past. Of late, there has been much interest in academic circles to revalue folklores, legends, and oral traditions in order to draw forth history from collective memory, which is a link that connects the present with the past, the individual with the collectivity.[10] The strength, integrity and cohesion enjoyed by the tradition depends greatly on the consensus that the tradition generates within the community; it also implies that the fixed forms of the tradition gradually and involuntarily get adapted to the contextual exigencies in the course of events. Tradition decisively had a pivotal role to play in the origin and development of Christianity. When Jesus instructed his disciples to "go out to the whole world and proclaim the Good News to all creation" (Mark 16:15), his emphasis was more on oral proclamation than on producing parchments and putting them into circulation. A case in point is what Paul's words represent as the end result of the proclamation by the disciples: "This is the tradition of the Lord that I received and that in my turn I have handed on to you." (1 Cor 11:23). In this process of handing on the tradition, the oral and written proclamations did not run parallel to one another, as all too often their paths cross one another. In the course of time, in many instances, the oral traditions came to be committed to writing and took shape as documents like epigraphs, books, and acts of synods and councils. Along with the Bible, the tradition is, for the church, one of the two sources of divine revelation.

One of the several components of the tradition of the early Christians was their shared belief that the Gospel had already been preached across the whole world. As far as the early Church was concerned, there was nothing farfetched or implausible about it since the Gospel carried numerous pointers to the prospect of the entire humankind being the addressees of the Gospel proclamation, despite the obvious insignificance, fragility, and numerical negligibility of the first announcers of the Kingdom. The Gospel promised that the Kingdom. God would grow "like the yeast . . . until the whole mass of dough began to rise" (Matt 13:33). In much the same way, the Kingdom could be likened to "a mustard seed, which a man took and sowed in his field. It is smaller than the rest of the seeds, but once it has fully grown, it is bigger than any garden plant; like a tree, the birds come and rest in its branches" (Matt 13:31,32). Jesus spoke of "people coming from east and west, from north and south" and that they would "sit at table in the kingdom of God" (Luke 13:29). Some of the statements of Jesus were explicit to the point that "this Gospel of the Kingdom will be proclaimed throughout the world for all the nations to know; then the end will come" (Matt 24:14). For the nascent Church, these scriptural texts were seminal for the spread of the view that the Gospel was to reach out to the entire world. The apostles themselves would later make it known that the Gospel had already been preached to the whole world, and as a result some of the first Christian communities looked eagerly for the Lord's second coming, believing that his return was imminent. "When the command by the archangel's voice is given, the Lord himself will come down from Heaven, while the divine trumpet call is sounding. Then those who have died in the Lord will rise first; as for us who are still alive, we will be brought along with them in the clouds to meet the Lord in the celestial world" (1 Thess 4:16–17). Harnack openly disdains these Pauline texts (1 Thess 1:8; Rom 1:8; Col 1:6,13) and summarily labels them as "deliberate rhetorical exaggerations" by St. Paul.[11] However, it is not necessary to denigrate these texts and their author, as they become quite intelligible when viewed in their proper historical perspective.

TRADITION ABOUT GOSPEL'S DIFFUSION IN EARLY CHURCH

The New Testament presents Jesus as one born in the Roman Empire (*oikoumene*) but who, towards the close of his earthly sojourn sends his disciples out into the whole world (*kosmos*) to preach the Gospel. Jesus's birth is presented as an unequivocal historical event in its real context: "At that time the emperor issued a decree for a census of the whole empire to be taken… So, the people travelled to their own cities, and Joseph set out from Nazareth of Galilee. As he belonged to the family of David, being a descendant of his, he went to Judea to David's town of Bethlehem to be registered with Mary, his wife, who was with child" (Luke 2:1,4–5). Luke concludes his Gospel with the mandate entrusted by Jesus to his apostles: "Then repentance and forgiveness in his name would be proclaimed to all the nations, beginning from Jerusalem. Now you shall be witnesses to this" (Luke 24:47–48). The spatial extension of the Gospel from the Roman Empire into the wide world through the instrumentality of the disciples is, in fact, the story of the church. The mission of the disciples took concrete shape when they moved out of Palestine in obedience to the command of Jesus, whose priority was for the proclamation of the dawn of the Kingdom "to all creation" (Mark 16:15). There are two related expressions employed anciently in the church that cast light on the tradition of the early Church that the Gospel had been preached to the entire humankind. The two expressions are "the whole world" and "the ends of the earth.".

"The Whole World"

The population in the Mediterranean region had a common *Weltanschauung,* a shared idea of "the world." They believed that they were at the Center of the World, as the etymology of the term "Mediterranean" goes to show. In fact, the term Mediterranean results from the putting together of the two Latin words *Medius* (= center, mid) and *terra* (fem. = land, earth), meaning the "Center of the Earth." In Late Latin, the linked expression *Mediterranean* was applied to refer also to the Mediterranean Sea, the almost land-locked sea separating Europe from North Africa, linking it with the Atlantic Ocean by the Strait of Gibraltar and with the Black Sea by the Bosporus, and latterly with the Red Sea through the Suez

Canal. In point of fact, the Mediterranean region functions as a kind of Center of the Earth, from which, the cardinal directions of north, east, south, and west have been and still are determined. For instance, we still keep on saying that India is an eastern country inasmuch as it lies towards the east of the Mediterranean region.

The Hebrews believed that their land lay at the Center of the Earth, as Ezek 38:12 says: "I will go against this people gathered from among the nations, who live by trading and are increasing their cattle at the centre of the earth." This explains the belief that it was from the Center of the Earth that Jesus sent out his disciples to proclaim the Kingdom to the peoples inhabiting the entire earth. It goes without saying that those days the earth was commonly understood to be flat, with most of the peoples subscribing to a flat earth cosmography. Accordingly, the flat earth was thought to have its own ends or confines. Thus, there appears the expression "The Ends of the Earth."[12]

"The Ends of the Earth"

"The Ends of the Earth" and other similar expressions appear time and time again in the Bible. "The ends of the earth" alone is used over thirty times in the Scriptures. As examples, one may cite (Ps 48:10): "Your praise reaches to the ends of the earth, as does your name, O God," (Isa 41:28): "Have you not known, have you not heard that Yahweh is the everlasting God, the Creator of the ends of the earth?, and (Jer 10:13): "When he raises his voice the waters pile up in the heavens. He calls the clouds from the ends of the earth; he sends lightening with the rain and from his storehouse sends out the wind." The words of Jesus to his disciples before his ascension, as reported in the Acts of the apostles, are particularly relevant to the present context: "But you will receive power when the Holy Spirit comes upon you; and you will be my witnesses in Jerusalem, throughout Judea and Samaria, even to the ends of the earth" (Acts 1:8). The expressions "Corners" or "Confines" of the earth too have the same connotation. The Book of Revelation 7:1 refers to the four corners of the earth: "After this, there were four angels standing at the four corners of the earth, holding back the four winds to prevent their blowing against the earth, the sea and the trees." The peoples of the Mediterranean region saw themselves as being at the Center of the Earth and, according to the early Christians, it was from the Center of the Earth that Jesus had dispatched his disciples to preach the Gospel to the ends of the earth. In other words, from the Mediterranean region, the Gospel was to spread out into the whole world or *kosmos*.

LANDS TOWARDS "THE ENDS OF THE EARTH"

The attempt to identify some locations that may be termed as pointers to the "Ends of the Earth" can prove to be a fruitful exercise. The First Book of Maccabees outlines the military exploits of Alexander the Great, when it says: "Alexander of Macedon son of Philip had come from the land of Kittim and defeated Darius king of the Persians and Medes, whom he succeeded as ruler, at first of Hellas. He undertook many campaigns, gained possession of many fortresses, and put the local kings to death. So, he advanced to the ends of the earth, plundering nation after nation; the earth grew silent before him, and his ambitious heart swelled with pride" (1 Macc 1:1–3). History shows that Alexander's subduing expeditions, in fact, concluded in Northwestern India. Thapar writes, "In 327 B.C., Alexander, continuing his march across the empire of Darius, entered the Indian provinces. The Greek campaign in Northwestern India lasted for about two years. . . . Alexander came to India in order to reach the easternmost parts of Darius's empire. He also wished to solve the "problem of Ocean" the limits of which were a puzzle to Greek geographers. And, not unnaturally, he wanted to add what was already being described as the fabulous country of India to his list of conquests. The campaign took him across the five rivers of Punjab at the last of which his soldiers refused to go further."[13] His conquest in North-western India (derived from the name of the river Sindhu—Indus river), thus came to be viewed as his success in achieving victory even at the "Ends of the Earth." Here the appellative "India" inasmuch as it stood for a location at the "Ends of the Earth" implied not only North-Western India but also the whole of India and the East. It was in this sense that the early Church had come to the belief that the Gospel had already reached the ends of the earth. The early Church had the tradition that India that lay at the "Ends of the Earth" had been the scene of the preaching activities and the martyrdom of the apostle Thomas. This was one of the rationales for the church to claim that the Gospel had already been preached to the ends of the earth.

According to the Gospel of Luke, Jesus tells the disbelieving crowds: "The Queen of the South will rise up on Judgment Day with the people of these times and accuse them, for she came from the ends of the earth to hear the wisdom of Solomon; and here there is greater than Solomon (Luke 11:31). In the parallel text, Mathew has it as the Queen of the South "came from the other side of the world" (Matt 12:42). The exact identity of the Queen of the South is a mooted point. However, she is commonly believed to have been the Queen of Ethiopia or Yemen and scholars opine that Sheba and Seba represent two regions in North-eastern Africa. If Sheba is identified as a kingdom in Arabia, it could be appropriately referred to as a kingdom of the South for the Palestinians. The visit of the Queen of Sheba to King Solomon has long been the subject of much embellishment and elaboration in the Talmud and the Quran as well as in the Ethiopian religious traditions. What is pertinent to our context is that the provenience of the Queen was from one of the Ends of the Earth. In other words, she is believed to have gone to meet King Solomon from one of the extremities of the earth. The Book of Esther places Ethiopia alongside India: "In the days of Ahasuerus—this was the Ahasuerus whose empire stretched from India to Ethiopia and comprised one hundred twenty-seven provinces" (Esth 1:1; see also 8:1). This collocation of the two countries is clearly indicative of the author's imprecise and vague geographical notion of the region. North-Western India, with its location at the end of the earth, was described as the culmination point of Alexander's military exploits. This India also represented the location of the preaching of Apostle Thomas and his eventual death and burial. This was a topographical endorsement of the church's tradition that the Gospel had already been proclaimed by an apostle at the end of the earth towards the south.

If these locations indicating the confines of the earth are situated eastwards and southwards of the Mediterranean, there is a conspicuous point on the western side of the Mediterranean named *Finisterre* that is particularly relevant to the subject under discussion. This toponymical designation *Finisterre* literally means *End of the Earth* and this location is found on the Atlantic coast of Galicia, Spain. Cape Finisterre (*Cabo Fisterra* in Galician and Cabo *Finisterre* in Castilian) is today a Spanish town with about 5,000 residents. The name *Finisterre* is originally derived from the Latin term *Finis terrae*, signifying "End of the Earth" and the Mediterranean peoples believed that it was the western end of the earth. For centuries, it used to be the final destination for the scores of pilgrims on *the Way of St James* or *O Camiño de Santiago*, to the Cathedral of Santiago de Compostela that houses the tomb of the apostle St James the Great. A distance of 90 kilometers separates Cape Finisterre from the cathedral of Santiago, which had been one of the most renowned pilgrimage destinations for the early Christians. That the tomb of an Apostle be situated at the western End of the Earth was particularly significant in many ways. It was an unconfutable proof for the church of the genuineness of the tradition that the preaching of the Gospel had already taken place at one end of the earth westwards of the Mediterranean.

These three locations, namely, Finisterre in Spain towards the West, the kingdoms of Sheba and Seba towards the South, and the last kingdom conquered by Alexander the Great in the East, namely India towards the east, clearly mirror the worldview of the peoples of the Mediterranean region, who saw themselves as being at the Center of the World. On looking around, the early Christians could point to the Ends of the Earth in the East (India), West (Spain), and South (The Horn of Africa) and proclaim that their religion had reached the whole world that was then known to them. It is nothing but anachronism to presume that the idea of the world that the peoples of the biblical period had is the same as that our contemporary world has. The Mediterranean peoples of the Biblical times had absolutely no idea about the continent of America, the Sub-Saharan Africa, the Far East Asia, and the Continent of Australia and their perception of the earth around them was limited to the Mediterranean region and to some vague notions about the east. They were also rather familiar with the natural features of North Africa as much of North Africa had been part of the Roman Empire. Northwestern Africa was referred to as Libya or Africa, while Egypt was thought to be part of Asia. But for some minor changes this perspective of the world would reign supreme until the seaway to the Americas and to Asia would be discovered towards the close of the fifteenth century. Accordingly, one sees the prevalence of the same mind-set and worldview through the New Testament as well as in the posterior ecclesiastical writings. The expression "ends of the earth" appears many a time in the Patristic writings. It had become so integral to the ecclesiastical tradition that one hears it echoing even in the early decades of twentieth century. A case in point is the apostolic letter *Maximum illud* of Pope Benedict XV, issued on 30 November, 1919. The pope writes: "Receiving this mandate, 'they went forth and preached everywhere' (Mark 16:20), so that 'through all the earth their voice resounds, and to the ends of the earth, their message' (Ps 18:5). . . .Even in the first three centuries, when persecution after persecution, inspired by Hell, fell upon the nascent Church in a raging attempt to crush her, even then when the whole of civilization was deluged with Christian blood, out on the far frontiers of the Empire the messengers of the Gospel went about, announcing their tidings."[14] The earth about which the ecclesiastical sources speak was basically the Mediterranean regions and not the one that would embrace also the immense territories that Spain and Portugal and others would "discover" in the decades after the close of fifteenth century.

There are in all twenty-seven allusions in the New Testament implying that the early Christians believed in the "worldwide" diffusion of Christianity in the first three centuries of the first Millennium. The citation of a few scriptural texts is in place here. Rom 1:8—"First of all, I give thanks to my God through Jesus Christ, for all of you, because your faith is spoken of all over the world." 1 Cor 11:23—"This is the tradition of the Lord that I received and that in my turn I have handed on to you." Col 1:6—"This Gospel, already present among you, is bearing fruit and growing throughout the world." Col 1:23—"Keep in mind the Gospel you have heard, which has been preached to every creature under heaven." 1 Tim 3:16—"He was shown in the flesh and sanctified by the Spirit; presented to the angels and proclaimed to all nations. The world believed in him: He was taken up in glory." Acts 17:5–7—"They came to the house of Jason, in an attempt to bring Paul and Silas before the people's assembly. Not finding them there, they dragged off Jason and some of the brothers to the city authorities shouting, 'These people who have turned the world upside down have come here also, and Jason has given them hospitality." This worldview circumscribed by the Mediterranean region, in fact, underpinned these ecclesiastical writers and they cannot be faulted for exaggeration or for overstating things. They were using the accepted language of the day. The uninterrupted trade between *caput mundi* and an end of the earth like India made such an apostolic mission verosimile.[15]

Viewed in its contextual angle, a Scriptural passage like: "Then he told them, 'Go out to the whole world and proclaim the Good News to all creation'. . . . The Eleven went forth and preached everywhere, while the Lord continually worked with them and confirmed the message by the miracles which accompanied them" (Mark 16:20) fully makes sense. That the Gospel had been preached to the whole world as then known, was taken for granted by these writers. And there is no record of anyone questioning the veracity of this shared belief. Even at the peak of doctrinal controversies, the protagonists accepted this common belief. Polemists would have certainly brought up the incongruences, if they had any knowledge to the contrary. That the entire world, including India, had been evangelized in the apostolic age had become the tradition of the whole Church, as the patristic tradition keeps reiterating it all through the first millennium. It is noteworthy that the testimonies originate from the different Churches, thus making them the voice of the then universal Church. One may refer to Clement of Alexandria (c. 150–215), Origen (c. 185–255), Ephrem (c. 306–373), Gregory of Nazianzus (329–390), Ambrose (340–397), John Chrysostom (c. 344–407), Jerome (c. 342–420), Rufinus of Aquileia), Gaudentius of Brescia (c. 387–410), Paulinus of Nola (c. 354–431), Jacob of Serugh (450–521), Gregory of Tours (c. 538–594), Gregory the Great (540–604), Isidore of Siviglia (c. 560–636), Venerable Bede (c. 673–735)[16] as some of the outstanding patristic witnesses to the tradition regarding Apostle Thomas's evangelization mission in India.

The ancient Church's tradition about the proclamation of the Gospel in the entire world was not merely a passively accepted datum within the various Christian communities. Instead, it was something that they used to celebrate fervently every year. The fact that Christian communities were making cultic commemoration of the various saints, including the apostles, provided every year the occasion to revisit the life and activities of the saints in the light of the knowledge to which they had access. Hence, if any information going against the tradition were available, such would have certainly undermined the tradition itself. For example, the *Didascalia* (The Teachings of the Apostles) compiled in Syriac in all likelihood at the turn of the third century represents the genuine expression of a widespread community's belief that India "received the apostles' Hand of the priesthood from Judas Thomas." In the hymns in honor of St. Thomas composed by St. Ephrem in Edessa (today's Urfa in Turkey), one finds the echoing of a whole Church's tradition. Edessa had then become a popular pilgrimage center because of the presence there of the relics of the apostle Thomas, which had been brought there and were held in great veneration. All through the ancient Christianity, one finds the tradition being transmitted integrally from generation to generation down through the centuries, reaffirming uninterruptedly that the Gospel had been preached in the whole world in the apostolic period and that it had fallen on St. Thomas, one of the Twelve, to proclaim it in India.[17] By way of confirmation of the tradition, these early Christians could point to the tomb of St. James and that of Apostle Thomas, both lying close to the Ends of the Earth (Finisterre in the West and Mylapore in the East).

THE ACTS OF THOMAS AND THE TRADITION OF INDIA'S ST. THOMAS CHRISTIANS

The Acts of Thomas had little influence on the origin and molding of the tradition of the St. Thomas Christians in India, even though the book had taken shape in the Syriac ambience in the third century itself. The Indian Christians, who had entered into fellowship with the East Syriac Church early in their history, did not feel the need of having the Acts to lean on, since they had their own feet to stand on. In fact, the apostle is named "Judas Thomas" all through *The Acts*, while such an appellation is totally alien to the tradition of the Indian Christians.[18] The name "Thomas" had struck such deep root in India that it could not be supplanted by the "Judas Thomas" of *The Acts of Thomas*. This signifies that the entry of the name of Thomas" into India preceded the appearance of *The Acts of Thomas* on the Indian scene. If the tradition of the Indian Christians goes back to *The Acts of Thomas*, there is no reason why the St. Thomas Christians in India should have retained only a half of their hero's name, rejecting wholly the other half. A perusal of the various versions of the tradition of the St. Thomas Christians shows clearly that by and large they are native to India as they are wedded inseparably to specific locations and people in the land, all characteristically Indian in origin. The Indian Christians never attempted to implant locally any of the personages or events borrowed from *The Acts of Thomas* into their own Indian environment. They have not made any attempt to identify Gondophernes of *The Acts of Thomas* with any of their own princes. Something especially noteworthy is the fact that the Indian Christians never presented *The Acts of Thomas* or even referred to it, when the inquisitive westerners pressed them for documentary evidence by way of substantiating their tradition. They kept on insistently restating that their claim goes back to the living tradition of their community.

The independence of the origin of the tradition of the Indian Christians from *The Acts of Thomas* notwithstanding, there are three key episodes in this apocryphal work that find their unambiguous resonance in the tradition of the St. Thomas Christians and that one may read as evidences for the genuineness of the tradition of the St. Thomas Christians. Firstly, *The Acts of Thomas* explicitly mentions that St. Thomas did not die in the kingdom of Gondophernes but that he had left this king's domain for another region in India and that it is there that the apostle had met with his violent death. The reference to his death in another kingdom in India is particularly significant and it fits in with the tradition that says that the apostle's death occurred in Mylapore in Southeast India. Even though there are allusions in different authors about the evangelization ministry of the apostle Thomas in other lands besides India, no Church or land has ever laid claim to have been the scene of his martyrdom. The locating of Mylapore as the unique site of the martyrdom of the apostle by the tradition of the Indian Christians, makes the tradition of the St. Thomas Christians unique and, therefore, distinct from all the other traditions. Besides, whatever be the source of the traditions, they all invariably refer to India, when it concerns the place of the apostle's martyrdom. In fact, this is an implicit reiteration of the tradition of India's St. Thomas Christians. Those days the West had no term but "India" in order to refer to the territory in Southwestern India where the St. Thomas Christians have had their domicile since centuries. Therefore, the India of Gondophernes or northwestern India could denote any other part of India as well.

Secondly, according to *The Acts of Thomas*, the body of the martyred Apostle was first interred in India where he had been killed and later it was exhumed and the remains were taken away to the "West" or "Mesopotamia" by a merchant.[19] This detail acquires its full significance when seen in the backdrop of the tradition that Edessa was playing host to the apostle's relics and that the place, in fact, lies westwards of the Indian town of Mylapore. *The Acts of Thomas* refers to the "thief of the relics" as "a brother," implying that his action had been lauded in Edessa, and that it had found favorable acceptance in the ambience in which *The Acts of Thomas* were composed, namely, in the Syriac Church. The Indian Christians, who customarily had their abode on the south-west coast of India, have been known for centuries to be making their way across to the distant land of Mylapore to venerate their "Spiritual Father" at the empty tomb on the eastern coast of India. Those who had been on pilgrimage to Mylapore were held in high regard in the community. They also had external signs of distinction. It is noteworthy that the disciples of St. Thomas on the south-west coast of India never tried to invent a tomb of their apostle in their vicinity or neighborhood, at a site easily accessible to them. Instead, they chose to undertake the hazardous journey to Mylapore in order to pay homage to their Apostle.

Thirdly, the pilgrims were wont to take away with them from Mylapore as keepsake or memento loose earth from the tomb and oil from the lamp that a caretaker would keep lighted at the tomb. It was incumbent on the caretaker to maintain constantly the supply of dust so that it would be readily available to the pilgrims. These relics were believed to have healing powers as they would be blessed by the clerics with a special prayer in Syriac and used by the faithful for procuring relief from physical ailments and maladies. *The Acts of Thomas* had already spoken of the miraculous healing powers of the relics from the tomb. The king wanted to get a piece of bone from the tomb for curing his son's infirmity. It was then discovered that the bones had been taken away to the west and so the king had to be content with some dust taken from the tomb. The story narrated by *The Acts of Thomas* and the long-standing tradition of taking recourse to the loose earth from the tomb clearly suggest that here we are dealing with the same tomb. Despite their independent origins, one may safely deduce that the pious use of dust from the tomb of Mylapore serves as a point of convergence between *The Acts of Thomas* and the tradition of the St. Thomas Christians.[20]

INDIAN CHURCH'S TRADITION, ITS CONCRETENESS AND COMPACTNESS

A close scrutiny of the tradition of the St. Thomas Christians about the origin of their community brings to light certain fixed points, which together impart a certain identity, concreteness and stability to the tradition itself.[21] Even though the precise details of the origin of the community still lie in the mists of time, there has been a remarkable consistency in the identity of the contents of the tradition and the way it has been handed down from one generation to another, as amply evidenced in the period after the history of the community began to be chronicled. This aspect of stability and consensus is remarkable especially when viewed in the angle of the rivalries, concurrences, power struggles, and issues of familial prestige that plagued the community during the several vicissitudes of its history. The tradition did grant a certain pre-eminence to certain families precisely because of their direct association with the apostle St. Thomas and this precedence was never challenged by the others. The traditionally attributed pre-eminence continued to command respect in the whole community. When a traditionally acknowledged locality happened to be deprived of its accessibility due to natural causes, there were no attempts on the part of the community to substitute it with another place. In sum, one may say that the tradition has remained intact and unaltered all through the documented period of the history of the St. Thomas Christians, suggesting that there are no reasons why the same could not have happened earlier also.

The particular relationship that India's St. Thomas Christians had with the East Syriac Church is revealing on several counts. Certain liturgical peculiarities of the Indian Christians evidently could not have reached them from the East Syriac Church. The way they held the feast of *Dukrana* shows their unique relationship with their Apostle Thomas. The third of July was not a solemn day of celebration for the East Syriac Church and its breviary had only a one-day commemoration in honor of Apostle Thomas. Instead, for the Indian Christians the *Dukrana* was and still continues to be a day of solemnity. Their breviary had a commemorative octave, thus proving clearly that it could not have been a mere import from the East Syriac Church.[22] The East Syriac Church has always expressly admitted that Apostle Thomas is the founder of India's St. Thomas Christians,[23] and has ever held in high veneration the apostle's tomb in Mylapore. They joined hands with the Indian Christians in paying respects to Apostle Thomas at Mylapore, and openly acknowledged that the relics they had with them, had reached them from India. Though they held South Indian Christianity under their jurisdiction, they never took exception to the South Indian tradition about St. Thomas. Were this tradition a mere myth, they would certainly have set their face against it in no uncertain terms. If the East Syriac Church had introduced Christianity into South India, as still some opine, the South Indian tradition would have been nipped in the bud. On the contrary, the authorities of the East Syriac Church accepted this tradition as being in line with their own.[24]

The long-established ways of exercising the office of the Archdeacon is a case in point. Among the St. Thomas Christians, the Archdeacon represented something much more than an ecclesiastical office inasmuch as he practically functioned as the head of the community. The Archdeacon was to be a member of a particular family that was believed to have been directly associated with the apostle Thomas. The entire community rallied around the Archdeacon and in no way questioned his authority that, in the ultimate analysis, went back to the personal and direct intervention of Apostle Thomas. The orderly and harmonious functioning of the office of the Archdeacon was, in fact, a permanent and uninterrupted restatement of the tradition of the St. Thomas Christians. The unfortunate events that unfolded in the wake of the Revolt of 1653 also reveal the privileged place enjoyed by the family to which the office of the Archdeacon had been linked. Both the rival factions chose members of the same family to head the respective party. The Archdeacon who had assumed the title of Mar Thoma could be unseated or his power neutralized only by another person hailing from the same family.

In much the same way, the still extant ramification within the church of the St. Thomas Christians into Southist and Northist communities is a telling case in favor of confirming the tradition of the St. Thomas Christians. There were moments when there was even bad blood between the two groupings, especially on questions regarding social prestige and precedence. However, neither of the two groups has ever called into question the genuineness of the tradition of the other. In fact, there have been in circulation several versions of narratives aimed at establishing a superior social ranking of one over the other; the stories are more like anecdotes recounted within a family to belittle or make fun of one another. Even in these light-hearted stories, the core of the tradition about the mission of St. Thomas and his apostolate in India is upheld by both the groups and the stories are inserted into the general context of this tradition. On the other hand, the tradition of the one leans heavily on that of the other for survival. This internal cohesion within the community as regards the tradition is something that cannot easily be brushed aside. Ever since the tradition came to be committed to writing, the tradition has remained intact and very much consistent as regards its contents.[25]

Another striking aspect of the tradition of the St. Thomas Christians is its concreteness. The tradition does not just state in vague and general terms that Apostle Thomas had reached India and preached the Gospel to the local population there. Instead, it points to a specific location of his arrival by sea and this location has been shown to be a center of ancient human settlement. Again, the tradition refers to seven communities established by the apostle in places that too are known to have been ancient human abodes. The case of Nilakkel, a place that was home to one of the earliest Christian fellowships is worth being cited in the present context. The place had become so unhabitable that the population quit the whole area. However, there have been no attempts to invent another Nilakkel or to rename the place. Nilakkel continues to find its place in the tradition and it still exists enveloped by the luxurious growth of the tropical forest. The concreteness of the tradition is evidenced also in the fact that certain family names have been faithfully retained by the entire community down through the centuries. These families are believed to have been in a special way connected with the apostle Thomas.

CONCLUSION

In sum, one may for sure say that the tradition of the St. Thomas Christians gave their community its identity, capacitating it to survive the diverse contretemps that came its way in its bimillennial history. A perusal of the history of the community particularly since the early sixteenth century shows that its tradition served it as the springboard providing it with inner strength, buoyancy, and resilience. The direct link with Apostle Thomas that the tradition claims is cited by the community time and time again as the prime reason for upholding its various customs and practices. These Indian Christians risked much and had to face extreme pressure from various quarters in order to remain true to their communal norms, rites, and customs. This is the rationale of the fact that the tradition of the apostolic origin of the community becomes ever more pronounced and articulated in the decades subsequent upon its encounter with the European missionaries. The stiff resistance of the St. Thomas Christians to the strategies of the European missionaries to constrain them into giving up their age-old customs and cultic observances and making them embrace the manners of the missionaries cannot be explained without taking into due consideration the conviction of the Indian Christians about the genuineness of the tradition of their Church's apostolic background. In fact, the history of the St. Thomas Christians will remain unintelligible and inexplicable without presuming the existence of such a tradition. One may, therefore, conclude saying that the tradition of the Indian Christians represents "a historical outcome, an *eventus*,"[26] that necessarily and intrinsically involves the presence and activities of Apostle Thomas in Southern India, his establishing of a Christian community, and his death and burial at Mylapore. "The ancient tomb of Mylapore, the *Acta Thomae*, the testimonies of ecclesiastical writers, and the constant belief of the different Churches serve as collateral evidences in vouching for this event. Inasmuch as it was the significance of its tradition that constituted this Christian community and sustained it down through its centuried history, it is entirely justified in inheriting its tradition, living it, celebrating it and handing it down to its posterity."[27]

ENDNOTES

[1] Adolf Harnack, *The Expansion of Christianity in the first three Centuries*, I, Wipf and Stock Publishers, Eugene (Reprint 1966), VIII-IX.

[2] Harnack, *The Expansion of Christianity in the first three Centuries*, II, 299.

[3] Samuel Hugh Moffett, *A history of Christianity in Asia*, I: *Beginnings to 1500*, Theological Publications in India, Bangalore, 1998, (revised and corrected edition), 25, describes the tradition of India's St. Thomas Christians as "one of the oldest and strongest traditions in Church history." In the sixteenth century, Christian Europe was pleasantly surprised to hear of the existence of a Christian community in India, that had survived for centuries at a great distance from Christian strongholds. Thomas Whitehouse, *Lingerings of light in a dark land: Being researches into the past history and present condition of the Syrian Church of Malabar,* William Brown and Co., London, 1873, 1: "The long-continued existence of an ancient branch of the Christian Church on the remote shores of Southern India, where it has for many centuries outstood all the changes and chances, to which every human institution is subject, is one of the most remarkable and deeply interesting facts of Church history."

[4] The two English translations of *The Acts of Thomas* often cited are: Albertus Frederik Johannes Klijn, *The Acts of Thomas: Introduction and, Text and Commentary*, Bill, Leiden, 1962; Günther Bornkamm, *The Acts of Thomas*, in E. Hennecke, *New Testament Apocrypha*, II, ed. W. Schneemelcher, English edition by R. M. Wilson, Lutterworth, London, 1965.

[5] John Faithful Fleet, *St. Thomas and Gondophernes*, in *Journal of the Royal Asiatic Society of Great Britain and Ireland* (1905) 227. In effect, *The Acts of Thomas* had actually built itself on the church's general tradition. "The important point for us is that a Christian tradition, current in Syria, Asia Minor, and all those parts as far as Italy, and connecting St. Thomas with Parthia and 'India', and with two 'Indian' kings whom it specifically names, is traceable back, at any rate, to the third or fourth century of the Christian era, and perhaps to the second quarter of the third century."

[6] Gondophernes, also spelled Gondophares, (flourished in first century A.D.), was an Indo-Parthian ruler in the region of Arachosia, Kabul and Gandhara (present-day Afghanistan-Pakistan) in c. A.D. 19–45. The first time his name gets a historical mention is in the apocryphal work *The Acts of Thomas*. *This apocryphal composition tells the story of the Apostle Thomas, who visited the palace of Gondophernes. The Apostle was entrusted with the responsibility of erecting a royal palace, but he was thrown into prison for having spent the money on charities, instead of building the palace.* In the meantime, the king's brother Gaddied, and the angels took him to heaven and showed him the palace that St. Thomas had built there by his good deeds. Gad regains his life and he and Gondophernes embrace the Christian faith. Coins of Gondophernes, some carrying his Indian name Guduphara, indicate that he may have reigned supreme over both eastern Iran and Northwestern India.

According to an inscription at Takht-i-Bhai (near Peshawar), Gondophernes ruled for at least twenty six years, possibly from about A.D. 19 to 45.

[7] Stephen Neill, *A history of Christianity in India. The Beginnings to AD 1707*, Cambridge University Press, London, 1984, 49: "Millions of Christians in South India are certain that the founder of their Church was none other than the apostle Thomas himself. The historian cannot prove to them that that they are mistaken in their belief. He may feel it right to warn them that historical research cannot pronounce on the matter with a confidence equal to that which they entertain by faith."

[8] Samuel Hugh Moffett, *A History of Christianity in Asia*, I: *Beginnings to 1500*, Harper, San Francisco, 1992, 25: "But the tradition is so ancient and the support so strong even in the normally sceptical twentieth century that it may be wise to admit that underlying some of the most improbable legends there often lies a foundation of fact."

[9] Stephen Neill, *A History of Christianity in India*, 30: "If the apostle Thomas, one of the twelve apostles of Jesus of Nazareth, had wished to take ship to and go to India, there was nothing to prevent his doing so. Ample evidence exists to show the range and vigour of the commerce between India and the western world in the first two centuries of our era."

[10] Cristiana Fiamingo, *Introduzione*, in *Culture della memoria e patrimonizzazione della memoria storica*, a cura di Cristiana Fiamingo, Edizioni Unicopli, Milano, 2014, 12: "Si assiste da qualche decennio, infatti, ad una evoluzione rapidissima del rapporto tra storia e memoria, e l'esperienza collettiva di *Facebook* e la moda dei *selfie* sono leggibili quali derive di un tale processo." See also Birger Gerhardsson, *Memory and Manuscript and Tradition and Transmission in Early Christianity*, (The Biblical Resource Series), William B. Eerdmans Publishing Co, Grand Rapids, 1998.

[11] Harnack, *The Expansion of Christianity in the first three Centuries*, II, 171.

[12] For a brief discussion on the use of symbolism of the Biblical world, see Othmar Keel, *The Symbols of the Biblical World. Ancient Near Eastern Iconography and the Book of Psalms*, A Crossroad Book, New York 1978, 15–60.

[13] Romila Thapar, *The Penguin History of Early India. From the Origins to AD 1300*, I, Penguin Books, New Delhi, 2002, 157–158).

[14] Benedictus XV, Littera apostolica *Maximum illud*, in *Acta Apostilicae Sedis* 11 (1919), 440.

[15] H. Idris Bell, *Egypt under the early Principate*, in *The Cambridge Ancient History: The Augustan Empire 44 B.C. – A.D. 70*, ed. S.A, Cook – F.E, Adcock – M.P. Charlesworth, Cambridge University Press, Cambridge, Port Chester, Melbourne, Sydney, 1971, (reprint 1989), 307): "During the reign of August us repeated embassies from India came to Rome, and under Claudius we hear one from Ceylon. The discovery of monsoons, perhaps about A.D. 40, gave a further impetus to the eastern trade, and great fleet sailed annually for India, to return laden with the merchandise of the East." George Nedungatt, *Quest for the Historical Thomas Apostle of India. A Rereading of the Evidence*, Theological Publications in India, Bangalore, 2008, 409, narrates a parable

of a sports champion and deduces, "Similarly, in the first century, a world mission of the apostles could not have been imagined leaving out India."

16 Adolphus Edwin Medlycott, *India and the Apostle Thomas. An Enquirywith a critical analysis of the Acta Thomae*, London, David Mutt, 1905, gives a rather comprehensive list of sources that associate Apostle Thomas with India; see also George Nedumparambil, *A Search of the Roots of Syro-Malabar Church in Kerala*, Media House, Delhi, 2015.

17 A. Mathias Mundadan, *History of Christianity in India*, I: *From the Beginning up to the Middle of the Sixteenth Century*, The Church History Association of India–Theological Publications in India, Bangalore, 1984, 23: "The earliest record about the apostolate of St. Thomas is the apocryphal: *the Acts of Judas Thomas*, written in Syriac in the Edessan circle about the turn of the third century A.D. Even though this work has been acknowledged as apocryphal, Gnostic in origin, and romantic in style, several scholars find in it a historical nucleus, which represents the second century tradition about the apostolate of St. Thomas in India. Besides, a number of fragmentary passages in other writings of the third, fourth and the following centuries speak in unambiguous terms about the Indian apostolate of St. Thomas. From the fourth century onwards, the major Churches are unanimous in their witnessing to the tradition."

18 John Nicol Farquhar. *Apostle Thomas in Northern India*, [reprint from *The Bulletin of the John Rylands Library* 10 (1926) 1-34] Manchester, 1926, 33,] concludes from a survey of various ancient sources: "Thus these quotations make it quite clear that, at least from A.D. 140, all Edessene Christians called their own apostle 'Judas Thomas.'" Klijn Albertus Frederik Johannes, *Edessa, die Stadt des Apostels Thomas. Das älteste Christentum in Syrien* (Neukirchener Studienbücher, 4), Neukirchen-Vluyn 1965., 67: "Jedenfalls steht fest, dass Thomas im gesamten syrischen Sprachgebiet als Judas Thomas bezeichnet wird."

19 Benedict Vadakkekakra, *Origin of Christianity in India. A historiographical Critique*, Media House, Delhi, 2007, 153: "The Church's accepted belief regarding Apostle Thomas's mission field finds corresponding echo also in the tradition concerning his relics. The first reference to the presence of the relics beyond the confines of India, to be more precise outside his original tomb, is found in the *Acta Thomae* itself. According to the *Acta Thomae* the transfer of the relics from the first tomb 'happened after a long time' following the apostle's martyrdom. When King Mazdai opened the grave 'he did not find the bones, for one of the brethren had taken them away secretly and conveyed them to the West.'"

20 Giuseppe Sorge, *L'India di S. Tommaso. Ricerche storiche sulla chiesa malabarica*, (Cristianesimo e Oriente), CLUEB, Bologna, 1983, 16: "Di fatti, nel rito siriaco-orientale, il rito di tutti quelli che allora erano cristiani di S. Tommaso, la polvere raccolta dalla tomba dei santi mescolata all 'acqua e all'olio veniva benedetta liturgicamente e usata nelle chiese e data da bere ai malati."

21 Cyril Bruce Firth, *An Introduction to Indian Church History*, (Revised edition), ISPCK, Delhi, 2001, 13-14, "The tradition stands by itself; and it ought

not to be lightly assumed that a tradition handed down from ancient times in a living community that still exists, is necessarily a worse historical witness than certain scanty, and often vague, statements in books written far away from India by men who evidently had little information at their disposal."

22 The elaborate octave celebration of *Dukrana* by India's St. Thomas Christians has been attentively studied by scholars. Henry Hosten, *Again the Dukrana of July 3*, Mannanam 1928, 17: "I have commented on it generously and have come to the conclusion that it is not only original, very ancient, earlier than the *Passio* (of 450–550 and perhaps much earlier), but of Indian growth. I have suggested even that it contains elements of a liturgy going back to the very beginning."

23 S.N. Wald, *Saint Thomas, the Apostle of India*, Sat-Prachar Press, Indore, 1952, 29: "But the greatest weight has the testimony of the Syrian church itself. The Syrian writers, in their hymns, canticles, panegyrics and chronicles unanimously profess that St. Thomas preached the Gospel in India. They further testify that he died a martyr in India and his relics were brought from India to Edessa in Syria."

24 Hermann D'Souza, *In the steps of St. Thomas*, St. Thomas Mount National Shrine, Madras, 1952, 29: Wilhelm Germann, *Die Kirche der Thomaschristen. Ein Beitrag zur Geschichte der orientalischen Kirchen*, Gütersloh, C. Bertelsmann, 1877, 46: "Es fehlt jeglicher Anhalt zu einer Entscheidung und es muss also auf sich beruhen bleiben, nur dass man die Übertragung selbst festzuhalten hat, für welche noch ins Gewicht fallen wird, dass die Edessener trotz des Besitzes der Gebeine niemals eine Tradition hatten, dass der Apostel bei ihnen gestorben sei, im Gegenteil auch die Syrer verweisen auf Mailapur."

25 Mundadan, *History of Christianity in India*, 61, speaks of "two monuments" that uphold the "South Indian claim to the apostolate of St. Thomas." The monuments are "the community of St. Thomas Christians with their living tradition, and the tomb of Mylapore, which is definitely identified as the burial place of St. Thomas at least from the fourteenth century onwards."

26 Michael Oakeshott, *On History and other Essays*, Southampton, B. Blackwell, 1983, 62: "By a historical event I mean an occurrence or situation, inferred from surviving record, alleged to be what was actually happening, in a certain respect, then and there, and understood in terms of the mediation of its emergence; that is, understood as an *eventus* or outcome of what went before."

27 Vadakkekara, *Origin of Christianity in India*, 347–348.

5

ST. THOMAS TRADITIONS IN ANCIENT CHRISTIAN FOLK SONGS

Byju Mathew Mukalel

INTRODUCTION

Though Christianity in India is the fruit of the pioneering and laborious work of St. Thomas the apostle, the assistance extended to it by the sister Churches in Syria and Europe is of great value especially in the context of unearthing the life and works of the apostle in India. Leaving apart the question of the possible formation of the *Acts of Thomas* in India or else-where, we have to give credit to the Syrian church that we were left with some early documents including *Acts of Thomas,* concerning the Indian Apostolate of *Marthomasleeha.* Again, the European writers like Amador Correia, SJ (1564), Francis Dionisio, SJ (1578),[1] and Antonio Gouvea (1603) made references to the ancient songs of the Christians of Kerala and wrote down the contents of the oral tradition of St. Thomas Christians making use also of the ancient folk songs. Therefore, with homage to the pioneering and farsighted services of the Syrian and European Churches, I would like to present ancient songs of the Christians of Kerala and the Thomistic traditions appearing in them.

These Christian ancient folk songs, most of which were formed in the Knanaya community[2] are sung even today during marriages, tours, family get-togethers, etc., that signifies its present-day relevance. A study on these songs would bring to light many horizons hitherto unknown regarding history, language, life-style, dress code, food habits, rituals, re-ligious traditions, etc. It may clarify the significant role of these songs in the devotional, religious, biblical, cultural, social, literary, and intellectual formation of Kerala as well. The European writers, as stated earlier ex-pressly mentioned that the ancient songs sung by the natives were one of the sources of their narration of the history of Malabar Church and as such they serve as an important and the earliest literary source of Kerala history too. Though everything contained in the ancient songs cannot be considered as authentic and true in historicizing, we can still utilize them as subsidiary sources and even as primary sources, if supported by other evidences, especially in the Kerala cultural and historical background where written sources are rarely available.

Our area of study in this paper is centered on the Thomistic traditions handed down through these songs. For study purpose, we shall divide these songs into two groups. Primarily, those songs having Thomistic traditions as their core content: 1. *Margamkalippattu*, 2. *Rampan Pattu*, 3. *Thomaparvam* and secondly those songs that have certain connection with St. Thomas like, 1. *Pananpattu*, 2. *Marthomman* song, 3. Historical songs, 4. Songs of churches, 5. Songs of *Parichamuttukali, Vattakkali*, marriage, etc. An analysis of the first group of songs indicates a common source, which I suppose would be the *Acts of Thomas* with the apparent similarities, though generated in different ages.

Sources

Folk songs being oral in nature, we don't have original text of the ancient songs and thereby its original epoch of composition is unknown. Yet an analysis of the literary genus and language of the songs as well as the references in the writings of the Europeans make us believe that many of these songs were composed prior to the arrival of the Europeans. Utilization of these songs for narrating the history of St. Thomas Christians by the Europeans is, however, an indication that the songs were already an object of study in that period itself.

The existing texts of the songs trace origin in the beginning of the eighteenth century. We are fortunate to have three such palm leaf texts (*thaliyolagrantham*) with more than 300 years of antiquity, which indicates that an urge for the collection and preservation of these songs was alive at least from that time onwards. The total palm leaves may arrive to 400 in number. It is written on both sides of the leaves. It shows clearly an edited work, song after song on the same leaves, which obviously indicates that yet another collection of songs in different loose leaves would have pre-existed.

In 1910, these songs were compiled and published by P.U. Lukas with the help and direction of Fr. Mathew Vattakkalathil with the title *Ancient Songs of the Syrian Christians of Malabar (Malayalathe Suriyani Kristianikalute Purathanappattukal)*. To the best of our knowledge, this book is the first printed collection of folk songs in Kerala. Now we have the eleventh edition of it. Even if we calculate a minimum of 500 copies per edition, some 6000 texts have already reached the hands of the readers in the last hundred years.

PREVIOUS STUDIES

It is sad to say that serious works based on the ancient songs are yet to come. Though European writers have made use of these songs for history writing and our older generations tried to preserve these songs from oral tradition into writing down on palm leaves and then to a published work, its usage as source of valid history remained almost unnoticed. Though Bernard Thoma (Alencheril) TOCD had utilized *Rampanpattu* extensively in his *Marthommakristhyanikal*, it cannot be considered systematic and scientific in the modern methodology of history. Jacob Kollaparambil made concrete steps in using these songs in historicizing especially in his *Historical Sources on the Knanites, Babylonian Origin of the Southists among St. Thomas Christians* and *Sources of the Syro Malabar Law*. Deepa SJC as part of her doctoral dissertation in the Mahatma Gandhi University, Kottayam under the guidance of Scaria Zacharia studied these songs on their folkloristic aspects. There exists an MPhil dissertation by Babu Thomas that however is concentrated on the cultural aspects of the songs.

My thrust in this study, however, is to consider them as a historical and linguistic auxilium, i.e., references, aids, and evidences that these songs would be able to help a historian of St. Thomas Christians or Kerala historian in finding out the historical Thomas the apostle, in the land of Kerala. I hope also that this would prompt all of us to have at least a copy of the text of the Christian ancient folk songs and to begin to dwell more on these songs so that with the cultural, intellectual baggage possessed by each one of us, we shall bring new lights and more comprehensive understanding of Indian church history.

GENERAL IMPRESSIONS

As indicated above, though we have to distinguish between the songs that have St. Thomas tradition as its prime content and the rest of the songs that occasionally mentions the apostolate of St. Thomas, one of the salient feature common to all is certain recurrent and identical expressions[3] like: his name–*Marthomman* or simply Thoma; the year of his arrival–A.D. 52; the seven churches established by him—Kollam, Niranam, Kokkamangalam, Kottakkayal, Chayal, Palur, and Kodungallur; his arrival–the place of martyrdom–Mylapore; the Episcopal succession–through Paul; the word *marthommanvazhi* (Christian way of living according to St. Thomas) and its usage in parallel to *Semayonkeppavazhi* in Antioch and Rome, etc. *Vazhi* is a Dravidian term denoting the way. The parallel Sanskrit term is *Margam* that, however is used very rarely in the songs, is an indication of the antiquity of the expression, since the Sanskrit influence in the Malayalam language came most probably from the eighth century onwards.

THE NAMES *MARTHOMMAN* AND *THOMA*

The names to denote St. Thomas the apostle used in our songs are either *Marthomman*, *Thomasleeha* or simply *Thoma*. *Thoma* is a Syriac proper noun. *Mar* means Lord and *Sleeha* means apostle in Syriac. However, the coined name *Marthomman* deserves special attention since it is a form of malayalamizing. The particle "an" at the end of *thoma* is a suffix to denote third person masculine singular in Malayalam. For example, Ramah (Ram+ah) in Sanskrit is made Ram+an (Raman) to make it Malayalam. Thus, even in the name *Marthomman* itself we see an inculturization process. We can observe that Syriac language and culture are melt into the Kerala culture so pacifically. In the *Pananpattu* we see a clear distinction between the names of Thomas, the apostle and Thomas of Knai, the merchant: St. Thomas the apostle is called *Marthomman*, whereas Thomas of Knai is called simply *Thommachan* or with the locative adjectival prefix Knai as *Knaithomman*.

SONGS HAVING ST. THOMAS TRADITION AS ITS MAIN CONTENT

There are three ancient songs that have St. Thomas tradition as the main content. *Margamkalippattu,* is in palm leaf manuscript form, while *Pananpattu* is collected from oral tradition. With regard to the *Rambanpattu*, to the best of my knowledge, the manuscript source is unknown. But Bernard Thoma gives the full text of it in his *Marthomakristianikal* of 1916.

Margamkalippattu

Margamkalippattu is the poetic literature of *Margamkali*, a marvellous performing art form and contribution of the Knanaya community to the Kerala artistic horizon. *Margamkali* used to be performed on the eve of marriage of the Knanites after the rituals of *Chanthamcharth* (*Anthamcharth*)[4] or *Mailanchiyiteel*,[5] and on the eves of parish fests or other festive occasions. It was performed by 12 male dancers around a lighted oil lamp, symbolizing Christ with his disciples.

Margamkalippattu has a total of 440 verses in 14 stanzas *(padams)* including an invocatory hymn. The invocatory hymn having twelve verses seems not to be an original part of the rest of the song. The style of language of the hymn and the rest are very much different. The invocatory hymn seems to be much ancient with archaic Dravidian words, while the rest contains many words borrowed from Sanskrit. For example, *vazhi*, a Dravidian word, is used to denote Christian faith in the invocatory part, whereas *margam*, a Sanskrit derived word is used in the rest of the part. Thus, it is possible that, an already existing song (invocatory hymn) would have been added to the rest of the part.

The invocatory hymn speaks of St. Thomas's martyrdom by the piercing of an arrow by a Brahmin *(vedyan,* one who knows the Vedas).[6] The Symbolic attribution to peacock in the hymn is interesting. Apart from the mural, mosaic, and iconographical Christian representation of peacocks symbolizing immortality (borrowed from the Greek mythology attributing no decay for the flesh of peacocks after death), in the Indian Vedic representations, peacock is the vehicle of Kartikeya or Muruga in the Dravidian context. Lord Srikrishna is depicted always with peacock feather on his head. Krishna is depicted also as having a flute in his arms, whereas St. Thomas is attributed to have a stick, better a scepter. So, the cultural paragonism is evident.

The *Margamkalippattu* is a poetic fictional narration of the missionary works of St. Thomas the apostle. It is the ardent desire of the King of Chozha Mandala (present day Tamilnadu) to have a palace similar to that of Solomon that made him send his minister Havan to the West in search of a carpenter (architect). At Mahosa (Maha Ûs? or Mahodayapuram at Cranganore?), Havan met with Jesus Christ, who sold St. Thomas to him. Interestingly the selling of important persons happened twice in the Bible: Joseph was sold by his brothers and Jesus was sold (betrayed for money) by Judas Iscariot. Both the sales turned to be good at the end. It was just because of the death of Judas due to his betrayal, that St. Thomas, himself a born twin, had to travel alone to India while all other Apostles travelled as couples in their missionary endeavors as lamented by *Marthomma* in the *Margamkalippattu* itself. Jesus, however, ensures St. Thomas that he should not think that he is alone and that Jesus himself will be with him.

Havan brought St. Thomas to the King of Chozha, who gave him much money and utensils to build the palace, which however was spent by St. Thomas for his missionary enterprises. Knowing that he did not do anything, the King got angry and put him in prison, meanwhile the brother of the King fell ill and died and his soul saw the beautiful palace prepared for the King by St. Thomas in heaven, and narrated the whole to the King while returned from heaven. So, the King was pleased and set free the apostle. The King, his brother and Havan got baptized. And, many others got baptized due to the works of St. Thomas. Later, he was asked to venerate Lordess Kali in the temple that was obviously refused.

Further the temple was put into fires by the words of St. Thomas that made the Brahmins infuriated and one of them killed him by a spear at Chinnamala.[7] His soul was taken to the heavens by the angels and the mortal body was put in a church as wealth of his children.

Dr. Jacob Vellian narrates in detail that how *Margamkalippattu* is very much influenced by the *Acts of Thomas* and by the homilies of Jacob of Serug in his *Margamkali Attaprakaram*.

Our expectation will be high if we pretend that a contemporary historical record on the apostolate of St. Thomas is offered in the *Margamkalippattu*. Yet, though we do not know the exact epoch of formation of this song except that it is prior to the European era in the Indian soil, we come across an account of the then prevailing tradition on the St. Thomas apostolate through it.

Marthomaparvam

There are many references to *Marthomaparvam* in many church history works of Kerala though very often it is referred as *Rambanpattu* or *Marthomaparvam* as if they are identical works. However, they are two different works. This is testified to by P.J. Thomas and Jacob Kollaparambil. In addition, to the best of my knowledge, there are two texts with the name *Marthomaparvam*. In his monumental work, *Malayala Sahithyavum Kristianikalum* (Malayalam Literature and Christians) of 1961, P.J. Thomas speaks of Edamarathu Victor as the author of this song written in between 1892–1897 and writes that it contains 1769 stanzas (of two lines) in three *padams*. He gives two citations also from this work.

Jacob Kollaparambil possessed a palm leaf manuscript of *Marthomaparvam* having seventeen folia.[8] The fourteenth folio of this manuscript is missing. Both the citations in P.J. Thomas, however, are not found in the palm leaf manuscript, and it is difficult to believe that both the citations appear in the missing fourteenth leaf itself. Further, the total number of stanzas may not be more than 270 in the manuscript even if we include the missing fourteenth leaf and the work is not divided into *padams*. The meter followed in the manuscript text is *Kalakanchi*, whereas the two citations from Edamarathu are in two other meters. Therefore, we are prompted to believe that there existed at least two different works with the name *Marthomaparvam*. We do not know whether the work indicated by P.J. Thomas is published or at least preserved. Further investigation is to be done on this.

It is better to consider *Marthomaparvam* in the manuscript form available to us as a literary work rather than a folk song. The language is of a much later period with many Sanskrit words, *parvam* itself bringing the idea of Sanskrit *kavyas*. It can be inferred that *Acts of Thomas* as well as the oral tradition of the soil have a direct influence in the making of this work. The colophon of the song is worth our study. The colophon makes it clear that it is the narration of the good story of Marthoma, the best *sanyasi* (religious one). Ample use of Kerala flora and fauna is found in the work. The works of St. Thomas at Kollam, Makothevar Pattanam, and the journeys to Mylapore and Chinnamala are narrated. There is mention of Naredra Gumpasnon that may be an erroneous transliteration of the King Gundaphor in the *Acts of Thomas*. It is a tiger that brings back the hand of the servant as in the case of *Margamkalilppattu*, whereas in the *Acts,* it is a dog. St. Thomas is martyred at the hands of the servants of the King in *Marthomaparvam* where as in *Margamkalippattu* it is executed by Brahmins on account of not venerating Kali, the Hindu Goddess. In *Marthomaparvam* no mention is made of the reason for the death of Thomas as well as how it was executed.

Rambanpattu

Since Thomas Koonammakkal gives a detailed account of *Rambanpattu* in this work itself, I shall restrain myself to certain passing comments only. We get the full text of *Rambanpattu* from *Marthomakristianikal* of Bernard Thoma and the study of this text by Bernard remains a landmark model of history utilizing ancient Malayalam literary works. Unfortunately, in these 100 years, it seems that he is left with no posterity in this field.

With the usage of many Sanskrit and sanskritized words, the language of *Rambanpattu* indicates a modernized language suggesting that it cannot be of prior to the sixteenth century. Most probably it is a single authored literary work propagated only among the learned ones just like *Marthomaparvam*. It did not get popularity or public reception like *Margamkalippattu* probably because of the fact that there was no performing art form attached to it.

SONGS HAVING CONNECTION WITH ST. THOMAS

The Ancient songs are divided into five categories, namely, *Penpattukal* (songs of the females), *Anpattukal* (Songs of the Males), *Pallippattukal* (Songs about the Churches), *Vattakkalippattukal and Vanchippattukal* in the published text itself. All these categories include songs that have some bearing with the St. Thomas tradition.

Pananpattu

Pananpattu (*Panan* song) deserves special mention here. Though not an integral part of *Purathanappattukal,* from the fifth edition onwards it was added to the published text. *Pananpattu* contains those songs sung by the Panan or Veeradiyan caste people who used to sing songs in palaces, noble houses and in war fields. We find mention of them in the *Samkham* literature and in the famous *parayipetta panthirukula aithihyam* (legend of the twelve tribes delivered by Paraya woman). There are several songs of them available today and many studies are done on their songs in the northern and southern parts of Kerala. P.J. Thomas added for the first time sixty-eight lines from the *Pananpattu* in his *Keralathile Kristheeya Sahityam* (Christian Literature of Kerala) in 1935. Jacob Vellian added the full text of the *Pananpattu* in the fifth edition of the *Purathanappattukal* collecting from Raman Panan of Piravom (275 lines) and Narayana Panan (175 lines) of Mulanthuruthy.

Only one *Panan song* related to the Christian community is available to us. It speaks of the relation between Cheraman Perumal and Knaithomman and their mutual helps and rewards.[9] The song describes the mediatory role that Knaithoma took in order to bring back the four working class people from Sri Lanka and the resulting awarding of seventy-two and a half privileges and land without tax for building Church and Streets. These privileges were written on copper plates and a copy of the same was made on a granite sheet and is kept in the northern gate of Kodungallur temple.

The attribution by many Kerala Church historians that *Pananpattukal* or *Veeradiyanpattukal* speaks of the works of St. Thomas the apostle, is therefore, not true. However, what makes us interested here is the mention of the name of St. Thomas as a witness to the grant donated by Cheraman Perumal to Knaithoma.[10] The Sun and the Moon are usually ascribed as witnesses in copper plates and other royal documents of Kerala. But the presence of an additional witness, St. Thomas the apostle is very suggestive. Why *Alaha Nayan* (God, the Father) or *Anpan Misiha* (Christ, the lover and founder of Christianity) is not made a witness? The King by himself would not have suggested inserting the name of St. Thomas. We have to believe that if the tradition related to St. Thomas would not have existed in Kerala, the King would have been unaware of such a tradition and therefore would not have inserted it in the copperplate. At least the Panans would not have inserted it in the song for the same reason. So, we have to conclude that the Apostolate of St. Thomas was already known in the Indian soil, or at least that Knaithomman would have insisted for its insertion. So, I think this insertion in a secular document (or at least in the song about that document) of *Marthommasleeha* is proof for the cognition of St. Thomas Apostolate in Kerala.

Marthomman song

Marthomman is a very popular song sung in any function of the Knanites as a prayer song. However, it is to be born in mind that it is not a prayer song, rather it is a song of a mother at the time of the marriage of her daughter expressing the anxieties and happiness of the moment. Leaving the middle part, the first 6 lines and the last 4 lines are sung to make it a prayer song. Here in the first stanza, the mother as well as the whole community says that we begin with the goodness of Marthomman, and so let everything be auspicious.[11] The next two stanzas are words inviting the presence of Jesus Christ and the Holy Spirit in the panthal (podium) of wedding. Here we see a preeminence of St. Thomas over Jesus Christ and Holy Spirit, which is theologically incorrect. But it shows how deep rooted is their faith in the presence and goodness of Marthomma, their father in faith.

Historical songs

The tradition of the Knanites always held the St. Thomas apostolate in India as valid. In fact, they anchored the motive of their immigration from Southern Mesopotamia as a missionary endeavor to strengthen the St. Thomas Christians. This tradition is found in many of the songs narrating their immigration. Thus, in the song *Innu nee njangale kaivitto Marone* (Lord, have you left us alone today) "Overcoming struggles and hardships, we arrived at Mylapore and Kodungallur of St. Thomas by the order of the One in the Trinity (= Jesus Christ) to enlighten the faith of the descendants of St. Thomas."[12]

The song *Nallororossilam thannil Nagariyil* (in the good city of Jerusalem) speaks of the order, blessings and the Holy book received from the Catholicos who is in the way/law of St. Thomas by Urha Mar Yauseph and his team before departing to India.[13] A historical song on Mar Abraham also mentions amply the apostolate of St. Thomas. This song in fourteen *padams* was written in 1724 about Mar Abraham, the last Chaldean prelate over the St. Thomas Christians who died in 1597. In the second *padam* of the song, after specifying that Simon was at Antioch and Paul at Western Rome, the places under the Law of St. Thomas are enumerated. They are Chinam, Makkam, Mayilapur, Ormis, Malakka, and Malanad (Kerala).[14] It is stated also that the Catholicos of Bagdad also belongs to the Law of Thomas. In the fourth *padam*, before specifying the arrival of Knaithomma and his team, mention is made of the arrival and death of St. Thomas.[15] The fifth *padam* specifies the missionary activity of Knaithomma towards the St. Thomas Christians.[16] In the sixth *padam*, which speaks about the arrival of the five Chaldean bishops in Kerala, there is mention of the seven churches (established by St. Thomas) as head churches[17] and it speaks of the sixty five St. Thomas Christian churches on their arrival that is described as a garden of jasmine.[18]

Though written very late, i.e. in 1908 by P.U. Lukas entitled *Brief History of the Suriani Church of Kerala Vanchippattu* also gives the same details.[19]

Song of Churches

Though of a later origin, *Pallippattukal*, which include songs on Churches and Crosses, serve a good deal as a valid source of history. Making a song soon after the construction of a church was a custom prevailing in Kerala that facilitated finding out the exact year–and possibly the date–of construction of the church. Usually the whole details of the construction are described in that song. It acted also as a catechesis on the biblical stories, on the history of the ancient Church in Kerala and on the history and heroic virtues of the heavenly patron of the parishes.

These songs on churches give ample testimony on the St. Thomas's apostolate as well. Though these songs cannot be considered as contemporary documents, yet their testimonies do indicate that a vibrant and all-embracing tradition regarding St. Thomas's apostolate was alive all through these ages. Thus, we get such references in the songs of Chunkom (1579), Kottayam Cheriya Pally (1579), Kallucherry (1580), Cross of Chunkom – Thodupuzha (1630), Punnathara (1635), Puthuppally (1640), Paingolam – Pala (1667), Kaipuzha (1813), Edakkattu – Kottayam (1821), etc.

In the Song of Four Churches—a song about Chunkom church dedicated to St. Mary—the *padams* fifth to eighth describe the history of the church in Kerala, in which the work of St. Thomas and the continuation in the Law of Thomas is expressed. In the fifth *padam,* of the song of the Cross—built in 1630—of Chunkom church, it is stated that the work of the Cross was finished on the feast of *Dukrana* of St. Thomas that indicates the celebration and importance of such a feast.[20] Further, in the song of Paingolam Church, it is stated that the Cross of Chunkom church was built by the handwork of St. Thomas.[21]

In the fourth and fifth *padams* of the song of Kottayam Cheriya Pally, built in 1579, we find ample references to the work and Law of St. Thomas.[22]

In the sixth *padam* of the song of Kallucherry church dedicated to St. Mary, after narrating the missionary works of St. Peter in Antioch and

Rome, the Churches of the Law of Thomas are enumerated that include Chinam, Makkam, Mayilapur, Urumees, Ilakka (Malacca), and Malanadu (Kerala).[23]

Punnathura church, built in 1635, is dedicated to St. Thomas. In the old song consisting of just 10 verses of the Church of Punnathara, the prayer addressed to St. Thomas is for protecting them like the mother who gave birth to them.[24] Again the seventh *padam* of the new song of the same church written by Thakadiyel Ittiyavira in the latter half of nineteenth century makes clear mention of the work of St. Thomas in India.[25]

In the fifth *padam* of the song of Puthuppally Pally, built in 1640, also there is mention of the missionary as well as episcopal activities of St. Thomas.[26]

Kaipuzha church, built in 1813, is dedicated to St. George and its song is written by Thakadiyel Ittiyavira. The fifth *padam* narrates the work of St. Thomas in India.[27] Kottayam Edakkattu church, built in 1821, also is dedicated to St. George. Thakadiyel Ittiyavira himself formed its song. The sixth *padam* of the song deals with the work of St. Thomas.[28]

Songs of *Parichamuttukali, Vattakkali,* and marriage

Many songs were sung for the *Parichamuttukali*, a warrior dance in circle with sword and shield performed by the Syrian Christians, since they had a good artillery similar to that of Nayars. Among these songs, there were songs related to St. Thomas and usually the *Rangapooja*, the invocatory hymn contains prayer to St. Thomas.[29]

Vattakkali means dance in circle. But unfortunately, we are unable to retrace its performance. However, a lot of *vattakkalippattukal* exists among the ancient songs. The first line of the song *Ettuthira Vattakkali*, starts with commemorating St. Thomas. The line speaks of the adorned bridegroom by the command of the words of St. Thomas (Law of Thomas) who shines in eight directions.[30]

In a collection of three songs related to marriage named *Kalyanapadangal*, the third song contains invocations to St. Thomas.[31]

CONCLUSION

A glimpse at the St. Thomas's Apostolate in India in various ancient songs of St. Thomas Christians was attempted. Main thrust of this article was to put together various original source materials related to this topic. It is found that we have ample such works, either published or in manuscript form and some even in oral forms. They vary in style, content, and length. But they offer us a positive answer to the question of the St. Thomas's Apostolate in South India, and particularly in Kerala. None of these songs negates the Legacy of St. Thomas's Apostolate in India. From these songs we can conclude at least that the Apostolate of St. Thomas in India is not an invention of the near centuries, but a belief handed over through various centuries. Of course, we have to bear in mind that none of these songs would have been in existence from the first century and thereby lacks contemporary evidentiary value. Still, these songs lead us to the most ancient and still existing written sources of our tradition. As such they manifest the belief of the people of that epoch and of the succeeding epochs.

The tradition on the Thomistic apostolate manifested through these songs all through these centuries is such dense, varied, yet unanimous, that a true and honest historian cannot ignore at all. Therefore, a serious higher study utilizing references and contents from these songs is a must of the hour for unravelling the obscure past of the St. Thomas Christians. Even a doctoral thesis is highly recommended to highlight such salient features and sources of history that hitherto was kept unearthed. The pioneering works of the Europeans, of Bernard Thoma, Jacob Kollaparambil, and Jacob Vellian are to be continued and strengthened.

ENDNOTES

¹ "I knew things written below from information received from old and trust-
worthy persons; and in these all are concordant, because they keep these as
firm traditions, and as written in books and sung in their songs." Fr. Francis
Dionisio, SJ, Report written to the Superior General of the Jesuits dated 4
January, 1578 in Portuguese language on the Christians of St. Thomas. Two
originals are extant in ARSI, Goa 12, II, ff. 439–441 and 442–443. Fr Wicki,
SJ has published the report in *Documenta Indica* (vol. XII, pp. 131–143). The
present citation is from the translation of Dr. Jacob Kollaparambil, *Historical
Sources on the Knanites*, in Dr. Jacob Vellian (ed.), *Symposium on Knanites
Conducted in Connection with the Platinum Jubilee Celebration of the Diocese
of Kottayam on 29ᵗʰ August 1986*, Jyothi Book House, Kottayam 1986, 6. For
further information, cfr. Dr. Jacob Kollaparambil, *Historical Sources on the
Knanites,* on ancient songs on p. 45.

² The Knanaya community or Thekkumbhaga samudayam consists of faithful
belonging to the Syro-Malabar Catholic Archeparchy of Kottayam for the
Southist people and to the Knanaya Jacobite *Bhadrasanam* of Chingavanam.
The Knanaya community and the Archeparchy of Kottayam have played
and still play a vital role in the history of the Syro-Malabar Church and of
the Indian church in general. According to the living tradition among the
Knanites, it had its origin from a colony of Jewish Christians of the Tribe of
Judah consisting of around 400 persons of seventy-two families of seven clans
who in A.D. 345 immigrated to Cranganore (Muziris, the renowned ancient
port of Kerala, now known as Kodungalloor) from Southern Mesopotamia.
The group, headed by a merchant called Knaithomman, included a bishop
Mar Youseph, four priests and some deacons. Their traditional belief attested
by the songs is that they came to strengthen and re-invigorate the ecclesial-
ly weakened St. Thomas Christians of India that they did by preaching the
Gospel mainly through their life. They built churches of their own and had
priests of their own and continued in the Catholic faith. They continued their
relation to the mother Church and obtained bishops from there. This community has played a vital role in authoring as well as in preserving the ancient
songs. The unique identity of this community is formed also through the act
of singing these ancient songs in a collective manner. Certain ancient songs
like *Nallororoslem, Munnam Malankara, Innu Nee Njangle,* etc. (P.U. Lukas,
Malayalathe Suriyani Kristiyanikalute Purathanappattukal, Manorama Press,
Kottayam 1910, 5-7 (hereafter *Purathanappattukal*) and *Pananpattu* are very
important from a historical point of view with regard to the community.

³ It is not in the sense that all of the songs utilise all these expressions, but only
in the sense that if utilized, they are identical.

⁴ The words *Chanthamcharth* (beautification) and *anthamcharth* (rite of puberty) are used interchangeably to denote the same custom at bridegroom's
house on the eve of the preceding day of marriage. In ancient times there was
the practice of early marriages. Usually the first shaving was done in connection with marriage. Shaving, oiling, and bathing are all acts of physical

101

beautification while an aspect of psychological and spiritual cleaning is also at work in the Knanaya practice of *Chanthamcharth*. Further, *Mailanchiyiteel,* the parallel custom at the bride's house, is also related to beautification, both physical as well as spiritual. Hence the term *Chanthamcharth* is relevant. The parallel term *Anthamcharth* also is correct. The term "*antham*" gets the meaning of common sense or intelligence in the common parlance of "*avano-ru anthavum kunthavumilla.*" (He doesn't have common sense or he does not understand.) Hence *anthamcharth* is be recognized as a custom equivalent to the rite of puberty practiced in many cultures. Through a symbolic ceremony of first shaving and ritual bath, the community recognizes the adulthood of the person and sanctions his maturity to lead a married life. The sister of the bridegroom prepares *pavata* (a special podium) in the barn or in the main hall of the house. She places a long roded or hanging oil lamp (*kolvilak-ku/ thukkuvilakku*) in front of the podium. The brother-in-law brings the bridegroom to the podium. After the evening prayers, the assembled sings '*Marthomman.*' When the song is finished, the barber approaches the bridegroom and asks the assembled, "*Pathinezhu parishacku melulla malorodu chodickunnu, manavala chekkanu chantham charthatte?*" (= I request those great men who are above seventeen castes, may I shave the bridegroom?). The same question is repeated thrice, and finally the audience gives the consent. The barber shaves the beard and oils the whole body with coconut oil. Thereafter the bridegroom is taken for ritual bathe and then returns wearing white dress. During the whole time the assembly sings "*Chanthamcharth* song" beginning with "*Maranisopathaviyile*" and other songs.

5   *Mailanchiyiteel* (smearing with henna) is one of the most important customs that takes place at the bride's house on the previous eve of marriage of the Knanites. The first part is more or less identical to that of *Chanthamcharth*. The bride comes to the assembled accompanied by the elder sister and sits on the podium. A lighted lamp is placed in front of her. After the evening prayers and the prayer song *Marthomman*, the audience starts the *Mailanchippattu*. The first strophe of the *Mailanchippattu* describes the creation of Adam and the second, that of Eve. The third contains the life style of the first spouses in paradise. The fourth deals with the sin of man and therefore the need of smearing with henna. Eve plucked the fruits with the hands and walked with legs to arrive there. This is the motive behind covering hands and legs with henna. While henna, used as a cosmetic, beautifies the bride, in the custom it is used as a symbol of inner purification, i.e., washing out all stains of sins from the bride before entering a new married life. The paternal grandmother is responsible to smear the henna. She smears it on the hands and legs in accordance with the verses of the song.

6   മെയ്ക്കണിന്ത പീലിയും മയിൽമേൽത്തോന്നും മേനിയും
പിടിച്ച ദണ്ഡും കയ്യും മെയ്യും എന്നന്നേയ്ക്കും വാഴ്കവെ
വാഴ്ക വാഴ്ക നമ്മുടെ പരിഷയെല്ലാം ഭൂമിമേൽ
വഴിക്കുറായ് നടക്കവേണ്ടി വന്തവരോ നാമെല്ലാം
അഴിവുകാലം വന്നടുത്തു അലയുന്ന നിൻമക്കളെ
അഴിയായ്വണ്ണം കാത്തരുൾവാൻ കഴിവുപേശുക മാർത്തോമ്മാൻ
മലമേൽനിന്നു വേദ്യനമ്പു ചാർത്തിമാറിലെന്നപോൽ
മൈൽമേലേറി നിന്ന നില കാണവേണം പന്തലിൽ

പട്ടുടൻ പണിപ്പൂടവ പവിഴമുത്തുമാലയും
അലങ്കരിച്ച പന്തലിൽ വന്നുതക വേണം മാർത്തോമ്മാൻ
അലങ്കരിച്ച പന്തലിൽ വണ്ണെഴുന്തരുൾക മാർത്തോമ്മാൻ
അലങ്കരിച്ച പന്തലിൽ വന്നരുൾതരേണം മാർത്തോമ്മാൻ

(P.U. Lukas, *Malayalathe Suriyani Kristiyanikalute Purathanappattukal*,
    Jyothi Book House, Kottayam, 2002, 10ᵗʰ edition, [hereafter
    Purathanappattukal], 143)

[The peacock feather adorned on body, the stature which seems better than
    peacock,
The scepter held, hands and the body everything shall remain for ever
All our community shall reign on Earth
We all came to walk on the Way with loyalty
Your children wandering due to the time of destruction
Marthomman, tell us the means to keep them up beautifully
The position of being on peacock is to be seen in the pandal
As if when the Brahmin shot with arrow on chest from the mountain
With silklike torso, privileged dress and pearl and coral chains
Marthomman is to be in the decorated pandal
Marthomman has to come in ceremonial procession into the decorated
    Pandal
Marthomman has to offer blessings in the decorated Pandal.]
The lines 3–6 of this invocatory hymn makes allusion to the Southist
    authorship.

7   "My pilgrimage (1ˢᵗ to 9ᵗʰ May 2018) in bicycle to Mylapore has widened my
toponymistic notions that are to be considered seriously, of course with care.
In the vicinity of Myalapore, the names of many places raise curiosity. The
distance from Mylapore to Chinnamalai is 7 kilometers. At a distance of 9
kilometers from Chinnamalai, there is a place called Tirusulam (Thirusuram,
Chathurvethimangalam) near to Chennai airport. Tirusulam etimologically
comes from (tatbhava form of) Sanskrit or Prakrit Trisul, the three headed
spears. Sri Viswaruba Vekkaliamman temple is one among the most important 8 temples surrounding Tirusulam all of that are dedicated to goddess Amman (Amman Koil). In *Margamkalippattu*, St. Thomas was asked to
venerate Kaliyar, and here we have the Kaliyamman temple and he was later
murdered by a spear. (The presence of this temple and usage of Sanskrit at
the time of St. Thomas is to be verified.) The name Chinnamalai, meaning
small hill in Tamil, is found in the *Margamkalippattu*. According to the local
tradition, it is in a small cave above that exists the present church that St.
Thomas sheltered himself while he was fleeing from persecution.

Mount St. Thomas, a place 5 kilometers away from Chinnamalai and 6
kilometers from Tirusulam, is identified by the Portuguese as the location of
the spearing and death of St. Thomas. According to the Portuguese version, it
is at St. Thomas Mount that the St. Thomas Cross (*Marthomasleeva*), a Cross
of Persian style and origin, is discovered. The Cross is kept at the center of the
Main altar wall of the National Shrine at St. Thomas Mount. The name with
which the hill is known presently is St. Thomas Mount, which is of English
origin. The former name of the hill is Parangimalai, which though Tamil in

language, calls for the presence of 'Parangis', the Portughese. So, this name also belongs to the European era."

The distance from Chinnamalai to Mylapore is just 7 kilometers. Santhome Basilica, which is believed to be built on the tomb of the holy apostle, is just one kilometer away from Mylapore. Santhome (Saint Thomas), a Portuguese word, and St. Thomas Mount never appear in our songs or in the oral tradition, which indicates that our songs are prior to the discovery of these locations by the Portuguese. In our tradtion and songs, the burial place of the apostle is always referred to as Mylapore. Myalaporepattanam was a flourishing port at the beginning of the Christian era and the capital of a local kingdom according to Fr. Thomas J. Mundackal, author of a book on St. Thomas's martyrdom at Mylapore and present Procurator of the National Shrine at St. Thomas Mount.

8   The manuscript, presently preserved by myself, was edited as part of the dissertation for my Master of Philosophy at Oriental Research Institute and Manuscripts Library, Kariavattam campus of University of Kerala. The same was brought to light as appendix in Jacob Kollaparambil, *The Sources of the Syro Malabar Law,* edited by Sunny Kokkaravalayil, SJ, OIRSI No. 403, Vadavathoor, 2015, 633–646.

9   ചേരാം പെരുമാൾ തമ്പുരാനുമെ
ക്നായ് നല്ല തൊമ്മച്ചനുമെ
അവർ തമ്മളില് വാണിരുന്ന
കാലമിപ്പോൾ പാടുന്നല്ലോ. (*Purathanappattukal,* 296)
[It is sung now on the golden era
Of mutual bondage between
Lord Cheraman Perumal
And Knayi Thommachan, the good.]

10   ആദിത്യനുമേ ചന്ദ്രനുമേ
മാർതോമ്മാശ്ലീഹായെയും
മൂവരുമെ സാക്ഷിയായി
ചെമ്പേടിന്മേൽ എഴുതിമാറി
കരിങ്കല്ലിന്മേല് പകർപ്പെടുത്തെടാ
കൊടുങ്ങല്ലൂരെ വടക്കെനടയിൽ
കമത്തി മൂടിഇട്ടു കല്ല്
ഏതു രാജാക്കൾ കണ്ടെന്നാലും
കുറവില്ലെന്റെ തൊമ്മച്ചായാ. (*Purathanappattukal,* 220-221)
[Wrote down on copper plate
Making witnesses all the three:
The Sun, the Moon
And Lord Thomas, the Apostle
A copy is taken on a granite slab
The stone is laid overturned and covered
At the Northern gate of Kodungallur
It is valid (forever), my Thommachan,
Even if any King examine it.]

11   മാർത്തോമ്മൻ നന്മയാലൊന്നു തുടങ്ങുന്നു
നന്നായിക വരേണമേയിന്നു. (*Purathanappattukal,* 1)
[By the grace of Marthomman, it begins
Let it be auspicious today.]

12   മൂവരൊരുവന്റെ കല്പനയാലെ മാർത്തോമ്മാൻ മൈലാപ്പൂർ
മുട്ടുപാടുകൾ തീർന്നു ഞങ്ങളെത്തി വന്നു കൊടുങ്ങല്ലൂർ
....

മാർത്തോമ്മാൻ തന്റെ ശേഷക്കാർ മാർഗ്ഗമങ്ങു തെളിപ്പാനായ്.
(*Purathanappattukal*, 8)
By the order of One among the Trinity, we are at Mylapore of Marthomman
After overcoming troubles, we arrived at Kodungallur
....

To enlighten the faith of the descendants of Marthomman.

13   നല്ലോരോരോശ്ശ്ലീലം തന്നിൽ നഗരിയിൽ
മരതകമുത്തു വിളയുന്ന നാട്ടില്
മയിലാടും പോലെ വിളങ്ങുന്ന മന്നൻ

....

മലനാടു വാഴുവാൻ പോകണം മന്നന്
ബാവായുടെ കല്പനയാലെ പുറപ്പെട്ടു
യാത്രവിധിച്ചുടനനുവാദവും വാങ്ങി

....

ശുദ്ധമാന തൃക്കൈയിലെ പുസ്തകവും വാങ്ങി
ശുദ്ധമാന കാസോലിക്ക മാർത്തോമ്മൻ വഴിക്കെല്ലാം (*Purathanappattukal*, 5)
[In the good city of Jerusalem
Where Emerald pearl is plenty
The Lord who shines like dancing peacock

....

The Lord wants to administer in Kerala
Departed with the order of the Bava
Got permission soon after the organisation of the journey

....

Got the Book from the holy hands of
The Holy Catholica in the way of St. Thomas]

14   മാനമുള്ളാരന്തിയോക്ക്യായിൽ നഗർതന്നിൽ ശേമമാൻ
മുനിവെല്ലും തമ്പിമാരും അവരൊക്കെ ഒരുമ്പാടായ്
മാനം വെച്ചരവരൊക്കെ കുലങ്ങളിൽ മാമ്മോസാ
മുതൃച്ചയാൽ പൌലോസും പടിഞ്ഞാറെ റോമ്മായിൽ
മാനമുള്ള നല്ല റോമ്മാ നഗർതന്നിൽ പകുതി
എടുത്തടിയാരെ മനം കരക്കോൾക തമ്പുരാൻ
ചീനം മക്കം മയിലാപ്പൂരും ഒർമ്മീസും മലാക്കായും
ചിതത്തോടെ മലനാടു മർത്തോമ്മാൻവഴിക്കെല്ലാം
ശിലിഹൻമാർ മുടിഞ്ഞെള്ളി അതിൽപിന്നെ മാമ്മോസാ
ചിതത്തോടെ അന്തിയോക്കിൽ കാസോലിക്കാ നടത്തി
കുലങ്ങളും വഴിപാടും ഉണ്ടു ഇണ്ടൽ പരിശിലായ്
അതുകൊണ്ടു കുലങ്ങളിലുമുശങ്ങൾ കൊടുത്തു
നാലുദിക്കും കാസോലിക്കാ പദവികൾ കൊടുത്തു
ബഗുദാശി കാസോലിക്കാ മാർത്തോമ്മാൻ വഴിക്കെല്ലാം
അലഞ്ഞുലഞ്ഞുഴലുന്നു മലനാടു വിധിയാൽ
അടിയാരെ വഴിപാട്ടിൽ കരക്കോൾക തമ്പുരാൻ. (*Purathanappattukal*, 225)
[In the famous city of Antioch of Simon the sage,
the younger brothers who surpass him all together in unity
Received baptism in clans with honour
Paul ventured in Western Rome as well
O Lord, receive in your mind we, your servants

Taking half of the famous and good city of Rome
China, Makkam, Mayilapore, Ormis, Malacca
And befittingly Malanadu on the Way of Marthomman
At the passing of the Apostles, the Catholicos
Rightly administered baptism at Antioch
Clans and Law of the Way are there, despair became a boon
Therefore rights were given to the clans
Catholica privileges were given in all the four quarters
By Catholicos of Bagdad who is in the Marthomman Law
Malanadu, unfortunately, is wandering and shaking to the bottom
O Lord, receive us, the miserables, in the Law of the Way.]

15 ആദിമുന്നമിമ്മലനാട്ടിൽ വന്നോരു മർത്തോമ്മാന്റെ
അല്ലലൊഴിച്ചു നന്മ വരുത്തി പിന്നെ മരിച്ചശേഷം
കാലം മൂന്നൂറാണ്ടതുശേഷം വന്നു കിനായിത്തൊമ്മൻ
കാസോലിക്കാ കല്പനയാലെ ആബൂനാൻമാർ വരവുണ്ട്
ഉന്നിയ ചേരകോൻ തൻ മലനാടു കൊടുങ്ങല്ലൂർ കുടിപുക്ക്
ഊനമില്ലാതൊരു പള്ളിയും പട്ടണമന്നു ചമച്ചു ജനങ്ങൾ
കൊല്ലമിരണ്ടും കൊച്ചി, മലാക്കാ, ഒർമ്മീസും, ചീനം, മക്കം
കോമളമായൊരു പള്ളിയും പട്ടണമന്നു സമത്തിനൊരുങ്ങി.
(*Purathanappattukal*, 226)
[When the earlier sorrows of Marthomman who came to this Malanadu
Were eradicated and brought goodness and he died
Kinayithomman came three hundred years after it
With the command of Catholicos,
inhabited directly at Kodungallur, the capital city of the King of Chera of
Malanadu
the people built without any fault a church and a city
The two Kollams, Kochi, Malacca, Hormis, China and Makkam
a beautiful church and city was completed equally.

16 പുതുമങ്കൾ തങ്കും മഹോതേവർ തന്നിൽ
പുതുമയാൽ വന്ന കിനായിത്തൊമ്മൻ
ഭീതിപെട്ടാരാഞ്ഞു മർത്തോമ്മാന്റെ
വേദനപൂണ്ട തരുതായ്ക്കൾക്ക്
എട്ടുദിശിയുമറിയിച്ചുംകൊണ്ട്
എത്തിച്ചുംകൊണ്ടു കൊടുങ്ങല്ലൂർക്ക്
മാർഗ്ഗവും പുക്കു വഴിപാടു നന്നായ്
മനോഗുണമെന്നേക്കും കൈക്കൊണ്ടാറെ. (*Purathanappattukal*, 226)
[In the city of Mahathevar of great novelty
Kinayithomman came for the first time
informed of with anxiety on the Orthodox desciples of Marthomma
who were in distress
Informing it in eight quarters
brought (a group of Christians) to Kodungallur
(The disciples of Marthomma) received the Way and the Law prospered
and received the blessing for ever.

17 കൊല്ലവും പാലൂർ കൊടുങ്ങല്ലൂർ കോക്കമങ്ങലം
കൊട്ടക്കായൽ നിരണം ചായൽ തലയോടേഴു മുമ്പുണ്ട്.
(*Purathanappattukal*, 226)
[Kollam, Palur, Kodungallur, Kokkamangalam
Kottakkayal, Niranam and Chayal, the seven head churches were already existing]

18 മല്ലികപ്പൂത്തോട്ടം നട്ടിട്ടും പന്തലിട്ടിട്ടും
വാട്ടം വരാതെയറുപതോടഞ്ചു പള്ളിയും
ചൊല്ലും പിമ്പേഴോടെഴുപത്തുരണ്ടിടവക
ശോഭയാലൊക്കെ ചമച്ചാരാ നാല്പതാണ്ടിട. (*Purathanappattukal*, 227)
[The garden of jasmine planted and flowered
sixty plus five churches without decay
with the existing seven churches together seventytwo churches
beautifully built within forty years.]

19 ചന്തമോടാനിശ്ചയത്തിൽ ശുദ്ധനാം മാർത്തോമ്മാശ്ലീഹാ
ഇൻഡ്യയുടെ പ്രേഷകനായി വിധിക്കപ്പെട്ടു
അൻപത്തിരണ്ടായ ക്രിസ്തുവർഷമതിൽ ക്രിസ്തുശിഷ്യ-
നൻപൊത്തിക്കേരളമാകും രാജ്യത്തിലെത്തി
ക്രിസ്തുവേദം നാടുതോറും പ്രസംഗിച്ചു വിപ്രരാദി-
മർത്ത്യരെയൊട്ടനേകം തൻ മതത്തിൽ ചേർത്തു
ഉള്ളിൽ വിശ്വാസമുള്ളോർക്കു പള്ളിതീർത്തു പല ദിക്കിൽ
കള്ളമറ്റ ഭക്തന്മാരെ ഭരിപ്പാനാക്കി
ക്രിസ്താബ്ദമറുപത്തേഴുമൊത്ത കാലത്തമ്മഹാത്മാ
വെത്തിനാൻ മയിലാപ്പൂരെന്നുള്ളോരാ ദിക്കിൽ
ഭിന്നിച്ചു ലോകരാ,ദ്ധൃത്യൻ ദുഷ്ടൻ കയ്യാൽ കുന്തമേറ്റു
ചിന്നമല തന്നിൽ വേദസാക്ഷിയായി തീർന്നു. (*Purathanappattukal*, 182)
[On account of that lovely decision, the holy Lord Thomas, the Apostle
is adjudicated missionary of India.
in fifty two of Christian era, the disciple of Christ
with love arrived in the Kingdom Kerala
Propagated Christian Gospel in all localities
many persons like Brahmins were added to his religion
Built churches in many quarters for those who believe in heart
made those devotees without wickedness as administers
in around sixty seven of the Christin Era that great soul
reached the place called Mayilappore
The people were divided, speared by an atrocious Brahmin
At Chinnamala he became a martyr.]

20 കോമളമാം നൽവരവും മാർത്തോമ്മാന്റെ ദുക്റാന
അന്നു നിറവേറി കുരിശാലാഹാ തന്നരുളാലെ (*Purathanappattukal*, 70)
[With tender good blessing, on the Dukrana of Marthomma
The Cross was finished with the order of God (the Father)]

21 അൻപോടു നല്ലൊരു ചുങ്കത്തില്
മുമ്പിൽ കുരിശു പണ്ടില്ലായ്കയാൽ
മർത്തോമ്മാന്തന്റെ കൈപ്പുണിയാൽ
വിസ്മയത്തിന്നിടകൂട്ടിയല്ലോ. (*Purathanappattukal*, 76)
[Since there was no Cross earlier
At Chunkom (which is) good and lovely

Since Marthomman did it with his own hand
There was occasion for a great surprise.]

22

ചെൽവമേറീടുന്നോരന്ത്യോഹ്യായും
ജന്മമാം വഗുദാശി റോമ്മായിലും
ചേലേറി നായൻ പിറന്ന കിനാനും
ചേർന്നുള്ള ദിക്കുകളൊക്കയിലും
ചെന്നങ്ങു നന്നായി നാടുതോറും
മാർഗ്ഗം വിധിച്ച വിധികൾപോലെ
ചേരവോൻ നാടായ മലയാളവും
ചോഴൻ വാഴുന്ന മൈലാപ്പൂരും
ചെമ്മയാൽ തൊട്ടതിൽ പകപ്പൊഴിഞ്ഞു
തോമ്മാ താൻ തന്നെ അടുത്തു വന്നു.
വന്ന ദിവ്യന്മാറാൻ കാലമഞ്ചിൽ പത്തോടൊന്നു രണ്ടീല്
വച്ചപള്ളിയടക്കമേഴിലടുത്തും പുനർ നാലല്ലോ
വൻപുയർന്ന കൊടുങ്ങല്ലൂരടുത്ത കോക്കമംഗലം
വർദ്ധിപ്പേറുമിടപ്പള്ളിയോടടുത്ത കൊട്ടക്കായലും
എന്നതെന്നിവയുള്ള മൂന്നുന്നാലും നന്നായി നിന്ന നാൾ
എന്തു പേകൾ നിറഞ്ഞന്തരാളമായി മാണിക്കവാശരാൽ
ഏകനതുകണ്ടു തിരുവുള്ളം ചെയ്തു തോമ്മാ തന്നോട്
ഉറ്റ ജനമുള്ളിൽ തോന്നുവാനത്തൽ തീർത്തു നല്ലനാൾ
ഉയിരു വെടിഞ്ഞുള്ളവരു പോലെയുള്ളിയുറച്ചായവർ
ഉത്തമനീശോ കവറുങ്കൽകൂടി ചെന്നവർ കുമ്പിട്ടു
ഉയിരിനടയവൻ ഞങ്ങളെ കാത്തുകൊള്ളുകെന്നൊക്കയും
ഒത്തു നിലനിന്ന താവഴിക്കൂട്ടം മുറയാലെയൊക്കയും
ഓടിയണഞ്ഞു വന്നാകുലം എന്നിൽ ചേർന്നു തഴുകുന്നിതെ
ഏതും മടിയെന്ന്യേയായക്കൂട്ടം കപ്പലേറുന്നു. (*Purathanappattukal,* 161)

[In the wealthiest city of Antochia,
In Bagdad, the native place and in Roma,
In the beautiful Kinan, where the leader is born
Arrived well in each of all these places
And preached as is ordered by the Way
Likely, the attractive and adjacent preaching
Of Thoma himself erased hostility
In Malayalam, the land of Cheravon
And in Myalapore, where reigns Chozha King.
The Saint who came in fifty two of Christian era
among the seven churches built, four are nearby
Kokkamangalam near to Kodungallore of great fame
and Kottakkayal near to Idappally which is increasing highly
At the time when these three and four kept good
Manickavasar who was filled with madness
The only One saw it and ordered to Thoma
In order that the own people feel within, the sadness was eliminated on a
good day
They were like those who were stiffened in heart as if they have lost life
They together went and bowed at the tomb of Jesus, the best
O Possessor of life, protect us, and everything of that sort
the bunch of clans stayed together in all the right way

ran and reached me with despair and embraced me
without any languor the group embarks the ship.]

23   നല്ക്കുരിശവിടെനിന്നു ചെന്നു പല പള്ളിയിൽ
ചീനം, മക്കം, മൈലാപ്പൂരു, റുമ്മീസുമിളാക്കായും
ചേരൻവീരൻ മലനാടു മർത്തോമ്മാൻവഴിക്കെല്ലാം. (*Purathanappattukal*, 73)

[From there the good Cross reached in many churches
at Chinam, Makkam, Mylapore, Urumees, Ilakka
and Malanadu of the heroic Cheran is on the way of Thomas]

24   അമ്പിനോടെ ബാവാതന്റെ മനോഗുണമതിനാലെ
ഇമ്പമോടെ വസിച്ചിടും പുന്നത്തുറയിൽ– മെയ്യെ
ഇമ്പമോടെ വസിച്ചിടും മുമ്പനായ മാർത്തോമ്മാനെ
അമ്പിനോടെ ഞങ്ങളിതാ കുമ്പിട്ടിടുന്നു
കുമ്പിടുന്നു ഞങ്ങളിനു അമ്പു ചെയ്യേണമെന്നിട്ടു
കുറ്റം പൊറുത്തടിയാരെ രക്ഷ ചെയ്യേണം
പെറ്റതായെപ്പോലെ തന്നെ രക്ഷിക്കേണമടിയാരെ
കൊറ്റവന്റെ പാദമണച്ചരുളീടേണം
മന്നിൽപ്പുകൾ പെരുകീടും പുന്നത്തുറ പള്ളിതന്നിൽ
മർത്തോമ്മാൻ ശ്ലീഹാ ഞങ്ങളെ കാത്തരുളേണം (*Purathanappattukal*, 80)

[On account of the love and Grace of Father
inhabits with love in Punnathura
Marthomma the great who inhabits with love,
We bow down with love
We bow down today, love us and then
Save we, the slaves, by forgiving our sins
Save we, the slaves, just like the mother who gave birth
bring us to the feet of the Leader
Marthomman, the Apostle, in the church of Punnathara,
very famous in the world, protect us.]

25   നാമമിരട്ടയതെന്നു വിളിക്കും മർത്തോമ്മായെ ഹിന്തുവിൽ
നമ്മുടെ ബാവാതന്നാലീശോമിശിഹാതന്നെയറിയിപ്പാൻ
കല്പിച്ചതിനാൽ പലരും മോക്ഷം പ്രാപിപ്പാൻ വഴിതാൻ കാട്ടി
അത്ഭുതമേറ്റം മലയാളത്തീശ്ലീഹാതന്നുടെ കയ്യാലെ
മാമ്മോദീസാ മുങ്ങി പലരും തിരുസ്സഭ തന്നിൽ ചേരുന്നു
നമ്മുടെ കർത്താവീശോതങ്കൽ വിശ്വാസത്തെയുറപ്പിച്ചു
മാർഗ്ഗമറിയിച്ചെല്ലാവരെയും സത്യവിശേഷം കേൾപ്പിച്ചു
സ്വർഗ്ഗം പ്രാപിച്ചധികവിശേഷം ചെയ്തതു ചൊല്വാനെളുതല്ല
പള്ളികൾ പല പല ദേശങ്ങളീ മർത്തോമ്മാതൻ നാമത്താൽ
ഉള്ളിൽ ഭക്തി മുഴുത്തിട്ടേറ്റം കൊണ്ടാടി സ്തുതി ചെയ്യുന്നു.
(*Purathanappattukal*, 88)

[Since God the Father ordered Marthomma who is called with the name
   twin
to Proclaim Jesus Christ in India
The way to obtain salvation was shown to many
Surprisingly through the hands of the Apostle
In Malayalam many joined the Holy Church receiving baptism
Anchoring faith in our Lord Jesus
Proclaimed the Way and made all hear the true news
It is not easy to narrate the extra deeds after obtaining heaven

There are churches in the name of Marthomma in various places
We praise at the most with overflowing faith deep at heart.]

26 മാർഗ്ഗമറിയിപ്പതിന്നു ശിഷ്യഗണങ്ങളും
വന്നു മാർഗ്ഗമറിയിപ്പാനിതു മാർത്തോമ്മാൻ മലനാടതിൽ
മാനമോടെ കൊടുത്തു പട്ടവുമങ്ങനെ മരുവുന്ന നാൾ
ക്ഷീണമായിതു മാർഗ്ഗമങ്ങതിനിങ്ങറിഞ്ഞും വിധിവശാൽ
ക്ഷീരവും പരിചോടെ തേനുമൊഴുകുന്നാടു കിനാനതിൽ
നിന്നു വന്നു കൊടുങ്ങല്ലൂർ ദിശി പുക്കു ക്രീസ്തുജനങ്ങളും
നീതിയുടയവനാണ്ടു മൂന്നു ശതത്തിൽ നാല്പതോടഞ്ചിൽ
ചേരകോന്തൻ തിരുമുമ്പിൽ ചേതസി
തെളിവോടെ കാഴ്ചയെടുത്തു ഭൂമി കൊടുത്തിതെ
വാങ്ങിയന്നവർ വച്ചു പള്ളി നഗരിയുമതിലേറ്റമായി
വന്നു വാണു പുതുപ്പള്ളിയിതിലെത്രയുമഴകോടുടൻ. (*Purathanappattukal*,
167)

[The bunch of desciples to proclaim the Way
Marthomman came to Malanadu to proclaim the Way
he has prestigiously given ordination and during this time
Knowing by fate that the Way is weakened
Christian people from Kinan, the place where flows abundantly milk and
    honey
came and they disembarked at Kodungallore city
In 345 of the year of the owner of justice
In front of Cherakon who delighted in mind
received the offerings and gave land
which they received and built church and city in it beautifully
and they came to Puthuppally and reigned it most lovingly.]

27 ഭൂതലമൊക്കയിൽ ശിഷ്യൻമാരിങ്ങനെ
വേദമറിയിച്ചു യാത്ര
ഉറഹാദിശിപുക്കു മർത്തോമ്മാതാനന്ന്
സർവേശവാർത്തകൾ ചൊല്ലി
അക്കാലം ചോഴന്റെ കാഴ്ച നിമിത്തമായി
പുക്കുവനീ മലനാട്ടിൽ
കണ്ടുപറഞ്ഞു താൻ ചോഴനുമായിട്ട്
വീണ്ടും വരുംപടി ചൊല്ലി
യാത്ര തിരിച്ചവൻ സഞ്ചാരവേഷത്തിൽ
ശാസ്ത്രജ്ഞന്മാരോടെതൃത്തു
അഴകലെ കോട്ടയ്ക്കുമൂറ്റമാം ഗ്രാമത്തിൽ
ഏഴാറു ഭൂസുരർ മറ്റും
വിസ്താരമായറിയിച്ചേകദൈവത്തെ
വിശ്വസിച്ചീശോയാൽ രക്ഷ
കേരളസഞ്ചാരം ചെയ്തുതാനിങ്ങനെ
കുരിശേഴു പ്രതിഷ്ഠ ചെയ്തു
കഷ്ടങ്ങളേറ്റു മരിച്ചീശോ രക്ഷിച്ചു
ദൃഷ്ടിയാൽ കണ്ടായതോർപ്പാൻ
മാർഗ്ഗമറിയിച്ചു മാമ്മോദീസായാലെ
സ്വർഗ്ഗമെന്നുള്ളവ കാട്ടി
കാലം തികഞ്ഞുതാൻ പാടുകളേൾപ്പാനായി
മയിലാപ്പുരെത്തി താൻ വീണ്ടും
പരലോകസമ്മാനഭാഗ്യാഗുണങ്ങളെ
പരമാർത്ഥമായറിയിച്ചു

110

കഷ്ടങ്ങളേറ്റു മരിപ്പാൻ മലതന്നിൽ
ദുഷ്ടരാം കാവ്യരാലന്ന്
വേലുകളേറ്റു താൻ നിദ്ര സമീപിച്ചു
ആലാഹാപദം വണങ്ങി
സത്യസ്വരൂപിയോടെബ്രായഭാഷയിൽ
ഇന്തുവാം മാനുഷർക്കായി
സ്തോത്രം തികച്ചു മുഴങ്കാലിൽ നിന്നുതാൻ
യാത്ര പരിശുദ്ധ ദേഹി
സ്വർലോകവാസികളാലെയെതിരേറ്റു
സ്വർലോകം ചേർന്നു സന്തോമ്മാ
പണ്ടു പറഞ്ഞൊത്ത സിംഹാസനം തനി-
ക്കാണ്ടവൻ ദാനമായി നൽകി.
കേരളവാസികളായൊരടിയാരെ
പരിപാലിച്ചെന്നേയ്ക്കും വാഴ്ക. (*Purathanappattukal,* 94)
[The desciples were in journey in the whole world
Procliming the Gospel like this
Marthomma reached at Urha city then
Proclaiming Almighty's news
Then with the the attention of Chozha
He reached this Malanadu
He met and told Chozha that
I will be returning, he assured.
He set forth on jorney as a voyager
he fought with the learned
in a village better than a fortress on account of beauty
fourtytwo Kings and all
Announced the One God elaborately
Believed that the salvation is through Jesus
Travelled Kerala in this manner
Consecrated seven Crosses
Undergone sufferings and died, and thus Jesus saved
With own eyes saw it, and to perpetuate the memory
proclaimed the Way, and showed that
Heaven is through Baptism alone
When the time was matured in order to receive the sufferings
He reached Mayilappore again
the rewards and worthiness of the other world
were informed categorically
Reached the Mount to die with sufferings
Through the piercing of lances of the wicked Brahmins
He went asleep
and bowed at the feet of God the Father
For the people of India
Glorified the one who is truth in his nature in Hebrew language
The journey in his legs
The inhabitants of Heaven
Received the holy soul
Saint Thomas joined to Heaven

God gave him as gift
the throne which was already pledged
You live forever protecting us,
Your Kerala resident servants.]

28

അരുളാലെ പോയന്നാറു രണ്ടു ശിഷ്യന്മാരും
ധരയിൽ നീളെ സത്യവേദമറിയിപ്പാനായി
അത്ഭുതത്താൽ മാർത്തോമ്മായെ ഹിന്തു തന്നിൽ
ശില്പിഭാവമായി വന്നു ചോഴൻ മുൻപാകെ
അമ്പതോടു രണ്ടുചെന്ന മാറാൻ കാല-
മിമ്പമായറിയിച്ചീശോമിശിഹാ തന്നെ
സപ്തസ്ലീബാ നമസ്കാരസ്ഥലങ്ങളും
സ്ഥാപിച്ചയാൽ സ്വർഗപ്രാപ്തനായ ശേഷത്തിൽ
വിശ്വാസികൾക്കിടയൻമാരില്ലാതായി
വിശ്വാസത്തിൽ ക്ഷീണം തട്ടി ഛിദ്രം കാരണം
താഴ്ചവന്നു മലങ്കരമാർഗ്ഗമെന്നു
കിഴക്കിനുടെ കാസോലിക്കാ ദൈവനിയോഗാൽ
അരുളിച്ചെയ്തു തൊമ്മൻ കീനാൻ തന്നോടന്ന്
കേരളത്തിൽ സ്ഥാപിക്കണം വിശ്വാസികളെ. (*Purathanappattukal*, 112)

[The twelve desciples went by the order of Jesus
To proclaim the true Gospel in all places of the earth
Surprisingly St. Thomas arrived in India
In front of Chozha King in the form of an architect
In the year of the Lord fifty two
He with pleasure proclaimed Jesus Christ
When the establisher of the seven Cross worshipping places
Was received into heaven
There were no pastors for the believers
Due to divisions the faith fainted
At that time the Catholicos of the East, entrusted by God,
Informed Thomman Kinan
That the Christianity in Malankara is declined
And (ordered) to establish believers in Kerala]

29

പണ്ടുതാതൻ തോമ്മാശ്ലീഹാ
തന്ന സത്യമാർഗ്ഗദീപം
താണു വീണു വണങ്ങുന്നു
സാദരം ഞങ്ങൾ തതീത്തിത്തെയ്
....

നാഥൻ തന്റെ ചുവടു നോക്കി
ദിവ്യദീപം കൈയ്യിലേന്തി
വന്നണഞ്ഞു നീയിനാട്ടിൽ
കടലുകൾ താണ്ടി തതീത്തിത്തെയ്.

[We bow down and rever with reverence
the light of true faith
which our Father St. Thomas, the apostle
gave us long time back
looking at the feet of the Lord
holding the holy light in the hands
You arrived in this land
Traversing the oceans]

In the *Acts of Thomas*, one may find certain references about his mission in North India. But with regard to his mission in South, there is a strong tradition that is prevalent even today. According to the South Indian tradition, St. Thomas came to India and landed in Cranganore or Kodunglloor in A.D. 52 and started his mission from there. It was the main port in the Malabar Coast.[4] Traditional songs like *Rabbanpattu*, *Pananpattu*, and *Margamkalipattu* that exist in South India contain a lot of historical accounts and they support the missionary work of St. Thomas there. Exact time of their composition cannot be ascertained from the works, but they are accounts of ancient events, transmitted orally among the St. Thomas Christians before they were written down.[5]

The churches that were blessed by the apostolic patrimony of St. Thomas are called St. Thomas Churches. The church in Persia and the church in India are St. Thomas Churches according to tradition. In course of time, the church in Persia was called East Syrian Church, Assyrian Church, Chaldean Church, Nestorian Church, Babylonian Church and Church of Seleucia-Ctesiphon because of various reasons. The church in India that originated in the St. Thomas heritage was divided into various denominations such as the Syro-Malabar Church, the Syro-Malankara Church, the Malankara Orthodox Church, the Syrian Orthodox Jacobite Church, and the Marthoma Church. All these churches are St. Thomas Churches as they share the common heritage of the apostolicity of St. Thomas.

THE APOSTOLIC CHURCH IN PERSIA

The Persian church believed that they received gospel from Apostle Thomas.[6] According to the tradition of that church, he preached gospel to the regions of the Orient first and then he moved to India. "A very old tradition represents the apostle Thomas as having brought Christianity to Parthia as well as to India—though later traditions mention only India. If we remember, however, that the Parthian Empire included present-day Afghanistan and quite a large portion of Northern India, then the two traditions are not irreconcilable."[7] St. Thomas preached gospel in East Syria. More precisely, he might have preached gospel in some parts of the Persian Empire and then commissioned his disciples to continue his missionary works. Therefore, Mar Addai, his disciple and Mar Mari, the disciple of Addai continued the work of the master.

The *Doctrine of Addai* tells that St. Thomas sent his disciple Addai (Thaddeus) to King Abgar of Edessa[8] and converted him and his people to Christianity.[9] Then Addai moved to Seleucia-Ctesiphon to evangelize the people. According to another Seleucidan tradition, Mar Mari, the disciple

---

30 എട്ടുദിശയും വിളങ്ങിന മർത്തോമ്മാൻ അരുൾപെറ്റ മാന്യമണവാളപ്പിള്ള താൻ.

(*Purathanappattukal*, 19)

31 കാർത്തരുളണമേ മമനാഥൻ നാമനാഥാ
മാർക്ഷകോമ്മായേ ശരണം
രക്ഷകനുടെ വഴി തൽക്ഷണം ഗ്രഹിതനാം
ശിഷ്യനായവൻ ബഹു ഗുരുഭക്തൻ
സർവേശ്വര തിരുമുറിവതിലംഗുലം
അരുളാൽ തൊട്ടൊരു കുതൂഹലവും
സർവഗുണാംബുധി മരിയാളുടെ തിരു-
ചമയച്ചരടു നീ വാങ്ങിയതും
അറിവേറിന ഗുജ്രത്രീനൃപർ മുതൽ
അനവധി നരരെയുമരുൾവഴിയേ
അറിവാക്കിത്തവ കരമതിനാലെ
ജ്ഞാനസ്നാനം നല്കിയതും
അരചനായ ചോഴൻ തരിക ധീരൻ
ഒരു സുകോവിൽ പണിന്തതും
അതിശയമിതു തവ കവിളിലടിച്ചവനെ
പിടിച്ചു വ്യാഗ്രലം കരത്തേൽ
ഒടിച്ചു വാങ്ങിയതും ശ്ലീഹാ-
മിശിഹായുടെ അരുൾവഴി അറിയിച്ചതും
ശ്ലീഹായുടെ തവ മരണമതും
മൈലാ എന്നൊരു ഗിരിയിൽ പെരിയൊരു
പുരിയിൽ ധനുമെഴുമൂന്നതിലും
ശുദ്ധത പെരുകിയ തന്നുടെ അസ്ഥികൾ
വച്ചിതു ഉറഹാപ്പള്ളിയിലും
കർക്കടകത്രീദിനമതുമോർത്തഴൽ
ഉൾക്കനിവാൽ സ്തുതി ചെയ്വതിനും
പരമനാഥ ശിഷ്യാ, തരിക രക്ഷ,
സരസമോക്ഷേ വസിപ്പാൻ
അനവധി മനഗുണവരനുടെ തിരുമന-
സ്സിടിയനിൽ വരുവതിനൊരുവഴിയായി മമ-
മാറാനുടെ വഴി മലയാളേ ബഹു-
കൂറാൽ നീ അറിയിച്ചതും
മാർഗ്ഗം നേടിയവർക്കു സ്തുതിപ്പിടം
ആക്കുവതിന്നായി സപ്തസ്ഥലേ
ന്തത്തിൽ പണിചെയ്തു നീ സന്തതം
കുരിശും ചമച്ചതിലൊരു സ്ഥലവും
ചായൽ പള്ളി വിചാരകനായ
മമനാഥൻ തവ കാരണവും
ശത്രുവായ വസ്തു കരിശനത്താൽ
തവ പുരത്തെ തൃജിച്ചരുൾ
പെരിയ പുനന്തുറയിൽ മരുവും ദേവാലയവും
ചമച്ചു വസിപ്പതോർത്തു തുണയ്ക്ക മാർത്തോമ്മാശ്ലീഹാ.

(*Purathanappattukal*, 140-141)

[Protect me, my Lord, the Lord of my name
St. Thomas, be my refuge
The disciple who is very devoted to the master
and instantly perceived the way of our Saviour
with the command of God, the Almighty,
The great surprise in touching with your finger in the holy wounds

that you received the holy cord of Mariya,
The ocean of all goodness
That you taught many persons
From the three Kings of great knowledge
The Way of our Lord
And gave baptism with your own hands
That you built a good palace
To give to the brave King Chozhan
That the Way of Lord Jesus was proclaimed
to the one who beat on your cheeks
whose hand was caught by a tiger
from whom the apostle took back it is highly surprising
The death of the Apostle
was on a mount called Myla, a great city
on the twenty first of Dhanu
the highly sanctified borns of him
is deposited in the church of Urha
On third of Karkadakom
in memory of that commemoration
remembering that sorrow
to praise you with heart
O disciple of the Supreme Lord, give me salvation,
so that I may dwell in beautiful heaven
That you proclaimed with great fidelity
The Way of my Lord in Kerala
In order that it be a channel that the holy will of the Noble
Adorned with many qualities be on me
Beautifully you built Crosses for ever
and made abodes in all the seven places
to make a dwelling place of worship
for those who entered the Way
St. Thomas, the Apostle, assist me
remembering that I stay at Punnathura, great for the Way,
building the existing church there of
Abandoning your city on account of you,
and of the things of the enemy
My Lord and Patron of Chayal church.]

6

THOMISTIC APOSTOLATE AND KNANAYA COMMUNITY

Mathew Kochadampallil

St. Thomas the apostle is considered the apostle of the East Syrian church and the Indian church. The St. Thomas patrimony of which these churches are proud of is a common factor. Though the primary documents that testify the mission of the apostle on those regions are lacking, traditions, references, and testimonies of the church fathers give ample support to this fact. The Christian migration under the leadership of Thomas Kynai in A.D. 345—that also does not have primary sources but supporting documents, ancient songs, and references—according to tradition, was a migration from one St. Thomas Church to another St. Thomas Church. All circumstantial evidences support the historicity of both these traditions. To understand the Thomistic Patrimony and the connection of the Knanaya[1] Community with the Apostolic Church of India, the history of the Persian church and Knanaya Immigration should be studied carefully.

St. Thomas and Missions

Jesus commanded the apostles to preach the gospel to all the nations in the world (Matt 28:18–20) and they set themselves out for mission. St. Thomas preached the gospel to the Parthians, Indians,[2] and other groups. A probable route of his missionary journey is the following:

St. Thomas started the journey from Jerusalem and after crossing many provinces and preaching to Parthians, Medians and Persians reached North India for evangelization. From where [*sic*] he went back to Jerusalem to attend the council of A.D. 49. And it was on his second trip to India (South India) that he passed through [the] Persian Gulf and Socotra reached Muziris (Malyankara) in 52.[3]

30 എട്ടുദിശയും വിളങ്ങിന മർത്തോമ്മാൻ അരുൾപെറ്റ മാന്യമണവാളപ്പിള്ള താൻ.

(*Purathanappattukal*, 19)

31 കാർത്തരുളണമേ മമനാഥൻ നാമനാഥാ
മാർത്തോമ്മായേ ശരണം
രക്ഷകനുടെ വഴി തൽക്ഷണം ഗ്രഹിതനാം
ശിഷ്യനായവൻ ബഹു ഗുരുഭക്തൻ
സർവേശ്വര തിരുമുറിവതിലംഗുലം
അരുളാൽ തൊട്ടൊരു കുതൂഹലവും
സർവഗുണാംബുധി മരിയാളുടെ തിരു-
ചമയച്ചരടു നീ വാങ്ങിയതും
അറിവേറിന ഗൂജത്രീനൃപർ മുതൽ
അനവധി നരരെയുമരുൾവഴിയേ
അറിവാക്കിത്തവ കരമതിനാലെ
ജ്ഞാനസ്നാനം നല്കിയതും
അരചനായ ചോഴൻ തരിക ധീരൻ
ഒരു സുകോവിൽ പണിത്തനും
അതിശയമിതു തവ കവിളിലടിച്ചവനെ
പിടിച്ചു വ്യാഘ്രം കരത്തേൽ
ഒടിച്ചു വാങ്ങിയതും ശ്ലീഹാ-
മിശിഹായുടെ അരുൾവഴി അറിയിച്ചതും
ശ്ലീഹായുടെ തവ മരണമതും
മൈലാ എന്നൊരു ഗിരിയിൽ പെരിയൊരു
പുരിയിൽ ധനുമെഴുമൂന്നതിലും
ശുദ്ധത പെരുകിയ തന്നുടെ അസ്ഥികൾ
വച്ചിതു ഉറഹാപ്പള്ളിയിലും
കർക്കടകത്രീദിനമതുമോർത്തഴൽ
ഉൾക്കനിവാൽ സ്തുതി ചെയ്വതിനും
പരമനാഥ ശിഷ്യാ, തരിക രക്ഷ,
സരസമോക്ഷ വസിപ്പാൻ
അനവധി മനഗുണവരനുടെ തിരുമന-
സ്റ്റിയനിൽ വരുവതിനൊരുവഴിയായി മമ-
മാറാനുടെ വഴി മലയാളേ ബഹു-
കൂറാൽ നീ അറിയിച്ചതും
മാർഗ്ഗം നേടിയവർക്കു സ്തുതിപ്പിടം
ആക്കുവതിന്നായി സപ്തസ്ഥലേ
ന്തത്തിൽ പണിചെയ്തു നീ സന്തതം
കുരിശും ചമച്ചതിലൊരു സ്ഥലവും
ചായൽ പള്ളി വിചാരകനായ
മമനാഥൻ തവ കാരണവും
ശത്രുവായ വസ്തു കരിശനത്താൽ
തവ പുരത്തെ ത്യജിച്ചരുൾ
പെരിയ പുന്നത്തുറയിൽ മരുവും ദേവാലയവും
ചമച്ചു വസിപ്പതോർത്തു തുണയ്ക്ക മാർത്തോമ്മാശ്ലീഹാ.

(*Purathanappattukal*, 140-141)

[Protect me, my Lord, the Lord of my name
St. Thomas, be my refuge
The disciple who is very devoted to the master
and instantly perceived the way of our Saviour
with the command of God, the Almighty,
The great surprise in touching with your finger in the holy wounds

113

that you received the holy cord of Mariya,
The ocean of all goodness
That you taught many persons
From the three Kings of great knowledge
The Way of our Lord
And gave baptism with your own hands
That you built a good palace
To give to the brave King Chozhan
That the Way of Lord Jesus was proclaimed
to the one who beat on your cheeks
whose hand was caught by a tiger
from whom the apostle took back it is highly surprising
The death of the Apostle
was on a mount called Myla, a great city
on the twenty first of Dhanu
the highly sanctified borns of him
is deposited in the church of Urha
On third of Karkadakom
in memory of that commemoration
remembering that sorrow
to praise you with heart
O disciple of the Supreme Lord, give me salvation,
so that I may dwell in beautiful heaven
That you proclaimed with great fidelity
The Way of my Lord in Kerala
In order that it be a channel that the holy will of the Noble
Adorned with many qualities be on me
Beautifully you built Crosses for ever
and made abodes in all the seven places
to make a dwelling place of worship
for those who entered the Way
St. Thomas, the Apostle, assist me
remembering that I stay at Punnathura, great for the Way,
building the existing church there of
Abandoning your city on account of you,
and of the things of the enemy
My Lord and Patron of Chayal church.]

6

THOMISTIC APOSTOLATE AND KNANAYA COMMUNITY

Mathew Kochadampallil

St. Thomas the apostle is considered the apostle of the East Syrian church and the Indian church. The St. Thomas patrimony of which these churches are proud of is a common factor. Though the primary documents that testify the mission of the apostle on those regions are lacking, traditions, references, and testimonies of the church fathers give ample support to this fact. The Christian migration under the leadership of Thomas Kynai in A.D. 345—that also does not have primary sources but supportive documents, ancient songs, and references—according to tradition, was a migration from one St. Thomas Church to another St. Thomas Church. All circumstantial evidences support the historicity of both these traditions. To understand the Thomistic Patrimony and the connection of the Knanaya[1] Community with the Apostolic Church of India, the history of the Persian church and Knanaya Immigration should be studied carefully.

ST. THOMAS AND MISSIONS

Jesus commanded the apostles to preach the gospel to all the nations in the world (Matt 28:18–20) and they set themselves out for mission. St. Thomas preached the gospel to the Parthians, Indians,[2] and other groups. A probable route of his missionary journey is the following:

> St. Thomas started the journey from Jerusalem and after crossing many provinces and preaching to Parthians, Medians and Persians reached North India for evangelization. From where [sic] he went back to Jerusalem to attend the council of A.D. 49. And it was on his second trip to India (South India) that he passed through [the] Persian Gulf and Socotra reached Muziris (Malyankara) in 52.[3]

In the *Acts of Thomas*, one may find certain references about his mission in North India. But with regard to his mission in South, there is a strong tradition that is prevalent even today. According to the South Indian tradition, St. Thomas came to India and landed in Cranganore or Kodunglloor in A.D. 52 and started his mission from there. It was the main port in the Malabar Coast.[4] Traditional songs like *Rabbanpattu, Pananpattu,* and *Margamkalipattu* that exist in South India contain a lot of historical accounts and they support the missionary work of St. Thomas there. Exact time of their composition cannot be ascertained from the works, but they are accounts of ancient events, transmitted orally among the St. Thomas Christians before they were written down.[5]

The churches that were blessed by the apostolic patrimony of St. Thomas are called St. Thomas Churches. The church in Persia and the church in India are St. Thomas Churches according to tradition. In course of time, the church in Persia was called East Syrian Church, Assyrian Church, Chaldean Church, Nestorian Church, Babylonian Church and Church of Seleucia-Ctesiphon because of various reasons. The church in India that originated in the St. Thomas heritage was divided into various denominations such as the Syro-Malabar Church, the Syro-Malankara Church, the Malankara Orthodox Church, the Syrian Orthodox Jacobite Church, and the Marthoma Church. All these churches are St. Thomas Churches as they share the common heritage of the apostolicity of St. Thomas.

THE APOSTOLIC CHURCH IN PERSIA

The Persian church believed that they received gospel from Apostle Thomas.[6] According to the tradition of that church, he preached gospel to the regions of the Orient first and then he moved to India. "A very old tradition represents the apostle Thomas as having brought Christianity to Parthia as well as to India—though later traditions mention only India. If we remember, however, that the Parthian Empire included present-day Afghanistan and quite a large portion of Northern India, then the two traditions are not irreconcilable."[7] St. Thomas preached gospel in East Syria. More precisely, he might have preached gospel in some parts of the Persian Empire and then commissioned his disciples to continue his missionary works. Therefore, Mar Addai, his disciple and Mar Mari, the disciple of Addai continued the work of the master.

The *Doctrine of Addai* tells that St. Thomas sent his disciple Addai (Thaddeus) to King Abgar of Edessa[8] and converted him and his people to Christianity.[9] Then Addai moved to Seleucia-Ctesiphon to evangelize the people. According to another Seleucidan tradition, Mar Mari, the disciple of Addai in Edessa, was sent to Seleucia and he evangelized the region.[10] But the Persian church, in general, believed that they received gospel from St. Thomas. There was a moment in history in which the Church of Persia proper would say to the Mesopotamian Church of Seleucia-Ctesiphon that the former was evangelized by St. Thomas[11] in order to assert its superiority[12] over the Church of Seleucia-Ctesiphon. By 310, the bishop of Seleucia-Ctesiphon assumed the title of Catholicos.

However, there were links between Christianity in Persia and in the little state of Orshoene on her western borders, whose capital city was Edessa.[13] Although the tradition that the King of Edessa, Abqar corresponded with Jesus or with the apostles, Thomas or Thaddeaus, or Simon the Zealot, and brought the faith to the city seems to be a story, it is established that by about 150 C.E. while Edessa was still part of the Parthian Empire, Christianity was already there. The summary of the tradition of the land, as stated by Bernard Ardura O'Prem, is as following:

> According to an ancient tradition, St. Thomas went to evangelize Syria, and later the city of Edessa. He converted Thaddeus of Edessa and then founded the Christian community of Babylon. He lived in this Mesopotamian city for seven years. According to Eusebius of Caesaria, the Apostle subsequently left the care of the Christian community in Mesopotamia to his disciple Thaddeus and pushed on to southwestern India where he arrived by sea in the year 52.[14]

The Jewish diaspora in Assyrian or Persian territory

When the Jews were expelled from their land in the first centuries, they moved to various parts of the world, where they established their settlements. Their migration to different parts of the world and their settlements helped growth of the church.

> Every territory in the plain of the Tigris and Euphrates, from Armenia to the Persian Gulf, as well as northeastward to the Caspian Sea, and eastward to Media, contained Jewish populations, and in some of these places, particularly Babylonia and Adiabene, these settlements were populous and strong.[15]

A large part of the Jewish population in the Mesopotamian region was converted to Christianity.[16] These Jewish Christians belonged to the Persian church. Based on these findings, J. Kollaparambil assumes that the Christians who migrated from the Persian church's territory to Kodungalloor in 345 C.E. were Jewish Christians and that they were part of the St. Thomas Church of Persia.[17]

The See of Seleucia-Ctesiphon

It is believed that Mar Mari appointed presbyters and bishops to the regions where he evangelized, but the See of Seleucia-Ctesiphon got predominance during the time of Mar Papa around 310 C.E. He was succeeded by Mar Simon Barsabbae. During the time of Shapur II, Mar Barsabbae and five bishops and a large number of Christians were killed on Good Friday in the year 344.[18] He was followed by Mar Shah-dost[19] who was also killed immediately.[20] It was during his tenure the event of the emigration of the Knanaya community took place according to the tradition, although one cannot establish a causal link between these two events.

EMIGRATION OF THE SOUTHIST OR KNANAYA COMMUNITY IN 345 C.E.

Regarding the Knanaya migration of 345 C.E. also, there are no contemporary written documents. However, there is a living tradition about the said event: a tradition strongly supported by a royal monument believed to have been granted by the then king, and attested by a number of ancient songs (*Purâthanapâttukal* or traditional songs).[21]

Tradition about the immigration

According to tradition, a group of Christians immigrated to Kodungalloor from Mesopotamia in 345 under the leadership of a merchant called Thomas Kynai and of Mar Joseph of Urha.

> The summary of the Southist tradition about their migration and the presence on the Malabar Coast is as following: The Church of India founded by St. Thomas was in a perishing situation because of lack of ecclesial ministers. When the Catholicos of the East–Seleucia-Ctesiphon–understood the plight of the Church of India, he decided to send a community to enliven the Church.[22]

This community consisted of "seventy-two royal" families from seven clans (or sects) numbering around 400 persons. The group was led by a Jewish Christian merchant called Thomas of Kynai and a bishop (*metran*) named Urha Mar Yausef (Joseph). These leaders, together with four pastors *(katthanars)* and many deacons came to India under the authority and instruction of the Catholicos of the East.[23]

Though the living Knanaya tradition in South India presents the above-mentioned history of their immigration, the primary sources regarding this migration are not yet discovered. Their history can be traced out from some original sources like ancient songs, an ancient short history of the St. Thomas Christians and the royal monument recorded on copper plates. There are reports and references by European and Indian authors that are drawn up from the above-mentioned original sources.[24] Circumstantial evidences confirm this tradition.

Possible inferences regarding migration

There are two inferences regarding the migration of the community: a) it was a missionary journey to strengthen the Indian church, b) migration was an escape from persecution. The tradition, recounted in the above-mentioned original sources and that is held by the church in Malabar, about the migration in 345 is that the disembarkation of the Southists or Knanaya community was a missionary journey in order to strengthen the St. Thomas Church in India. There is an argument in support of the above statement that the Persian church was one of the greatest missionary churches and the merchants had an important role in taking missionaries to distant lands.[25] "When Christianity became established in the Persian Empire, Christians, either as missionaries or traders, spread the faith up and down both sides of Persian Gulf."[26] Missionaries of the Persian church were supported and guided by merchants on their way to the East, most probably because the merchants were acquainted with sea routs to different shores. Therefore, the bishop, priests and lay leaders might have got the support of a merchant leader in 345 C.E. Migration for evangelization was the only theory regarding migration until twentieth century.

There was another opinion that emerged in the twentieth century that connects the migration to the persecution of that time.[27] It goes like this in summary form: during the time of Shappur II, in Adiabene, Beth Garmae, Khuzistan, and many other provinces in which Christians were settled, local leaders started organizing slaughter of believers.[28] Consequently, Christians of the place might have moved to other places in Arabia and other parts of Asia, as many believers of the first Christian community fled from Jerusalem to escape persecution. However, this is a conjecture that the migrant Christians of 345 were escaping persecution; the link between the two events is not established. The narrations found in ancient songs say that the emigrant community departed from their hometown with blessings and permission of the Catholicos. They set out after a farewell.[29] A Christian group with a bishop, priests, deacons and faithful certainly form a liturgical unit. This representation and farewell would not be possible if they were running away in danger of death and persecution.

RELATION OF THE COMMUNITY WITH ST. THOMAS CHURCH IN INDIA

Southist community who believed to have emigrated from Middle East to India could easily integrate itself to the Christian community of the land. Migrants admitted the tradition that the church in India had an apostolic origin; in other words, the St. Thomas origin of the Indian church was never challenged by the migrant community, rather they accepted it.

St. Thomas—connection of Knanites in traditional songs

According to tradition, Southists who emigrated to Kodungalloor had special devotion to St. Thomas. It was evident in their traditional songs called *Purathanapattukal*.[30] The ancient songs of St. Thomas Christians contain relevant information about Thomas Kynai and his community. These songs are conserved and sung till now, especially among Southists. Francis Ros rightly observes that St. Thomas Christians "have no books of ancient history but only traditions of the ancients, to which they cling tenaciously."[31] One has to infer and trace out history from those songs with a critical mind, as in the case of any ancient text. If one closely studies the ancient songs, one can find certain references that point to their devotion to St. Thomas. The reference to St. Thomas found in *Pananpattu* (about Thomas Kynai) that the king promised privileges to Thomas Kynai placing Sun, Moon and St. Thomas as witnesses testifies that Knanites had devotion to St. Thomas the apostle.[32] Otherwise he would not be mentioned as a strong witness to the event of the grant of those privileges. Margamkali that was prevalent among the Knanaya community begins with a prayer to St. Thomas.[33]

The ancient song *Muvaroruvante kalpanayale* says that the immigrant community built a church at Cranganore (Kodungalloor)[34] after venerating St. Thomas of Mylapore. Internal evidences of the song indicate that the building was in the name of St. Thomas. But clearer information can be collected from reports of the European missionaries. Diogo do Couto, who was in India from 1567 to 1616, was the official historian and keeper of the archives of Portuguese India. He reported.

> And after that the same king gave him the field of Cranganor, where now is our fortress where Thomé Cananeo ordered to make the Church at the place where it now is, under the invocation of the same Apostle; and afterwards he made two others: one of the title of Our Lady, and another of St. Cyriac, Martyr.[35]

Though Francis Ros also indicated that Thomas Kynai and his people built a church in Cranganore,[36] a remark about the name of the church is found in the report of do Couto. The document MS Sloane 2748-A, supposed to be written in 1676 says that Thomas Kynai was the one who built and founded the first church of St. Thomas in Cranganore.[37] From these data and facts, it can be concluded beyond doubt that Thomas Kynai and his people had deep reverence to St. Thomas, the apostle of India and of their former home land. Otherwise Thomas Kynai would not have built a church in honor of Apostle Thomas.

In short, Knanaya community that had a Thomistic origin respected and recognized the Thomistic tradition of India; in other words, Southists or Knanaya Christians gladly accepted the apostolic origin of the Church of India and incorporated itself into the tradition in India.

Testimonies in ancient writings

The name St. Thomas Christians is mainly found in the writings of European missionaries. They preferred to present the Christians of the land as St. Thomas Christians that would distinguish them from Latin Christians. By *St. Thomas Christians,* they meant both Southists or Knanites and Northists. A. Monserrate who had been working among St. Thomas Christians for many years reported in 1579 that there were two groups of people among St. Thomas Christians. The first group descended from the disciples of St. Thomas and the other from Thomas the Syrian.[38] Francis Ros who was the first Latin bishop of St. Thomas Christians of Angamaly gives another piece of information. He reported that long before the coming of Thomas Kynai there were St. Thomas Christians in Malabar. But after describing the lineage and the story of the land about Thomas Kynai, Ros reports: "The Christians of St. Thomas who have descended from Thomas Caneneo [Kynai] are few. They are in Udiamper, the great church of Carturte [Kaduthuruthy], the great church of Cotete [Kottayam], and at Turigure [Thodupuzha]."[39] Here one can very well see that Francis Ros calls Knanites or Southists, St. Thomas Christians.

MS Sloane 2748-A, a document kept in British Museum catalogue[40] calls the forefathers of the migrant community as indirect disciples of St. Thomas. This report of 1676 says: "They say that he was a native of Canaan, disciple of St. Thomas, i.e. not a direct disciple, but disciple of the disciples and their descendants."[41] It is certain that the author was not an authority to say categorically that they were the lineage of the disciples of St. Thomas. But he was reporting the belief of the land or sharing the view of the native people. According to the tradition of the Persian church their father in faith was Apostle Thomas and the community migrated from that land rightly was called sons of the St. Thomas Church of Persia (Canaan[42] of MS Sloane 2748-A). Vincent Maria of St Catherine of Siena observes in 1672 that St. Thomas Christians are gifted with better quality and discernment. "They are divided into two factions, the one called *Vadakumbagam* or Northerners are more numerous and the other *Thekumbhagam* or Southerners have but few churches."[43]

The reasonable assumption one can arrive at from these references is that mostly Europeans called the Syrian Christians who claimed the apostolic tradition of St. Thomas as Marthoma Christians. Under that name they included both Southists and Northists. These European missionaries were well aware of the fact that there were two groups among Christians in India, one from direct descendants of the people converted by Thomas the apostle and the other from the progeny of immigrant people. But they called both groups Christians of St. Thomas.[44] Since both the communities had relations with Thomas the apostle, the name was appropriate to both of them.

Contributions of Knanites in the growth of St. Thomas Church in India

Immigration of Knanaya community in 345 C.E. was a landmark in the history of St. Thomas Christians in India[45] especially in establishing its relationship with the East Syrian Church, though one cannot pin point the exact period of the beginning of the Syrian rite of worship in Malabar. Privileges that the immigrant community received from the ruler of the land were extended to all Christians.[46] "He [Thomas Kynai] united many Christians both the old ones and the new whom he himself had made Christians. He obtained from the king many incomes for the church, and from that time on the Christianity prospered."[47] The community respected and recognized the leadership of Syrian bishops and native archdeacons all through the centuries and they cooperated with the whole. There was tension between the two communities only when their identity came under threat.[48]

The Knanaya community that also constituted part of St. Thomas Church in India stood hand in hand with the whole Christian Community in the history of the church. During times of trouble in 1550s, when the king of Vadakkumkur tried to arrest bishop Mar Abraham, due to insinuations of Portuguese missionaries, they defended the bishop as he sought asylum in Thekkenkur (Thekkumkur) Kingdom. The letter of Carneiro, a Jesuit missionary, dated December 24, 1557 gives a description of those events. Bowing to pressure of the Portuguese missionaries, the king of Vadakkumkur tried to take Mar Abraham under custody; but around 2000 St. Thomas Christians came forward and defended him and freed him[49] risking their lives and possessions. Here both the communities were united in protecting their bishop.[50]

When St. Thomas Church was divided into two in 1653, Knanaya community was also divided into two and they had a key role in deciding the course of the two factions. Anjilimoottil Ittithomman Kathanar of Kallissery Knanaya parish supported Archdeacon Thomas and forged letters for the archdeacon's episcopal ordination.[51] Thus, Knanites of *Puthenkur* division[52] remained faithfully with the faction of St. Thomas Christians under Archdeacon Thomas. Knanites of *Pazhayakur*[53] division were the pioneers who rejected Archdeacon Thomas and they were together with the other St. Thomas Christians who supported the validly ordained bishop. When Roman Apostolic See was ready to ordain a St. Thomas Christian as bishop in Malabar, Knanaya Catholics promised their obedience and loyalty to him.[54] Thus, Mar Chandy Parambil was ordained bishop at Kaduthuruthy Valiyapally of the Knanites. These events show that Knanites acted together with the whole St. Thomas community in historical moments of the church.

Under the leadership of Mar Kariattil, when the whole St. Thomas Christians desired reunion of the separated brethren, Knanites cooperated with the attempt wholeheartedly. Ittikuruvila Tharakan of Neendoor (a Knanite) contributed financially to the journey and accompanied the delegates till Tharankanpati.[55] After the unexpected death of Mar Kariattil, when Fr. Thomas Paremmakkal was made the administrator, Knanaya Community recognized his leadership. They also participated in the general assembly at Angamaly.[56] Among the twelve canons of Paremmakkal, there was a Knanaya priest called Illickal Punnoos or Stephen from Chunkom (Thodupuzha).[57] In nineteenth century, when St. Thomas Christians desired to get a Chaldean bishop, a small part of the knanites—the churches under *Padroado* jurisdiction, very particularly Kaduthuruthy Valiyapally—cooperated with this venture. Therefore, Mar Rokkos gave priestly ordination and other orders to many in Kaduthuruthy.[58] These attempts and cooperation of the Knanites with the other St. Thomas Christians helped the church to affirm its identity and, of course, to grow.

Even after erection of the Vicariate of Kottayam in 1911 for Knanaya Catholics, Knanites worked for the provision of permission for use of Antiochean liturgy for the reunited faithful in the Catholic Church. As a result, the Congregation for the Oriental Churches gave permission to continue Antiochean Rite in the Catholic Church for the reuniting Jacobites.[59] This permission has a pivotal role in the reunion of Jacobites and later Malankara reunion.[60] Thus, Knanaya Community work as a catalyst, to some extent, for the long cherished desire of the whole church—reunion of the whole St. Thomas Christians.

CONCLUSION

St. Thomas Church of India had liturgical and administrative connection with the Persian church and the migration under the leadership of Thomas Kynai in 345 C.E. was migration from a St. Thomas church in the Middle East to another St. Thomas church in India. Their homeland was believed to be evangelized by St. Thomas the apostle and his disciples like Mar Addai and Mar Mari. The immigrated community recognized the St. Thomas tradition in India. They maintained their identity recognizing the leadership of East Syrian bishops and archdeacons.

The devotion of the Knanaya community to St. Thomas was evident in their traditional songs. European missionaries included Knanites also among St. Thomas Christians considering their relation to the apostle. During the troublesome period of schism, the Knanaya community remained together with the other St. Thomas Christian community both in *Puthenkur* division and in *Pazhayakur* division, although Knanites and Northists maintained their separate identity and uniqueness. Their attempts for reunion of separated Christians also contributed to the good of St. Thomas Christians as a whole. Thus, Knanites incorporated and recognized the St. Thomas Apostolate in India because they were also part of St. Thomas tradition.

ENDNOTES

1   The term Knanaya was used in the twentieth century to denote the migrants under Thomas Kynai and Mar Joseph of Urha. They were called Southists or *Thekkumbhagar* in the reports and references of the European and Indian writers until nineteenth century.

2   Eusebius of Cesarea, *Ecclesiastical History* III, chapter 1: PG 20, 214–215 as found in J. Kollaparambil, *The Sources of Syro-Malabar Law*, S. Kokkaravalayil ed., Kottayam 2015, 64.

3   J. Puliurumpil, *Muziris Turned Kodungalloor Capital City and Metropolitan See*, Irinjalakuda 2016, 75.

4   K. M. Panikkar, *Malabar and the Portuguese: Being a History of the Relations of the Portuguese with Malabar from 1500 to 1663*, Bombay 1929, 4.

5   M. Kochadampallil, *Southist Vicariate of Kottayam in 1911: History and Importance*, Delhi 2019, 25.

6   T. J. Lamy, ed., *Bar Hebraeus, Chronicon Ecclesiasticum*, tom. III, Paris 1877, 5–6. "Nimirum liber "doctrinae sanctorum Apostolorum" nos edocet Christi evangelium ab initio per divum apostolum Thomam in regione orientali annuntiatum fuisse, anno ascensionis Domini secundo. Cum per eam transiret in Indiam perrecturus, populous evangelizavit varios, Parthos, medos, Persas, Carabaeos, Bactrianos, Margos et Indos."

7   R.E. Waterfield, *Christians in Persia*, London 1973, 16.

8   G. Phillips, *The Doctrine of Addai, the Apostle, now first edited in a complete form in the original Syriac with an English Translation and Notes*, London 1876, 5.

9   A. S. Atiya, *History of Eastern Christianity*, Notre Dame, 1968, 243–245. F.C. Burkitt, *Early Eastern Christianity*, London 1904, 16.

10   J. Kollaparambil, *The Sources of Syro-Malabar Law*, S. Kokkaravalayil ed., 99.

11   J. Kollaparambil, *The Sources of Syro-Malabar Law*, S. Kokkaravalayil ed., 98.

12   T. J. Lamy, ed., *Bar Hebraeus, Chronicon Ecclesiasticum*, tom. III, Paris 1877, 172. "Nos Thomae apostoli discipulis simus, et nihil nobis cum sede Maris commune est."

13   R.E. Waterfield, *Christians in Persia*, 16–17.

14   Bernard Ardura O'Prem, *The Need of the Involvement of the Church in the teaching and Research of History*, Key note address in the International Seminar (30.01.2018) on "St. Thomas Christians through the Ages: A Historiogragraphical Approach" on 30 January-01 February 2018, Mannanam 2018, 1.

15   J. Neusner, *A History of the Jews in Babylonia I*, Leiden 1969, 15.

16   J. Neusner, *A History of the Jews in Babylonia III*, Leiden 1968, 12. "It is reasonable to suppose that most Babylonian *minim* [Jewish apostates] were Jewish Christians of some sort."

17   J. Kollaparambil, *The Babylonian Origin of the Southists among the St. Thomas Christians*, OCA (241) Rome 1992, 123.

18 S.H. Moffetti, *A History of Christianity in Asia* vol. I, New York 1992, 140. See also K. Smith, *The Martyrdom and History of Blessed Simeon bar Sabba'e*, New Jersey 2014, xx–xxiv.

19 W.A. Wigram, *An Introduction to the History of the Assyrian Church*, New York 1910, 68. He was of the opinion that that Mar Simon Barsabba was killed in 339. But Moffetti basing on the work of Bedjan, *Acta Martyrum et Sanctorum II* holds the view that the said event took place in 344.

20 R.W. Burges, "The Dates of the Martyrdom of Simeon bar Sabba'e and the 'Great Massacre'," *Analecta Bollandiana* 117 (1999), 9-66, 43–44.

21 A report of Francis Ros, written in 1603/1604, contains a Portuguese translation of the Kynai Thomman copper plates with the privileges granted to the immigrant community. The original of the report is kept in the British Library (MS Add. 9853, 86–99). This text is edited and translated into English by Vincenzo Poggi and Jacob Kollaparambil and published, together with the Portuguese original, in George Nedungatt, ed., *The Synod of Diamper Revisited*, Rome 2001, 299–367, for the translation of the copper plate see 309–311. See also the detailed report of the Latin missionary Damiao De Goes in 1566 on the Kynai Thomman copper plates and their history, and the circumstances in which their Portuguese copy was made, in Jacob Kollaparambil, *The Sources of the Syro-Malabar Law*, 311–314.

22 J. Kollaparambil, *The Babylonian Origin of the Southists among the St. Thomas Christians*, XXIV.

23 R.E. Frykenberg, *Christianity in India; from Beginning to the Present*, Oxford 2008, 108.

24 J. Kollaparambil, *The Sources of Syro-Malabar Law*, S. Kokkaravalayil ed., 130.

25 H.D. Owens, "Nestorian Merchant Missionaries and Today's Unreached People Groups" in *Syriac Studies*, http://www.syriacstudies.com/2014/10/22/nestorian-merchant-missionaries-and-todays-unreached-people-groups-howard-d-owens-2/, accessed on 31 December 2017.

26 R.E. Waterfield, *Christians in Persia*, 40.

27 J. C. Panjikaran, *The Syrian Church in Malabar*, Trichinopoly 1914, 22. The theory of migration because of persecution is not proved through documents in the book but it can be considered as a possible assumption.

28 J. Neusner, *A History of the Jews in Babylonia: iv the age of Shapur II*, Leiden 1969, 24–25.

29 P.U. Lukas, *Purathanapattukal*, Kottayam 2016, 5–7.

30 P.U. Lukas, *Purathanapattukal*, 1.

31 F. Ros, "Report on the Serra (1603/1604)," edited and translated by V. Poggi-J. Kollaparambil, in G. Nedungatt, ed., *The Synod of Diamper Revisited*, (*Kanonika* 9) Rome 2001, 299–367, 307. The original of the report is in the British Library *MS. Add. 9853*, 86–99 (525–538).

32 P.U. Lukas, *Purathanapattukal*, 220–221.

33 J. Vellian and C. Choondal, *Margamkali Attaprakaram*, 5th edition, Kottayam 2015, 12.

34 P.U. Lukas, *Purathanapattukal*, 9.

35 D. de Couto, *Decada Da Asia XII*, Lisbon 1788, 283. "o mesmo Rey o chão de Cranganor, onde agora está a nossa Fortaleza, onde o Thomé Cananeo mandou fazer a Igreja no lugar, emque hoje está da invocação do mesmo Apostolo; e depois fez outras duas: huma do orago de nossa Senhora, e outra de S. Cyriaco Martyr."

36 F. Ros, "Report on the Serra (1603/1604)," in G. Nedungatt ed., *The Synod of Diamper Revisited*, 309. Also J. Kollaparambil, *The Sources of Syro-Malabar Law*, S. Kokkaravalayil ed., 153.

37 MS Sloane 2748-A, 6ᵛ as quoted in J. Kollaparambil, "Historical Sources on the Knanites," in J. Vellian ed., *Symposium on Knanites conducted in connection with the Platinum Jubilee Celebrations of the Diocese of Kottayam*, Kottayam 1986, Part I, 1–40, at 37."Este varão Apostolico foi que fabricou e fundou a primeira Igreja de S.Thome em Cranganor ...." Also, Francesco de Souza, ed., *Oriente Conquistado a Jesu Christo*, vol 1, Part II, Division II, Lisbon 1710, 114, para 16.

38 Letter of A. Monserrate to Jesuit General dated 12 January 1579 in J. Wicki, *Documenta Indica* XI, Rome 1970, 505–528, 525.ᵛ "La más particular ocupación mia sido con los christianos de la Sierra, que vulgrmente se dizen de S. Thomé. Acerca de la origen destos christianos hay duas opinions, una es que todos descienden de los discipulos del apóstol S. Thomé, otros dizen que solamente de un Mar Thomé, suriano."

39 F. Ros, "Report on the Serra (1603/1604)," V. Poggi-J. Kollaparambil, ed., and tran., in G. Nedungatt, ed., *The Synod of Diamper Revisited*, (*Kanonika* 9) Rome 2001, 299–367, 313. Original is in the British Library *MS. Add. 9853* ff. 86–99 (525–538), 88.ʳ "Os Christãos de S. Thome descendentes de Thome Cananeo são poucos. Estão no Udiamper, e na Igreia grande de Carturte e na Igreia grande de Cotete, e em Turigure."

40 J. Kollaparambil considers Fr. Mathew of St. Joseph as its author. J. Kollaparambil, "Historical Sources on the Knanites," in J. Vellian ed., *Symposium on Knanites conducted in connection with the Platinum Jubilee Celebrations of the Diocese of Kottayam*, Kottayam 1986, Part I, 1–40, at 36.

41 MS Sloane 2748-A, 6ᵛ as quoted in J. Kollaparambil, "Historical Sources on the Knanites", 37. "E dizem que foi natural de terra de Canaan, discipulo di S. Thome, nã o discipulo dos antigos, mas discipulo do discipulos e descendentes dellas."

42 The name Canaan is not the Cana of the New Testament and the Canaan of the Old Testament but Kynai, the place of Thomas Kynai.

43 Vincent Mary of St. Catherine of Siena, *Il Viaggio all'Indie Orientali*, Roma 1672, 143. "Li Christiani di S. Tomaso, frà li Malavari, sono li dotati di miglio qualità, giuditio, e conditioni. ... Si dividono in due fattioni [so in the original], l'una detta Baregumpagam, ò del Norte numerossima, l'altra Tegumpagam, ò del Sul, di poche chiese, cioè Diamper, Cotette, Turugli, Carturte."

44 P. Da Trinidade, *Conquista Espiritual do Oriente,* written between 1630 and 1636, Lisbon 1964, vol II, 322. "Destes cristãos que vulgarmente se chamam de S. Tomé...."

45 ARSI, *Cottayam-Franciae,* 1005, fasc. 4, 25. "A Short Account of the Sudist Syrians" sent to Lavigne by Mathew Vattakalam dated 13 April 1907.

46 A. M. Mundadan, "What the Leadership of Thomas Cana (and the People who possibly came with him) gave to the Early Christian Community in India," in J. Vellian ed., *Symposium on Knanites conducted in connection with the Platinum Jubilee Celebrations of the Diocese of Kottayam,* Kottayam 1986, part II, i–vii, at iv.

47 "Relatio P. Dionysii S.I. De Christianis S. Thomae" dated 4 January 1578 in J. Wicki, *Documenta Indica* XI, Rome 1970, 131–143, 137. "E juntou hai muitos cristãos assi dos antiguos como outros novos que elle fez, e ouve d'el-rei muitas rendas pera a igreja, e dahi por diante foy em crecimento esta cristandade. . . ."

48 ARSI, *Goa 48,* 92.ʳ⁻ᵛ Letter of J. Compori to Aquaviva dated 9 January 1604. "Estas duas castas de que falavamos cada huma dellas pretende proceder da verdadeira molher fazendo outra filha da eserava. E assy huma casta não se casa com a outra, e nos bazares tem differentes Jgureias adonde acodem todos cada hum comforme a sua geração, aindaque no mais se communicão, mas com tudo entre sy sempre ha differenças e rixas. Este anno entre dous bazarss destas duas castas começerão tão grandes discordias, que numqua foy possivel comporlos, e assy chegou o negocio a tal que ouve (92v) ferimentos, e mortes de parte a parte, e depois o Rey de Cochim em cujas terras moravão mandou seus naires no bazar dos mais culpados destruindoo e pondo o a saco. E como estes duos bandos não se quietavãose grandissimas mortes e trabalhos em todo a christandade; mas com o favor divino e commedo dos Reis da terra a tudo atalhou o S.ᵒʳ Bispo, que neste tempo ia estava em Cochin chamadoo do Rej por certos negocios." Translation is from J. Kollaparambil, "Historical Sources on the Knanites", Part I, 21–22.

49 Letter of Melchior Carneiro to Ludvico Gonçalves from Goa dated 24 December 1557 in J. Wicki, *Documenta Indica* III, Rome 1954, 792–802, at 800–801. "Huyendo el Obispo nestoriano de donde estaba, por miedo que los portugueses no le prendiesen, por ser un lugar donde estaba junto a un rìo, y yéndose para el reyno de la pimienta, teniendo ya nosotros concertado con el rey que lo prendiese para entregárnoslo, y abiendo ya el rey embiado mucha gente para le buscar, se juntaron más de dos mil christianos y se hicieron amocos del Obispo, los quales lo defendieron y libraron, con costarles mucha parte de su hacienda. Y estos christianos se yndignaron contra los portugueses, porque les querían prender a su Obispo; de manera que andábamos en mucho peligro de que nos matasen, por andar nosotros tanbién entre spesuras y bosques y sin saber los passos de la tierra."

50 M. Kochadampallil, *Southist Vicariate of Kottayam in 1911: History and Importance,* Delhi 2019, 43.

[51] APF, *SOCG* 234, 355ʳ. For the references of the forged letter by Ittithomman, see also, P. Podipara, *The Thomas Christians* in Kalayil, T., ed., *Collected Works of Rev. Dr. Placid J. Podipara CMI* vol. I, 383.

[52] Those who separated themselves in 1653 and supported Archdeacon Thomas.

[53] Those who continued their loyalty to Archbishop Garcia.

[54] J. Sebastiani, *La Seconda Speditione All'Indie Orientale*, Roma 1672, 146–147. "Detto principale di Turgolin [Pachikara Tharakan of Thodupuzha from Chumkom parish] mi disse più volte in quel medesimo giorno, che sperava in Dio di vedere presto tutta la Serra soggeta al nuovo Vescovo, sapendo tutti esser legitimo; loro Nationale, e sì virtuoso; ma che quanto à Christiani e Chiese del mezzo giorno, egli permetteva, e s'obligava tenergliele sempre obediente, quando anche ogn'altre l'abbandonasse, senza guardare, che non era di Tecumpagam. Per gradir questa offerta raccomandai caldamente in sua presenza esso, i suoi Christiani, e Chiese à Monsignor di Magara, quale disse che riconosceva dal loro zelo, e fervore, e che sempre l'haverabbe protetti, aiutati, e serviti con la medessima vita e molto piu, che gli altri chiamati Barecum pagam o Tramontani (onesta denominatione di Australi o Tramontani est ratione situs antiqui non moderni)." See also APF, *SOCG* 234, 16ᵛ-17ʳ.

[55] Cathanar Thomman Paremmakkal, *Varthamanappusthakam*, tran. P.J. Podipara, (OCA 190), Rome 1971, 75 and 77.

[56] Thomman Kathanar Paremmakkal, *Varthamanappusthakam*, Kottayam 1989, 482–483.

[57] Thomman Kathanar Paremmakkal, *Varthamanappusthakam*, 483.

[58] Bernard of Thomas, *Mar Thoma Kristhianikal* II, Mannanam 1921, 270.

[59] ACO, *Rubr. 40*, prot.no. 6004, Letter of Marini to Pisani dated 5 July, 1921.

[60] J. Kollaparambil-B. Mukulel ed., *Thekkumbahaga Janathinuvendi Visuddha Paththam Pius Sthapiccha Kottayam Athirupatha: Sathabdi Symposiyangal*, Kottayam 2014, 276.

7

ACTS OF THOMAS VERSUS RAMBAN PATTU

Thomas Koonammakkal

Acts of Thomas contains two different stories, each centering on a king. As a result, there is an underlying disagreement in the text. This two-structured narration of Thomas's mission in the kingdoms of Gudnaphar and Mazdai has already been pointed out by scholars.[1] As the text is analyzed further a triple structure is found: Thomas's landing at the royal city of *Sandaruk*, story of a heavenly palace for Gudnaphar and martyrdom under Mazdai. Is this inconsistency a result from the intention of the author to extend Thomas's mission to South India?[2] Are Gudnaphar and Gundaforos one and the same person? Can the South Indian Thomas stories—oral or written—however late they are, help us to explore this supposed extension of Thomas's mission? Can we altogether reject the possible historicity of an oral tradition that happened to be written down recently? Historical worth of written sources need not compel us to discredit the value of orally transmitted stories. The present paper is only an introductory study based on the so-called Song of Thoma Ramban[3] (for which I have observed eleven stages of development), with special reference to the above mentioned three-structured story of the Acts of Thomas. I do not want to repeat what has been already explained in two of my former studies on Suryaya Hendwaya in the Harp XX: 2 (2006), 295–304 and the Passover (Parole del'Orient 41 (2015), 223–238. A detailed discussion of the present paper is to appear in the Harp XXXIII (2018).

I identified Sandaruk with Malyamkara in the year 1987; I came to that conclusion from the name of a city called Helioforum (literal translation of Pakalomattam), the city where the See of Thomas is still (c. 4th–6th) kept.[4] These two identifications are enough to prove the historical value of a lost document of the second century compiled by the second generation disciple of apostle Thomas in South India. *Acts of Thomas* is based on

original and authentic South Indian stories that were transmitted orally
and in writing. South Indian oral traditions and their modern written versions are historically and geographically more important than *third* century Acts that are total disarray. Sufficient indications of a more than one
written document are mentioned in the Ramban Song that used earlier
written and oral sources.

THE SONG OF THOMA RAMBAN

This Malayalam song is written in 1601 as the author claims in the text,
though the year of composition has been disputed or doubted on the basis
of no textual-critical reason.[5] There were some nine manuscripts in 1930
(at present I have access only to a photocopy made in 1987 and I do not
think that all of them survive today! Many of them had important colophons. It is crucial to discover them and other copies as well). Mingana
ruled out any historical value for this song as he considered the text as a
late forgery.[6] He is entirely mistaken to reach such a view. Others suspect
that the author was using *Acts of Thomas* and even Latin *Passio*.[7] Their
"post hoc ergo propter hoc" argument is illogical, unhistorical, and totally unacceptable. Similarities are no reason to argue that these are all
due to later introduction. An early written text may not be older than an
oral tradition that happened to have no corresponding written version.
There are enough indications suggesting the existence of a common older
South Indian oral (as well as written, but lost) source for all these adapted stories. This song is based on the vestiges of some original oral—later
written but lost source. Between the oral and written stages there are considerable gaps that may mean an older written and a later written version
and additions and updating did occur. An initial literary scrutiny of the
song, supported by internal evidence proves the date of present composition plausible. But the more crucial issue about the source used by Thoma
Ramban·48 has never been traced. He speaks about his source: "For the
use of simple and uneducated people I have simplified and put together in to a song *that history* written by Māliēkal Thōmā Rambān II who
lived forty eight generations ago": Thoma Ramban II (c. 70–c. 140) is the
nephew of Thoma Ramban I who was baptized by Apostle Thomas. How
do we reach the period of Ramban II? The younger/youngest son of the
younger/youngest brother for 48 generations leads us to the second half of
the first and first half of the second century, following a clue in the song.
The song contains many such secret codes and clues.

Whatever be the exact historical situation under which Thoma
Ramban II wrote down the *history* there are indications about the existence of a written source that was used by Thoma Ramban 48. A series
of Thomas songs existed even before the present song. They were all

based on two or three sources that are mutilated beyond any possibility of re-construction: One in Sanskrit (?) and a more or less identical text (most probably a Syriac/Old Tamil version) made after the composition of *Acts of Thomas*. The original Sanskrit/Syriac/Tamil text was written between or before A.D. 140–160 on the basis of oral, local stories of a few families like Kadapur (near Kuravilangad), Maliekal (*Niranam*), and hence older than any other Thomas stories.[8] The oral stage seems to go back to the period between A.D. 50–140. Four families from *Palayur* (Kalli, Kalikav, Sankarapuri (moon city?), and Pakalomattam (Helioforum, Sun-city, Sun-field/Sun-forum?) had their own orally transmitted family stories which became more popular. Probably Sankarapuri (moon city?) came from *Mylapur* region (?). Many families had similar orally transmitted private stories associating them with Thomas. These stories were often re-vised and updated with new additions and almost all historical elements are untraceable, lost, or unidentifiable. Since they were glorifying the past of some families, others did not have access or knew them easily; in due course some lost their former prestige, financial status, position, or im-portance and they left out these stories because of their shame unable to claim a share in the lost glory and role. No wonder that such stories were kept secretly in oral form. A later written form does not mean a forgery; even forgery has some reasons and persons who remain behind the cur-tain of forgery.

Many written sources about Thomas mission in India did disappear in the aftermath of Diamper in 1599.[9] But the written source of this song is lost centuries ago, after leaving some fragments for our author. The song as well as the variant colophons contains references to these fragments. Absence of written source did not affect the oral transmission from one generation to another. The song is characterized by a surprising consis-tency of narration, very primitive and undeveloped Thomas legends that cannot be a later forgery based on Acts *of Thomas*. Doctrinal con-cerns of the *Acts* are unknown to the author. Some similarities with the Gospels, Acts of the Apostles (and Paul) are clear. But any influence of *Acts of Thomas* is not clear though common elements seem to come from a common oral or written source. There were certain orally transmitted family stories unknown to the public at large. The whole text is divisible in to units or 16, 8 and 4 lines as a result of which even the very few variant readings do not create a serious problem. Here I give a small survey of the text and its main contents:

FIRST 16 LINES CONTAIN A PRAYER CUM INTRODUCTION PROPER

I: "The WAY of the Son of God" in *Keralam*. Apostle Thomas arrives at *Mālyamkara* in the year A.D. 50. After 8 days Thomas "went in great hurry" to *Mailāpūr* where he "preached" for four and a half months. Then he went to China for four and a half months. When he came back to *Mailāpūr* he received money (for a second time?) to "build something" (—a palace later!). He went about preaching and giving away the money to the needy...

II: The nephew (who was also the son-in-law) of the King of *Thiruvanchikulam* (*Chēra king*) came to Thomas and because of the royal request Thomas came back to *Mālyamkara* in A.D. 51. Thomas mission lasted for one and a half years, and he baptized the royal family, 3000 or 4000 *Kāvyar*[10] along with forty Jews who had been living in *Keralam*. A *sliva* and a 'house' (for worship a *beth sliva*) got established. 'With the permission of all' Kepa the royal nephew and son-in-law of King Antrayos (*Andropolis* of Greek Acts may mean the city of Andrew, the *Chera* capital and port city?) became a deacon/priest. Then a series of missionary travels within the boundaries of Chera Kingdom follow. Kepa (like Simon Kepa) remained always at the side of Thomas (as an interpreter or royal patron without which the establishment of Christianity in the traditional seven Brahmin strongholds is impossible). Historians are still to find solution to the statues of a *Pallivanaperumal* (with a chest cross and cross staff in right hand) from the *Nilamperur* temple. A stay of one year and a conversion of a negligible number (1100, 1400, 1600, 1750, 200, etc.) who are given a *sliva* and a "house" (*beth sliva* for worship). *Kollam, Trikpālēswaram, Malanagaram* (mount-city) *Chāyal, Niraṇam* (where the paternal uncle of Thoma Ramban II is made priest), *Gōkkamangalam, Kōttakkāyal* are mentioned. Thomas made a "third' visit to *Mālyamkara* and then went to *Pālūr*. This section contains undeniable historical contents prior to the *Acts of Thomas*.

III: The agent of *Chōlan* came to inquire about the "building of the palace," and Thomas went back to *Mailāpūr* in A.D. 59. The rest of this section is more or less as in the *Acts of Thomas*. Within two and a half years Thomas baptized the royal brothers and some 7000 people. The kings of *Chandrapuri*[11] (moon-city) were Patrose and Paulose (the converted royal brothers of *Chōla* dynasty?). Thomas gave *guruppattam* (episcopate/priesthood or teacher post called Ramban or Malpan) to "Beautiful Paulose" (*Chundaran/Sundaran/Chanthiran*) appointing six priests under him. All gave up their property to Thomas who made arrangements how it should be administered. Here the similarity with the first disciples of Jesus and the first generation of Judeo-Christians can be posited.

IV: Thomas was travelling by land along with "angels" and he reached *Malayāttūr* where he baptized 220 people in two months. Thomas spent one year re-organizing the "seven" (royal) Churches appointing priests, ordering to erect "house" (*beth sliva* for worship), at the end of all giving *rūhāvaram* (gift of the Spirit to call and bring down the Holy Spirit (priesthood) to continue baptism and Eucharist, but not confirmation as some like Mundadan have suggested. Confirmation did not take shape as a separate mystery in the East Syriac Church before the year 392. Along with Thoma Ramban I of Niraṇam Thomas went to *Chāyal* where "he gave his garment to Kepa. Kepa wore this mantle. It reminds us of OT prophets Elijah whose mantle was given to Elisha as a sign of succession in the role of prophet. Thomas placed his hands on Kepa's head and ordered all to accept Kepa as Thomas himself." Thomas revealed that he is going to "make his last journey" (departure from them as well as from the world). This filled all with great grief and all wept at this touching farewell. But Thomas gave the "position of Rambān" to Māliēkal Thōmā whose family is going to have priests in every generation. This Rambān was given 'The Book of Remembrance' (the gospel according to Matthew in Aramaic or some of the Old Testament books or scrolls, the skin book—*thukal pusthakam*—of Thomas, the chronicle, or Diary of Thomas, etc.). The colophons of the manuscripts of the song give these details. But it is a near impossible task to recover more than nine manuscripts available up to ca. 1930. Apostle Thomas accompanied by bishop Kepa and Thoma Ramban I travelled along the "mountain-passage" (in so-called Western Ghats; this very term shows that most of the people of Malankara coast are emigrants from the region between two Ghats). The *malavazhi* or *Pandivazhi* led Thomas to Pāndi (the third South Indian kingdom whose capital was Mathura) along with "angels" in 69 C.E. Unlike the *Acts of Thomas* our author is ignorant about the mission in Pandi (Mazdai's kingdom?); but he concedes a three-year gap before the martyrdom of Thomas. Nothing in the song indicates anything about Gundaforos, Mazdai, and any other personalities of the *Acts*. But we hear about Avan, the Jewish converts, seven royal churches, some royal conversions, palace built in heaven, bishops, priests, deacons, voluntary renunciation of private property by the (clergy?), Thomas going to China for a very short period, his earlier preaching in many other countries (perhaps a hint on the Parthian mission), long list of miracles, successor of Thomas, personal and family names, confrontation in a temple, martyrdom, heavenly vision are all indications of a story different, earlier and independent of the *Acts*.

V: A fantastic interpolation of the innumerable miracles worked 'through the sign of the cross by that hand that was adorned with the miraculous blood' of Christ.[12] None of the miracles are explained, but only just enumerated. All numbers begin with 'two' for poetical reasons (?) The extra ordinary number of miracles (29 dead raised to life, 260 demoniacs, 230 lepers, 250 blind, 220 paralytics, 20 dumb and 280 incurably sick were healed) is a pre-Song development, but not based on *Acts of Thomas*.

VI: The whole number of converted people in *Keralam* (?) is given as 17480 (17450, 17500, etc.) with some sub-divisions according to various castes the existence of which in those days is a matter of dispute. But the total population of Keralam was about one lakh. Such a small number of conversions argues for the historicity. Two *Perumāls* (royal title; they may be important officials serving the Kings or even members of the royal family), became bishops/heads (one in *Keralam* and the other in *Chōlam*?). "Seven *gramams*" were given one priest/bishop each. Among these seven priests four were made Rambāns: Families of Māliyaka or Māliyekal, and Kadapūr are explicitly mentioned in the song; but the other two are implicitly pointed out as Kālikāvu and Pakalōmattom. There is also an allusion to Sankarapuri, probably emigrants from Chola kingdom in the first century itself (?) and this is to indicate that Thoma Ramban II was writing after the death of Kepa and episcopate/role of headship (perhaps episcopacy came to a full stop after the death of Kepa?) was taken up by the Pakalōmattam family. Three deacons (?) were appointed in each of the 'Seven *grāmams*' in order to administer the public property. (The "*grāmam*" had no private property after conversion?). A first or early second century historical situation of the apostolic community is reflected here. Common sharing of the property existed only in the beginning of the apostolic period. Local traditions say that priesthood came to a halt 93 years after the martyrdom of Thomas (A.D. 72). So Persian connections began; Pantaenus was brought in for a particular occasion and earlier commercial contacts with Alexandria facilitated this. It does not mean any Alexandrian mission work behind the origin of South Indian church. Dihle has not pointed out any concrete evidence for his theory.

VII: Thomas's martyrdom in the kingdom of Chōlan. In A.D. 72 on 3 July, Thomas encounter some *Embrāns* (Brahmin priests of Tamil origin) in a Kāli-shrine. Thomas was thrust with a *sūlam* (a fork-like lance associated with Kāli-worship). Chennembranmar Brahmins were created by the pathetically wrong reading of the text: chennu + embranmar. Thomas "fell on a stone in that thicket which is near the sea shore." "Angels" reported this to bishop Paulose who gave a glorious burial to Thomas. That bishop's royal brother too was there. "Angels" brought the news to bishop Kepa who went to Mailāpūr accompanied by two Rambāns Maliekal from Niranam and Kadapur (from *Kuravilangad* near that there was an ancient port that is still to be identified through archaeological excavations; sea was nearest to Kaduthuruthy (eight kilometers in between) and Kuravilangad in those days through small rivers or water ways. Today's *Valiyathodu* (literally big canal) of Kuravilangad is a very tiny one without water for most of the year and hence no more boats there; but it was once more than 14 meters wide, full of water and boats were usual means of transport at least up to the Kadapur region; the canal went through famous Kadapur the native place of navigators of legendary fame. The ship of Jonah, their votive offering to Kuravilangad, which they alone are entitled to carry in annual procession is a unique relic of their past glory as sailors. Hundreds of Kadapurians carrying the boat in procession as if they are navigating along with the unfortunate Jonah, acting out the tempest engulfing the ship of Jonah until he is thrown out of the ship, is unique annual event in Kuravilangad. The three spiritual leaders—Kepa the successor of the apostle, Maliyekal Ramban and Kadapur Ramban traveled by the land route (easy to use in those days) and reached the Palli (later a church; but originally a Buddhist term for their assembly, later associated with royalty and deity) where Thomas was already buried. Their arrival at Thomas's tomb was on 21 July. For ten days all kinds of worship and prayers were offered without any interruption. Then Thomas made a miraculous appearance in a heavenly palace. Bishop Paulose (like St. Paul) could identify this as the one that he saw once! A glorious epiphany of Thomas is reflected in the narration of this "vision." Finally, all departed. Here one may see parallels with ascension and Pentecost.

Epilogue:

Thoma Ramban 48 wrote this song for simple/humble or uneducated people, removing the "details" (and defects) from that history written by Māliyēkal Thomā Rambān II. This song is placed at the feet of Apostle Thomas on July 1 (or 3?) in A.D. 1601.

First century Keralam was the coastal region between Kollam and Palghat; all the seven royal churches are within this boundary; but it extended up to Coimbatur-Salem region. South of Kollam was part of Pandi. North of Palghat belonged to Mooshika. The easiest passage between Keralam and Cholam was through Bharathapuzha or Palghat to the east; it was the favorite route for the international traders. Then there was the sea route encircling the southernmost tip of India. But the travelers could follow *Mala vazhi*—hill path—or *Pandi vazhi* (Pandi road) which had three branches: from the port city of Muchiri through Periar—Ankamaly—Malayatur-Kothamangalam—Munnar; from further south through Meenachilar—Poonjar—Chayal; southernmost border Kollam—Niranam—Pampa—Chayal. These threefold hill paths of Chera kingdom of first century were connected with the land routes and river ways with all important trade centers and sea ports of South India. But the Pandi were gradually occupying Meenachil and Pampa river routes; the destruction of Nilackal/Chayal and the emergence of two small Pandi kingdoms—Poonjar and Panthalam—were the final result of this Pandi incursion into Malanadu/Malankara of Cheras who were also from Kongu Cheras of South India. The Vanchi or capital of Malanadu Cheras was on the Periar estuary.

Planting a *sliva* and building of a house or a roof over the *sliva* (for worship) is the typical way of Thomas's procedure. Apostles travelling about and planting a *sliva* is known to us from a fourth century (?) text.[13] There is a wrong belief that Christians began to use the symbol of the cross only after the so-called discovery of the true cross. Very search for the true cross is an indication that already that symbol was important for them. Why should they seek for a thing if it meant nothing for them? There are enough texts in Gospels, Acts and Pauline corpus in support of this. Cross was used as a sign (in pre-baptismal anointing, liturgical gatherings, etc.) since the days of the apostles not a fourth century development. Later Christianizing interpolations in the original Sanskrit text of the second century are clear.[14] There is a series of rather puzzling phrases scattered throughout the song; a number of these phrases escape all our attempts at an accurate translation. Some of the "numbers," astronomical data and geographical details are worthy of further study. We shall enumerate a few of such words after explaining one of them in detail:

(23): *Arivan paraven* means You know my saying. In the first reading nobody may suspect anything behind this phrase that is apparently coming from two Malayalam verbs: *ariyuka (to know) and parayuka (to say)*. Here Thoma Ramban 48 is giving a clear allusion to the source he is using. It is true that this Malayalam verb has been repeatedly used in the song. But soon after the "introduction" as well as twice in the "epilogue" the terms *arivin* (most probably *Arivan or Araven* was wrongly written by a scribe), *Arive* (document, knowledge, information) and *Arivan* (that—we/ they—may know), *Arivil* (in a written document) were used; one of the manuscripts give the title of the work as *Arive*; but when *Arivan* occurs a third time in the epilogue even in the very last line we can suspect and ask why soon after the introduction, as well as in the epilogue this term appears 4 times at least in two cases where they seem rather absurd from a linguistic point of view. One of the oral traditions I came across two months ago has *ariyuka, parayka* (know, tell). Thoma Ramban 48 is just alluding to the term (*rbn* can stand for *ramban* and *arabana*, *arban*, *aravan*, etc.) that became *ARVAN*, *ARAVAN*, etc. in Malayalam. None of the modern Malayalam lexicographers or grammarians admits the existence of such a Malayalam term formed from Syriac. But this term existed until last century and the term (but not the document) was known to Gundert. Though he knew this term, in all probability he could not detect the real meaning and hence he refers to (some) *Syriac document* in a very vague manner.[15] But in Syriac it can mean "papyrus," "translation of Bible," etc.[16] This special term was applied to the "history" written on "ôla" (specially prepared palm leaves as the typical writing material) because it was kept along with "the Book of remembrance."

There are two similar Dravidian terms: *Aravam and Aravan* whose origin and exact sense is a matter of dispute.[17] *Aravam* can mean "half," "low," "Tamil language," etc. *Aravan* means "a virtuous man," "a Buddhist or Brahmin monk of South India," "name of caste (?) who lived in Kerala c. fourth century A.D. and who were more respected than Brahmins," etc.[18] But who are these people? Most probably Thoma Ramban 48 who knew more is playing with all these meanings around the terms *aravan*, *ramban*, *Habban*, *Avan*. But until someone finds out, why and how Gundert happened to connect an apparently Malayalam term with some Syriac document, which we have not yet identified or come across we cannot be certain; if anyone can discover more than half a dozen books on Thomas by Paremmakkal Thoma kathanar (+1799) we may get more information. Some other terms that play on some original Syriac words, we leave out for the time being. There is a very subtle development based on the terms *urha* (way) and *avana* (palace, mansion), connecting them with John 14: 2–23 where we have the same terms. The whole palace-building story is indeed a theological interpretation of some lost or distant historical content. The Way to the Heavenly Mansion is another motive. In the present study we leave out further details.

Playing with entirely different meanings or slightly different meanings of some Malayalam, Sanskrit, Syriac terms is a literary technique of TR 48; for the sake of brevity we leave out this section from the present paper and proceed to the second part of our study.

ST. THOMAS IN THREE KINGDOMS

Acts of Thomas envisages three kingdoms—imaginary or real—to situate the Thomas's mission. Attempts either to identify these kingdoms or to rule out the entire story as a Gnostic romance are well known to us.[19] Song of Thoma Ramban is indeed a seventeenth century adaptation that can shed some light into this much disputed Thomas's story; the source from which the song drew is not an "extended Thomas tradition"[20] and hence it is necessary to re-examine the story behind the *Acts of Thomas*.

The royal city of Sandarūk that is reached by sea-route remains a riddle for many. As a possible location scholars propose Egypt, Sindh, Indo-Parthian border, Socōtra, ancient Andhra kingdom (whole borders extended up to the Northwestern region of modern India), etc.[21] But those who see *Acts of Thomas* as a Gnostic romance prefer the term *Andrapolis/ Andropolis* see it as an imaginary place: *man city*[22] or *people city*.[23] A comparative study of all variant readings, confirm Sandarūk—the shore where sandal wood is found or the mountain lend where sandal grow, clearest indication to the Southwest Indian coast—as the original term and this rules out the term *Andropolis* from the original story whether imaginary or historical.[24]

All South Indian Thomas traditions—written or oral—argue that St. Thomas landed in Kodungallūr in A.D. 52.[25] But as a notable exception the song argues that Thomas disembarked in "Māliyāmkara" in the year A.D. 50.[26] A critical study of this difference of opinion eventually supports the existence of a "Rambân tradition" behind the song, an ancient and "independent" tradition. It is based on the family history of Maliekal settled in Niranam; it had a collection of books associated with the mission of Apostle Thomas. In every generation it had priests as promised by the apostle. Some of its precious books were kept inside the wooden walls of their house as a talisman. Wooden houses might last a few hundred years; after more than ten generations who is going to remember this hidden treasure; we do not know how many times this process was repeated; we hear about the fragments of a parchment ('skin kook of Thomas') even in the late eighteenth or early nineteenth century. That is the latest we hear about this secret collection of books from the manuscripts of the Ramban song: "If so and so tries he will be able to tell more about the skin book of Thomas." We know that most of the Maliekal family emigrated to Paravur, Palayur, Ankamaly, and other places. As an aftermath of Sliva-Oath of Mattanchery in 1653 the most important remnant of Maliekal family migrated to Kuravilangad because they wanted to be with Pazhayakur. Those who remained at Niranam joined the Puthenkur; eventually many of them joined the Mar Thoma Church. Every migration meant a break with the past and forgetfulness of the lost glory of the family. Since no central meeting of various family branches has been established further details could not be collected. Even their contact with the Ramban song was very scanty, though some of them knew about it.

Today there are two places called *Māliyāmkara and Mālippuram,* close to the ancient royal city of Chera kings. Not far away there is a place called *Urakam; Malyamkara* is near *Ur (uraduthulloru* in one of the songs). *Ur* is very common ending in South India and I have found rather surprising number of its usage. Here Ur stands for the capital city. Districts of Trivandrum (111+), Kollam (96+), Alapuzha (64+), Kottayam (53+), Idukki (24+), Eranakulam (80+) have altogether more than 428 places ending with *Ur. Kannur, Palayur, Paravur, Perumpavur, Perur, Ettumanur, Kilirur,* Puthur, Punalur, Avittathur, Kanthallur, Omallur, Kothanallur, Kumaranallur, etc., are only a random selection. Hundreds of *Ur* ending geographical names can be found throughout South India. Nearby places of Malyamkara include *Chennamangalam,* Sringapuram (*Chingapuram*), etc. Without some archaeological studies under water the exact location of this royal capital is risky. But in all probability is in Vadakekara. The ancient *Māliyāmkara* literally means "Land of sandal wood." *Māleyam*[27] is a Sanskrit term coined from Dravidic term *malai* or *male* meaning "mountain" or hilly place that came to be applied to Western Ghats where sandal wood grew and hence called the birth place of sandal wood. Our initial study reveals that the term *Māleyam* was coined in ancient *Keralam* by those Aryan emigrants where from the later Nampūthiri Brahmins emerged.[28]

The term *Sandarūk* can be a literal translation of *Māleyamkara* or Land of sandal wood. Sandar/sandal ultimately goes back to a Sanskrit word *chandana* that means sandal wood, the product of mountains or malai.[29] Thus, *māleyam* and sandal/sandar are one and the same. The last two letters of *Sandarūk* seem to come from *uruk, ūr, ūrak, ūrakam, ōram (maly), kara, sea-shore, riverbed,* etc., and they indicate "a town" or "the land close to the sea or river." Thus, the term *Sandarūk* seems to be the royal port that became a second or later capital of Chēra kings. I came to this conclusion in 1987. Because of my negligence I did not go through the copious notes of Klijn, though I had gone through his translation of the Acta. I identified Sandaruk with *Malyamkara* (Hilly Seashore), *Maliyavumkara* (Riverbed land), *Maleyamkara* (Sandal land). But I came across his important observation—Sandaruk originated from sandal— only a decade later and that gave me an additional support. *Sandaruk* is *Andrapolis* in Greek. It is the royal port city where Thomas landed in A.D. 50. There existed no Andropolis anywhere in India. It has nothing to do with Andhra region of India. We have three interesting variants in three manuscripts. In manuscript H it is *Enadrokh*; in G *Enadokh*; Z gives *Edron*. Klijn concludes that there is a fusion between two independent texts: (mss A B C D F T X P U V Q R S V) longer text closer to the Syriac text and a much shorter text (mss GHMZ), and the shorter text is not a summary of the longer text. Mss H, G and Z give very curious variants to *Andrapolis*.[30] Ignorance of the name and geography is clear. Klijn comes closer to our conclusion though he did not identify the city: "It also may be a derivation from sandal-wood, thus the place where the sandal trees grow."[31] *Maleyamkara* means exactly the same: the land of sandal trees. The whole southwestern coast was called *Maleyamkara*; it is obvious the term was translated wrongly into Syriac. It could have been "hilly land" rather than "land of sandal trees." Perhaps the confusion came from two similar words: maleyam (sandal) and *malayam* (hilly). *Maliyavumkara* (maly means land close to the shore of the river) can stand for plot of land or a port

Acts of Thomas situates the "palace-building" in Gudnaphar's kingdom where he could not situate Thomas's martyrdom because of the relationship between Thomas and Gudnaphar. But the author of *Acts* had some vague idea about Thomas's mission in a third kingdom for which he supplied "a king Mazdai." As we critically evaluate the legends, stories, miracles, inconsistencies, etc., of the *Acts of Thomas* in the light of 'Rambān tradition' (available only in song) a crucial question about the "wandering" of Thomas's mission emerges: Did the author of Acts of Thomas draw on some "wandering legends from South India" in order to combine Thomas's Parthian mission[32] and Indian mission? In the song, there is nothing about Thomas's mission work in a third kingdom. If the song is drawing on *Acts of Thomas* the legends and kingdoms merge is to one unit that is against the mind of the two authors and this ultimately competes to deny Thomas's mission in India that in fact both writers want to establish.

The Greek version did not translate Sandarūk, but translated another Sanskrit term: Purushapuram (man-city) that is the modern Peshawar. "Purusha" is man or person. "Puram" is town. "Purusha" (Pururavas) is also the name of the famous Indian king whom Alexander, the great, encountered. This "Purusha" created a lasting impression in the Greek world about India. But "Purusha" was known to the Greek world as "Pores." All Indian kings were considered only as descendants of "Pores." The "King of Indi" (Pāndi) and his kingdom has been confused with King Pores and Indo-Bactrian region.[33] If the author of Syriac Acts is trying to explain Thomas's Parthian mission depending on wandering oral traditions from India[34] the "confusion" as well as the term "Andropolis"[35] are explaining a story behind the composition of *Acts of Thomas* itself. Since the "palace-building story" was transferred to Gudnaphar's kingdom he had to situate the "martyrdom and tomb-story" in the third kingdom inventing "Mazdai."[36] The Rambān tradition about Thomas's mission in the three South Indian kingdoms—Chēra, Chōla, and Pāndi—gets miserably confused in the *Acts of Thomas*. The doctrinal motives of the author prompted him to rewrite the oral traditions (?) that could have easily reacted Edessa or elsewhere towards the end of second century.[37]

As we put together the Syriac, Greek and Latin versions of Thomas's story we get some interesting details. "De Miraculis" speaks of the (Sandarūk mission) thus: *exeuntes de navi ingressi sunt primam Indiae civitatem*.[38] This first city is "first emporium" of India,[39] which is near the Chera capital called Vanchi. "Passio" mentions a mountain "Gazus" between "Andranopolim"[40] and "Elioforum" (apparently, the city of Gudnaphar).[41] Between Chera and Chōla kingdoms the mountain "Ghat" exists. This cannot be another accidental similarity. The author of 'Passio' misunderstood "Elioforum" as a city. This "Elioforum" is "Helioforum" as we observe from variant readings. "Helioforum" is a literal translation of "Pakalōmattam," the most celebrated Brahmin-Christian family. "Pakalōn" means "sun"; "mattam" is "forum." Wherefrom did all these South Indian details crept in to these Latin versions? In the present paper we leave out further details about this problem.

The Syriac Acts ends the Sandarūk mission thus: "And he (Thomas) left them (the royal couple) and went away. . ... And they (the royal couple, the flute-girl, etc.) taught the king too, and collected a number of brethren, until news was heard of the apostle (being) in the realm of India; and they went to him and were united unto him."[42] The song speaks of Thomas going to their place where he had landed first. "De Miraculis" has the following parallel:

> *adulescentes autem praedicabant verbum dei ita ut omnis populus per eos converteretur ad dominum. Sed et ipse rex qui erat pater puellae compunctus corde credidit in dominum Iesum Christum, et audiens beatum apostolum in ulteriore Indiam commorari abiit cum omnibus qui crediderant, et* __pervenit ad eum, et procidens ad pedes eius rogavit ut__ *eos omnes baptismatis gratis consescraret... ipse quoque rex rogavit sibi caput totondi, et diaconus* __ordinatus est__*, et adhaerebat incessanter apostoliene doctrinae.*[43]

(The young people preached the word of God so that all the people through them converted to the Lord. And yet the king himself, who was the father of the maiden, with repented heart believed in the Lord Jesus Christ and, hearing that the holy Apostle was staying in the inner India, he, has gone out with all those who had believed and, has come to him, thrown at his feet, and has asked that he consecrate them all in the grace of the baptism . . . . The king himself asked to receive the tonsure and was ordained deacon and adhered unceasingly to the apostolic doctrine).[43]

All the phrases underlined in these two citations had literal contact with the "source" used by the song. The Indian oral traditions mention no such migration by the disciples. "Passio" has some additional information that strengthens our identification of Sandarūk as "Māleyamkara":

*post non multum vero temporis <u>misit</u> unum ex discipulis suis quem <u>pres-</u>
<u>byterum ordinans</u> ita constituit, ut <u>in eadem civitate</u> consistens <u>ordinaret</u>
<u>ecclesiam</u>, in qua multus est deo populos adquieitus, <u>et est ibi sedes Thomae</u>
<u>apostoli</u> et fides catholica usque in hodiernum diem. <u>Ipse</u> autem <u>puer</u>
Dyonisius nomine <u>episcopus factus</u> sponsamque suam Pelagiam nomine
sacro velamine consecravit quae post obitum euis duplex martyrium tenuit,
unum quia virum habere contemsit, alterum quia sacrificare idolis noluit,
atquae his duabus ex causis sententiam decollationibus accepit. Et super
tempulum eius Graecis sermonibus et litteris ita scriptum est: 'in hoc loco
requiescit sponsa Dionisii episcopi quae est filia Thomae apostoli'. . . Cum
autem esset Hieroforum apostolus Indiae civitatem ingressus, Abbanes ad
Gundaforum regem nuntiavit Thomam...* [44]

(After some time, he sent one of his disciples and, after having ordained him priest, he stated him to reside in the same town and establish a Church there, in which large is the people faithful to God: there is the seat of Apostle Thomas and the catholic faith until today. The same young man named Dionysius, once became bishop, consecrated as nun his wife Pelagia, who received after his death a double martyrdom: one because she refused to marry, the other because she did not want to sacrifice to idols and for both these reasons, she received the condemnation of beheading. On his church in Greek language and characters it is writ-ten: "In this place rests the spouse of the bishop Dionysius, daughter of Thomas the apostle" . . . .. Being the Apostle of India arrived in the city of Hierophorus, Abbanes announced Thomas to the king Gondaphores).[44]

The phrases underlined in the above text had a better contact with the "source" behind Song of Thoma Ramban. The phrases with inter-rupted underlining support our identification of Sandarūk. *Sedes Thomae Apostoli* is said to be in "Andranopolin."[45] It is the city whose king became Andrayos according to the Rambanpattu. Yroforum, hiroforum, hiropho-rum, hieraforum, (he)lioforum, ilioforum, hieropolim, hieroporum occur as witness to the confusion of the author or copiests., Vat. Syr. XXII writ-ten in A.D. 1301 speaks of "the Seat of Apostle Thomas" in "Shengale" that is identified with Kodungallūr. The Syriac Acts mentions a "deacon Xanthippus" who was given charge of the community before Thomas left for Mazdai's kingdom.[46] "A deacon" who assists Thomas is mentioned in another context.[47] In "Transitus Mariae" Thomas is gone to India "to visit" or "to baptize" some members of a royal family: a "sister" of the king, her "son," "a royal nephew," etc., occur.[48] All these are just confused references to the royal son-in-law and nephew of the Chēra king mentioned in the song. It is this royal nephew who goes to Chōla kingdom to "bring back Thomas kissing his feet" and asking pardon for some initial dishonor suffered by Thomas.

One of the most popular Christian names of Kerala is *Umman* (architect, carpenter, skilled builder, etc.), who is none other than "Thomas" because of the "palace-building" tradition. The palace is the church built in heaven by the good works of Christians. Apparently, there was well-established Judeo-Christian community in the first Christian era in Malankara coast. The *Acts of Thomas* uses the same term, but never as a proper name for Thomas.[49] Some of you from the Syriac Churches may be able to find out whether it is used elsewhere as substitute for "Thomas."

CONCLUSION

Acts of Thomas was written with some special doctrinal motives connected with encratism. In the very first Acts ascetical terms like *nukraya*, *xenos* (alien, stranger), ascetical fasting, attitude towards marriage bridal chamber, contrast between temporal and eternal, etc., occur. The author combined two Thomas's missions using the reports only from the South Indian mission. When the traditions about Thomas's mission in the Chēra, Chōla, and Pāndi kingdoms of South India reached Edessa/Nisibis region by means of travelling merchants the original story got an unrecognizable color. Both geography and personalities were confused or changed. When this story was used to combine the Parthian and Indian missions adding the doctrinal propaganda of the author, a series of inconsistencies mutilated the "history." Syriac translation of South Indian oral or written source translated Maleyamkara into Sandaruk; the same land of king Antrayos got into Greek as Andropolis/ Andrapolis. Syriac Gudnapar and Greek Gundoforus are two different persons. But Song of Thoma Ramban, based on the lost second-century "history" of Thoma Ramban II helps us in some way to re-examine the story concealed and confused by the author of the Acts of Thomas in all its versions. Long lost original versions had access to a triple linguistic written tradition as well.

ENDNOTES

1. A.F.J. Klijn, *The Acts of Thomas* (Leiden 1962), 28–29.
2. L. Brown, *The Indian Christians of St. Thomas* (Cambridge 1956, 2ed) 43–46; A Dihle, *Neues zur Thomas-Tradition*, JAC 6 (1963) 54-70; A.F.J. Klijn, 28–29. Brown is using a modern novel (concerned only with recently re-formed group) and can see only through European view of history through Portuguese documentary evidence. Like Brown many European scholars and some Indians too presume that Acts of Thomas is the source of all Indian Thomas stories. Post hoc ergo propter hoc argument is totally unacceptable. An earlier written down version need not necessarily discredit the antiquity of an oral tradition. Written form may be later and oral form may antedate its written version.
3. Rambān is only the Indian pronunciation (as old as Biblical Aramaic) of *rabban*. A few similar examples are *humba, renga, qandiša, 'endân, šambah*, etc. For further details see my forthcoming "Acts of Thomas Re-examined in the Light of the Song of Thoma Ramban," The Harp XXXIII (2018), 1-42. Other articles to follow: "The Acts of Thomas versus Rambanpattu"; "The Song of Thoma Ramban: A Forgery"? See also, "Marthomma sliha Bharathathil," in Awarnaniyadanangalute Suwarnawarshangal, Golden Jubilee Souvnier, Diocese of Palai (Palai 2001), 33-49; see the 11 stages of development behind Rambanpattu.
4. In my article in The Life and Nature of the St. Thomas Christian Church in the Pre-Diamper Period, ed. Bosco Puthur (Kochi) raised this issue years back.
5. Bernard of St. Thomas alone. All others give only a misleading summary. Short studies have been made by Placid J. Podipara, E.R. Hambye, P.J. Thomas, T.K. Joseph, V.C. George, L. Brown, A.M. Mundadan, Chummar Choondal, etc.
6. A. Mingana, *The Early Spread of Christianity in India*, BJRL 10 (1926), 509.
7. L. Brown, 49 n.1.
8. This I call 'history' of Thoma Ramban II that in its later oral/written form (?) was used by Thoma Ramban 48 in order to compose this song.
9. This is known from the writings of P. Maffei, Du Jarric, Gouvea, etc.
10. *Kapora* is *kāvōra* according to Indian Syriac from which the Malayalam term *kāvyar* originated. (Some wrongly suspect an Arabic origin! If it was from Arabic it would have been Kafir).
11. R. Caldwell, *A Comparative Grammar of the Dravidian or South-Indian Family of Languages* (London 1875) 10, 20, 24, 35. A city near river *Chandragiri* once in *Chōla* kingdom is a possibility.
12. St. Ephrem, Comm. *On Diates*. XXI, 18; W. Strothmann, *Jakob von Sarug, Drei Gedichte uber den Apostel Thomas in Indien* (Wiesbaden 1976) I 11-12, 49, 196 (= 29, 34, 58).
13. W. Wright, *Apocryphal Acts of the Apostles* (London 1871) II, ix, 58.

[14] Cf. P.J. Thoma, *The South Indian Tradition of the Apostle Thomas*, JRAS Cent. Supplement (October 1924), 213–224.

[15] H. Gundert, *Malayalam-English Nighandu* (2ed; Kottayam 1962), 76.

[16] I. Low, *Aramaeische Pflanzennamen* (Leipzig 1881), 54–55; R. Payne Smith, *Thes. Syr.* I, 366–367.

[17] R. Caldwell, 92–95.

[18] S.G.P. Pillai, *Šabdatārāvali* (10 ed., Kottayam 1983) 247, cf. 14, 16.

[19] F.C. Burkitt, *Early Eastern Christianity* (London 1904) 193–194, 206.

[20] Cf. The legends underlying Song of Thoma Ramban are more primitive and rudimentary.

[21] A. Dihle, 59.

[22] R. McL. Wilson, *The Acts of Thomas* in W. Foerster, ed. *Gnosis: A Selection of Gnostic Texts* (Oxford 1972) I, 338.

[23] M. Lafargue, *Language and Gnosis: The Opening Scenes of the 'Acts of Thomas'* (Harvard Dissertations in Religion 18, Philadelphia 1985), 71.

[24] A. Dihle, 59

[25] Muchiri, Thiruvanchikulam, Makōthai, Mahādēvarpattanam, Shingly, Shengale, Muyirikkōdu, Kodungallūr, etc. refer to one and the same geographical location near modern 'Māliyamkara'.

[26] Bernard of St. Thomas, 79.

[27] H. Gundert, 729, 743: R. Caldwell, 20, 21, 27.

[28] F. Day, *The Land of the Perumals* (Madras 1863) 299–300.

[29] C. Brokelmann, *Lex. Syr.* (2ed. Göttingen 1928) 484, 633; 107, 422.

[30] A.F.J. Klijn, 5.

[31] A.F.J. Klijn, 164.

[32] Eusebius, *Hist. Eccl.* III.

[33] R. Caldwell, 15f.

[34] The "relics" of Thomas reach Edessa from India, and some "legends" too?

[35] The Greek Acts complete the process started in Syriac Acts is transferring Indian legends in to "Parthia."

[36] There is no detail of Pāndi mission in the song, though Thomas travelled via a third kingdom.

[37] Cf. U. Monneret De Villard, *La fiera di Batnae e lu Traslezione di S.Tomaso a Edessa,Rendiconti delle Sedute dell' Accademia Nazionale dei Lincei*, Ser. VII, vol. VI, 3-4 (Roma 1951), 74–104.

[38] M. Bonnet, *Acta Thomae* (Supplementum Codicis Apocryphi i, Lipsiae 1883) 98; K. Zelzer, *Die alten lateinischen Thomasakten* (Berlin 1974), 47.

[39] This identification is a most probable one.

[40] M. Bonnet, 140, 144; K. Zelzer, 6, 18.

[41] Concept of 'grāmam' could be easily misunderstood by a foreign writer. Cf. V.A. Gadgil, The Village in Sanskrit Literature, *Journal of the Bombay Branch of the Royal Asiatic Society,* New Ser. II, 2 (1926), 150–166.

[42] W. Wright, 155, 159; A.F. J. Klijn, 72f.

[43]   M. Bonnet, 101; K. Zelzer, 49.

[44]   M. Bonnet, 139; K. Zelzer, 11.

[45]   M. Bonnet, 135, 139.

[46]   A.F.J. Klijn, 99.

[47]   M. Bonnet, 90.

[48]   A.S. Lewis, *Apocfrypha Syriaca: The Protoevangelium Jacobi and Transitus Mariae* (Studia Sinaitica XI, London 1902) xiv, 31, 28.

[49]   E. Beck, Texne und Texnites bei dem Syrer Ephräm, *OCP* 47 (1981) 295–331. Syriac Acts has the term ummana/umman and it is used also by Jacob of Serugh. But here is a whole interchange of both.

8

THE TRADITION OF SEVEN CHURCHES

James Puliurumpil

INTRODUCTION

In compliance with the command of Christ, the apostles went around the world preaching the Gospel to all the peoples. They distributed among themselves the regions of the world.[1] Accordingly, as Origen testifies, St. Thomas received Parthia (India).[2] The journey of St. Thomas to India, the farthest land,[3] was not something unimaginable or unthinkable in the first century A.D. India was known to the western writers even from the fifth century before Christ. The Roman trade with the cities of the western coast of India is well attested in the writings of Pliny, Ptolemy, Strabo, Arrian, etc. Thomas, accompanied by Habban, as *Acts of Judas Thomas* narrates[4] reached Broach in Gujarat and started missionary work in India. During his missionary journeys in South India he established communities in different places. Seven of them are important that are known in the history books as "the seven churches." One of the important evidences to attest the Indian apostolate of St. Thomas is the so-called "tradition of seven churches."

KERALA IN THE FIRST CENTURY A.D.

Kerala in the first century formed part of Thamizhakam, which is constituted of the three kingdoms of Chera, Chola, and Pandya. Chera included the present-day Kerala except south of Trivandrum. All these three were not always independent kingdoms; sometimes Pandya held supremacy over the other two and sometimes Chola. The Chola kings held sway even over Sri Lanka. In all these three kingdoms, there were many small kingdoms under their patronage, which were often loyal to them but at times revolted against them.[5] St. Thomas during his second missionary journey in South India founded communities in these three kingdoms that constituted the areas in between the western and eastern coasts of India known as the Malabar and Coromandel coasts.

It is the living tradition of St. Thomas Christians that the first communities formed by St. Thomas in Kerala were in seven places. These seven Christian communities that appeared in the first century A.D. were Kodungalloor, Palayoor (Palur), Kokkamangalam, Kollam, Niranam, Nilakkal and Paravur. Of these Palayoor, Kokkamangalam, Kodungalloor and Paravur were in the Chera Kingdom and Nilakkal, Niranam and Kollam in the Pandyan kingdom. Another important Christian center in South India, Mylapore in the Coromandal coast, which is not counted part of the seven churches, the place of martyrdom of St. Thomas is in the Chola kingdom. It is on the basis of the information given in *Periplus of the Erythrean Sea* that the territorial limits of Chera, Chola and Pandya kingdoms were ascertained. According to the author of this work Naura (Cannoore), Tyndis (Ponnani) and Muziris (Kodungalloor) were in Chera kingdom, whereas Nelkunda (Niranam) and Barake (Purakad) located on the banks of the river Baris (Pampa) were in Pandyan kingdom.[6]

Fertile river valleys

Of these Christian settlements Kodungalloor, Palayoor and Paravur are located in the fertile valley of River Periyar and Niranam in the valley of River Pampa. Kokkamangalam is on the border of the backwaters of Kuttanad. These seven places and their adjacent regions were the prime Syrian Christian centers until their migration to other places in the first decades of the twentieth century. Although some of these lost importance like Kokkamangalam and others like Nilakkal that ceased to exist, the Christians always held the tradition of the seven churches in high esteem.

The early centers of St. Thomas Christians had a different geographical distribution. They were the maritime centers of exchange, namely Kodungalloor, Paravur, and Kollam. In Kodungalloor they seem to have expanded to the hinterland to take maximum benefit out of the fertile plains of Periyar. Similarly, Parvur, Kollam, and Palayoor that though belonged to the coastal belt, had fertile cultivable hinterland. Kokkamangalam was connected with the backwaters of Vembanad, while Nilakkal and Niranam were located in the fertile valley of Pampa.[7]

Maritime trade centers

Among these seven settlements, Kodungalloor, Paravur, and Kollam were more exposed to the maritime trade links. It is also probable that some of the converts of these places were Greek or Jewish settlers; but the majority were indigenous people who were predominantly following Buddhism or Jainism, the principal religions of South India in the early Christian Era. The new converts should have resorted to agriculture because of the increasing demand for agricultural products. This created by Roman traders from the Mediterranean world brought them to experiment with new crops that ultimately led the Christian converts to develop cultivation as their major occupation. Generally speaking, the settlements of the early St. Thomas Christians were scattered around the expanding agrarian zone lying between Palayoor and Kollam.

The principal region where pepper was grown in large quantities was called *Kottanarike.*[8] Both Pliny and Ptolemy write on *Kottanarike*, which should be Kuttanad or the regions surrounding Pampa river. Earlier days this seems to have been a vast pepper growing area, even though now it is a waterlogged area on account of the frequent geophysical changes that took place on the coastal Kerala in general and in Kuttanad region in particular. There was a slow but gradual expansion of agricultural activities from Purakkad to regions south of Niranam and more and more areas were brought under pepper cultivation in this process.

KODUNGALLOOR, THE CAPITAL CITY

It is beyond doubt that Muziris was the most important city of Kerala (the Malabar coast), and of the whole of India in ancient times. Pliny refers to Muziris as the most important port of India (*primum emporium Indiae*).[9] But the writers are not unanimous in attributing a single name for the city. The city is differently called by different writers in different languages; such as *Muchiri, Muziris, Muchiricodu, Muchiripatanam, Mahodayapuram, Mahadevarpatanam, Vanchi, Thiruvanchi, Thiruvanchikulam, Malankara, Malyankara*, etc.

Muziris, situated on the river bank of Periyar, was destroyed by a flood and as a result, the nearby small city of Kodungalloor (in the extreme end of Periyar) became important. In history we also read that in ancient times ships were coming only up to a few miles away from Muziris and through boats things were taken to ships. The fact that Muziris is situated 4 kilometers away from Kodungalloor, the port city that is on the estuary, adds credibility to the above finding. Therefore, ships might have come till Kodungalloor, whereas the important city was Muziris, away from the sea-shore, on the banks of the river Periyar. It is not necessary that the port should be in the city itself. It can be a few miles away from the proper city.

(As Muziris was the most important port of India it was also called the gate of ancient India. It served as an emporium of trade for the Phoenicians, Egyptians, Greeks and the Romans and a port of entry to the foreigners and foreign traders. According to some writers Muziris is the second most important port city after the city of Bharukacha or Broach in Gujarath. Muziris was also a very rich city due to the enormous foreign trade. Many writers of ancient times refer to the phenomenal prosperity of Muziris especially in the days of Roman trade.[11])

The author of *Periplus of the Erythrean Sea* and Ptolemy speak of Muziris as a great port. According to them, this harbor was crowded with ships of all kinds, with large ware-houses and extensive bazaars adjoining it and royal mansions and places of worship in the interior. The author of *Periplus* writes:

> The kingdom under sway of Kerlaputras, Tindis is subject, a village of great note situated near the sea. Muziris which pertains to the same realm is a city at the height of prosperity, frequented as it is by ships from Ariarke and Greek ships from Egypt. It lies near a river at a distance from Tindis of 500 stadia, whether this is measured from river to river or by the length of the sea voyage, and it is 20 stadia distant from the mouth of its own river.[12]

The Tamil poem *Akananuru* describes Muziris that is situated near the mouth of Periyar as follows:

> The thriving town of Muchiri, where the beautiful large ships of the Yavanas, bringing gold, come splashing the white foam on the waters of Periyar, which belongs to the Cherala kingdom and return laden with pepper.[13]

(The river Periyar served as the most important means of transportation of pepper and other spices produced in the hinterland to this port city of Kodungalloor. These items were exported directly to Alexandria, "the pearl of the Mediterranean." Products from North-eastern parts of India, Ceylon, China, and the interior parts of Tamil Nadu and Gangetic regions were brought to the port of Kodungalloor for onward shipment.[14] Another Tamil poet Paranar refers to the brisk trade in pepper at the port of Muziris:

> Fish is bartered for paddy, which is brought in baskets to the houses. Sacks of pepper are brought from the houses to the market. The gold received from ships, in exchange for articles sold, is brought on shore in barges at Muchiri, where the music of the surging sea never ceases, and where Chenguttavan presents to visitors, the rare products of the seas and mountains.[15])

According to Basnage, the close intercourse between the East and the West resulted in the arrival of the first Jewish contingent on the Malabar coast, of course at Muziris, in Solomon's fleet of merchant men. Rabbi Benjamin informs us that, in his day, the place contained about

1000 Israelites, and no wonder, because that was the location of the first Hebrew colony and it remained there till its desolation in 1524 and the final dispersion and the emigration to Kochi in 1565.[16]

Emergence of Kodungalloor

As we go through the ancient documents on Kerala history, we can notice one thing that the name Muziris is gradually abandoned in favor of Kodungalloor. From the tenth century onwards or exactly from the time of Al Biruni (970–1039) Kodungalloor is seen more used. Again, one thing is clear in documents that the exact word "Kodungalloor" is seen used from the fifteenth century. Therefore, from tenth till fifteenth centuries other names, but all referring to Kodungalloor, were in use. Whether the different names refer to the same city or to many cities is a question of further discussion and study. We are inclined to believe that either Muziris itself or the present day Kodungalloor (till recently called Cranganore) or some other city very near to it or a portion of the big city is in reference.

The present condition of Kodungalloor is indeed deplorable. Till the middle of the fourteenth century Muziris remained a very prosperous, rich, and important city. Kodungalloor was already on the decline when the Portuguese arrived in India. Kodungalloor was shorn of her history, not by the work of anybody, but due to the geological instability of the coast.[17]

KOLLAM, THE SECOND IMPORTANT CITY IN KERALA

The second city where Thomas preached was Kollam that was an important city in the Pandyan kingdom. In the medieval Islamic documents Kollam is called Koulam Mali.[18] Thomas reached Kollam not directly from Kodungalloor. He preached in different places in between. Gouvea writes that after having built up the Christian community of Kodungalloor, the apostle went across the entire coast of Malabar up to Culao (Quilon) where too he halted because it was a noble and principal city, making many Christians there in.[19]

Kollam, formerly called Quilon, was the second most ancient trading center and port of Kerala. It was at one time a great commercial and political center and also a center of Christianity. A number of travelers who visited this place or heard about it have written about the Christians of this place and the church that existed in that city.[20] Kollam had trade relations both with the East and the West. It enjoyed a large trade with China and the Middle East. Its port has been described by early travelers as one of the largest in the world, and its market, the first in India. With the arrival of the Arabs and the Portuguese in Kerala and the rise of the ports of Kozhikode and Kochi as commercial competitors, its importance began to decline, its manufacturers became neglected, its harbor gradually lost its natural facilities for shipping and it came finally to be reduced to a third rate port.[21] The beautiful fort at Kollam, called Fort Thomas, which was built by the Portuguese, was also destroyed by the Portuguese themselves due to a clash between them and the Queen of Venad.[22]

"Thomas who reached Maliankara to preach the Gospel, after founding a church there, with the disciple Cepha came to Kollam and there too preached the Gospel" is the narration in *Ramban Pattu*. Certain Church Fathers while describing the Indian Mission of St. Thomas write about Kollam as one among the ancient Christian centers. There are a lot of literary evidences too in this regard. Till the ninth century, a Church of the St. Thomas Christians existed in the town, which was destroyed by a flood. The local people say that the remains of it can be seen even today a few hundred meters away from the shore.

NIRANAM

Niranam was an international trading center in the first and second centuries. It was also a port city. A trade route starting from Madurai, the Pandyan capital, ended in the port of Niranam. Niranam was very close to the sea in former times. In course of time the seabed was formed into land and certain places came up that we find today in between Niranam and Alappuzha beach, which are of a later origin. All these places today are known as Upper Kuttanad. The rivers Pampa, Manimala, and Kovilar make this land fertile.

The antiquity and importance of Niranam can clearly be seen in many ancient documents. The ancient writers Ptolemy and Pliny refer to the city. The author of the *Periplus of the Erythrean Sea* (A.D. 60) also testifies to this fact. They all say that it is a trading center and a port city. In *Periplus of the Erythrean Sea* we read: Niranam (Neyconda) was 500 stadia (50 miles) away from Muziris and 120 stadia (12 miles) from Beraka or Purakad. In Pliny's *Natural History* written in A.D. 77. Niranam is called by another name "Neandinton." Ptolemy (A.D. 150) uses the name "Nelkinda" and *Periplus* "Neyconda" or "Nikinda." Niranam is mentioned also in *Unnineeli sandesam*. This again adds to its antiquity and importance. Gundert uses another name for Niranam, i.e., *Neermannu*.

The city of Niranam had trade relations with the ancient civilizations of Greece, Egypt, and Rome. The Roman coins of Augustus Caesar discovered in Niranam, a few decades back, is a clear proof of this fact.

St. Thomas, the apostle of India, who landed in Kodungalloor, preached the Gospel in many places, especially in the port cities of Kerala. Niranam is one among them, where St. Thomas founded a Christian community.[23] The northern part of Niranam is called *Kottachal*, where St. Thomas is believed to have landed. This place is also called "Thomakadavu" or "Thommathukadavu." The first Christian community founded by St. Thomas was in the place of the present-day Mar Thoma Church (Jerusalem Mar Thoma Church). Because of the resistance of the local people a church could not be built there at that time. Therefore, the first church was built in the place where today we find the St. Mary's Syrian Orthodox Church (Niranam Valiyapally). There are evidences to say that in 1259 a big church was built there, and in its place a third one in 1912. The present-day church in Niranam is the fourth one, rebuilt in 1930. The granite cross in front of the church is of the thirteenth century.

NILACKAL

Nilackal was an important town and a prominent trade center of ancient Kerala. Nilackal had a privileged position in Venad, which was the most important region of Chera kingdom. Nilackal was the entrance to Pandya kingdom, as it was the eastern most city of *Keralanadu* or kingdom in ancient times. The remains of a road or pass leading to Madurai, from Kerala passing through Nilackal can be seen even today.

The first source to study the history of Nilackal is the Sangam literature. We can find references to Nilackal in *Chilappathikaram* and *Pathittippattu*. Chilappathikaram describes the migration of Kannaki from Puhar to Madurai, the Pandyan capital. After the mistaken killing of Kovilan, she ran to Kodungalloor (Muziris) via Nilackal. The mountain pass was near Kumily. This route between Madurai and Muziris passing through Nilackal was a brisk trade route in ancient times.

In *Pathittipaattu* we read that the servants of Pandyan King came to Chera kingdom, to the areas of Nilackal and the surrounding towns, which is today the district of Pathanamthitta[26] to purchase gold and silk. An etymological study of the place names of many towns or villages of Pathanamthitta district reveals this fact. For example, the places called Kaippattoor, Omalloor, Koduman, Chandanappalli, Thattasssery, etc. Kaippattoor is a combination of three words: *kai* = hand, *pattu* = silk, *oor* = land, i.e., the place of handmade silk. Omalloor: *om* = good or fine, *mallu* = thread, *oor* = land, ie the land of good or fine thread. Kodumann: *kodu* = gold, *mann* = land, i.e. land of gold.

It is the strong belief of the Keralites that St. Thomas during his journey and missionary work in Kerala should have founded a Christian community in Nilackal too. St. Thomas's journey to and from Mylapore should have been through this town as it was on the route from Kerala to Tamil Nadu.[27] But the Christian community founded by the apostle could not withstand the test of time. According to many historians Nilackal church was destroyed in the civil war between 1311–1315 and Christians migrated to nearby places. Already from the tenth century people of Nilackal was suffering a lot due to the continuous wars fought in their land as it was the border region of Chera and Chola (Pandyas). There may be other causes for the flight of the people from this place, like diseases, attack of wild animals, etc. Anyhow, from the beginning of the fourteenth century onwards we do not find Christian communities in the region of Nilackal. Many churches or Christian communities in Travancore today claim their origin from the migration of Christians from Nilackal. For example, Chengannoor, Venmani, Thumabmon, Kozhanchery, Omalloor, Kanjirappalli, Poonjar, Kadambanatt, Ranni, etc.

(In 1957, the remains of the Nilackal church were traced in the Sabari forest of today. Then in 1983 an ancient cross was found by the workers while they were working in a farm. Following this finding, in 1984 a church was built in Thevarmala, in the mountainous region of Nilackal. This church, called St. Thomas Ecumenical Church is owned by the important Christian groups of Kerala and that stands as a monument of the historicity of the ancient Nilackal Christian community.)

This important trade center began to decline in the tenth century; and by twelfth century Nilackal and the neighbouring industrial area lost their importance. As a consequence of the Chera-Pandya conflict, already in the tenth century Nilackal and neighboring regions became Pandyan territory under the rule of Panthalam Rajas. The literal meaning of Panthalam is Pandyan settlement (pandya + *alam* = settlement). The worship of Ayyappa (of Sabarimala) and Kannaki are due to Pandyan or Tamil influence on Chera or Kerala.[28] At the end of 100 years' war between Chera and Chola (including Pandya kingdom) in 1102, Kerala suffered the worst damages. Venad became independent of Kulashekhara dynasty of Chera kingdom. The two kingdoms of Venad, Panthalam Rajas and Poonjar Rajas became extension of Pandyan kingdom or Chola empire. Thus, from the twelfth century, Nilackal was no more enjoying its former position of an important trade center.

(Another reason for the decline of Nilackal was a civil war that occurred in the thirteenth century. Though Kulashekhara dynasty tasted defeat at the hands of Cholas, after almost 200 years they defeated their enemies and returned to power. Ravi Varma Kulashekhara in 1299 unified the whole of South India under his power, and in 1312 he declared himself the emperor of South India. But his successors were inefficient and thereby the Kulashekhara dynasty or the Second Chera empire again lost its power and the different small kingdoms depending on it lost their political importance.)

PARAVUR

Paravur or Parur is an ancient Syrian Christian stronghold. Today it is called North Paravur in order to distinguish it from South Paravur. In ancient times it was also called *Kottakkavu* that means "a temple inside the walls." This city was not far from the ancient capital city of Kerala, Muziris, and was considered to be on the banks of river Periyar in ancient times. It was a port city and trading center, where St. Thomas founded a community and it is the tradition that it is from Kottakkavu that he left to Mylapore, where he succumbed to his enemies.[29] The Portuguese missionaries, testify the importance of this place in their writings during the early Portuguese period.[30] The third church in Paravur was built in 1308 that was destroyed by Tippu Sultan in 1789.[31] The present one is blessed in 1938. Bishop Francis Roz is buried in this church.

PALAYOOR

In history we read St. Thomas the apostle went from Kodungalloor to Palayoor (also called Palur) and converted many into Christianity there. The descendants of some of the ancient families are seen even today with the same family names. For example, Pakalomattam, Sankarapuri, Kaliyankavu, etc.[32] The archdeacons in the Malabar Church till 1653 were from the Pakalomattam family and all nine Mar Thomas (from 1653 till 1817) were from the same family. The tombs of some of the archdeacons can still be seen in Pakalomattam, a place two kilometers away from Kuravilangad, on the M.C. road side.

Palayoor is the northern most of the seven ancient Churches; while Kollam is the southernmost. This was a trading colony in ancient times like Kollam and Kodungalloor. The presence of Jews in this place can be evidenced from the name *Yoodakunnu* meaning "the mountain of the Jews" that is another name for Palayoor. After having converted some Brahmin families into Christianity St. Thomas converted a Hindu temple into a church.[33] Even today one can note the surroundings of the ancient church as those of a temple. It is believed that in consequence of the desecration of the village by the apostle, the Brahmins who remained true to their faith cursed the place as *Sapakad* meaning "the forest of curse" and went to the neighboring villages.[34] Palayoor that is also called as Chavakad is the derivation of *Sapakad*.

KOKKAMANGALAM

Kokkamangalam, also called Gokamangalam and Kokkothamangalam, is in the southern most coast of Vembanad lake. According to Collinsey, a French governor of Malabar, Kokkamangalam is in the bay of Kollam, i.e., the part of the sea extended from Kodungalloor to Kollam. Ships going from Kodungalloor to Kollam were passing through the straits of Kokkamangalam. St. Thomas after his mission in Kodungalloor travelled southwards and reached Kokkamangalam.[35]

St. Thomas converted a lot of Brahmins, almost 1600 according to tradition, into Christianity.[36] But due to objections from the other Brahmins the Christian community could not flourish there.[37] The later history testifies that it flourished in the neighboring regions of Pallippuram and Kaduthuruthy.[38] A cross found later in the small island of Mattel, which is to the east of Pallippuram, which is on the other side of Vembanad lake, is a testimony to the presence of Christians in those regions. That cross is kept today in the parish church of Pallippuram. The present church of Kokkamangalam was built only in 1900, and only a few Christians are seen today in this area.

CONCLUSION

The Indian apostolate of St. Thomas is often a question of debate and discussion. It is not clear what prompts some writers to raise this issue and bring it to the public. Many and varied are the documents to prove the historicity of the Indian apostolate of St. Thomas. The tomb at Mylapore and the work *Acts of Judas Thomas* are the most important ones among them. The next important proof could be the 'tradition of seven churches' that is dealt with briefly in this article. If one is honest in his approach and if disposed to go through the existing scientific documents the Indian apostolate of St. Thomas is not at all a problem to be discussed upon.

ENDNOTES

1   In the introductory part of the text of *Acts of Judas Thomas* we read that the
     world was divided among the twelve apostles. For details see A.F.J. Klijn, *The
     Acts of Thomas: Introduction, Text and Commentary* (Leiden 1962).

2   Origen associates the apostle Thomas with Parthia in his *Commentary on
     Genesis*. His original work was lost; but this statement has been preserved by
     Eusebius of Caesarea in, *Ecclesiastical History* III, 1.

3   Herodotus, *Thaleia* Book 3. For details see J. Puliurumpil, *Classic India*
     (Kottayam 2016), 89.

4   See Acts cha. 1. *Acts of Judas Thomas*, tr. & ed. by W. Wright (Amsterdam
     1968), 146.

5   For details see, Jose Mullankuzhy, *Sanghakala Kristavar* (Mal.), (Kanjirapally
     2007), 53–59.

6   Lionnel Casson, *Periplus of the Eritrean Sea* (Princeton 1989), 83.

7   L.W. Brown, *The Indian Christians of St. Thomas* (Cambridge 1956), 52.

8   Lionnel Casson, *Periplus of the Eritrean Sea* (Princeton 1989), 85.

9   Pliny, *Natural History* 1, 6.

10   K.P. Padmanabha Menon, *History of Kerala*, Vol. I (New Delhi 1989), 305.

11   In the first century A.D., there were many other port towns too that had very
     brisk trade with the Romans. See R. Mukerji, *Indian Shipping: A History of
     the Sea-borne Trade and Maritime Activity of the Indians from the Earliest
     Times* (New Delhi 1999), 135.

12   J.W. McCrindle (tr. & ed.), *The Commerce and Navigation of the Erythrean
     Sea* (London 1879), 104.

13   *Akananuru*, Akam 148, as quoted in A. Sreedhara Menon, *A Survey of Kerala
     History* (Madras 1988), 50.

14   K.S. Mathew & Pius Malekandathil, *Kerala Economy and European Trade*
     (Muvathupuzha 2003), 5.

15   *Paranar*, puram 343, as quoted in K.P. Padmanabha Menon, *History of
     Kerala*, Vol. I (New Delhi 1989), 307.

16   K.P. Padmanabha Menon, *History of Kerala*, Vol. I (New Delhi 1989), 313.

17   K.P. Padmanabha Menon, *History of Kerala* vol. I (New Delhi 1989), 326.

18   S.D. Goitein, *Letters of Medieval Jewish Traders* (Princeton 1972), 64.

19   Pius Malekandathil (ed.), *Jornada of Dom Alexis de Menezes: A Portuguese
     Account of the Sixteenth Century Malabar* (Kochi 2003), 6.

20   Abu Salih, *The Churches and Monasteries of Egypt and Some Neighbouring
     Countries* (Oxford 1895), 300.

21   K.P. Padmanabha Menon, *History of Kerala*, Vol. I (New Delhi 1989), 270.

22   Narration of the siege of Kollam fort is described in V. Nagam Aiya, *The
     Travancore State Manual*, Vol. I (Trivandrum 1906) 289–290.

23   There are many stories connected with the origin and development of a
     Christian community in Niranam. For details see L.M. Zaleski, *The Apostle
     St. Thomas* (Mangalore 1912), 170–171.

[24] Sr. Prassanna Vazheeparambil, *Thomaslehayude Niranam* (Changanasserry 2005), 97.

[25] Sr. Prassanna Vazheeparambil, *Thomaslehayude Niranam* (Changanasserry 2005), 42.

[26] The word Pathanamthitta is a combination of three words: *Pathu* = ten, *inam* = items, and *thitta* = place or terrace, meaning place of ten items; probably these items are industrial products.

[27] For details see B.S. Ward & H. Connor, *Memoir of the Survey of Travancore and Cochin* (Trivandrum 1898), 56.

[28] Dr. Alexander Jacob, Nilackal St. Thomas Church—A Historical Review, in *St. Thomas at Nilackal—Past and Present*, K.U. John (ed.), 12.

[29] For details see A.E. Medlycott, *India and the Apostle Thomas.* (London 1905), 134.

[30] Diogo de Couts, *Da Asia* (Lisbon 1856), 16.

[31] L.W. Brown, *The Indian Christians of St. Thomas* (Cambridge 1956), 53.

[32] L.K. Ayyer, *Anthropology of the Syrian Christians* (Ernakulam 1926), 2.

[33] L.W. Brown, *The Indian Christians of St. Thomas* (Cambridge 1956), 53.

[34] A.C. Perumalil, *The Apostles in India* (Patna 1971), 95.

[35] A.E. Medlycott, *India and the Apostle Thomas* (London 1905), 133.

[36] L.K. Ayyer, *Anthropology of the Syrian Christians* (Ernakulam 1926), 6.

[37] A.C. Perumalil, *The Apostles in India* (Patna 1971), 94.

[38] L.W. Brown, *The Indian Christians of St. Thomas* (Cambridge 1956), 53.

9

PATRISTIC EVIDENCE ON THE APOSTOLATE OF ST. THOMAS WITH SPECIAL REFERENCE TO ST. EPHREM

Johns Abraham Konat

The apostolic mission of St. Thomas to India has been a strong tradition both among the Christians of Malabar as well as in the West. It is believed that he evangelized the Malabar cost, met with his death near Chennai, and was buried in Mylapore. But there are scholars who doubt and even deny the mission of the apostle to India. Here we intend to discuss the patristic evidences related to this tradition, giving special emphasis to the works of Ephrem. According to the tradition prevalent in Malabar, Thomas arrived in A.D. 52 and worked for twenty years. He landed first in Craganore. He ordained priests from four Brahmin families of Malabar and established seven (or 7 and a half) churches. Later he travelled further east up to China to preach the Gospel. Coming back to India he was martyred in Mylapore by the Brahmins in A.D. 72.[1] Outside Malabar the first document that gives a detailed description of the works of Thomas relating him to India is the Apocryphal text known as the Acts of *Judas Thomas* written around the middle of the third century.[2] Most of the later Fathers of the church rely for their narratives on the story as told in the *Acts of Judas Thomas*.

ACTS OF JUDAS THOMAS

The Acts of Thomas has thirteen acts.[3] There are many theories regarding its original language. There are scholars who believe that it was written in Syriac[4] and others who opt for Greek. Some propose that the original was in Greek that was translated early into Syriac and afterwards the Greek text was lost except for some fragments. So later Greek versions are all translations of the Syriac version.[5] The text describes how the apostles cast lots and Thomas got India as his mission field. He was reluctant to go because he was weak and did not have enough strength.[6] He also says that "I am a Hebrew; how can I teach the Indians."[7] But Christ himself appeared and strengthened him. He accepted and he was sold as a slave to Habban the merchant. Habban brought him to India, to the palace of King Gondaphorus. The text describes the various miracles he worked and how he built the palace in heaven for king Gondaphorus. Thomas received money from the king for buiding the palace but he utilized it for helping the poor. Then Thomas begins his work in the kingdom of another king Mazdai. He attracted the enmity of the king because Thomas taught that marriage is sinful and even the king's wife became a follower of the apostle, rejecting marital relations. The text ends by describing his martyrdom. He was put to death by the soldiers of king Mazdai, according to the king's command. Soldiers took him to a mountain and before his death Thomas was allowed to pray. He ordained a priest and a deacon before his death. He was then pierced by spear.[8] He was buried in the sepulcher in which ancient kings were buried. It also mentions that his relics were carried away to the west before the death of the king.[8a]

Medlycott says that the description of certain customs found in the *Acts* point to South India. The description of royal women being carried around by servants in a sort of palanquin, ritual bath before taking part in a meal, saluting the king at early dawn, etc. are examples.[8b]

DIDASCALIA APOSTOLORUM

The work known as *Didascalia Apostolorum*, written in Syria around A.D. 250 says: "India and all its places, and those around it, up to the last sea received the apostles' hand of priesthood from Judas Thomas who was guide and commander in the church that he built there and ministered there."[9] The document also mentions that, what Thomas had written from India has been received and read in churches in every place just like what James had written from Jerusalem, Simon from Rome, etc.[10]

OTHER PATRISTIC TESTIMONIES

The earliest patristic witness regarding the mission of Apostle Thomas is found in a *Commentary on Genesis* written by the Alexandrian Father Origen (Book III).[11] It is dated around A.D. 224.[12] "The holy apostles and disciples of our savior were scattered throughout the whole world. Thomas, as tradition relates, obtained by lot Parthia, Andrew Scythia, "This narrative reflects the Alexandrian tradition on the apostolate of Thomas. The original of this work is lost. We find this mention as quoted by the early historian of the Christian church, Eusebius of Caesarea (early fourth century).[13] Historians Rufinus (end of fourth century) and Socrates (fifth century) relay on Eusebius[14] and affirm that the mission of Thomas was in Parthia.[15] P.J. Podipara says that in those days a good deal of Northwest India was included in Parthia or was under Parthian Princes and thus there is nothing wrong in assuming that Parthia included India also.[16] Even though the question which part of India was evangelized by Thomas still persists, it does not exclude South India.[17] J. Puliurumpil also is of the opinion that Parthia was an elastic term in those days and could include India.[18]

Eusebius connects Bartholomew to India.[19] India was also a vague term in those days that might signify almost any region beyond the Roman Empire's Southeast frontiers. While mentioning Bartholomew, Eusebius might have had in mind one of the countries bordering the Red Sea. Some references mention that Thomas preached to the Parthians, Medes, Persians and went up to India and was martyred and buried in Calamene, India.[20]

Medlycott says that not only Syrian Fathers like Ephrem and Jacob of Serugh, but also Greek and Latin Fathers like Gregory Nazianzen, John Chrysostom, Ambrose, Jerome, and Paulinus of Nola explicitly connect Thomas to India.[21] But the references made by these Fathers, except Ephrem and Jacob of Serugh, are very scanty. They connect Thomas to India when saying something else, as a passing note.

Gregory of Nazianzen, in a sermon preached in Constantinople against the Arians in 380, mentions the name of Thomas associating it with India. He says that the apostles were strangers among the nations and countries committed to them: "What had Paul in common with the Gentiles, Luke with Achia, Andrew with Epirus, John with Ephesus, Thomas with India, Mark with Italy? What had all the others . . . with the people to whom they were sent."[22]

Ambrose of Milan (+397) in his work *De Morbis Brahmanorum*, tries to narrate about the country, customs and life of the Brahmins and speaks a lot about India, its people, the city of Muzuris and about St. Thomas. He testifies that Thomas preached in India and Mathew in Persia.[23]

Jerome (+420) in his work *Epistola ad Marcellam* answers the question, did our Lord abide always with his apostles saying, "He (Christ) dwelt in all places: with Thomas in India, with Peter in Rome, with Paul in Illyricum . . . with each apostle in each and all countries."[24] In his *De Viris Illustribus*, Jerome says; "The Apostle Thomas, as it has been handed down to us by tradition, preached the Lord's gospel to the Parthians, the Medes, the Persians, the Carmans, Hyrcanians, the Bactrians and the Magians. He slept in the city of Calamina, which is in India."[25] Puliurumbil affirms that Jerome knew India and its culture to a certain extend and thus what Jerome means by the word India is our present India. The Indian mission of Thomas was at that time a known fact and a popular theme.[26] Paulinus who became bishop of Nola in 409, while describing the mission of apostles to different places says: "Parthia receives Mathew, India Thomas, Libya Thaddeus, and Phrygia Pilip."[27]

Jacob of Serugh (+521) has written two *memre* on Apostle Thomas and his mission to India.[28] In the first *memra* he describes the casting of lots and how Thomas was reluctant to accept his mission to India. He says the people there are dark and fearful. They do not have a god. The fact that Thomas showed reluctance is attested in the Acts, but the mention of a dark and fearful people is not found in it.

As both Ephrem, Jacob and the *penquita* prayers affirm this point it cannot be considered as mere poetic imagination. Jacob says that Indians are dark on both sides and their sight is hateful.[29] People of India are qualified further by names such as evil ones and black.[30] At last Christ himself appears to Thomas and convinces him to take up the mission.[31] The second *memra* begins with the arrival of Thomas in India in the guise of an artisan for building a palace for the king. Jacob describes how he takes money and distributes it to the poor, etc. The basic narrative of Jacob is a combination of what is described in the *Acts of Thomas* and what we find in the writings of Ephrem.

EVIDENCES SEEN IN THE WORKS OF EPHREM

St. Ephrem the Syrian (+373) was a prolific writer who has used poetry to expose the faith, to comment the Bible, to write biographies, to give moral exhortations and fight against the heretics. It has been remarked that his writings are like the ocean whose boundaries cannot be seen. It is estimated that he wrote more than three million verses. He lived at least for ten years in Edessa, the city where the mortal remains of St. Thomas are kept. Still no direct evidence could be found in his writings about the labor of the apostle in India.

REFERENCES IN *CARMINA NISIBENA*

Ephrem's hymns on Nisibis, *Carmina Nisibena*, composed most probably to be sung at the public services of the church, with a refrain at the end of each strophe,[32] contain some references connecting St. Thomas to India. Especially in hymn 42, Ephrem imagines the Devil as saying:[33]

"The devil cried out where shall I flee from the righteous; I provoked death that I might kill the Apostles; that by their death I might escape their blows. But now I am beaten harder; The Apostle I killed in India has preceded me in Edessa; he was here and there also everywhere I went; here and there to my grief I find him.[34]

Blessed is the might which dwells in the glorious bones."

"That merchant carried the bones is it not he (himself) they carried. Behold they (Edessa and the merchant) had mutual profit, what gain did I get while they had mutual profit; both brought me loss. Who will show me the casket of Iscariot, for I acquire power from it; the relicerium of Thomas killed me for a hidden power that resides on it tortures me."[35]

In the third stanza, Ephrem goes on to describe the profit of the bones that he repeats was transported by a merchant. Ephrem does not give the name of the merchant. Medlycott identifies him as Khabin on the basis of the Chaldean Martyriology.[36] Ephrem further compares Patriarch Joseph of the OT with Thomas and says:

"Moses the chosen carried the bones (of Joseph) in faith for profit; and if that great prophet believed, that there is help in the bones, the merchant did believe well, and it is good that they called[36a] him merchant; the merchant made gain and grew and reigned; his treasure has made me very poor; his treasure was opened in Edessa and has enriched the great fortress with benefits."[37]

In the fourth stanza, Ephrem describes the treasure house that kept the relics of Thomas.

"I wonder at this treasure house, for its treasure was small at first; and behold no man took from it; the spring of its wealth was poor; but when many had surrounded it and plundered and looted its riches; how much it was plundered so much its riches increased for if an enclosed spring is sought out; if pierced flows mighty and abounds."

REFERENCES IN THE *MADRASHE*

References are found in at least three *madrashe* of Ephrem.[39] They do not have any special titles. In the first *madrasha* there are seventeen stanzas and 11 to 17 contains direct references to Thomas. Ephrem praises Thomas,[40] and says that he has purified by baptism a tainted land, a land of dark people.[41] Ephrem continues to narrate that Thomas was sent by the Great King (Christ) and calls India as the dark bride. Thomas has rescued her from the error of sacrifices. Once again, he alludes that the mortal remains were brought by a merchant and praises him for having brought this precious pearl to a place that needed it.

Stanza 11 says:

"Blessed are you Thomas, twin is your beauty; twin is your spiritual beauty; your beauty is not one alone, neither is your name one; behold your beauties are many and shining; renowned is your name among apostles and is preached; in my lowly state, I haste to sing your word with my ugly mouth."[42]

Stanza 12 says:

"Blessed art thou, O Light, like the lamp, the sun has sent in the midst of darkness; to go and enlighten the land darkened with fumes of sacrifices, 'A land of dark people fell on you in order that these you should clothe white in glory, (and) in baptism) you cleansed her and made her white; he whitened the impurity."[43]

Stanza 13 says:

"Blessed are you, who proceeded like the ray from the sphere of the great Sun, and dispelled by your dawn the painful shadow of India; Great lamp, one of the twelve, who was filled from that oil of the cross, and enlightened the dark abyss of India by that light."[44]

Stanza 14:

"Blessed are you whom the great king has sent to espouse India to his only begotten; and you cleansed the black one and made (her) white, better than snow and pure linen; you are blessed the hated one because, beautiful and radiant, to her groom she might enter."[45]

Stanza 15:

"Blessed are you for you have confidence in the bride from the pagans, whom you rescued from demon's errors and enslavement to sacrifices; you cleansed her with saving bath, you made fair she who was black from sun burn; the cross of light effaced her dark shade."[46]

Stanza 16:

"Blessed are you O merchant for you brought the treasure to the land which needed; you are the wise man for you found the good pearl; and he sells all he has to acquire it; it enriches and ennobles him, for he found it; truly a famous merchant who became rich and (enriched) the world."[47]

Stanza 17:

"O blessed fortress, you are blessed for you received the pearl, because you could not find a better pearl in India other than this. Blessed are you for you were worthy to guard in your treasure the chosen stone, nothing resembles it; the Son of the Good one, full of all goodness, whose grace His adorers praise."[48]

The second *madrasha* that mentions Thomas is also found in Lamy's edition.[49] There are eight stanzas in it, stanzas 4 and 5 do not mention our theme. The first stanza contains two specific references. One to the feast of Thomas that was started by a pontiff and the second a shrine that was erected by a king. This might be a reference to king Mazdai, the one who ordered the assassination of Thomas. He opened the tomb of Thomas. Finding nothing in it he took some soil and healed his son with it.[50] Probably this king might be the first one who erected a church over his tomb in Mylapore.[50a] Ephrem also speaks of the wonders that were being performed by Thomas both when he was alive and after his death.[51] By his prayers, diseases are healed, the demons are driven out and the dead come back to life.[52] Given below is a translation.

Stanza 1:

"Thomas which is your lineage that you become so illustrious, a merchant brought your bones, a priest assigns you a feast, a king erects a shrine."[53]

According to Chronicon Edessenum, the bones were transferred to Edessa in 394.[53a] But, there is an inconsistence because Ephrem's date of demise is fixed as 373. Some scholars push it further upto 379.[53b] Even this later date would not make it possible for him to know the date of the transfer of bones of Thomas, if it happened only in 394. The description in *The Acts of Thomas* also suggests that the bones were brought to Edessa during the life time of king Mazdai.[53c] Medlycott says that 394 mentioned in the *Chronicon* might be the date on which the bones were transferred from its first resting place in Edessa to the newly erected church in honor of Thomas.[53d]

Stanza 2:

"The merchant who brought your bones was vigilant externally and in secret they (watched over) him; of all things he traded he never fell upon something like this."

Stanza 3:

"So many times, he entered India and came out, all the treasures which he found in it he considered as dung with the eyes of (compared to) the bones which he found.

Stanza 6:

"Something else was given in addition, which was neither promised nor hoped for; behold in India your wonders and in our land your lienor and everywhere your remembrance."

Stanza 7:

> "While alive you did signs, which you did after your death (also) through the toil in one region you healed and without toil behold you heal everywhere."

Stanza 8:

> "As you were commanded you healed with the sign (of the cross) and with oil. You persecute the evil spirits without a sound, and without a word you heal and without prayer the dead are raised."[54]

The fourth reference is found in the next hymn. It consists of six strophes of which three are important.

Stanza 1:

> "The First Born chose His Apostles and among them He chose Apostle Thomas; and He sent him to baptize the perverse and dark gentiles; the night was spread over India and there was grief and like the ray of the sun he went and dawned and enlightened it."[55]

Stanza 2:

He alludes to the building of the palace in heaven.

> "Who has ever seen an earthly one building above except Thomas the Son's Apostle; while he was below he reaches out and builds the foundations high above in heaven; on the earth he was wise than all, that while being in the depth he builds with his wisdom and is crowned in the high by his command."

Stanza 5:

> "The faithful does not need men to praise him for a big crowd of his witnesses are near his bones as well as near his sufferings, and by his honor he is believed and by his signs he is preached, for it lives for the Indian; supplicate in his honor, whoever doubts his bones."[56]

Even though the words of Ephrem do not describe the mission in detail, the main facts of Thomas's mission, that he, one of the twelve apostles, came to India where people with dark complexion lived, that he baptized them. He illuminated a place filled with sacrifices. He purified the bride from evil errors, for the Only Begotten. His dawn removed India's darkness. He suffered martyrdom in India and was buried in India and his bones were later transferred to Edessa by a merchant, who was blessed for having brought such a priceless treasure to Edessa, the city that really needed the relics. It was the greatest pearl that India could yield. Thomas suddenly becomes famous because great wonders happen because of his bones. A Pontiff starts a feast in his name and a king builds a shrine to his memory. His power was felt in both places and his feast is kept everywhere. When he was alive, he could work wonders only in one region, but after his death miracles happen in his name everywhere. It is mentioned that he did wonders with the sign of the cross and oil. Ephrem mentions the palace built by Thomas saying he designed on earth and built in heaven. All these facts are evident from these few lines.

Most of these details point to the fact that Ephrem was well versed with *The Acts of Thomas*. But we also find certain points that are absent in the Acts. The detail that the bones of Thomas were carried to Edessa by a merchant, is not found in the *Acts of Thomas*, which mentions that it was carried by one of the brethren (Wright, 297–298) Here Ephrem might be depending upon the Edessan tradition.

The description of Ephrem, especially his repeated insistence that it was the land of dark people who used to offer sacrifices, etc. points to South India. This detail is not found in the Acts. So, it should be an additional information gathered by Ephrem. After him, Jacob of Serugh also repeats the same. By the first century A.D., the Arians, a people with a fair complexion had started inhabiting the northern part of India. We can more or less affirm that while describing the mission of Thomas, Ephrem had South India in his mind, because neither in Persia, Parthia nor in North India did a people with dark complexion abide during that time.

One should bear in mind that whatever we find in the writings of Ephrem are not his personal opinion alone. He is actually narrating the tradition prevalent in Edessa regarding the mission of Thomas. The details reflect the mind of the church of Edessa. Thus, the words of Ephrem carry more weight.

REFERENCES IN THE *PENQUITA*

The *penquita* in the West Syrian tradition mentions almost the same ideas found in Ephrem and the *Acts of Thomas*. The prayers reiterate that India is a land inhabited by dark people, and that Thomas was reluctant to go to India the fearful land of Hindus.[57] In the evening prayer, it is pointed out that India is a land without God.[58] The people there has a shameful appearance;[59] they are black. In the hymn of Ephrem the names of Habban and Gondaphorus are mentioned, as well as the palace built by Thomas.[60] In the prayer for the night describes the sale of Thomas[61] and how he converted the people of darkness.[62] The dream of the king of India who saw the palace, the assurance of Christ; to be with him wherever he goes, etc., are other themes found in the night's prayer. In the morning office we find mention of the death of Thomas with a spear and how his mortal remains were divided and taken to the four quarters of the world.[63] One of the miracles attributed to Thomas in which a dog tore off the hand of a man who unnecessarily struck Thomas;[64] and the details of the measurements that he carried out for the construction of palace; the mention that he will build only in winter, etc., are also seen in the *penqita* prayers.[65] What we find here is mostly the influence of Ephrem, Jacob of Serugh, and the *Acts*.

CONCLUSION

Except a few references, most of the Fathers of the church associates Apostle Thomas with India. According to some specialists the association of Thomas with Parthia does not exclude India. Evidences start from the first half of the third century onwards. It is of course true that most of these traditions originated from the same source, *The Acts of Judas Thomas*. But the fact that they were prevalent in the east, the middle-east, and the west, gives more valor to basic assumption that Thomas was the apostle of India. The references of Origen, Eusebius, etc. connecting Thomas to Parthia need not exclude India as his mission field. By all probability, India referred to by Ephrem is South India where the Dravidians lived in the first century A.D.

ENDNOTES

1. C.B. Firth, *An Introduction to Indian Church History*, ISPCK, Delhi, 2013, 3.

2. Firth, 8.

3. For an English translation from the Syriac version see; W. Wright, *Apocryphal Acts of the apostles*, vol. II, London 1871, 146–298.

4. Based on the inference given by F.C. Burkitt, Medlycott affirms beyond doubt that the original is Syriac, A.E. Medlycott, *India and the apostle Thomas*, London 1905, 221.

5. M.R. James, *The Apocryphal New Testament*, in, *gnosis.org/library/actthom.htm*

6. Wright, 147.

7. Wright, 146.

8. Wright, 295–296.

8a. In some versions it is stated that the bones were carried away to Mesopotamia. M. R. James, 8b. Medlycott, 277–280.

9. Syriac text; W. Cureton, *Ancient Syriac Documents*, London 1864, 33; Medlycott, 35ff.

10. Cureton, 32.

11. Origene, *Homelie sur la Genese*, ed. L. Doutreleau, in Sources Chretiennes 7bis, Paris, 1976. This Homilie was pronounced in the fourth decade of the third century when Origene was in his sixties, says the editor, 13; Firth, 6.

12. J. Puliurumpil, *St. Thomas in India: Patristic Evidences*, Kottayam 2012, 249. The opinion of Doutreleau is different. See note 11.

13. For a Latin version see, Origene.

14. Heras, H, *The Two Apostles of India*, Tiruchirapalli 1944, 1.

15. P.J. Podipara, *The Thomas Christians*, St. Paul Publications, Bombay 1970, 15.

16. Podipara, 16.

17. Podipara, 18.

18. J. Puliurumpil, 248–249.

19. Eusebe de Cesaree, *Histoire ecclesiastique*, ed. G. Bardy, in Sources chretiennes 41, Paris 1955, 40. He says that when Panteanus came to India there were already Christians in India and they had a Gospel of Mathew in Hebrew, and that Barthelomew was their apostle.

20. Firth, 7.

21. Medlycott, 42–46.

22. Gregory Nazianzen, *Contro Arianos* XI, *PG* 26, 28; Puliurumpil, 262–263.

23. Puliurumpil, 265–266; Migne, *PL*, 14, 1143).

24. Puliurumpil, 45. *Jerome, Epistula LIX, ad Marcellum*, ed. Migne, PL XXII, cols. 588, 589.

25. Jerome, *De Viris Illustribus*, PL XXIII, col. 721; Puliurumpil, 270–271.

26. Puliurumpil, 273.

27. *PL* 61, col. 514.

[28] *Homiliae selectae Mar Jacobi Sarugensis*, ed. P. Bedjan, vol. III, Paris-Leipzig 1905–1910, *On Apostle Thomas*, 724–762; and *On the Palace Built by Thomas*, 763–781.

[29] Bedjan, *On Apostle Thomas*, 229.

[30] Bedjan, 309.

[31] Bedjan, 449.

[32] Puliurumpil, 219.

[33] Ephrem, *Des Heiligen Ephrem des Syres Carmina Nisibena*, ed. E. Beck, CSCO Syr 102 (240), Louvain 1963.

[34] Ephrem, 37.

[35] Ephrem, 37.

[36] Medlycott, 23.

[36a] See the varient and *Carmina Nisibena*, 38.

[37] *Carmina Nisibena*, 38.

[38] *Carmina Nisibena*, 38.

[39] Ephrem, *S. Ephraemi Syri Hymni et Sermones*, vol. IV, ed. Lamy, Mechliniae 1902.

[40] Ephrem, Stanza 11, 700.

[41] Ephrem, Stanza 12, 699.

[42] Ephrem, 699.

[43] Ephrem, 699.

[44] Ephrem, 701.

[45] Ephrem, 701.

[46] Ephrem, 701.

[47] Ephrem, 701.

[48] Ephrem, 701.

[49] Ephrem, 703.

[50] Wright, 297–298.

[50a] Medlycott affirms that it was Mazdai himself who built the church over the tomb, 27–28, Note 2.

[51] Lamy, 703.

[52] Lamy, 705.

[53] Lamy, 703.

[53a] Puliurumpil, 232–233.

[53b] John Kunnapillil, Mar Aprem Malpan, Oriental Institute of Religious Studies, Kottayam 1992, 73–74.

[53c] See above note, 8a.

[53d] Medlycott, 27, Note 1.

[54] Medlycott, 705.

[55] Medlycott, 705.

[56] Medlycott, 707.

[57] *Kthobo d'penquito d'hudro sathonoyo,* ed. Abraham Konat, Pampakuda 1962, Vol III, 222.

[58] Medlycott, 223.

[59] Medlycott, 223.

[60] Medlycott, 224

[61] Medlycott, 225

[62] Medlycott, 226

[63] Medlycott, 228

[64] Medlycott, 230; Wright, 150, 152–153.

[65] Wright, 160.

10

GUIDELINES FOR REBUILDING MISSIONS OF APOSTLE THOMAS AND A REASSESSMENT OF ACTS OF THOMAS

Pierre C. Perrier

THE SOURCE OF TRADITION TO BE TRANSMITTED IN THROUGH JESUS ALONE

In this report have been used the works conducted in France in a framework of a work-group study to better explain the historical elements especially related to the Early Church; they have led us to define both social and temporal environments of the apostolic missions in the wake of those of Jesus.

It is assumed, that following the Pentecost, Jesus' series of teachings was similarly continued by the apostles. It is, however, important to note that this is merely a logical conclusion; since the sermons by the apostles could not stray from the specifics they had received from Jesus in the course of the three years of daily following him. They must have been well aware of first doing, what they had learned at his side.

Well, during the first year, apostles listened, learned, and participated as mere students, witnessing to the mission of Jesus and later, having been chosen, they embarked on their first mission. It consisted of reaching out to as many Hebrews as possible, in the places that they had already visited with Jesus. This corresponds to assigning one of the twelve tribes to each of the twelve apostles.

This is only visible in Peshitta text of the Gospels through individual assignment (MT and Lc) or assignments in pairs, but primarily always to the principal seat of the tribe–*mdintha* (Mc 6:11). This entailed the initial order specific to these assignments; they would go there as representatives

Study carried out within Chaire de recherche sur l'Eurasie with the support of the Auvergne Rhône Alpes Region.

175

of Jesus and then, during the second year, while being themselves established as the apostles of the first instance, they would bring their disciples (hence, 72), so Jesus might choose those who would compose the second level. These 72 disciples having been thus established to assist each apostle in a group of disciples, they had to first and foremost instruct the them in the teachings of Jesus, so they could then collaborate with them on a mission. Finally, in the third instance, they themselves would send the 6x12 or 72 disciples (six by six assigned to each of the apostles) so that the missions could continue among the tribes, and then shared with the members of the tribe's Diaspora, whom they would receive or had received[1] after being trained for the mission in the company of Jesus. But there were also those to whom they had passed on the Good News during the Pentecost, those who came from their families, from the Diasporas on pilgrimage to Jerusalem in the year 30 or in the sabbatical year of 33–34.[2]

Thus, from one intimate to another, the ensemble of Hebrews in Palestine would receive, at least in the principal seats of the tribes, the first teachings concerning the Kingdom explained by the oral texts. They would flock in their houses to them for the growth of faith in the heart of their families toward all and in all places. The Twelve and their seventy-two disciples, assisted by the Holy Spirit who had come down to them, would go on establishing churches founded to illuminate the memory of each and would give birth to the evangelization of the outside world.[3] They would become the continuators of their One Lord in accordance with this tree-like model. Such rapid organization of evangelical activity is well described and acknowledged by many[4] of those who worked in the Holy Land but not by others[5] who are too unfamiliar with the specifics of the missions that followed the Pentecost.

A FORM OF ORAL LITERATURE THAT HAD SOME DIFFICULTY TO BE UNDERSTOOD IN THE WEST

The *Acts of Thomas* take us into the form of oral Mesopotamian literature, with ties to the Holy Land, to memorizing through oral tradition so remote from what has been preserved in literature, that became prevalent in the West during the last centuries before twenty-first century. Therefore, Western tradition is not helpful in analyzing the first century in Palestine, especially if we start out with the later western copies that have reached us in greater numbers[6] than the sources from Mesopotamia.[7]

The writings of the first century in the Greco-Roman world are actually even more remote from the Mesopotamian literary tradition than those of the Chinese. The latter have preserved within their great written culture much more powerful traces of oral tradition that goes back to their first great civilization that of the Imperial Han elites. This historical culture reliably recorded the monarchs of the dynasty, as well as some written accounts describing the life of elites in the Chinese empire, all the while preserving a popular tradition that included tales and legends.[8] In the West very few collections of legends have been preserved and even less tales and myths, especially those employed in the religious and educational domains, so were so abundant at that time.

The Mesopotamian literature, however, is practically unknown to us after the clay tablets in cuneiform had been inscribed for the last time. This is due to the systematic destruction of its great libraries by the first and the third generations of Muslim rulers. Thus, this literary tradition including its biblical corpus, the only compilation to have preserved[9] the near entirety of the eastern Peshitta in Imperial Aramaic, is underappreciated in the West. We are unable to reconstruct these writings and can only become indirectly aware of them in the Greek and Latin compendium that came down to us in a modified and rewritten form, well after the last prophets, from Tobias to Jonas,[10] had been compiled into the Hebrew Testament. This literary tradition is based on analogy while calling on the whole range of techniques used in the times of the last biblical writers, that is to say, stories destined to make one understand the recommendations of the wise men and possibly derived from both proverbs and specific historical information that has not reached us.

Moreover, there are historical accounts of a slowly elaborated legal and religious[11] documentation conveying cases that could be very specifically referred to narratives and teachings having resulted in sentences.[12] One therefore, must take into consideration the Mesopotamian legal tradition that presupposed an entirely oral account in depositions conserved by the scribes after the ruling. Actually, the legal tradition of the Parthian Empire goes back to a thousand-year-old oral tradition followed by recordings made by tribunal scribes in what concerned the most exemplary sentences. In these oral documents, the customary usage was to string together texts on the same topic or from the same story in a necklace, in a way of ensuring the veracity in the coherence between a large number of these basic texts that had been thus compiled. In the East, truth is always provided to the listener through complimentary repetition of explicitly or specifically similar stories ensuring the historical construction of protagonist's experiences or of a legal and a religious topic; this can be observed in the *Acts of the apostles*, the martyrs and especially in the *Acts of Thomas*.

The usual model is to string[13] the texts together into a necklace by groups of five to ten documents composing a thematic and chronological unit in keeping with a common mnemonic method of fingers on a hand that does not require the author to call upon his writing skills. The scribes used to pile up tablets.

If we analyze the beginning of the first necklace in the *Acts of the apostle Thomas,*[14] we will observe that it actually cannot be understood without dividing its structure into 2x5 parts, which we can discern, based on the division of the Aramaic text published by W. Wright and the notations made by M. Bonnet. The latter can serve as a point of reference, but does not provide a breakdown by themes or by a similarity of scenes. This often results in passages of variable length in the narratives and in what concerns the long texts, provides a fairly apparent subdivision into three, which happens to be traditional. If we consider that these subdivisions cover a still more important number of subsets than the evangelical verses: the content is often much more prolific and is generally subdivided into 2 or 3 sub-paragraphs. An elaborately expressed prayer, a specific sermon had to be explained to the listener with a sufficient amount of details so that the imagination would fill in the details specifically provided for the events happening in places manifestly unfamiliar to the listener.

In the oral tradition, we call these textual units "pearls," although the Aramaic term *marganitha* is singular (the plural is generally the same) it also encompasses a magnificent necklace of pearls as *"in pendants such as in deacons' necklace having over 100 beads and over 10 strands of pendants."* In the East, such necklace of pearls is considered beautiful when its structure assembles several pearls in a regular order and varying in "weight" (the length of a text to memorize) but identical in pendants; hence a string of words is assembled like the one in pearls, often numerous and organized into sub-necklaces, into pendants to be put around the neck, by analogy around the throat, of the narrator who does know the stories by heart.

THE FIRST NECKLACE INTRODUCING THE PROBLEM OF THE ACTS: INTRODUCTION OF A CHRISTIAN RELAY TO SANDARUK

The first necklace in the *Acts of Thomas* describes his arrival in the principal seat of an empire called Sandaruk. Obviously, this is a deformation by oral tradition of one of the many stopovers and later military implantations of Emperor Alexander, whose name can be surmised from it, and that to this day is known as Sandracosta, for Al Sandracosta, "which is related to Alexander." Through ignorance of numerous "Alexandrias" in Persia, it was translated for Western readers as Alexandria in Egypt. It is located at the crossroads leading eastward or northward and to the Caspian Sea across the Urmia lake, where roads are nations separated to attain different peoples of the Caucasus: Georgians, Armenians. In this "Sandaruk" then, near the tomb of the two of the three Magi kings, lives a large community of Assyrian and Chaldean Christians. The southeastern route allowed one to reach the Indus valley by going across what is a present-day Afghanistan. Sandracosta was truly a vital communication hub, when one decided against going to Bactra and changed direction for Taxila, or any other land easier to reach by crossing the lake near the city of Urmia; where an important Hebrew community used to resided until the medieval period, its existence has then been continued by the Judeo-Christians who are still present there today.[15]

Thus, by analogy, the marriage celebration, and the revelation to a young Israeli girl, unattached to the spiritual path preached by Thomas, already point to the first illustration of the main theme in all of the Acts. However, it remains clear that this first pendant somewhat echoes the story of Tobias celebrating a marriage in Nineveh.[16] In it are directly linked to this city, the Hebrew Diaspora from Ecbatana on the route to the East; the farthermost western suburb of the great city of Nineveh from whence Judas-Thomas arrives in the beginning of the Acts. The ancient center of the great northern capital, since long time mostly in ruin, extended westward protected by a fortress (*bg*). The former city of kings (*sar*) of the North[17] is the present-day Mosul. We know that the main seat of Hebrew merchant community had been established there since its deportation by Sargon. In the first century the influence of this network would stretch much farther than Ecbatana in the book of Tobias: as of the reign of the Western Han dynasty, around 200, it would extend to China, however, its support base would always remain in the western suburb of the great Nineveh;[18] Bartholomew and Thomas had converted Nineveh-Mosul in 37–40, so they were the first to renew the "sign of Jonas" over the ancient capital of the North. However, the return of the two apostles to Jerusalem in the sabbatical year of 40–41, would be quickly followed (martyrdom of James) by a subsequently the beginning of much more distant missions than that of Sarboug that would remain their support base: the two would have to separate whereas the first time together Bartholomew and Thomas had actually fulfilled Jonas's[19] prophesy. Apparently, through their sermons, they managed to make accept the conversion by the larger part of the Hebrew community; that had begun with the pilgrims arriving from the East in the year 26 and baptized by John the Baptist upon their entry into the land of Israel and after in 30 and more in sabbatical pilgrimages of 33-34.[20] In fact, their names are placed together in such a way, that the name of Thomas opens the line after the six apostles disciples of John the Baptist, of whom Bartholomew is the last, as if to initiate the mission of the two to the first great historical city in the Fertile Crescent. They are also juxtaposed in the list of the 12 apostles provided by the *shouraya*–the introduction to the text based on the order given in Matt 10:3, but not in Mark or Luke (where the name of Matthew precedes that of Thomas). We can also observe that Juda Thomas is not called by his proper name to distinguish each of the three Juda amongst the Twelve, which identifies this text as one that was composed by the eastern diaspora.

Today, we can assume that the mission of Judas-Thomas, without his "partner,"[21] Bartholomew who went north, began in Sandaruk-Sandracosta—manifesting the decision to separate according to the northern and southern routes in the Himalaya massif, while deserting the one to the east. This decision is to be situated later than 41 in the year 45, the date of Sassanid military defeat at Bactra,[22] the next stage in their journey together on the direct route from Nineveh, so that as seasoned travelers they could reach the Chinese Far East (the Gog and the Magog depending on their nomadic name in Aramaic, qualified as "brutes" having respectively originated from inland or coastal regions of the Far East) by a land route. We can then understand that it was to preserve the final goal on the march to the East,[23] the same way as James reached the *finis terrae* in the West. However, he traveled to a much better known and a less distant extreme west—Spain, by a much more rapid maritime route used by Phoenicians for centuries.

It is precisely this beginning in the *Acts of Thomas* that tells the story of Thomas's own missions. This story begins for the two apostles with the parting of their way, Thomas being the youngest and the first in the line of six disciples who had not been trained by John the Baptist. The story involves an entire half of a previous septennial, between 41 and 44–45, in the wake of the mission from Antioch in 37-40-41. When their informants, who were probably merchants, told them that the Kushans had cut off the summer silk route through the direct passage of Pamir, they had to abandon the idea of setting off together on this second stretch of the journey. This marks the beginning of the *Acts*, the place, and the rationale.

By going to the shores of the Caspian Sea, Bartholomew chose to take the Armenian winter route through Siberian steppes that comes down to a quick trip without great mountain ranges, although, it is only accessible when the great currents taking their source in the Himalayas and the northern foothills opening on the plain remain frozen. However, he died as a martyr in Albanopolis, east of Armenia before his departure, probably because of the merchants unwilling to reveal the details of their trade to this disciple of Christ.

In what concerns Thomas, he came down from Sandaruk and headed to Indus taking the alternative southern land route of the Himalayas that leads from Indus to Ganges, in order to continue by feet his mission in the East. But initially, this mission had to pass through the entire Indus valley as described in the text of the Acts.

After these clarifications on the causes for the separations of the two apostles who felt their calling for a longer journey on foot, we can follow the first ten pearls in the first necklace. Allow us to remind you that in Aramaic, the term *Marganitha* does not only designate one pearl but also the whole necklace of pearls consisting of "pendants of pearls" assembled in one big text with several pendants; this ensemble is divided into "ordered" segments (put in a succeeding order) of a story, to provide the listeners of the Acts with a given oral narrative, as a detailed account that step by step explains, the global mission of Thomas in the Far East. The is perceived in its enunciations depending on the stage in Thomas's journey to the East; first Judas-Thomas needs to follow "a merchant" who leads him along one of the most important trade routes in Eurasia, where each stage prepares the next foundation; first it inspires him to call on a young woman to serve the Lord, then on the newlyweds, it is something that would become a repetitive pattern in the Acts in order to demonstrate that basis to establish first: a new "beit" (house) founded by a covenant in wedding, in the course of founding the new church. The points of reference for the segments in the text belong to Bonnet;[24] they are given between quotation marks and set in italic type:

I- The first pendent after the founding of mission in Mosul:

1   *(2-3)* the reliance on a merchant and the first passage across the waters of lake Urmia;

2   *(4)* Thomas at the wedding in Sandaruk;

3   *(5-6,1)* the flute player;

4   *(6,2-7,2) Wedding hymn (with the Church)*;

5   *(8-9,2a)* the flute player testifies;

6   *(9,2b-3)* miracle and a royal invitation;

7   *(10)* Judas prayer; the calling of the Hebrew flute player;

6   *(10)* Thomas's prayer for the calling of the newlyweds;

7   (11-12) the sermon on the real spiritual marriage (cf. Tob 8:5);

8   *(13-14)* incomprehension of parents;

9   *(15)* the confession of the husband;

10   *(16)* incomprehension then conversion of the King and in the city.

The name "Thomas" is rarely if ever used in the Aramaic texts, because in India, there is no need to distinguish between the three "Judas" among the Twelve, since only Judas Thaddeus responsible for Babylonia[25] could lead to confusion.[26] We can notice that the text visibly tries to make us understand that the choice of first relying on the young musician[27] is that of an inspired Judas starting the local mission in respectable house-holds even before, he began to discretely convert the husband. Hence, his discrete presence is implied only upon seeking the acceptance of evangelization from the monarch of the people. Thus, in accordance with true love of family, the Eastern Church has first invested into relying the Good News inside a home and primarily before married couples: their conversion being preceded, if possible, by that of saintly windows devoted to Christ, who in accordance with the love of God, were waiting for the Husband who must come, the Son of perfect love. The two callings complete one another to enthrone the tradition of family love for children[28] in the first place.

The issue of the original language does not exist in this first "pendant"; here we note the high number of specific professional terms or of terms related to trades specific to central Eurasia. For example the list of terms for semi-precious stones between the fourth and the ninth verses of the "Hymn of the Pearl" provides a faithful description on the origins of gems and metals that a jeweler like Thomas knew; it gives how to identify the nations by their Aramaic names; the same goes for the Hymn of the Alliance in the fourth pearl. The Greek text is powerless to make its Western reader penetrate both highly oriental ecclesiological and liturgical terms known by the missionaries to the Far East.

Outside this Western classification, the spiritual importance of the rites in the New Alliance can be explained by the choice of a *madrash* mode, using analogical comparisons that originated in everyday life. For example, the common words employed in the Aramaic to make eulogy of a bride come from similar biblical evocations but they are taken into the context of a common tongue used during wedding celebrations in the East.

The presence of unequivocal names of the Twelve and their Seventy-two disciples in the fourth pearl, nevertheless, demonstrates the emphasis placed on the New Alliance of the Gospels with prophecies in keeping with the Christian ternary: love, faith, and hope. However, this entirely Mesopotamian form, suggests an originally oral composition, addressed to listeners from this culture capable of appreciating the systematic use of analogies and evocative compounds proper to it. What the apostle says indicates its presence throughout his whole tradition, a fairly ample knowledge of an ensemble of texts from the Judeo-Christian necklaces that Thomas received prior to his departure from Jerusalem and later from Antioch in 37, greatly summarized in the Acts. In the course of his mission, he would later redevelop it more formally into a local language,[29] for example, into ancient Persian terms in Sanatruc. Hence, all would be deduced from the original texts in the Imperial Aramaic, the original common tongue for the majority of writings. *We, therefore, remind you that in the first centuries, all oriental texts in local languages get their writing from the deformation of the Aramaic Mesopotamian cursive.*

Hence, the memory of the apostle's original sermons could be very faithfully relayed everywhere among the neighboring nations living in the vicinity of major cities that he attempted to evangelize and not merely in the last of the princely courts where dynasties conserved Greek from their distant Hellenic roots as a scholarly tongue. The catechisms that pace the Acts are exclusively relayed in Aramaic texts. In order to be able to attribute these texts to Thomas himself or to his disciples (of higher order), it was necessary to first verify whether through oral play[30] these Peshitta texts, permitted to generate these midrashic developments into easily derivable *madrashés*,[31] here on the subject of the Alliance.

Indeed, these first texts are *"madrashé"* that were derived straight from the Gospel texts and the Old Testament hymns (notably the Song of Songs). The *Acts of Thomas* also possesses some precursors among the various texts by the late Diaspora prophets, recognizable by their similar form.[32] It is these very dense midrashic texts,[33] the first to be produced by the church in Aramaic language, that in the past thirty years the French working group has precisely and unequivocally set out to find as a substitute for the mediocre contents of the source Q such as it is esteemed in the West. The latter could not possibly permit the writing[34] of elaborate catechism texts provided in the Acts[35] to convert the nations.

As we will see later, this presupposes the bearers of the great oral Hebrew tradition as well as writers particularly well trained by Jesus in keeping with the context of the Mesopotamian tradition for preserving the oral word in writing. Yet, the evangelical source for these first necklaces recorded in this initial dense form[36] precedes the Gospels; the evangelists themselves were actually the compilers and writers of Matthew's Gospel.[37] They kept in touch in their centers of writing in keeping with this very specific mode of expression that has no equivalent in the Roman world of the first century. In fact, documents in the Greco-Roman world, whether in Rome or in Alexandria were henceforth composed with a quill in hand, thanks to other effects of writing. They no longer possessed this *domino* effect of words and phrasings that are typical of the catechisms and songs from the *Acts of Thomas* and could be obtained by assembling formulas operating in the world of oral tradition. Actually, this Western civilization, while ahead in the domains of writing and innovation, was losing a part of its methodology of thought as it had been anticipated by Socrates in Timaeus.

So, outside of the Hebraic world in Israel, the purely oral works, arranged as commentary-midrash, in accordance with ancient forms, could only be viable in the Mesopotamian Diaspora, rather than any other place. We can, therefore, understand the essential place of the Hebrew flute player as an assistant to Thomas's instruction: used to improvising on popular musical themes, used to accompanying a narrator of traditional texts, she would constitute the essential basis of the instruction that Thomas needed so badly[38] and progressively turn into the Mother of Memory.

One should then carefully listen to the epilogue of this pendant: having met the apostle on his evangelical path, the flute player joins the young newlyweds and joyfully follows him to relay the catechism of apostles, of whom Thomas is the bearer of reference and the Word would blossom beneath their feet.

Second pendant in Taxila

The theme of this second pendant is quite clearly explained through the parallel in its first pearl. It corresponds with a building project becoming a parallel in stone for a church composed of spiritual men; inside this building the saintly assembly celebrates liturgy that is what provides the beginning to this new binary theme of five plus five pearls as fingers together, described in an analogical fashion as building of a celestial palace associated to the liturgical celebration in an earthly palace.

For Judeo-Christian missionaries, the Temple of Jerusalem was no longer a new and a unique place of worship; it had to be replaced by new edifices in the nations, combining the place of assembly (a synagogue) with a place of *qurbana*, which would be proper to each nation. The introduction to the journey leading to this building project in the royal capital advances the analogy with a merchant carrying the Word and roaming the roads. Hence, it is the road from Sanatruk to Taxila, where the palace of a Greco-Parthian king Gondophares was located. We can easily trace this monarch through coins minted under his reign.

On a hill outside the city, one can still find traces of a building (naturally recovered by other more recent constructions)[39] that has been archeologically proven to date to the first centuries. It was built on top of a cave[40] with a present-day oral tradition mixing Christian, Buddhist and even Muslim contributions. The archeological investigation turned to the cave that had been first covered up in the first century, before a more recent second edifice was constructed on syncretic foundations of the Great Buddhist Vehicle going back to the reign of the Kushan king-emperor Kanishka (after 125), then in the fifth century, India reverted to Hinduism before the arrival of Islam.

The city has conserved Islamic legends albeit from a later date, concerning Jesus' visit to the city upon his Resurrection that coincided with loosing evident trace of its Christian community due to Muslim persecutions after the thirteenth century (according to local traditions, however the city's bishopric had been gone by the eighth century[41] probably during a Hindu crusade to suppress Buddhism).[42] Once on location, it becomes evident that the scraps of ancient traditions are a smoke attesting to real historical events, without justifying incoherent legends stemming from Quran's ambiguities on the subject of Jesus. Moreover, the reputedly Buddhist crypt or cave has no roots in traditional Buddhism; it can only be certainly more ancient, before precise datation, than the buildings that stood unawares on its top.

This second necklace after Sanatruc can be thus described:

II 1   (*17*) the appeal to Thomas;

   2   (*18*) the construction program from October to April;

   3   (*19*) Apostle's sermon in words and deeds;

   4   (*20*) King's refusal of the spiritual palace;

   5   (*21*) King faced with acceptation of his brother and his death;

   6   (*22-23*) King's remorse;

   7   (*24-26,1*) conversion of the two brothers and Judas' prayer of the act of grace;

   8   (*26, 2-27*) *rushma* of the two brothers;

   9   (*28*) Judas' sermon to the many in keeping with Matt 6;

   10   (*29*) The inauguration of *qubala*[43] for instructions on Sundays, the last *qubala* before the departure and a calling to go East.

We will note in particular the reminder to separate the instructions[44] conducted during summer mission (pearl 3) from the "winter school," "from the Feast of Booths to Easter celebration" (pearl 8), followed by the long sermons open to all (pearl 10 with the access to *qubala*). The presence of the cave on the hill confirms the founding of a church with its own hierarchy modeled after that of Mount Saint Thomas in Mylapore in a course of a half of septennial. However, the center of modern day Taxila has shifted; it is no longer the ancient capital of Gandhara but a small town. The Kushan capital was initially located in Begram and would be later re-established on the right bank of Indus at Peshawar, to the detriment of Taxila and the links to Ganges and the city of Patna. Later we will observe that the opposing typology of a king frustrated to abandon the idea of a beautiful palace turned into immaterial temple for the poor and the conversion of his brother accurately corresponds with the one of the historical missions to China. We have to assume that for Thomas this pendant in ten pearls played a prophetic typological and historical role. Persecutions experienced by the local Christians in the second century at the end of Kanishka's reign (around 150), when this Kushan monarch decided to impose a form of syncretism elaborated on the basis of Buddhism by equally combining both Buddhist and Western theories (especially those derived from stoicism and dating after the third century B.C.), come after the creations of *Acts* and confirm their antiquity. In referring to the days of the apostle and commemorating the Christian king Gondophares, whose kingdom had vanished toward the end of the first century succeeded by the Kushans, the writers of the Acts could not overlook these unnatural persecutions attributed to the successor of a Christian monarch through introduction of mandatory syncretism of all religions centered around Buddhism, with no God, no personal and collective sacrifice.

The ending of this pendant can be situated in the year 47, before the sabbatical year of 47–48, if we follow the hebraïc "three and half years rule" for establishment of a church at the seat of each new nation, in keeping with length of Jesus' own predications; so there are two new establishments between the sabbatical years.

A PENDANT RECALLING THE MEMORY OF AN UNPLANNED MISSION NECESSITATING EXORCISMS

The theme of this third group of peals wants us to acknowledge the great number of satanic possessions at the root of opposition to establishment of the church in north-west of India; however, it also attempts to explain the temptation of the apostle to distance himself from the long-term goal of his mission, in order to fight one by one the multitude of satanic enterprises, something that should have been left to his successors.

The second sentence of the first pearl clearly shows that: "having gone in the direction shown by the Lord (the East, the road to the Ganges valley and Pataliputa-Patna) and having walked the two miles that were required of him, the apostle made a turn to resurrect a handsome youth."

He invoked the Lord but wondered whether this was not a temptation as the rest of the story would abundantly prove it to be. And yet, he took this turn to the right, to the near-south and over which no one had asked of him to do. A snake appeared and Judas-Thomas would be drawn into a fight against all demons, something that the Lord had never suggested. The third pendant is marked by parallels explaining the struggle against "black snake" that attacked a young church, headed by the "handsome youth," a young convert. By betraying the purity of alliance with God who acknowledged his baptism, he had made it waste away. However, the apostle guides him to repentance and allows him to lead this church to its resurrection:

III 1   *(30)* Thomas takes a turn for a "handsome dead";[45]

   2   *(31)* and makes a black snake[46] come out;

   3   *(32)* the snake turns out to be the tempter of all;

   4   *(33) present* exorcism by Thomas at the request of the crowd;

   5   *(34-1a)* Thomas resurrects and revives the young man;

   6   *(34-1f)* adolescents confession;

   7   *(35)* God's Mercy;

   8   *(36)* the teaching for the adolescent;[47]

   9   *(37)* preaching of Thomas on hope in the spiritual struggle;[48]

   10   *(38)* conversion of the community.

The pendant does not evoke the transparent waters of Indus River on their arrival from the mountains at Taxila but the muddy delta where Thomas travels downstream in order to reach Pattala, a port located on the Indian Ocean. What we have here is an analogy of sin after the rush of reviving baptismal waters. Thomas's preaching probably began with a core of Christian converts from Taxila, who had settled down in Pattala, having typically branched out from the capital. However, when Thomas arrives to visit them, he discovers that the young church has wasted away. Instead of continuing his journey to the East, he has to offer help to the northern community in order to prop up the young church. Certainly, Thomas's instruction introduces God's Mercy for the sinners who while living in the world had betrayed the purity that allowed them to be closer to God and it begins with exorcisms, and acts of spiritual discernment making the "dead consciences" aware of their sin.

Of course, the choice of passing by Pattala would have allowed Judas-Thomas to take a boat from the port of Maïshan to Jerusalem for the Pentecost in 48, and even to be back for his mission in the summer of the same year, after the third gathering of the apostles. It also would have permitted him to consecrate the third septennial to following through on his long-term mission. But, as the Hymn of the Pearl clearly explains, Judas was confronting "demons of India" and would continue with his exorcisms. Instead of going to Judea, he remained in Pattala for half of the septennial (from 47–48 to 50–51). It is there that he would receive a letter urging his return to Jerusalem: The Mother of Jesus or the Mother of the Eastern Church, or according on a shorter formulation the Mother of the East had ascended to Heaven and…he was not there. Yet,[49] from the time he was recalled to his late arrival, Thomas probably like other apostles coming from distant lands, was struggling to overcome the growing opposition to conversions, the same applies to Matthew who was likely in the Ethiopian plateau.

And behold, Thomas abandons the idea of moving forward to Patna the Indian capital on the Ganges. He came to a land that had been evangelized before him, but was unable to withstand the attacks of the "slanderer" (Satan) and its young church was as if dead. The content of the pendant is historically accurate enough to situate Indus River flowing downstream on the right side from the road to the East. Yet, the sending of this urgent letter is only signaled in the middle of the ten pendants of the second part.

The urgency in this letter can be easily heard. There was a constant movement of boats up and down from Pattala, connecting the spice routes from Muziris through Pattala to Maïshan (a port that today has been succeeded by that of Basra). In order to get back to Jerusalem, Thomas had to pass through Maïshan. One might think of the apostle Simon who while evangelizing in the vicinity of Maïshan, in the estuary of the two rivers at the mouth of the Persian Gulf[50] had founded the church in this port city as of the year 40, probably with the help of Mari, one of the seventy-two disciples.[51] Meanwhile, a bit farther to the north, apostle Judas-Thaddeus was evangelizing Chaldea. Thomas most likely contacted with widows, settled at each missionary church of sufficient size, hence in that of Maïshan, most likely by Simon the Zealot. In keeping with the Eastern tradition, these widows received missionaries visiting the port, most certainly prayed for those who were passing through the city and received the accounts on the past missions. If the mission of Nathaniel-Bartholomew and Judas-Thomas to convert the Hebrews of Nineveh took place in the north, the Nineveh records surely must have existed, however they have not reached us. Still, we have several Indian chronicles of Judas-Thomas (in southern India) that could have been compiled in Maïshan, by the mothers of memory in light of the founding traditions, which are a faithful description based on a more ancient text, the direct source for the three first pendants in 30 pearls of the first part.

A PIVOTAL TEXT OF THE STRUCTURE: THE APOSTLE RETURNS TO JERUSALEM AND THEN GOES BACK TO INDIA

This series of five pearls composes the middle of the *Acts of Thomas*, with the exception of one appendage, which as we will see, illustrates Apostle's mission to China. This first series of five pearls, recounts his voyage to Jerusalem where he similarly returns on a donkey's back recalling Jesus' last week that ended with his death, the descent into She'ol and his Resurrection; thus begins Thomas's pilgrimage to Jerusalem that he left ten years earlier, fleeing like Peter the city of the false messiah: Herod Agrippa who had James the Great put to death upon his return from Spain.

Thomas himself corresponded with his "brothers"[52] the apostles, of whom the core was back in Zion, following the persecutions in the course of 37–44, as well as other surviving apostles, even those from distant lands, acknowledged by all traditions to have returned to commemorate Mary. The later years of the surviving Apostolic Church saw the deployment of the complete Memory of the Mother of the Church when liturgical and catechist texts of reference would be finalized. Thus, the fisherman who took flight when the soldiers came to arrest his Rabbi in the Gethsemane, until the time when he recognized him as his Lord and God, could henceforth establish much better structured Churches. This is what the Acts reveal by placing at the center of the narrative on the churches established by Thomas, this voyage to Jerusalem where he readied himself for a new twenty-one years mission (from 51–72), in the wake of the one among the tribe assigned to him during the first septennial (probably in the vicinity of the "*mdintha*" of the tribe Ephraim) in Antioch in Nineveh in 37, before his first and second visits to Jerusalem.

However during his voyage to Jerusalem in 51, he finds Peter,[53] John and James the Less, two fishermen and a cousin of Jesus with six others, since three apostles who had already died as martyrs and Mary became the center of the Heavenly Church, it is they who worked to return to the oral source of the composition of the four gospels in France[54] has been based.

Surprisingly, few deny apostle Thomas the credit for his missions from Nineveh to Indus, but many refuse to credit his work in the "second stage"—in the course of missions in 51–72. Yet, more and more valid archeological research and written documents confirm this, the latter more so than the first.

There is no place for ambiguity in the description of Thomas's voyage to the Holy City, which "shows" him reliving the memories of the Holy Week in his conversation with the donkey and the one with himself while returning to his former life once again in order to go back to his difficult task of missionary work in India and beyond, in the East and the Far East. If we are to believe what is narrated in the Hymn of the Pearl, since he had not gone back during the previous sabbatical year in Taxila, it was only then that he learned about the martyrdom of Bartholomew and Andrew.

This historical reconstruction allows us to shed some light on the discontinuity between the pendants III and V, but not on that in pendant IV, which without discontinuing presents us with a strange miracle; we do not know the reason why this miracle occurs when the apostle explains the miracles of conversion that the Lord allowed him to perform in the course of his missions:

> "On the way while he was speaking with the crowd of the Kingdom of God, a colt of a donkey (again a quote from the Gospel of Matthew (Matt 21:2) came and stood before him."

One should understand that this miracle of giving speech to a donkey commemorates the rest of Thomas's life. The description of the pilgrimage to Jerusalem when Thomas retraces the entry of the Lord into the city likens the apostle to Him as it is recalled in the genealogy of Mary. The text mixes the commemoration of Christ with that of apostle Thomas who is reliving this entry to Jerusalem by "A son of a great family" (Lc 19:12)" and reminds the crowds that accompanies him of the Might of his Lord in having chased multitudes of demons from India in order to bring them into the Kingdom of the Son of God.

This pendant is faithfully described in the following manner based on the Western points of reference in M. Bonnet:

IV 1 (39,1) Arrival to the City and the encounter with the donkey;

2 (39,2) Praise to the Son in Trinity;

3 (40,1–2a) Revelation made to Thomas as to the reasons of this passage in the Holy City;

4 (40,2b–3) The humility of Thomas faced with a century-old mystery (ThoraNb 22);

5 (41) Thomas mounts on the donkey that carries him to the gates of the city and dies. Judas unearths his memories.

This breakdown of this text into five instead of ten parts seems problematic since it comprises only five parts and the total length of this pendant is half of that of the texts from other four pendants. We will return to this observation below.

And yet, this very dense text in five parts is at the core of the VII pendants in the first part, which describes a conversation that Thomas has with himself. He is surprised by compulsion to give thanks for the help throughout his missions that he continuously received from Jesus. Then he recalls the declaration he made to his "Lord God" as prophecy of Truth he received at the contact with the wound in the side of Christ. It offsets the horror of the scene[55] he witnessed and engraved in his memory: the lance piercing the side of his Rabbi on the cross (Cf. below). In this fashion, he receives the justification for the urgency of this commemorative voyage to Jerusalem from India for the third septennial and all the more so because he had learned about the Departure of Mary, whose pre-eminent role as the Mother of the Church he recognizes. The donkey that in the oriental anthropological tradition is a parallel of the apostle's body, explains to Thomas his role as a humble conveyer for the Lord:

> "Thy lord also and teacher sat upon one that appertained unto me by race. And I also have now been sent to give the rest by thy sitting upon me: and (that) these may be confirmed in faith and unto me be added that portion which now I shall receive by thy service where with I serve thee; and when I have ministered unto thee, it shall be taken from me."

This text actually hints at the necklace of Mary's Mercy where she compiled the teachings of Jesus on the gifts bestowed on each man and each woman for the purpose of his mission; first, the gift of speech to bear witness to the evangelizing Word abundantly given to the apostle, as his *Acts* clearly demonstrate. But what is added and is "the best part" specifically given to him, according to the verifications made by our work group is "The Gospel of Mary": the four Gospels including the last that concludes them thanks to the work of Luke and Mary. Even before the late return of Thomas to Jerusalem in 51, the author of the Acts acknowledges the special place of women in the evangelization of the people that Thomas attributed them according to the necklace of Mercy.[56]

This quote explicitly provides the entire mystery revealed in the collection of the four Gospels in Aramaic language: according to the research conducted by our group, this entire mystery could be delivered to "those" who live in still more distant places and whom he still has to evangelize upon his return, from his base in the south of India.

Hence, it becomes easier to understand why this pendant draws the classical analogy between a donkey carrying a humble traveler in Jesus' stead, the dead body of a youth in the East and that of Isaac's lamb led to sacrifice. By giving his own body then, Thomas wishes to undertake the second part of his eastern mission until the time for his martyrdom. Having received the entire fruit of compiled traditions in a *qanone*[57] concerning the Coming of the Son of God, that he would then be able to relive and make his disciples relive. The entry into Jerusalem is at the center of the first part of the *Acts*, and there as we will see, a text complementary with the five pearls that would explain what the apostle received in Jerusalem and what he would bring on the second part of his mission once in the East,[58] is missing.

If we accept the time line of the *Acts* by solely settling on its division into groups of seven years between each sabbatical year and of three years and a half for half of a septennial in keeping with the recommendations given by Archangel Gabriel to Daniel, we will have to situate this return to Jerusalem in the year 51, and the Assumption of Mary, something that is confirmed by the information given in the beginning of *Transitus Mariae* (The twenty and first year...) that sets it in the middle of the summer mission.

The classification in the order of sabbaticals now allows us to attach to the intervals of sabbaticals (S) and half septennials (HS) the following succession of the two dates associated with missions also corresponding with the return to India (this time in the south) in the year 52:

S26	HS30	S33	HS37	S40	HS44
S47	HS50	51	S54...		

Jesus	Israel	Antioch	Nineveh	Sanatruk	Taxila
Pattala	Jerusalem		Kerala...		

We should also observe that the beginning of sabbatical years begins with *resh shana* (hebrew rosh ha shana) the celebration of the booths around October) while the new sabbatical year begins with Easters. It appears, as a result from these dates, that Thomas did not return to Jerusalem during the sabbatical year of 47-48 for the gathering with the other eight apostles who were still alive[59] at that time. There were five of them without him in the summer of 51, we were able to clarify this in the text through the continuity in the narrative between pendants II, III, and IV.

We should also specify that the voyage back to India did not consist in a return by the North on foot through Sanatruk and then to the Indus-Pattala valley or the voyage on foot and then by sea to Muziris the main spice port of Kerala in the first centuries. If one, however, decides to travel by sea, this choice allows one to go farther and faster: in choosing not to travel through Sanaa, but from vicinity of Babel to Maïshan and after the Persian Gulf to the south until the latitude of Muziris in the port of the spices was compelled to take another option (initially in the company of Matthew who was martyred in 48 in the Upper Nile valley that he wished to travel in order to reach Alexandria) and then through Socotra island the direct route to Muziris.[60] This voyage to reach the East by sea, followed the traditional Mesopotamian navigational route under the stars, which is something he could not have done, had he chosen to stay and fight the demons in Pattala who had spiritually extinguished the mission from Taxila. We should remember that at each stage there would be new evangelists helping the apostle in his mission to the capital city of the next kingdom.

The arrival of Thomas in Zion in the year 51, in order to receive the Testament of gentle compassion and theological rigor from the initial apostolic group centered around Mary and to appreciate its vital[61] necessity (and incidentally central in the composition of the Acts of Thomas) for its saintly Tradition. In fact, that the rabbinical Jews in Rome and Alexandria had to maintain the same kind of cultural and linguistic integrity in order not to "loose their souls."

WHERE WE LEARN THAT THE STAY IN KERALA WAS LONG BUT IT WAS FOLLOWED BY THE ATTEMPT TO GO EAST

The analysis to Indian tradition show that these three pendants, following Judas visit to Jerusalem, which should have corresponded to three periods or to three half-septennials that is about a ten year period, do not cover the entire timeline from the year 52 to the year 64, the date that the Han chronicles attach to the arrival of a Chinese boat that came to pick up Thomas in the south of India. However, the Indian chronicle[62] points the first mission to the Far East, when Thomas attempted to take the land route from Ayutha to the south of China, a mission that led him to evangelize the kingdoms of Kerala in a course of the summer of 54. It is quite likely, knowing, that Thomas as a proficient traveler on foot had initially followed land paths, probably intending to take the southern Himalayan road via Ganges. He had to abandon this plan without ever leaving Taxila at the outlet of the river in the east of India. However, the path to China from Ayutha was cut off by wars in the 50's, same as that going through Merw that had become impracticable in the middle of the 40's.

We can then understand why the text is continued in this fashion by the fifth pendant that describes the developments in the wake of the abandoned mission to Chine in the years 52–64 or the three six-month periods that could be roughly broken down into: 52–53/54–57 and then 58–61 and finally 61–64.

The mentioned themes are further described in ten basic pearls. The fifth pendant is developed along these lines:

V 1 (42) one woman calls the apostle who has returned to fight demons of India;

2 (43) the temptations by men;

3 (44) Judas denounces the malice of the snake;

4 (45) demons respond;

5 (46) the demon leaves;

6 (47) but Jesus is a hidden reviving mystery;

7 (48) Jesus is the sublime path;

8   (49) baptism and *qurbana* of the exorcised;

9   (50) 14f the descend of the Holy Spirit;

10 (50,3) making the sign of the cross over bread and communion

The choice of the comparative form is also very instructive as to the tonality of the mission: we can partially discern a variety in reading of the pearls contingent on literal or analogical interpretation that we decide to attribute them. Here are, for example, the subtitles given in the Greek version according to the first separation of the text due to Bonnet. It shows a more ambiguous interpretation that quickly attributes a sectarian or even heretical meaning to the work, as analyzed below:

1-the call for help by an Indian woman + 2-the distress of adulterers + 3-identification of the enemy + 4-complaints of demons explained + 5-threats and flight of the demon

The analogy used here, comes from the Hebrew tradition on the adultery with false gods and the enforcement of divine intervention through clairvoyance and prayer of the apostle. He often had to chase demons hiding among the multitude of Indian divinities. This analogy was borrowed from the Hebrew tradition and further reinforced here by the allusion to the intervention of Prophet Daniel in order to spare Suzanne surprised in her bath from condemnation. This allusion shows the close ties that the authors who made their contributions to the *Acts* had with the Babylonian tradition that are further emphasized by the use of Imperial Aramaic.

The sixth pendant is also clearly situated in Kerala confirmed by the absence of any mention concerning the journeys to Jerusalem in the sabbatical years of 54 and 61. This is why we must situate the three half-septennial cycles corresponding to the three necklaces V, VI and VII between the years 54 and 64.

Here we have the sixth necklace in its ten pearls:

VI 1   (51) a damming communion and murderer's confession;

2   (52) exorcism of the murderer;

3   (53) prayer for the killed woman;

4   (54) the woman resurrected by the saved assassin;

5   (55) She'ol in fire;

6   (56) She'ol of the impure;

7   (57) She'ol of liberation and compassion;

8   (58) sermon of Judas-Thomas;

9   (59) Judas heals;

10 (60) Praising Jesus

Finally, the seventh pearl opens with a mission in the south of India (Sri-Lanka) that would proceed in the following fashion ≈ by sea on a Chinese vessel prior to the return to India by the same route. This is how it is broken down:

VII 1   (62) arrival of a general asking to heal two women;

    2   (62,2) a woman at a wedding;

    3   (63) woman and daughter killed;

    4   (64) by a possessed man;

    5   (64,3) possessed for three years;

    6   (65) general converts and asks for healing;

    7   (65,3) the church is assembled;

    8   (66) sermon and the announcement of departure;

    9   (66,3) hope in Jesus Christ for the community;

   10 (67) prayer, imposition of hands of the clergy (Xanthippe).

We will not elaborate any further on these three necklaces because they would require very close collaboration with the Saint Thomas Christians to introduce them for an in-depth analysis following the first works conducted in a perfunctory fashion. We now possess the tools to analyze such oral traditions, but should avoid referring to the Indo-European languages such as Malayam-Aramaic in the conduct of examination, as we have done by drawing directly from Chinese and Aramaic sources for the Chinese chronicles: the first study being conducted in 2008, together with Xavier Walter, a professor of Chinese language at the university of Nanterre and well known for his long collaboration with the Chinese[63] and consultations with the Saint Thomas Christians of Malabar–Syriac denomination in Kerala.[64] Indian texts of oral tradition have served the basis for this study and are provided in reference, it now remains to study and complete the work that has already been done…[65]

WHERE WE PERMANENTLY RAISE THE VEIL ON THE AUTHORS OR THE AUTHOR BEHIND THE CONCLUSION OF THE ACTS BY EXAMINING A VIEW ALMOST CONSTANTLY TURNED TO THE CONVERSION OF WOMEN AND THEIR *RUSHMA*

It is a constant state of affairs, except for the Gospels, to observe that written history and its conclusions are generally made by historians who are men or at least by those who explain it as for the major part resulting from the work of men alone or from factors beyond their control. This is the reason why, the *Acts of Thomas* seem so puzzling and also probably why the commentators have almost always tried to postpone its dating in order to find traces of later heresies. And yet, the resurrection of Tabitha in the year 35 (Act 9:36–42) became a strong sign for Peter during the first years of evangelization, a sign served as an indispensable precedent to opening up the sermons to the non-Jews residing in the land of Israel: a major turning point of opening up the evangelization process to the world of nations that did not obey to the laws of Moses.

Announcing the Good News given in inheritance to the circumcised from great families, to foreigners and their loved ones (the "house" of centurion Cornelius) residing in the Holy Land, provoked concern even among the wisest of them all. Today, it is no longer obvious for many, that in his teachings Jesus chose and wished to provide the instruction in spoken word, that in addition to the guidance open to all that would firstly be relayed in a home, from one heart to another, in accordance with oral tradition: this implies the existence of the first very faithful works, generally summarizing the great sermons of Jesus or compilations of spiritual wisdom, to be repeated individually word for word.

These treasures to be placed by one heart into another, were first proposed inside the homes, and if one aimed at their memorization, from one generation to another, to be "understood later on." These treasures were carried by chaste widows in service of the mothers; this development was parallel to the dangerous missions undertaken by men; Holy Spirit, having inspired them to do apostolic work in Jerusalem in these early years. These texts were recited both to children and their parents. Less visible by their nature, these visitations had to be prepared by "Tabithas," or "widows in the world" and required their conversion from the very start of apostolic activity as a relay for the families, if the church was to survive.

We remarked in the beginning of the *Acts of Thomas*, on the presence of the Hebrew flute player when Thomas joins a group of merchants in order to travel, be fed and finally be accepted upon his arrival; but as we discover all the financial aid received from the leader of the merchants passes from Judas hands into those of the paupers who receive it through the feminine intervention on the part of the flute player, and most of all accompanied by the riches of Good News for their hearts. Hence, there is no need to look for heretical "encratist" ways in Thomas's mission initially targeting widows in order to build a network of mothers and "widows." On the contrary, as we have the common sense to acknowledge the reason for this strategy toward women, shall to be thankful to the authors less centered on the activities of men surely liable to provoke their persecution by authorities, to the benefit of providing us with information that other texts deemed worthy to omit.

A DEPARTURE OF THE APOSTLE FOR CHINA THAT WE SHOULD ACKNOWLEDGE AS CLEARLY CONFIRMED IN RELIABLE AND VALUABLE CHINESE CHRONICLES OF THE EASTERN HAN

We might wonder about the itinerary of Thomas, whether he had first, as tradition tells us, attempted a voyage to Insulindia from the north-east of India? Above, we have declared it possible. Unfortunately, Thomas, as it has been pointed out, must have learned that the land route allowing him to enter Sichuan in the great Chinese plains by south-west had been once again cut off due to military activity as it is recorded the Chinese chronicles.

As this voyage clearly shows Thomas's ultimate goal was to reach the East China Sea, that is, according to the *Hymn of Acts*, to give the pearls of the Kingdom to the pearl divers in the sea of the rising sun, at the easternmost extremity of the world. Then, at the gathering of the apostles in Jerusalem, he had learned of the martyrdom of Barthelomew and Andrew. He had to wait for the assistance from the Providence and prepare the sea voyage. Hence, Thomas did not return by Muziris, where he had been warmly welcomed but by the westernmost port for the Chinese vessels, located in the first century at Taprobana.

As Muziris, located to the west with its entry to the Red sea, this port allowed to voyage East following the stars to Qalah at the entry to the strait of Mallaka. One can assume that while in Kerala Thomas had learned that Taprobana provided him with opportunity to expand his mission to the extreme confines of the world, to the East China Sea.

The seventh pendant speaks of the church that was established in the port of Taprobana with the leader at its head and of the mission sent on the orders from the emperor Ming-di in 64 following a vision he apparently had at the spring equinox of the same year, to go seek and bring the writings of the God from the West. We can assume that the mission in Taprobana must have lasted until the end of 64 and that the Chinese boats with translators speaking Aramaic were going to ensure the opening up of the Chinese Empire to the Gospels in the year 65. Thomas could not have hoped for a better development.

The fifth pendant seems to cover at least the years 54(S) to 61. The length of this pendant is almost double of the preceding pendant and corresponds to much more dense volume of teachings and coinciding with a longer period of time of establishing churches on the coastline:

In its first part Thomas makes a long prayer to Jesus before a new exorcism and the *rashma* prepared for the victims of demons; baptism and anointing are followed by the *qurbana* and a description of the long prayer to the Holy Spirit before the signing of the bread with a cross. It also confirms that the custom of praying to the Trinity dates back to the first apostolic sermons. Then the second half of this pendant begins with a miracle of the dried-up hands, protecting the holy Eucharist from the communion of an unrepentant sinner. There is also the murder that has thus come in to light, leading the apostle to cure the sinner and resurrect his victim. It is followed by the teaching of Judas-Thomas on Sheol after the victim describes what she saw in the place where the souls of sinners could be amended and perfected.

It is evident that the teachings of Thomas take on a greater scope compared to those prior to his visit to Jerusalem. Their stronger ties to the definitive form of the four Gospels could be the cause. The definitive condensed addition of the four Gospels hints at an access to more diverse doctrinal contents that nurture the sermons of the apostle.

However, this text should be studied in concert with work conducted in Kerala since it might be confirmed by a more diverse local tradition.

AN INTERVAL OF TIME WHERE WE REALIZE THAT THE MISSION IS BEING PURSUED IN INDIA, FARTHER SOUTH AND THAT ITS FAME SPREADS EVEN FARTHER THAN INDIA

In fact, we are confronted to a conclusive testimony of one necklace in seven pendants of ten pearls, strung according to the breakdowns in the pearls and in the locations of missions:

s	I	II	III	IV	V	VI	VII
1/	2–16	17–29	30–38	39–41	42–50	51–61	62–67
	Ant/Nineveh Kerala	Sandaruk Tabropana	Taxila	Pattala	Jerusalem/East		Kerala
	37/37–40 57–60	41–44 61–64/ 65	44–48	48–51	51/52		/52–53/53–56

Pendant VII could be succinctly described in the following manner:

VII 1   (62) arrival of a general asking to heal two women;

    2   (62,2) a woman at a wedding;

    3   (63) woman and daughter killed;

    4   (64) by a possessed man;

    5   (64,3) possessed for three years;

    6   (65) general converts and asks for healing;

    7   (65,3) the church is assembled;

    8   (66) sermon and the announcement of departure;

9   (66,3) hope in Jesus Christ for the community;

10   (67) prayer, imposition of hands of the clergy (Xanthippe).

Hence, in this seventh necklace we learn of a meeting between an Aramaic-speaking "general" and Thomas. Apparently, it took place in Taprobana, the port situated in the north of Sri Lanka. The general's name or rather a nickname is Siphur or the trumpet, but this is a title given to royal squire or general of the royal guard in the Parthian army in Aramaic. This is probably what became the source of a confusion that should be clarified because, all seems to show that this misunderstanding on the part of the author or collector of the pearls of this necklace led to a representation of Siphur as a general of the Parthian army who arrived in India from the north-west. It would have then been a description of the encounter between Thomas and a Parthian general on the west coast of India in the north of Sri Lanka. But this comes from ignoring the fact that Chinese imperial cavalry originated from the Wusun kingdom (the rich plains of Ferghana) where big horses were being raised, a kingdom administered by Hebrews from the tribe of Manasseh who spoke Aramaic including in the running of the cavalries.

Multiple clues in the necklace point to southern Mesopotamia as the place of its creation, in any case not far from Maishan, a destination where the boats from Taprobana would arrive. It was also used by traders and emissaries to China and served as a relay for boats relaying information coming out of that country. However, this exchange seized in both China and Parthian kingdoms before the persecutions by Shapur I and the great age of trade with China under the Han, this is before the pontificate of Catholikos Abrahma of Kashkar (159–171), no later than in the second half of the second century.

And yet, two chronicles on Chinese emperors from the Han dynasty, associate the presence of the said Siphur with the half-brother of the Chinese emperor nicknamed Ming-di, that is to say, the Sun Emperor nicknamed like Louis XIV the Sun King. This perfectly corresponds to the Aramaic translation of Ming-di as Mazda-ï. But who are these Siphur and Wang Ying that the chronicles place together and whose persons are well known? Wang Ying with his squire or his general Wang Zun, is the half-brother of emperor Ming-di who had been sent on a mission to a small kingdom west of China, situated outside of both empires and more ancient than Parthian empire. This small kingdom was Ferghana (Wu Sun in Chinese) located on high-altitude plateau and exporting the big horses so vital for the Chinese military in their fight against Mongolian cavalry atop their small horses.

This half-brother of the emperor who commanded the Chinese army had married Manassar—a "Hebrew princess" the daughter of Ferghana king descending from the tribe of Manasseh. All these names mentioned in the Han chronicles as well as those of courtiers of the Chinese emperor and of a few other characters are transposed in the second half of the *Acts of Thomas*. We must admit: Siphur is the one who is described in the Chinese chronicles: a Hebrew from Diaspora who would become a Judeo-Christian general in the Chinese imperial guard of Ming-di. He came with his cavalry from Ferghana (the land of horse flies in Aramaic) to serve in the Chinese army under the command of prince Ying, the half-brother of the emperor. He then spoke Aramaic; at least with his wife and his cavalry guard.

This prince most certainly, was not sent on a mission charged with bringing to the emperor Ming-di the disciple of a God with a halo that appeared to him in royal Parthian travelling garments in the spring of 64[66]; however the order of the imperial mission demanded to bring copies of the parchment scrolls that the divine King had over his shoulder inside a Parthian bag for documents (a Persian bag that looks like a bag for golf clubs). All that was needed was a translator and providentially the imperial demand ordering this voyage, opened the door of opportunity for Thomas in the course of his meeting with Siphur. This "general" looking for "the disciple of this King that had appeared unto him" did everything to make the mission to Chine possible for Thomas who had dreamt so long of accomplishing it. All this was necessary in order to go to China, but a prince, the Chinese Marys and Marthas to meet were also indispensable.

We can now understand that those who compiled the traditions of the seventy other texts from ten pendants in the second part of the *Acts* did not possess a very good geographical and human knowledge in respects to the ancient Eurasian Far East. This was also the case for the readers of the *Acts* from the West in the last century. They ignored the very existence of such dynamic exchanges between distant lands that prevailed during the course of two centuries on the maritime route from China to Taprobana and Mylapore. This route did not go directly to Muziris as archeological digs show us. This explains the place of the same Chinese names in the account of Thomas's martyrdom as in the entire second Chinese part of the Acts.

This also shows the disintegration of the ancient Aramaic ties by land, not between China and Ferghana (in present day Kirgizstan) but between Israel and China by the land route from Nineveh and Bactra. This tends to prove that Chinese traditions of the second pendant could not have been compiled via land route or in Maishan after its reestablishment in the second half of the second century but from the mouth of Thomas himself settled in Mylapore before it was brought via Muziris to Maishan. These Chinese traditions prior to the end of the restoration of communications by land through the path of Pamir could not be confirmed in the third century during the reign of Wei, the prosecutors of Christians on the Silk route that had become more complex due to it annexed by the Kushans.

After that the two traditions of Kerala and Mylapore had been joined together, we can no longer have doubts on both of them due to the standards of the Chinese tradition attested by the imperial Han chronicles. Our present-day historical knowledge on the East can no longer make it possible to accept their displacement to late Edessa; however, the same does not apply to their late Greek translation. There could be no other collection of ancient legendary traditions that was so amply documented on the missions to the Parthian empire on the northwestern outskirts of India even if we forget the key role played by Maishan, which the texts of the Acts cite on several occasions.

The decisive help of the emperor Ming-di's vision that made possible the apostle's mission to his capital at Luoyang, could not have reached us from the accounts in later documents that are less informed on the subject. It is only attested by the providential assistance attributed to Siphur that this "general" sent on the orders of the Chinese emperor provided to Thomas. The absolute consistency of the accounts results from the emperor's wish to comprehend this Arrival of the Messiah that the Chinese auguries announced and that were bolstered by the Hebrews present at the imperial court. It was certainly of great importance to the flow of silk and other products from the empire that were being traded via maritime and steppe routes since the closure of old roads passing through Taklamakan and the Pamir.

A SUMMARY OF THE PROBABLE FINAL DRAFT HARMONIZING THE TWO PARTS OF THE ACTS

It is evident from the start that the five pendants forming the ensemble are the first volume in fifty pearls and its addition with its new central part and its new linkage to the second part of seventy pearls. This first volume narrating the traditions of the apostle already told us of a specific feminine attitude that existed in the early second century at the latest, and provides us with a valuable account on the feminine involvement in the Life of the Early Church. However, there is also the second part of the *Acts* that could have included three dates for the three remaining parts of the *Acts of Thomas* once it is separated from the necklace in five pendants compiled in the initial works below:

— one for the part between the texts numbering from 82 to 161 that includes ten additional pendants but only seven pearls, we once again have 70 pearls or texts.

— then one conclusion that is a pendant in the style of the first part in exactly the same form in ten pearls as the pendants. This ellipsis has for the goal to cover the sermons between the beginning of Thomas's missions in 69 and his death in the year 72 by combining additions to the second part in order to provide a common conclusion as to his martyrdom.

Finally, we can remark that one can extract from this pendant parts 3, 4, and 10 that are added to the seven other parts comprise a specific ensemble with a Madrasha of twenty-one praises to the Glory of the Father and of the Son, form a typically Mesopotamian conclusion in homage of the apostle, a *hutama* (the final blessing) added at the very end to the middle of each of the two parts of the texts compiling the accounts given by the disciples of Judas-Thomas that were written down in Maishan. Similarity that exist between this Madrasha and the "Madrasha of the Pearl Necklaces (Marganitha)" or of the general dogma of the Good News (Suartha) clearly points out the contributions most likely originating from the volumes of texts copied or adapted from the writings of the apostle himself.

In order to more easily understand its place in the timeline of writings and witness accounts, we must first take the final pendant in ten short pearls and put it together with the other events that took place in India. Its lack of dates as to the return from China to Mylapore has made the combining of the two at the end of Thomas's missions (in China) necessary in order to understand the assortment of characters and facts in this pendant on the martyrdom. Facts, it seems, ignored by the author who wrote the conclusion of the *Acts*. Without this distinction we can better understand the combining of facts into one conclusion that includes his martyrdom and a later miracle. This is clearly an addition to the 70 pearls of the first part that has been analyzed here above; however, we must observe that it comes in keeping with the rules of the Mesopotamian oral tradition that did not allow going back within the narrative. Of course the structure of this text changes to eleven pearls but its analysis shows that this addition was made in accordance to the mode in ten pearls of the first part that would have had to be reduced to seven if it had been written without the knowledge of the first part or would have had a different content, if it was initially a part of its seven pendants in ten basic pearls.

THE PART OF THE ADDITIONAL PENDANT RECOUNTING THE
MARTYRDOM OF THE APOSTLE

It is developed as a witness account in ten pearls:

XVIII (161–170)

1 (161) Judas-Thomas in prison;

2 (162) where it appears that Judas has gone through the closed doors to preach to the woman outside of prison;

3 (163) Trial where he repeats the Name of Jesus the Messiah;

4 (164) The king takes him to the mount to be transpierced;

5 (165) he gives thanks to the God and professes his faith in God the source of life;

6 (166) having ascended the mount he once again professes his faith;

7 (167) he prays for the king and his son and tells "My Lord and my God" and one last prayer;

8 (168) he then calls the soldiers, they transpierced him with lances;

9 (169) Judas appears after his death and to encourage in faith those he has ordained;

10 (170) through the contact with his relics the king is seized by remorse and wishes to cure his sick son but there is only dust from his tomb that exorcises the king's son who converts (171) a conclusion or *hutama*: "The acts of Judas Thomas who was the apostle of Jesus Christ and was massacred in India . . ."; some manuscripts end with *hutama*-eulogy to the apostle more or less developed in Aramaic.

This conclusion presents a problem, it becomes incomprehensible if we confuse the monarch of Mylapore with the one to whom Siphur took the apostle from Taprobana in the pendant VII of the first necklace, unless we situate the ten pendants in Mylapore. Moreover, it is clear that the final form is in ten parts while we observe that the martyrdom of the apostle Judas could have been provided in first seven pearls. The text numbered as 168 is very short and could have been included in the 167th; we remark that in the final count of the necklaces *hutama* (171) is generally the last of the more or less developed pearls. We can also note that the cure by dust from the collected blood of the martyr is included in the pilgrimage tradition to Mylapore that could not have come from China before his martyrdom or during the reign of Zhangdi (75-88), son and heir of Mengdi who ascended to the throne in 75. As we will see in the course of the analysis of ten pendants in the second part that confusion as to the events in China in 71 and those in Mylapore in 72, both seen from Maishan, is possible.

Historical information provided in the seventy texts of the second necklace numbered 82 to 161, concerning five people from different nations encountered by the apostle in China during his mission in the years 65 to 68 that appear in the Acts are then further cited in this last pendant. What's more, text 169, of the conclusion in the second part appears to be associated with the name of Migdonia, according to the wish of the apostle and Migdonia:

> "When they (king Mazdaï and Karish his relation) perceived that they (Migdonia and Tertia, their wives) obeyed them not, suffered them to live according to the wishes of their soul."

This is how for the first time, in a text of the Early Church in keeping with the wishes of Jesus, women are clearly given the freedom to choose their path to God, this freedom of faith also apparent in the oral Christian tradition of Kerala.

In 170 we remark the following phrase: "Mazdaï went and opened the sepulcher, but he found not the bones of Judas there, for one of the brethren had stolen[67] and taken them to the West." This could only mean the preservation of the relics during the persecutions against Christians in Mylapore in the second and third centuries their conservation in Mesopotamia in Nineveh, and their subsequent departure via Armenia, Nisbis and Edessa (with a fifty-year stay at the School of Edessa from 362-410) to the island of Chios near Ephesus and Smyrna and then under the Mongols to Italy. Is it only then that the Roman canon "elevates" Thomas just after James and John? And in the East appear the images of Christ in the company of Peter and Thomas? Peter is represented carrying the book of Gospels and Thomas with Jesus, who is holding the apostle by his hand so he could touch his side. This is how the texts of the *Acts* are being complimented by both art and liturgy in the East.

This however does not make them date later than the information received in the Parthian empire from India and China, but merely shows that the ties with the East were still maintained in Chaldea, even after it was written down and complied always following the mnemonic numerical rules of Mesopotamian tradition that was unknown to the authors using the linear Greek method. It is important to confirm in this last text that religious freedom going all the way to the imperial family was a part of the Han culture at its zenith in the first century.

Let us also note that the Parthian name Migdonia draws a clear parallel with Magdalena-Magdaleita, the evangelical Magdalene who instructed widows during her mission in Gaul that took place at the same time as that of Thomas's in China, just like the echo in the cave of Kong Wang Shan parallels that in Sainte Baume.

In order to better comprehend the confusion made in Chaldea, one must look at the two Chinese chronicles concerning the people holding functions at the court of the Chinese emperor Mingdi (57-75) and who are represented on the Chinese frieze sculpted no later than three years before the martyrdom of Thomas. Here we have the first century representations unparalleled elsewhere, that can corroborate the second part of the *Acts* as well as these two long Chinese chronicles of the Han.[68] Spotting them among the hundreds of figures engraved in granite of Kong Wang Shan does not present a problem.[69] To this day, we possess no other similar historically datable example confirmed by the Chinese archeological excavations thoroughly conducted by the archeologists from the University of Beijing that allows to identify the images of the Chinese personalities from the second half of the first century as well as a bearded missionary in liturgical vestments surrounded by a total of over twenty objects exclusively of Judeo-Christian origin. Since all the confusion with Buddhism was excluded by the conclusions of the second archeological research by the University of Beijing[70] we now possess a framework for the mission in India that has been described by these excavations, the *Acts*, as well as by the Greek manuscript Oxyrhynchos 413 dating to the first half of the second century.

None of the above could be applied to the last missions of the apostle in India, if we are unaware of the incapacity of all those who compiled the scenes described in the ten pendants to establish a real timeline for the three and a half year mission in Chine beyond the initial account on the process of missionary instruction to be respected, certain events and people, provided by the apostle himself just before his death and the persecution of Wang Ying (the princely brother not the son of the emperor) in 72 in China[71] and that of Thomas, transpierced by lances in the east of India at the end of the same year on the twenty-first of Kisleu of 72[72] according to the oral accounts of travelers, probably merchants, all speaking in Aramaic. The final form under which this pendant in ten pearls was added to the text of the initial seven pendants had to remain centered on problems of the apostle who wished to ensure the perpetuity of the catechistic tradition after his departure by confiding it to women more apt to pass it on to their children and loved ones as did Virgin Mary until her Assumption.

However, the arrival to Jerusalem for the Assumption represents the return to Israel outside "old Jewish sabbatical year" but it is still in keeping with the half septennial gaps in the timeline suggested to Daniel by Gabriel that corresponds to the Easter of 30. The journey must have taken place via Maishan (as is recalled in the Canticle of the Pearl)[73] same as the arrival of the relics that left Mylapore during the wars of the second and third centuries in India. All that for a rather simple reason, the facility of travel between Maishan, Muziris, and Taprobana as can be demonstrated on all the maps of the East as well as by the artifacts discovered at these ports.[74]

And yet at the time when the great Alexandria of Egypt hid the forest of Alexandrias in the Parthian empire, there were also researchers who imagined a passage from Alexandria in Egypt to India (to begin with Nödeke who nevertheless jutted down the old Aramaic of the Hymn) and even the arrival of the relics to Edessa via Alexandria without passing through Nineveh.

This arrival of limited duration in Edessa, (some fifty years) was due to violent persecutions of Christians as far as Nisbis, it preceded the refuge on the Ionian island of Chios and then in Ortona in 1258. In 1566, Turks destroyed the tomb without touching the relics that have been preserved to this day.

After arriving from Maishan, they probably remained in Nineveh (where a part of them is still kept)for over a century, before their larger part was taken via Armenia and Edessa to the sanctuary in Italian mountains, away from prosecution; an itinerary with no relation to the land of the authors or the collectors of traditions that traveled from the East to the shores of the Indian Ocean that compose the *Acts of Thomas*.

It is the number of nationalities and ports located beyond the passage through the Strait of Malacca that explain the disconnection of the Indian and the Chinese compilations. We observe the loss of historical Chinese context in favor of a simplified version based on conversions of women starting with the wife and daughter of Siphur, the wife of Karish and the ladies at the imperial court. This compilation follows the same direction as that of "Indian missions" primarily centered on future conveyers of the Good News from one generation to another, hence–women. This is clearly present in the Chinese tradition where women, who often escape the persecution, ensure its continuity through word and specific information provided today by archeological excavations.

Observations of the additional necklace in ten pendants and Thomas's mission in China

This is a summary of archeological research conducted on several occasions between 1980 and 2010 and finally dated by Chinese archeologists to be consistent with the Han chronicles to the first century in Haizu, an ancient imperial port on the sea of China with the three times the traffic of those on the Mediterranean. Kong Wang Shan hill confirm datation 65-70 C.E. of the complete site and truly bears the name of the Prince Ying. Today the site is accessible in Lianyungang in the Shanghai. The report on excavations and historical texts allow to see the importance of these discoveries, their dating and value are available in Chinese language only for archeology and in translation for the main texts.[75]

The arrival of the Chinese boat[76] to take Thomas to China, dates, names (see below) that coincide even better than for the mission to king Gondophares where there is no historical documentation. While we know there is a translated Chinese copy of religious texts brought to China by SchliheMoten and ShoufarLan (Aramaic names misspelled in Chinese of our Apostle and Siphur) and offered to the emperor for his approval in 67.

In China, archeologists have finally abandoned the initial Buddhist hypotheses in view of textual evidence and sculptures, but Chinese authorities prefer to attribute it all, dated and described by reliefs to "pre-Taoism" (no Taoism before the fourth century). So, the accurate attribution is left to the Westerners.[77] The file contains over twenty clearly Judeo-Christian references.

Political issues are considerable because they mark a major contribution to the first great culture of the Han Empire before its zenith and a clearer recognition would become grave matter as in the conclusion of the previous chapter on freedom of faith.

This is not a place to detail the second part of the *Acts* here. It is enough for the Saint Thomas Christians to know that while it does not directly concern them, its development in ten pendants of seven pearls and the appeal to woman for evangelization in the second necklace are the inversion of the first part in seven pendants for ten texts. This is due to the same author or possibly his successor's attempt to echo the first part in the second: there is the possession conversions and of a married couple, the Hebrew general of Chinese army, turned translator for Thomas whose wife and daughter are exorcised and converted then a princely couple and two married women forced to fight for their faith in a society closely controlled by men.

Here is the general pattern:

VIII/1 68–70 the voyage of Judas and Siphur pushed by the winds: needed confidence;

IX /2 71–81 exorcism of demons, preaching on Beatitude, Praises

X /3 82–90 Migdonia, sermon on humility, offer of Peace;

XI /4 91–98 Migdonia's conversion, felicity of small ones, dispute with Karish;

XII /5   99–107   Karish complains to Mazdaï, arrest of Siphur, Thomas is flagellated;

+++++++HYMN and PRAISES++++++++++

XIII /6   114–121   dispute with Karish, Migdonia's husband; Mygdonia's Rushma;

XIV /7   122–130   Dispute and Judas on trial for persuading Mygdonia and Tertia;

XV /8   131–141   Conversion of Mazdaï's wife, failure/ Judas' trial by fire;

XVI /9   142–148 imprisoned Judas Hymn and long Prayer for the imprisoned with him;

XVII/10   149–160   Rushmafor Mazdaï's son and his cured wife_

Siphur (trumpet or royal squire–shofar in Chinese = Greek and Aramaic–shiphur) with a wife and a daughter (in Chinese a general heading military expedition to the Parthian kingdom); translator–the trumpet, a Chinese of Aramaic origin: a Hebrew from Wusun (Ferghana kingdom ruled by a Hebrew king from Manasseh tribe).[78]

Migdonia, the wife of Karish Chinese—in Aramaic from Mygdonia (a mix of Macedonean macdonita with magdalaita from Magdala as in Mary Magdalene).

There is also a problem with the name of Mingdi's son who ruled as Zhangdi in 75-88; but the half-brother of Mingdi is Prince Liu Ying, both sons to Wudi, the founder of the East Han dynasty in Luoyang; this creates confusion between Wizan and Wang (prince) Ying married to Mannasar the Hebrew princess of Ferghana. Karish apparently wanted to assassinate him as a follower of a foreign religion. Prince Ying was forced to commit suicide by his half-brother Mingdi in 71 because having converted to Christianity; he financed the construction of cathedral and the frieze in Haizhou. Possibly in Maishan, his[79] relation to the emperor and his martyrdom in 71 were somewhat confused with that of Schlihe Thomas.

This factual link could only be established after the unwilling reattribution to Christianity made by Chinese archeologists (stopping at "pre-Taoism" in their official reports). We now have history backed up by facts, little modified by phonetic translation in two important passages from Han chronicles and later texts arbitrarily attributed to Buddhism that had to wait two centuries before being compiled under the Wei.

Details of excavations in Haizhou and Kong Wang Shan hill that bears the name of the prince who built the monuments mentioned in the archeological reports provided in reference.[80]

It must be underlined that today this is the biggest archeological site in the world attesting to apostolic mission in the years 65–70 and it was conducted by Thomas from his base in southern India as of 52. Its history is well dated and documented in numerous Chinese texts if we want to expose lesser facts based on partial Western[81] accounts limited to non-Christian authors.

Here we solely point to the historical characters attested in imperial Han chronicles and whose portraits are on the frieze engraved into the granite hillside of Kong Wang Shan. The second half of the *Acts of Thomas* presents well attested historical characters that can be identified among the 107 figures of the Chinese frieze. It conserves the memory on the main stages of Thomas's mission in China and contains the scenes of Christ, Nativity, an image of *qubala* and *qurbana*, and the gift of the translated copy of the Gospels to the emperor in 67. Most importantly it conserves the image of Thomas witnessing the piercing in the side of Christ by a centurion, and another one worn and less visible of his hand in the wound of the resurrected Christ. Moreover, there exist few variations in the oral Aramaic tradition:

We can then indicate the difference in the interpretations of pendant XVI (162–171) concerning the martyrdom of Thomas. There is a false link confusing Mylapore in India with Luoyang in China the capital of the emperor Ming-di and the two martyrdoms close in time but taking place in different locations;

In 71	In 72
Prince Wang Ying disciple of Judas-Thomas	Apostle Judas-Thomas
In exile from Luoyang, China	chased from Mylapore in India
Condemned to poison himself by Mingdi	Pierced by lance by Mazdaï
While his son the future Zhangdi converts	while the son of Mazdaï is cured by his relics
(when Thomas converts Siphur Wang zun)[82]	(the name of Mazdaï's son converted by Judas is Wizan)

The author of the pendant on martyrdom oblivious to geography confuses the persecution of prince Ying and the first Christians in China with that in India.[83] As a result the Greek translation would create the conviction in the West that the *Acts of Thomas* do not mention the mission in China or existence of the Chinese church in the first century that does not correspond to the position of the leaders of Mesopotamian Church that maintained strong ties with Chinese metropolitans.

In this situation we must examine why eastern texts have maintained that the "madrasha of the pearl necklace" in Aramaic or The Hymn of the Pearl of Matt 13:46 was composed by Thomas in his Mylapore prison. This is what is suggested in the five pendants that comprise the second part of the Acts! To understand this, we must study this hymn again, as they say in the West.

HYMN OF THE PEARL AND GLORY TO THE FATHER COMBINED WITH PRAISE TO THE SON

Hymn of the Pearl is typical by its Old Aramaic without Hellenized Syriac variations of the fourth century, something that was first noticed by Nöldeke and by the number of ancient Persian and Sogdian words pointing to a Parthian-speaker and the reestablishment of the Post-Seleucid Palestine in the Mesopotamian culture of the first century. There is also a strong implication of Parthian world in the Judeo-Christian culture.[84] Moreover, the West ignores that its oral compositions is so "countable."

Let us then start by enumerating the texts (as in the Aramaic verb matmat, hence the Greek mathematics). The text consists of 52 double pitgamés designed to be recited and meditated, probably on the first day of each week. It is composed of five sub-necklaces or pendants that give us:

	I 1-20 (20v)	II 21-40 (20v)	III 41-65 (25v)	IV 66-85 (20v)	V 86-105 (20v)
East /3	3	1	2	-	-
Pearl /8	(unique)	3	3	-	1
Letter /4	-	1	3	-	-
Voice /5	-	-	3	-	2
Splendid vestment	2+toge	-	1+toge	1+toge	
Door /2	-	-	-	1	1
Father/son /9	1	/3	3	2	2
Second/brother /3	-	-	1/1	1	
Mother/child /4	2	-	2	-	
Roi/royaume /13	2	1	4/1	2	3/1
Egypt/Egyptian /8	2	3	3	-	-
Snake /3	1	1	1	-	-
Liturgy /11	1	-	2	3	5
Dream/awakening /14	-	2	9	1	2

This frequency table shows a five-step progression of selected themes in fourteen key words highlighted by the recitation of the verse. We have clear guidance (this is not a Gnostic or heretical teaching) seemingly used by Thomas to remember what he had learned on his pilgrimage to Jerusalem on the traces of Jesus: reliving the Holy Week close to his Lord and God, in the course of 3 septennials, he would lead the quest for "the sense to find" (madrasha) in what is called the Hymn of the Pearl in five parts of four to five verses.

Hutama does not reveal the sense of the hymn, instead calling it a *madrasha*—a text to help understand the deeper sense based on evocations from the Scriptures. What is the connection between "Marganitha" –Pearl and the Scriptures, if madrasha is an explanation through comparison and a link (shri)? The sense is clear in Aramaic similar to Babylonian. First, it's not one pearl; there is repetition and a model to follow to reveal the glow—the rgâ, from the ensemble of existing discourses—ithâ, like pearls out of water reveal their "glow": Who is now beside the Father and the Son if not Mary, Mother of her son's Church? The middle of *Madrasha* tells: "That which comes from Your Father . . . ." It is a recitation to understand (*madrasha* (ma = do, explain and derash = explain (*midrash* in Hebrew), at its center the unmasking of the Evil one and the ancient Ophra of Benjamin's tribe where Jesus retires before the Passions, a place near the desert where he was tempted and Thomas prepares to die with Jesus John 11:16).

"That which comes from Your Father the King and your Mother Queen of the East and your brother our second" (in Thrinity) (M41). For Thomas on his arrival to Jerusalem, Mary is exalted in Heavens with the Father and the Son, but the text assures that she is now the Queen of the East by blood (Madrasha 60), the King's mother who can relay his requests thus the Queen of his missions. She made the holy vestments such as the weaving at the Temple, at home she as embled the Gospel necklaces and left them divide in Four Karozualthâ as well as the canonical form of Liturgy in word, speech, and ornaments.

Thomas explains to himself, that he is not to offer in the valley of Indus and its estuary (same Aramaic word for Nile valley and that of Indus) the deliverance to all the possessed as he did in Pattala that prevented his sermons. Meanwhile in Zion, instructions needed for establishing of Churches were being finished, given the final form in four texts that he understood since he recognized the living word of Jesus. Thus, the liturgical catechism, that Thomas was to spread in the East, had been completed.

The fifth verse repeated by Thomas to analyze his past and future missions, since he is to follow the spiritual process as a reinterpretation of the first three septennials of mission after the Pentecost: he first dons cheif of the priests' vestments of his tribe received from the Lord, and analogy to those actually given to Ephraim the third year, now openly celebrated in the capitals of the Nations. Then the high priest vestments he is to don among the Eastern nations appears more clearly, they are in three layers like those of cheif of the priests but bearing the sign of a cross and embroidered with its image (mad. 86) with tokens in precious stones from different tribes and nations (mad 82–85) on the outside a chasuble gown in silk embroidered in gold and inside in purple like the heart and like three fabrics from the Holy of Holies in the Temple torn from the top to bottom as by Christ on the Cross. Here Thomas must realize that he is "in Persona Christi" (mad. 78) in the Qurbana Canon (mad 105) to approach and touch the Body and the Blood of the new People of God in the Nations of the East.

What is extraordinary in this progressive revelation of the meaning in *"Madrasha* of Pearl Necklaces" is that it can now explain the part of catechism (mad 102-103) and of *qurbana* liturgy engraved on the frieze of Kong Wang Shan and in the plan of the cathedral discovered by the archeological excavations in China (Cf. below). We can ask the following question: was this *madrasha* composed by Thomas, recited to his Indian and Chinese disciples turned priests to explain the liturgical tradition arrived from Jerusalem in 51 and to be used as the example?[85]

Hymn of the Pearl (108-113) and Teshbon'thâ to the Glory of the Father and the Son (Act 113B ref 1 to 1-21 and 22-24) could find their true place in the completed *madrashâ* as already composed texts. As we have suggested their place is essential but now, we see them as clarified and sacralized when this madrasha and praises are inserted in pendant IV and between pendants XII and XIII and bringing the Chinese mission necklace to eleven pendants.

It is developed in five parts as a parallel to the Eastern oral tale where the apostle goes looking for the Pearl (mentioned eight times) fighting the Snake (mentioned three times) on two occasions, first time followed by sleep, then in a letter urging his return (mentioned 3 times) encouraging to resume the quest for the Pearl and receive "splendid vestments" given as a reward (mentioned four times) for being received at the Heavenly Gates that are the Tent of Holy of the Holies where *Qurbana*-Meeting takes place.

However, the Hymn of Glory and Praise repeats an ensemble of additional Glories to the Father and Praises to the Son 21 times amassing the qualifiers for the one and the other in reciprocity of both qualities repeated three times, dependent on the five qualities recited twice and five qualities pronounced once that provides the echoing shimmer over the twenty-one repetitions of the praise.

These two very Mesopotamian plays on "orality"[86]were most likely composed separately earlier on or so the second among them could be included in the end as an additional pendant into the big necklace in ten pendants of ten pearls with an aim to recall the features of successive missions of the apostle.

But it is the enormous necklaces of seventy pearls that should draw the attention of researchers wishing to reconstruct missions of the Early Church. The first is more important because more ancient and because the real story on the first preachings in China shows this later collection provides examples on initial conversions of women while omitting the more general context that the author ignored. Today, historical research should allow us to better reconstruct the specifics.

These are common specifications wished by Jesus during his missions that the Twelve and the Seventy-two learned by his side while he was preaching to twelve tribes of Israel and relayed to their Diasporas and all the lands in Eurasia and its confines. Today they are also serving as important example for reestablishing the new foundations. We will note in particular the catechistic necklace of Barnaby and Saul compiled by Luke 14:31–33[87] allowing us to learn the form that Paul's sermon took in the Acts of the Apostles.

FINAL PATTERN IN PROBABLE COMPOSITION OF ACTS

Could be thus resumed (in typically Babylonian calculation)

a	I	II	III	IV	V	VI	VII				
b	10	10	10	5	10	10	10				
c			(+MM/HP 12345)								
d	VIII	IX	X	XI	XII	L XIII	XIV	XV	XVI	XVII	
e	7	7	7	7	7	7	7	7	7	7	
f											XVIII-11
g											L 10?

In a: first septennial;
In b: length of pearls except the central 5
In the first septennial (lines a-b) composed around the hymn to the Pearl
(line c in 5 pendants identified from 1 to 5) completing to 10 le pendant IV.
Then composed centering on praise (= L; en 5 petites parties)
The 2 necklaces of 10 pendants in 7 pearls (d-e), then the martyrdom (lines f-g),
bringing the total to 17+ one pendant or 18 pendants and 150 pearls.

Proposed conclusions on dating and composition of different parts of the Acts

The progress made in history of evangelization in the East of Roman Empire and identification of procedures in composition of Mesopotamian oral tradition and oral validation in *qanone* prior to written recorded conservation have renewed modern dating criteria. This resulted in initial oral compositions in Imperial Aramaic being conserved in written documents more recent than oral compositions. These are major testaments to go before the tribunals, especially the Great Jerusalem Tribunal. The only ones to be accepted are those of oral recollection since they maintain the capacity for narration by heart without omissions or repetitions and variations before the tribunal and its scribes who immediately produce written records for all future comparison that is what was observed with the texts of the Early Church.[88]

For the older part of the first seventy pearls in these Acts, the oral Aramaic form, and its account on missions in India done in Aramaic from the ports of Southern India bring together the compilation and elaboration of the first long necklace in Aramaic sustained by Scriptures and the Peshitta of the four Gospels. Prat-Maishan based on oral narration, was composed by female authors, probably widows, in the Persian Gulf, judging by importance given to purity of heart and body. This dates the first necklace to the times of Catholikos Abraham of Kashgar and his successors between 160 and 201 at the latest, and the end of reign of the Christian King Gondophares at the earliest, around 70s. An additional pendant on the martyrdom being filled with mistakes confusing China and eastern India, suggesting that communication for verifications had seized that situates them earlier than persecution of Indian Christians and earlier than the end of Han, well before the beginning of Wei or the end of the second century.

The reception of martyr's relics must correspond to persecutions in Mylapore around the same time prior to those of Shapur II in 240. But there is no connection between the journey of relics saved in Mylapore and the texts of *Acts* addressing catechetical and liturgical issues concerning the church in Kerala and China by identifying congregations founded by Thomas between 52 and 68. On the other hand the incorrect elements leading to confusion between Thomas and Ying suggest accounts of disciples near Thomas commenting on his Chinese mission before his death and carrying both accounts first from Mylapore to Kerala and from Miziris to Maishan spreading false information. Destruction of Jerusalem also halts pilgrimages in the course of sabbatical years 75 and 82 but not the maritime ties.

We can then place the compiling and writing of two parts to the end of the first century at the latest for the first and beginning of the second century for the accounts coming from China corresponding to activity of Mari and Abres (121–137) or received as of Christian generations instructed by the seventy-two, chosen by Jesus himself and by circles close to the younger 500 disciples. Probably, the second necklace in seventy pearls should date to the same period, but the oral plays in the two last texts (madrasha and praises) could have only been composed before or after 159 at the latest either closer to the revolt of Babylonian Jews around 135, or Roman repressions between 137 and 159 and not under Mar Papa in 317–329. The transfer of the relics of the apostle to Armenia, Edessa and Italy is indicated too late around 320, after the prosecutions of Shapur II and must correspond to the great Sassanid persecution in 350–363.

To recap there is no other possibility outside of the first part being composed and relayed by the nuns of a "widow's house" in Maishan later or during mar Abres (121–137), same as for accounts on the martyrdom, with vaguer echoes on foundation of the church in China at the latest under Abraham of Kashkar (159–171) and possibly before due to amazing homogeneity in the ending of two parts.

SPECIAL THANKS

It was with particular pleasure that we have participated in this international conference on the Saint Thomas Christians that was based on the historical approach. This conference directly touches on this work by this particular group of French researchers as well as on the new Indian and Chinese works that own a particular debt to the impulsion provided by Father Lagrange in Jerusalem and especially by Cardinal Tisserant. For one century in-depth studies have been conducted in Rome and in France on the Eastern Churches of the Roman Empire, long time ignored by Catholic and Orthodox Churches as well as by multiple Protestant denominations. Today, they are still sidelined, however they are the ones to have kept the tradition of Jerusalem alive more so than the local Greek churches that only crave for intellectual preeminence tied to the Roman authority after Constantine before being defeated by other powers. However, there remains the western fascination for the intellectual activity requiring unbreakable attachment to what is real, so as to prevent the creation of new ideologies or impose the methods of thought to other churches of different culture or civilization. The success of western inventors of industrialized societies, much richer and more efficient was responsible for allowing many of our intellectuals to impose much less attainable ideologies than the system for producing goods and services (supply of energy, transportation, or healthcare or games and spectacles).

In what concerns religion, there are the anti-religious or amoral pressures, the refusal to consider different spiritual paths, or values that challenge habits and customs shared in the West[89] especially when this proves suitable. This was not the case for the Eastern Churches that take their root in Judeo-Christianity born of apostolic sermons or those by the first generation of 500 outside the Greco-Latin culture, and nourished by the very wise Mesopotamian civilization, and Hebraic culture. In the West, what was missing is the anthropology of oral tradition and the ternary human decision-making involving the compassionate vision of She'ol and the theology that would encompass the mysteries, according to an expression coming directly from its Judeo-Christian apostolic sources, traditions went straight with the apostolic missions. These missionaries to the East of which apostle Thomas mystically was and is the most extraordinary representative.

Cardinal Alencherry and Patriarch Catholikos Sako are today the leading figures of two churches—one in full missionary vigor and the another more than ever suffering its passions and attempting to revive with the remaining fragments of its civilization and Judeo-Christian culture despite the destructive will that has slowly reduced the congregation of the faithful compared to what it used to be during its incomparable medieval expansion.

We, the French determined to quickly establish the truth in the relativist, even decadent world, are working toward the revival of the burning faith firmly soundly set on Truth–Shrarâ of the church that has for two centuries refused its death, often and only from the inside. Recently we have been experiencing its revival in many places. It is still tentative but it is growing, relying on the past rich in saints—our examples for reaching out to the hearts of our contemporaries who are being drowned in a world, both too rich and too poor in spirit. We are becoming visible to all the "little ones" who are still a majority in France and do not yet know that they only have to unite and join that which is in the process of reborn everywhere with Mary.

BIBLIOGRAPHY

The group of French researchers

G1   Lagrange J-M., *La méthode historique,* Paris 1904

G2   Tisserant E., "L'Eglise nestorienne ," Dict. de Théologie catholique, XI, 1930

G3   Jousse M., *La Parole le Parlant et le Souffle,* Gallimard ed. 1976

G4   Jousse M., *Dernières dictées,* Assoc. Jousse ed 1999 (à paraître en anglais en 2à18

G5   Daniélou J., *Théologie du Judeo-christianisme,* 1966

G6   Khoury-Sarkis G., "Projet de restauration de la liturgie de Jérusalem,» *Orient syrien,* X–1965

G7   Dauvillier J. *Les provinces chaldéennes "de l'extérieur ,"* ÌC Toulouse 1948

G8   Dauvillier J. *Les temps apostoliques au premier siècle,* Sitray 1968

G9   Alichoran F. *Missel chaldéen, histoire de l'Eglise de l'Orient,* Concordia ed. 1982

G10 Monier P., *Conversations et paraboles* 1968

G11 Perrier P., *Karozoutha,* Mediaspaul 1986

G12 Perrier P., "Structures orales de la Pshytta,» Or chr. Analecta, 236, 1990

G13 Perrier P. *Les colliers évangéliques,* ed Jubilé 2003

G14 Perrier P., *KWS l'apôtre Thomas et le prince Ying,* Jubiléed, 2012

G15 Charbonnier J.–Perrier P.–Moreau R.–Ramelli I.–Xi-lin D. – Yevadian M., *L'apôtre Thomas et le christianisme en Asie colloque AED 2013.*

G16 Perrier P., *L'Evangile de la Miséricorde,* E.auC. ed. 2015

G17 Perrier P., *L'Evangile pour les petits,* Jubilé ed., to appear in 2018

G18 Perrier P. *L'Evangile de l'oral à l'écrit,* Jubilé ed. 2000

G19 Walter X et Perrier P. *Thomas fonde l'Eglise en Chine 65-68* Jubilé ed. 2008

Works in English (or accesible in English) with open vision in late 20th century

E1   Amphoux C. and C. Parker, Codex BezaeStudiesfrom the Lunel colloquium, Leyde, 1994

E2   Amphoux C., L'Evangile selon les hébreux source de l'Evangile de Luc, Apocrypha,1995.

E3   Bie Buyk D., The words of the Land teaching through proverbs, E.J. Brill 1996

E4   Black M., An aramaicapproach to the gospels and acts, Oxford UniversityPress 1967

E5   Bagatti B., La communitagiudeo-cristiniane, Libr. Ed. Vaticana 1981

E6   Bagatti B., Alleoriginidellachiesa,Lib . Ed. Vaticana 1982

E7 Edersheim A., The life and times of Jésus the Messiah, Hendrick –son pub. 1995

E8 Fitzmeyer J., A wandering Aramean, Missoula ed, 1979

E9 Gerhardsson B., Tradition and transmission in Earlychristhianity Coniectana Neo-Test. XX, Copenhagen 1964

E10 Hambye E.R., "St. Thomas in India," The Clergymonthly, XVI

E11 Hausen K. Oakman D., "The Galilean Fishing Economy and Jesus tradition," BTB-1997

E12 Mancini I., Archeological discoveries franciscan, Printing press, 1984

E13 Metzger B., The early versions of the New Testament, Oxford University Press, 1977

E14 Robinson J., Redating the New Testament, SCM Press, 1981

E15 Schmala R. Fisher R., The messianicseal of the Jerusalemchurch, Tiberiade, 1999

E16 Schürer E, The history of the jewish people in the age of Jesus-Christ I-II Clark ed, 1979

E17 Testa E., La fededella Chiesa Madre di Gerusalemme, Dehoniane 1995

E18 Zimmermann F., The aramaïcorigin of the four gospels, Ktav Pub. 1979

E19 Bagatti B., The Church from the circoncision Franciscan, Printing Press, Jerusalem, 1984

E20 Lagerwey J., Religion and Chinese Society, EEFO Hong Kong, 2004

E21 Kelber W. The Case of the Gospels: Memory 's Desireand Limits of HistoricalCriticism, vol 17, Issue 1 2002

E22 Kelber W. The oral and Written Gospel Indiana University, 1983

Basic book in English for sound analysis of the Aramean Oral composition referred to Marcel Jousse's work is referred in JM with comprehensive french bibliography in JM 1 p.401 and usual Fench publication JM 2

JM1 Jousse, The Anthropology of Geste and Rhythm, translated from french by Prof. Sinaert E. of Univ. of Natal, Center of oral studies Durban South Africa, 1997.

JM2 Marcel Jousse, L'Anthropologie du Geste, Gallimard ed. Paris 1974.

Basic books of publication and analysis of the available manuscripts of the *Acts of Thomas* referred AT1 et AT2 in English and AT3 in French

AT1 Wright, W, Apocryphal Acts of the Apostles, (syriac and english translation), London, 1871, 2 vol.

AT2 Lewis, Agnes Smith, Acta Mythologica Apostolorum, Collection Horae Semiticae, III, London, 1904

AT3 Poirier, Paul-Hubert, L'Hymne de la Perle des Actes de Thomas, Introduction, texte, traduction, commentaire, Louvain-la-Neuve. Centre d'histoire des religions, 1981, 462. Coll. Homo religions; Louvain 1980.

Apocryphal literature

Armenians apocryphals, ed. Č'rak'ean, 1904: Č'rak'eanK'ervpē, (*Écrits apostoliques non-canoniques)*, Venise, ed. Mekhitariste, 1904.

Armenians apocryphals, tr. Leloir, 1986-1992: Leloir Louis dom, *Écrits apocryphes sur les apôtres, traduction de l'édition arménienne de Venise*, Turnhout, Brepols, CC, series Apocryphorum, 3 et 4, 1986-1992.

Calzolari, 2011: Valentina Calzolari, *Les Apôtres Thaddée et Barthélemy, aux origines du christianisme arménien*, Turnhout, Brepols, Collection: "Apocryphes no 13,» 2011.

Christian apocryphalwritings, I, 1997: Bovon François et Geoltrain Pierre (dir.), *Écrits apocryphes chrétiens, I [sélection d'écrits apocryphes sur Jésus et Marie, sur Jean-Baptiste et les apôtres, et des visions et révélations]*, Paris, Gallimard, "Bibliothèque de la Pléiade no 442,» 1997.

Christian apocryphalwritings, II, 2005: Geoltrain Pierre et Jean-Daniel Kaestli, *Écrits apocryphes chrétiens II, Contient une sélection d'écrits apocryphes sur Jésus et Marie, sur Jean-Baptiste et les apôtres, et des visions et révéla-tions*, Paris, Gallimard, 2005.

Lipsius-Bonnet, 1959: Lipsius Richard A. et Bonnet Maximilien, Apostolorum Apocrypha, II volumes en 3 tomes, Hildesiem-New York, Georg Olms, 1898-1959 (réédition anastatique), 320.

Armenian Gospel of the Infancy, trad. Terian, 2008: Terian Abraham, *The Armenian Gospel of the Infancy, with three early versions of the Protevangelium of James*, Oxford University Press, 2008.

Bovon, 1978-1979: Bovon F., *Les Actes apocryphes du christianisme et monde païen* faculté de théologie Univ. de Genève, 1978-79.

ENDNOTES

1. Cf. Lc 4.3; 6, 12; 9, 12; 10, 4; 22, 30.
2. Cf. E8, E22.
3. Cf. G13, 835–848.
4. Cf. G1, G8, E3, E5, E6, E9, E17, E19, E22.
5. Cf. E2, E7, E13, E16, E18, AT1, AT2, AT3.
6. Cf. JM 1, 246–326.
7. Cf. G1, 57–180.
8. JM 2, 541–546, 685.
9. We recall that examples in Syriac dialect exist in Syria (for example Harklean or Phyloxanian) while we possess no variations on Oriental texts even prior to deformations and anti-Macionian corrections; such variants only concern the correction of the ambiguity variable of Greek in some of its versions denounced by Marcion in 140, cf. E1. So the French Group give us preference to the Pschytta antiquity.
10. Cf. G3.
11. See The Anchor Bible dictionary for Scribes.
12. G18 III, 69–85.
13. G18 II, 43–65.
14. G13 XIII, 387–398 and 410–420.
15. Cf. Müller–Simonis, From the Caucase to Persian Gulf/Urmia Missions, UCA, ed. Washington 1892.
16. Cf. Tobias 9:1–18 and G8.
17. The fortress of Sargon II, Sarboug or Dur-Surrakin, the present day Khorsabad, is some fifteen kilometers away from Mosul, where Sargon II used to reside. He had deported the ten tribes from the Kingdom of Israel after the fall of its capital Samaria in 722. This was the start of the Hebrew community which through work of its members in trade and smuggling became the source of wealth originating in the network of trade that he allowed to progressively establish from the East to the West in the northern part of Eurasia.
18. The ruin of Nineveh was announced by the prophet Nahum (Na 2–3) who was deported to Alqosh but was originally from Kfar-Naum, the principal seat of his tribe, the most open to the nations in the first century.
19. Matt 12:39; 16:2-4; Mc 8:12; Lc 11:29.
20. We would like to recall that John the Baptist first baptized those arriving to Judea by the road from Jerusalem, the capital of the South: Sarbug Babel by Euphrates and letting Babelon the left to go right to Jerusalem; a flow of pilgrims from the Chaldean Diaspora had mixed with traders from Chaldea and Jews from Palestine who did not plan to go back.
21. Cf. Mc 6:7.
22. This defeat is dated in the Chinese chronicles by the westward movement of the Kushans who had invaded Bactria as far as Bactra, having themselves been displaced by an invasion of the Yue-Tche tribes from the north and drawn to the Tarim basin.

23   Matt 28:19 and Mc 16:20.
24   AT3, 20-50.
25   Cf. G2.
26   The nickname Thaddeus (aram. Taddaï) to designate the last among brothers is common; however, it could give and has given place to confusion among the Greeks with the common name of Addaï which belonged to the successor of the apostles in Nineveh and who was one of the 72 disciples. This error is identified in a text of a Greek speaking writer then spread among Syriac speakers introducing false attributions and confusing Assyria and Chaldea.
27   Cf. Mt 9:23, et 11, 17.
28   Cf. Mt 18:13 and the strings of the young in G13.
29   Cf. JM 1, 472–488.
30   Cf. JM 2, 213–236.
31   Cf. JM 1, 607–619.
32   G11, 146–156.
33   Cf. G17.
34   G13, 611–629.
35   Cf. E4.
36   G12.
37   Cf. Strings composed by Mathew probably with the help from James in the chapters 5-6-5, 19 and 25, also see G13 chap VI and XVI.
38   Cf. MJ 1, 213–229 and 371–391.
39   Cf. Marshall J., Taxila structural remains I; University Press, 1951.
40   G16, 440-444.
41   Cf. G7.
42   G16, 446-448.
43   Cf. G13, 413.
44   Cf. G18, IV.
45   Cf. Lc 11:24-26.
46   Cf. Is 34:15.
47   Cf. Mt 23:33.
48   Cf. Mt 10:18.
49   On the Latin side, in the fifth century, the apocrypha on the Assumption was compiled into a collection under the title of Transitus Mariae which dates the event to the year '51. In the East it is celebrated on the fifteenth of Ab, the middle of summer, hence the date of the celebration is August 15, '51. This tradition overlaps the key dates of the Seventy years–20+51 announced by Archangel Gabriel to Daniel as containing a framework doubling the time for the Coming of Messiah. The tradition on Thomas arriving late to the gathering of the seven surviving apostles alongside John has been attested in a tradition reported by John of Damascus as coming from Juvenal the bishop of Jerusalem who was present at the council in Chalcedon.
50   G11, 564-568.

51 The tradition concerning Mari has been clarified by the Acts of Mar Mari published by C. and F. Jullien in the CSCO 234-235 Peeters, Louvain 2003, the traditions attributes to him the recognition of the young Chaldean Church by the King of kings and the construction of the Church of Chore (between 79 and 116 according to the dating of the river flow) between Seleucia–Ctesiphon, the double capital of the Parthian Empire, where his remains were kept as those of one among the 72 disciples and an acknowledged successor of Jude by Aggai and of Simon. He would travel to Jerusalem and Nineveh to collaborate with Addai (one of the 72 as well but acknowledged by Bartholomew). He brought a copy of the Pshytta in cursive letters and the relics of Jesus in Zion in order to ensure their survival from Roman prosecution and from mesopotamian plains to the mountains of Assyria, later from Mazdeans opposed to Christian faith. It is probably a comparable journey that the relics of Passions and then those of Thomas would undertake from Jerusalem and Mylapore under Mar Abres from the family of Joseph (121–137). They would for a time reside in Maishan explaining the close link of this city to their celebration, before being taken to safety in the north.

52 Due to the name "brother" given in aramaïc families to the second generation of the children issued from the ancestor as well for the first generation, it is clear that in the church the new brothers are selected in reference to God the Father of Jésus but also in reference to Mary the mother of Jesus

53 We often minimize both concrete and theological competence of Peter who like John accumulated the concrete experience through his work (cf. E11) and the teaching provided by John the Baptist and later by Mary.

54 Cf. G6 and G9.

55 It is so strongly engraved in his memory that he has it included in the frieze of Kong Wang Shan, which is deciphered in G14, 52 fig. 106 on the far right: Thomas turns his head while the lance strikes the side of his Rabbi.

56 G16, 316–388.

57 Texts composed by the apostles and their disciples, witnesses to predications in speech and in the acts of Jesus, go through the process of "canonization" in definitive necklaces comparable to the bamboo stems (qanona) solidly attached by stitching of texts to be learned by heart without forgetting to check the group's memory with the mother of "memory" for whom Mary is the example of coherence of all the evangelical memories. cf G16, introduction.

58 Thomas's courage to confront different cultures on his return to India and that of Peter in Rome once they are well equipped, has been wonderfully analyzed by Jousse in G4, soon to be translated.

59 to follow the plausible timeline of other twelve apostles, please refer to G11, 656–657.

60 The present day digs in Patanam seem to have identified the main spice port which in the West is called Muziris, however its coastline has changed. The digs were able to show the important levels of trade with the Red Sea and the Persian Gulf. The shortest route departs from the island of Socatra allowing the most direct and fast voyage under the stars and with favorable winds (in keeping with the Babylonian custom and the same latitude).

[61] Cf. G17, Conclusion.

[62] Here we follow the short form of the oral tradition given in G19 annex 24, 278–279 pending a thorough oral study to be conducted in Malayalam with the Christians speaking that language.

[63] Cf. G19, VII. It is certain that according to the Chinese historian Fan Ye, the study of text needs to be completed with Chinese scholars with competences in the domain of the second part of the Acts in Aramaic.

[64] Cf. G19 annex 24 and especially the text on 278–279 providing the core of the oral tradition in a French translation.

[65] This translation needs to be gone over in Aramaic translated from the Malayalam and in its original language in order to conduct a comparative critical analysis "in situ." We remind the reader that such oral analyzes have always provided much more solid support to historical and archeological research than the reliance on translations produced in keeping with western criteria, especially because of epistemological bias, which are rather important for the authors who have not conducted the in-depth ethnological verifications on local terrain.

[66] Cf. G19, 248: However, not a single of emissaries of the emperor Mingi could reach the Parthian empire by the silk route on land in the years 64/65.

[67] Cf. E10.

[68] Partially translated texts and references in G14, G15 and G19.

[69] G14, 128–131.

[70] G15, 115-122 and E18, 491–492.

[71] G15, 104–105.

[72] This is the liturgical date celebrating the martyrdom of Thomas in Mylapore and Kerala. It overlaps in the Roman West by the Byzantine liturgical tied to the celebration of the relics arrival in Edessa on the 3rd of July of 363 with the School of Nisbis fleeing the Persians during the persecutions of Shapur II; in the Latinized West of the ninth century, the 18 Kisleu (one week before Nativity the 25 Kisleu), moved to the 21st of December; however the original date was attested by a miracle of the seeping blood on the great cross on the Saint Thomas Mount in Mylapore on the 18th of December in 1558 repeated on several occasions in the course of Martyrs celebrations in Mylapore and reestablished as of 18th of December 1955, one week before the 25th of December, conserving the date of 25th of Kisleu of the ancient Hebrew calendar which was initially followed by the St. Thomas Christians.

[73] HP 104–105 the finale of the Hymn of the Pearl on the Gate of Resurrection.

[74] Report of the excavations available at the museum of Muziris.

[75] References in G14, G15, G19 and E18.

[76] G19, 51–56 and 59.

[77] Cf. G15, 97–111.

[78] Current research indicate the presence of Manasseh tribe in Ferghana prior to its incorporation into the empire of Darius, it would contribute to trade with China, due to the reputation of their "celestial » horses, supplied for the Chinese cavalry, which explains Manassar (a Manasseh princess in Aramaic),

the wife of prince Ying Mingdi's half-brother sent there by his father the emperor who ruled before the arrival of Thomas. In the first century, this kingdom had ties to northern Bactria, before YueThche pushed the Kushans westward and cut the west Silk road that passed by Tarimbasin; popularity of the name Manasseh, that of many royals, as well as giving birth to the multi-secular saga of Mans, told by the Kyrgyz to this day and wine production point to Judeo-Christian presence.

79   Cf. G19 annex 22 concerning prince Liu Ying (wangying or Wizan?) and his destiny as the founder of Church in China and a martyr for the faith in 71, one year before Thomas.

80   Reference to the documents provided in G14.

81   Cf. E14 as rare defenders of short chronologies linked to the apostles.

82   The prince (Wang) Liu Ying, the half-brother of Liu Ming, commanded the right wing of the army with Hebrew cavalry under his general (named Siphur = trumpet) who was Wang's second in command (zun). He was accused of plotting the rapid spread of Christianity and condemned to exile and death. However, Mingdi (the emperor) converted and Ying was rehabilitated, his relics buried by Liu da, the son of the emperor Zhang di (75–88) favorable to Christians if not a Christian himself.

83   This second persecution called the plot of "yellow turbans" by Han chronicles and literature took place in the second century, well after the persecution in Mylapore that lead to removal of Apostles' relics to Mesapotamia.

84   Cf A3 here we follow a very thorough analysis of the Hymn of the Pearl in A3; especially (33-81) (1871–1904) and 82-129 (1905-1933) containing historic and literary aspects attempting to reveal the typical and always late forms of Alexandrian gnosis or less constructed deviating middle eastern theologies. We can uphold such conclusions based on Greek but not on the Aramaic which always closely parallels the Peshitta of the New Testament allowing recognizing entire phrasal fragments as well as the psalms and the prophets of Diaspora. Finally, we can situate conclusions as they are in the Hymn of the Pearl (159) between Egyptian Encratism and the Pseudo-Macarius resulting in a thousand-page of editorial texts (159). However, an in-depth research into the origin of Parthian words (211–248) draws us to a text from the Sassanid period while introduction of ancient Persian and Sogdian words often confirm much more ancient employ often overlapped by Greek that this text seems to avoid. Hence it is possible to propose an origin that contradicts (275) the first hundred pages and derived from multiple Eastern influences over the text in Imperial Aramaic, a multi-leveled composition in Syriac composed in Edessa linguistically already greatly cut off from the identified Eastern Sassanid culture.

85   Cf. G6 and G9 but also see Maronite canon Sherer.

86   JM1, 555-570.

87   Cf. G13 XIII, 403 and 413.

88   Cf. Act 4, 1-2:5, 17, 42; 7, 1, 60; 12, 1-5.

89   Cf. E21 demonstrating the return to oral sources in US.

11

HISTORICAL, APOCRYPHAL, AND THEOLOGICAL SOURCES FROM THE ARMENIAN CHURCH ABOUT APOSTLE THOMAS AND INDIA

Maxime K. Yevadian

Nowadays, the Indian church is undoubtedly one of the great apostolic churches founded by an apostle, as it was the case for the Armenian church, during the extraordinary missionary movement that took place in the second third of the first century A.D., a peaceful and free movement that reached a far greater part of the ancient world than we had imagined. Besides, that church presents the rare trait of having seen all its manuscripts taken and destroyed by other Christians, the Portuguese, who wanted to Latinize that church and enforce a Roman Catholicism,[1] which caused public burnings similar to those we saw under Hitler and also in Turkey, under Erdogan.

In the absence of sufficient and old enough direct sources, the historian has to rely on three kinds of indirect sources:
- the sources that were discovered after that period of destruction,
- the known sources that were re-interpreted after having been ignored so far, due to misinterpretation,
- and the analysis of the constitution of a new corpus in other traditions, which allowed a better understanding of the image this church conveyed.

We shall examine the three types of approaches that bear witness to the vitality of the studies relating to Thomas's presence in India.

Study carried out within Chaire de recherche sur l'Eurasie with the support of the Auvergne Rhône Alpes Region.

The first aspect is illustrated by a review of the *Papyrus Oxyrhynchus 413*, the text of which attests that a Christian church did exist in South India during the first decades of the second century, probably in the Port of Muziris.

The second axis in this study consists in re-interpreting some texts we already know, *Thomas's Acts* in our case, texts that have apparently been written in the Syriac language, before being translated into Greek and Armenian. Such an analysis is based on the latest archaeological findings in China designed in fact as a report by a Community of Widows in Maïchan (South Mesopotamia), an entry port for trade with the Indian sub-continent, according to the data collected in the course of exchanging information with the Indian Christians. Once it has been read over in this light, the text could upstream with amazing accuracy some relevant information concerning Thomas's missions in Asia.

The third and last aspect is probably the least dramatic one, as it is not based on one unique document we would have completely read or re-read. The point here is to collect several texts from the whole literature of a particular church, the Armenian church, in order to try and re-constitute the vision the Armenian Fathers had of Thomas's action in India as well as of the foundation of a Christian church in this country. We shall open up our analysis by adding a few texts showing the Armenians' devotion to Thomas and his sanctuary in India. In that respect, we shall examine first the traditional Armenian texts about the apostle Thomas, insisting on the texts conventionally called apocryphal, which have been preserved in Armenian. Secondly, we shall examine the Armenian sources concerning the relationships between Armenia and India until the Islamic conquest, basing our study on a brief analysis of the Silk Road.

THOMAS IN THE APOCRYPHAL ARMENIAN TRADITION

The fundamental texts of the Armenian tradition have been partly translated into Armenian, either from the Syriac or from the Aramaic languages. *Apostle Addaï's Doctrine*, particularly, is a text written probably in the fifth century by an author otherwise unknown, Laboubna, Senaq's son.[2] The text is very famous since it relates the apocryphal correspondence exchanged between Jesus and Abgar, Manou's son, and king of Edessa.

Special ties with Edessa

The text has been translated into Armenian at an unknown date, probably between the late fifth and seventh centuries. The latest person who translated it into French, V. Calzolari, has not proposed any particular dating, and simply stuck to a synthesis of the former dates mentioned. In fact, the

Armenian version is faithful enough, as far as the essential text is concerned, but it progressively deviates from it in the second part, as it just ignores the elements relating to the apostle's death, which makes us think that the apostle might as well have gone to Armenia after he had evangelized the Edessa Kingdom.

Laboubna, *Aposle Addaï's Doctrine* Syriac version, § 93	Laboubna, *Aposle Addaï's Doctrine* Armenian version, § 93
They were all appalled by his [Addaï's] dying.[3]	And they were all appalled by his departure and by the fact that he was leaving them.[4]

In this text, the importance given to Thomas is considerably limited and is actually reduced to the following unique mention:

Laboubna, *Apostle Addaï 's Doctrine* Syriac version § 7	Laboubna, *Apostle Addaï's Doctrine* Armenian version, § 7
After Christ's Ascension into heaven, Judas Thomas sent to Abgar the apostle Addaï who had been one of the seventy-two disciples.[5]	After Christ's Ascension to heaven, Judas Thomas sent to Abgar the apostle Addaï who had been one of the seventy-two disciples.[6]

The text endorses the benediction of the Edessa city, a city that was never forayed by any army, thanks to a divine protection. But that situation changed, in A.D. 609, when the Sassanid armies invaded it. Then we had to do with another text, which was not translated into Armenian.[7] Actually, for the Edessenes, the apostle of Edessa is Thaddeus, not Thomas. The Armenian Fathers had very well understood it when they translated it into their own language and when they composed original plays about Thaddeus. Therefore, in *Armenian Thaddeus' martyrdom,* where Thomas is not even mentioned.

Meditation of the Gospels

There was a strong relationship between Armenia and the Syrian part of Mesopotamia in the early Christian period, because St Gregory the Illuminator, the Armenian apostle, had two groups of young men who were planned to enter the priesthood learn the Syriac language. Later, about 405–407, Mesrop Marchot's, who invented the Armenian alphabet, went to Edessa and Amida,[8] with the hope of finding there the help that would allow him to complete his project for that discovering or for inventing a new alphabet for the Armenian language, and he sent his disciples to that same area so that they may translate the Bible into Armenian.[9] Once the work had been completed, the Armenian prelates, when they had to deal with Syriac or Armenian manuscripts, translated a synthesis of the best Greek or Syriac Patristic texts. In the theological tradition of the School of Antioch, the Armenians used passages staging Thomas. In the Synoptic Gospels and *Acts of the Apostoles*, Thomas's name appears only on the lists of the apostles: Matthew 10: 2–4), Mark 6:7, Luke 10:1 and Acts 1:16. In the *Gospel by St. John*, which is given much importance in the Armenian church, he has been mentioned three times. There, Thomas displays enthusiasm and loyalty when announcing Christ's death and saying: "Let us also go, that we may die with him!" (John 11:16). His desire to fully understand is emphasized during the last supper (John 14:4). And finally, thanks to his disbelief, so useful for the people with no faith at all, he was able, after he was convinced, to go to the end of the world (John 20:24–29). The fact of having touched and believed through his experience of Christ's resurrected body became an evidence of Jesus' full humanity and, singularly, of the reality of his body. Read *The Book of Letters*, the Armenian church's official Compendium, and you will understand that, between the fifth and the twelfth centuries, and maybe even later, the apostle Thomas held a prominent place in the theological discussions, more particularly in the Christological ones.[10] It is the same for *The Seal of Faith*, a treaty composed by the Catholicos Komitas (618–628) and designed as a compendium of quotes to be used in the course of Christological discussions.[11] Among the texts selected, those from St. John's Gospel include many quotes where Thomas is featured.[12]

Thomas in Armenian literature

Beyond this text from the biblical tradition, which can be read and understood, Thomas is not given a significant part in the windfall the Armenian translations represent. He does not even appear in *Mesrop Marchot's Life* - the first original work composed in Armenian by his disciple Goriun, between 441 and 443 - or in the first *History of Armenia,* or in *Buzandaran,* composed about 460. In Agathangelos's *History* wrote during the decade of 470, he plays only a minor role. That text, which served as a basis for the Armenian theology and the history of that population, comprises a narrative section where the author relates the story of the conversion of king Tiridates III, known as Tiridates the Great, and of his family and his Court, by Saint Gregory the Illuminator, towards 294–295.[13] Somewhere in the middle of that work, *Teaching of Gregory* was inserted. It is a pre-baptism speech, theoretically pronounced before Tiridates and his Court to prepare them for their baptisms. This famous theological piece, which was progressively completed, until the early seventh century, mentions the apostle Thomas together with the other apostles in its § 686.[14] The enumeration is based on Mark 6:7 and Luke 10:1 gospels, as it mentions the apostles in pairs, but the order it follows is nearer to the one Matthew 10:2-4 chose. In any case, Thomas does not hold an important place in it, nor does Saint Bartholomew either.

But he is clearly designated as the apostle of India in the *Armenian canonical collection* (Կանոնագիրք Հայոց) compiled by the Catholicos Yovhannēs Awjnec'i: "Թովմաս ի Հնդկաց—Thomas [Apostole for the] Indians."[15]

In fact, we'll have to wait for Philon Tirakatsi (P'ilon Tirakac'i), in 695-696, as specified in the translation colophon,[16] for a translation into Armenian of Socrates Scholasticus' *Ecclesiastical History*. The history has been preserved in its Armenian translation in two census records, a short literal one, and a longer one leaving great scope for rewriting.[17] Both versions include chapter 67: "*Concerning the shrine of the apostle Thomas and events at it.*"[18] This chapter will be food for thought for the Armenians and create a taste for the apostle. Movses Khorents'i (Movsēs Xorenc'i fifth or eighth century?), will use that text and the Armenian version of the *Apostle Addaï's Doctrine* in his own *History of Armenia* (II 27-34, 33 mainly), which will strengthen further more that interest for worshiping the apostle[19]. Some parts of Stepanos Asoghik (Asołik) de Taron's *History*—he was a late tenth and early eleventh centuries historian- closely follow Movses Khorents'i' version, and certain elements from *The Apostle Addaï's Doctrine* have also been incorporated into it. To give an example, Jesus asks the apostle to write the letter in response to King Abgar.[20] He also mentions the fact that Armenia is a part of the mission that Thomas and Bartholomew have been entrusted with.[21] Finally, a quote by Thomas, in *Gospel of St. John's*[22] was used during the tenth century Christological controversies.[23] The tenth century historian, Thomas Arcrouni, reproduces the history of Christianization under the same scheme,[24] Thomas, after de ascension of Jesus sends Thaddaeus to Edessa. For this contemporaneous the Catholicos and historian Yovhannēs Drasxanakertc'i (899-929), the narration is the same.[25]

So, there are good grounds for considering that the tradition relating to Thomas was, for the Armenian Fathers, independent of Edessa, and that the only document evoking it is the revised Armenian version of *Addaï's Doctrine*, which is regularly quoted. It is at least the way the Fathers would have understood it. The centerpiece relating to the apostle Thomas's case is with no contest and for all the Christian churches, *Thomas's Acts*, which were written in Syriac before being translated into Greek, Armenian, or into any other language.

Thomas's Acts in Armenian tradition

The Armenian translation, which included *Thomas's Acts,* is no longer available. The Armenian tradition holds five apocryphal concerning Thomas; they were edited in the vast corpus of the *Extra-canonical apostolic sources* the Mekhitarist Priest Cherubin Tcherakian (Č'rak'ean) published in Venice in 1896 and 1904.[26] The first volume contained the texts dedicated to Peter and Paul, to Andrew, and to James and John. As for the second volume, it contained the texts concerning Philip Bartholomew, Thomas, Matthew, James, Jesus' brother, Thaddeus, Simon the Zealot, and the lists of all the apostles.

G. Tcherakian collected these texts in books of homilies (*tonakan)* from the Mekhitarists Fathers of the Venice and Vienna convents. The texts were completed with some other manuscripts, mainly from Jerusalem. They are therefore consistent with a specific style, abundantly represented in the Middle-Ages Armenian literature, which we would rather expect to have produced short texts partly reproducing some events in the saint's life while summing up the other ones, in order to have these texts read in the monasteries all along the liturgical year.

Dom Louis Leloir, from the Abbaye of Clerveaux, translated these two precious volumes into French with analysis. They appear in the volumes 3 and 4 of the *Apocryphorum Series* of the *Christianorum Corpus* edited by Brepols.[27] The texts we are interested in, referred as VII a (BHO 1211); VII b (BHO 1215); VII c (BHO 1212); VII d (BHO 1214) and VII e (BHO 1219), are collected in Volume 4.[28] The five texts comprise two sets, on the one hand, the VII a, VII b, VII c and VII e, which are revised excerpts or *Thomas's Acts* that have been abbreviated and condensed, the other set (VII d) being an Armenian composition.

This set of four volumes arises some comments. On the one hand, they all deal with a part of *Thomas's Acts,* the other Acts being at times abruptly summarized. Dom Louis Leloir has been able to prove that the whole set of texts, contrarily to what G. Garitte thought, are all dating back to a translation of *Thomas's Acts* that has not been kept in its complete form.[29]

For example, the same process occurred for Ireneus de Lyon's *Adversus Haereses,* his books I to III having partly survived only in some quotations, whereas his books IV and V have been entirely retained. On the other hand, the same researcher has shown that the Armenian version had probably been written from the original Syriac, or Aramaic, document, and not from the Greek version.[30] At last, confirming what we have already said, at no moment in this set of texts is there *any mention of the Edessa city.*

Here follows a table of the Acts and of them having been transmitted in the four Armenian works preserved:

Actes	§	Éd. Bonnet, p.	*VII.a*	*VII.b*	*VII.c*	*VII.e*
Acte I	1-16	99-124	x		x	x
Acte II	17-29	124-146	x		x	x
Acte III	30-38	147-156	x			
Acte IV	39-41	156-159	x			
Acte V	42-50	159-167				
Acte VI	51-61	167-178				
Acte VII	62-67	178-185	x		x	
Acte VIII	68-81	185-197	x		x	
Acte IX	82-118	197-229	(x)*			
Acte X	119-133	229-240				
Acte XI	134-138	240-245	x			
Acte XII	139-149	245-258	(x)**			
Acte XIII	150-154	259-263	(x)**			
Acte XIII	155-158	264-269		x		
Martyre	159-171	269-288		x		

* *The § 82-101 contents are condensed in four lines.*
** *The § 139-149 contents are condensed in a few lines.*

Reading the table requires some comments.

On one side, the reworking of the texts has been so important that now the entire Acts written in Armenian have been lost (V, VI and X). Similarly, in response to the use that was made of them, the texts essentially allow for a narrative leeway and the compilers have omitted the prayers and speeches, which are an important component of the original text. Such was the case for the famous hymn called "Hymn of the Pearl," whereas the Act 'VII, a' ends where the text begins. In the same way, the *Teshbuhta* featured in the Syriac text, right after the hymn called "Hymn of the Pearl," has not been retained either. On the other hand, the parts that have been best preserved are the *Acts* I and II and the account of the martyrdom (preserved in the *Acts* VII a, c, and e). The *Acts* VII and VIII have also been attested in Armenian. Our only regret is that the integral text is no longer available, but the passages preserved in several dozens of manuscripts prove that worshipping Thomas was a widespread tradition in the whole area of the Armenian plateau. Another sort of available text, called the *Synaxarions*, shows there was an Armenian devotion to Thomas, but before studying them, a last piece remains to be examined, the *Act* VII d.

Entitled *Discovery and Transfer to Armenia of Thomas's mortal remains* (BHO 1224), the text is an Armenian composition aiming at explaining how Thomas's remains were taken from India to Mesopotamia before the reign of Constantine (§ 3), and how, in Julian the Apostate times, the chest containing the relics was stolen by a General of the Sassanid army who thought he would find a treasure there. Since what he found were only bones, he just threw them at the feet of his horses, which at once became very agitated (§ 7–8). A man from his suite, called Joseph, had a vision. He collected the relics and went to Armenia to keep them safe from harm (§ 6, 9–11). When he arrived there, he asked for being baptized (§ 12) and the relics were allotted to two monasteries, the Paɫivank monastery and the Saint-Thomas monastery, in Řešouni, south of the lake of Van, (§ 12–13). The story is also mentioned in the summary of the text VII e, from the Armenian collection. In that version, we learn that the Sassanid lord is Joseph (Usuf), who left Iran to carry away Thomas's relics and have them safe (§ V–VI).

This story is also mentioned in a third version, contained in the *haysmavouk* (*Armenian synaxarion*). The *Armenian synaxarion* was originally a version translated from the Greek at the very beginning of the eleventh century, and it was progressively enriched with texts that were either composed or reworked. The text of that *synaxarion* was officially published in Constantinople in 1834. This edition was used by G. Bayan used for his French translation published in the *Oriental Patrology*.[31] It is a survey of the text VII, d. In some ways, it is more complete and more precise. That excerpt from the *haymavouk* (synaxarion) gives us the route Thomas followed:

"*Իսկ ինքն երանելին Թովմաս քարոզեաց Պարթեւաց եւ Մարաց՝ Պարսից եւ Կրմանաց, Բախտրիացւոց եւ Մոգուց՝ մինչեւ ի Սինեցւոյս, ընդ ամենայն տեղիս առնելով նշանս եւ սքանչելիս անուամբն Քրիստոսի եւ դարձուցանելով զբազումս ի Հաստոս ճշմարտութեան, Հաստատելով եկեղեցիս եւ կարգելով պաշտоնեայս ի տեղիս տեղիս:-* Blessed Thomas preached Parthians and Medes, Persians and Kirmans, Backtraits, and Mages, and went all the way to China, performing miracles and marvels in the name of Christ, converting a lot of people to the true Faith, founding churches with their appointed religious officials in several countries."[32]

The same text ends with a recall of the Armenian pilgrimage to Saint-Thomas's sanctuary in Chennai. We shall return to this later:

"*եւ զերեզման սուրբ առաքելոյն է Հոչակաւար ուքաստեղի մինչեւ ցայսор ժամանակի, յորմէ բազում բժշկութիւնք կատարին ի վարս Քրիստոսի:-* The holy apostle's tomb is a pilgrimage place famous to this day, where many healings occur in the name of Christ."[33]

Recently, the Holy See of Etchmiadzin has published, under the direction of the Archbishop Eghia Petrosyan a new version of the *Synaxarion*, in twelve volumes, including notes to be read during one month of the Liturgy.[34] To each text is presented in a synoptic presentation of six versions with all the manuscripts that contain it, but they unfortunately lack a critical apparatus. It is however a stunning working tool. The story of Apostle Thomas appears in the Volume of October.[35]

This first series of texts bears evidence of the progressive rise in the worship of the apostle Thomas and it is largely similar to the worship of the Armenian Apostle Saint Bartholomew. The series also confirms that the Armenian church possessed a version of *Thomas's Acts*, large excerpts of which have come to us. At last, for the Armenian Fathers, Thomas is, above all, India's apostle and his links with Edessa are insubstantial.

THE ARMENIAN-INDIAN RELATIONSHIPS UNTIL THE CONQUEST BY ISLAM

The Silk Roads

The historical relationships between Armenia and the Indian sub-continent go back a long way, dating back to the Achaemenid period at the latest. In fact, the King of kings, Darius I (521–486 B.C.) reorganized and developed what was called the Royal Road. This road was built and maintained in order to serve as a link between the main cities of the empire and facilitate a free circulation of people and goods. It went from Susa to Sardis and covered 1677 miles.[36] It crossed the Euphrates River at the level of Southern Armenia, and three stations had been established in that country: Ad Aros Tomisa, Kharpet, and Amida (Cf. Figure 1). In the first century A.D., the Greek geographer Strabo indicated that the road went on from Sardis and up to India,[37] thus being an important communication channel between both countries, which was part of a larger network called the Silk Roads.

May be I should remind you of what is usually called the Silk Road, which in fact was a triple network of distinct trade routes (Cf. Figure 2). The main roads started from Chang'an (Xi'an), built in the Han's period (206 B.C.) to the end of the Tang period (A.D. 904, probably with some interruption periods).[38] On the Han Chinese territory (206 B.C. to A.D. 220), there was a relay station every nine or twelve miles on all the land routes. On that Silk Road, we can mention the Chinese cities of Dun-Huang, Zhang-Xie or Wu-wei.

The *central road* is best known. It is a transcontinental land road that went across the Pamir high mountains via high altitude passes, two of

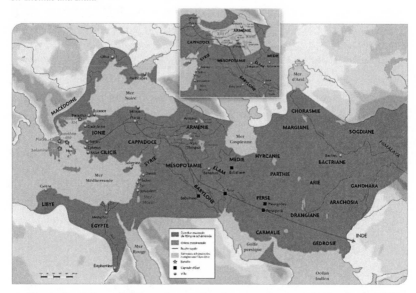

Fig. 1: the Achaemenid empire, under the reign Darius I (521–486 B.C.)[39]

which being at an altitude of about 16,000 feet. Travelling that road meant you had to transfer the goods twice, in order to use animals capable of climbing that high while carrying a heavy burden. This route, which made the Kingdom of Parthia a mandatory intermediary between China and the Mediterranean coastline of Antioch, in Syria, was not very convenient, finally, due to the high passes it went through. So, it was cut off during the invasion of a Yuezhi tribe from Pamir around A.D. 20 and again, later, during the invasion of their successors the Kushans.

Then, there was a *sea road*. It went around India, crossed the Red Sea, and went up the Nile River as far as Alexandria in Egypt (cf. Figure 3). The Greeks on one side, and the Indians and the Chinese on the other side, controlled that route from the second century B.C. onwards. Sailing it depended on the monsoon and on its required winds, but it also represented a constant sinking risk for the other boats, and a rotting risk for the goods transported.[40]

The *northern road*, or the Steppe's Road, as René Grousset calls it, went through the Northern part of the Caspian. Opened during the winter months, it led to Greater Armenia. It served as a direct way to the fairs organized in the capital city of Great-Armenia, Artaxata.[41] It was in fact the only all-weather road in place, since no pass there would be higher than a mile. Therefore, this route must have absorbed a significant part in the global trade of Chinese goods. During the winter, the frozen ground offered a trafficable trail and the streams were still safer ways, whereas in

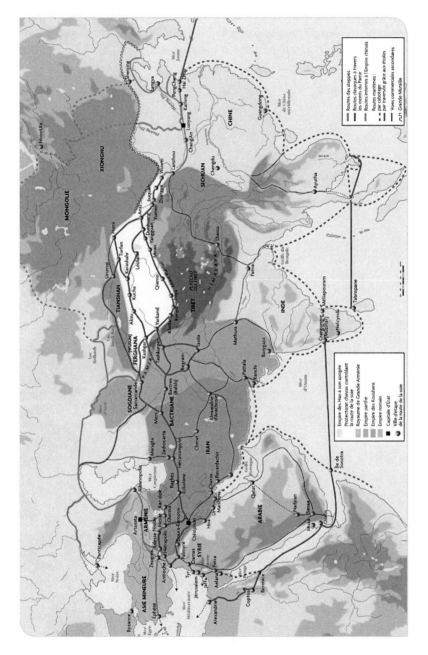

Fig. 2: The Silk Roads in the middle of the first century[42]

summer, thawing made this transit route impracticable. So, the caravans had to reach Armenia before the thawing period. This is the probable context in which the Greek geographer Strabo, a contemporary of the emperor Augustus, could have written the following passage, which had been unsatisfactorily explained so far:

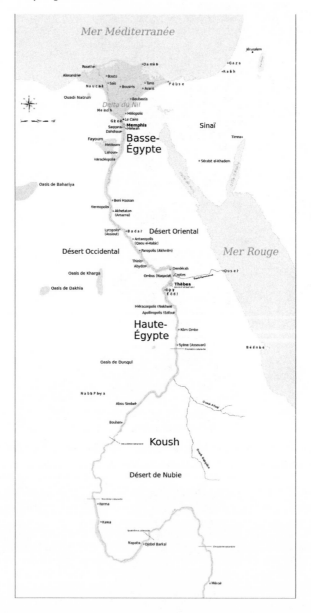

Fig. 3: The Silk Road (sea road) from Alexandria to Bereniké[43]

236

In the farther provinces of the North of Armenia, an enormous quantity of snow will fall down, apparently due to the proximity of the Caucasus and the Iberia or the Colchis Mountains. It is not unusual, as some people assure, that entire caravans were caught in avalanches when the snow fell over the passes or the narrow routes of the mountains, and they would stay buried there. But in order to be prepared for that risk, all travellers, they say, would not forget to carry with them long sticks that, in case they had that sort of accident, they would push forward to attain the higher levels and be able to breathe and warn those who would come after them, and who would inevitably help them and save their lives by pulling them out."[44]

The Northern part of the Armenian Plateau was particularly subject to avalanches when the first snows came or at the end of winter, when the snow melted. The passage evoked probably concerned the late arrival on the Armenian Plateau of caravans from China, at the beginning of Spring.

The Apostles Bartholomew's and Thomas's preaching

The existence of the three silk roads helps better understand the obvious apostolic dispersal to the Eastern world. The second chapter of the *Andrew' Acts* offers, according to our analysis,[45] the most complete version of the world having been split among the apostles:

> They stood up and drew lots to know who was going to "spread the word" and where they would go and preach to which population. Peter's lot was the coastal area, James' and John's wee the eastern area, Philip's lot fell on the cities of Samaria and Asia, Bartholomew's was Albanopolis, Matthew got Parthia and the Murmenide city, Thomas's lot was the Greater Armenia and India, Lebbeus and Thaddeus were assigned Beronicide, Simon the Canaanite was assigned the Barbarian countries and, after each of them had got his lot drawn, Andrew got Bythinia, Lacedomonian and Achaia."[46]

Apostle Thomas was assigned Parthia—which also included Armenia in A.D. 66—and Asia. He was sent to the East together with Bartholomew. The two apostles had to part when they realized that the Kushans had blocked the central road. Thomas went southwards and headed for the sea road, in order to go to India and then to China. As for Bartholomew, he tried to avoid the Kushans by going northwards. He probably went across Armenia, since his evangelical activity there was reported in sources from the entire Christian world. He was probably put to death in *Albanopolis*, a city of the Southern Caucasian Mountains.[47] The place was one of the last stages before he was to go around Southern Caucasus, in the coastal plain of the Caspian region. That is where he must have suffered martyrdom while he was considering going further on the Steppe Road.

Fig. 4: The probable itinerary of the apostles Thomas and Bartholomew[48]

The Armenian missionaries in Europe and Asia (fourth–seventh centuries)

One of the consequences of converting Armenia to Christianity was that it gave momentum to the preaching of the Christian religion in the East about A.D. 402, as attested by the Greek historian Sozomenus's *Church history*:

> Then, among the neighbouring populations, religion and belief gathered pace and people came in greater numbers, and I think that the beginning of the conversion of the Persians was owing to their intercourse with the Osroenians and the Armenians, for it is likely that they would converse with such Divine men and make experience of their virtue."[49]

The Armenian policy, as Tiridates' letter we mentioned earlier confirms it, was a groundswell movement in the history of that Church. Missionaries were sent to the four cardinal points, to Georgia and the Caucasus, as well as to Persia, right from Gregory the Illuminator's lifetime, and then to Europe (Italy, Gaul, and Germany).[50] The vast Asia also experimented the itinerant preaching of the Armenian missionaries. About the years 550, the White Huns (the Hephthalites) were a mission land for an Armenian bishop named Macarius. On two occasions, and together with his group of priests, the bishop devoted himself to evangelizing the Huns, as reported in the contemporary text that follows:

> After twice seven years came another bishop named Macarius, who was Armenian too. He behaved rightly and came voluntarily, and some priests came along with him. He (Macarius) built a church of bricks, planted trees, sowed various sorts of vegetables, performed miracles,

and christened a lot of people. Seeing there was something new, the chiefs there wondered, they were very pleased with these men and revered them, each one of the chiefs inviting them in his own region to see his people, and pleading for him to teach them. And see! They are still there."[51]

We can't exclude the possibility that an echo of the preaching survived in Central Asia; it could partly explain the conversion of the Keraït tribe in 1009, a major event that played its part at the time of the Mongolian epic of the thirteenth century. The Keraïts' Khan asked Ebedjesu, Merv's metropolitan, to find a priest or a bishop that would baptize him. The letter he wrote to the patriarch of Bagdad, John VI, has been kept and is dated 1009.[52] We would all the more expect that the bond between the Armenian church and the Keraïy region had remained vivid, because in 1324, in what is now called the Kyrghyztan, in the Pishpek oasis, John the Armenian served as a bishop.[53] The epitaph on his tomb, written in Armenian and summarized in Syriac, was actually discovered in the nineteenth century.

Knowing the Indian geography

The movements of men and goods between India and Armenia helped the Armenians gain a rather precise knowledge of India and its *Geography*. So, the geographer Ananias of Shirak, who died in 690, composed a vast geography after the text of the learned Greek Claudius Ptolemy. The text survived in the form of two reviews, a short one and a longer one to which were added some prints, which have now been lost. India is mentioned nine times in the whole text and here is the most complete description Ananias de Shirak gives of it:

> The thirty-fifth country of Asia is India, east of Ariana and Scythia by the Imaeus Mountains. [It extends] from there as far as the Aemodae Mountains and the border of China, and divided into two parts east and west of the River Ganges. Ptolemy shows seven rivers here, each with its own name, [...] The Gymnosophists feed only on fruit, rice, and sugar; they are called the Shaman and Brahmin nation by the Persians. They abstain from women and meat and in the morning, they worship the sun saying: "We believe you [to be God], but if there is any other superior to you, to him do we render our workship." Here are found animals witch the Persians call *šarpašank*. There are seventy-two nations east to Granges River [extending] as far as the land of Sinae. Here are other districts called the "Golden" and the "Silver." In their capital are found crows, white parrots, and bearded roosters. Two other districts are also called the "Golden" and the "Silver" and another, the "Copper" district. Here are found elephants and tigers which they say are subdued by magic and are as fast as the wind. Here are found peper, and aromatics [such

as] *boačaŕs, axiri-boyek, goziboyek, agisboyeak, cassia, dwałak, šahaworar, k'akołak,* witch eats camphor, sandal, nayiboyeak, several medicines and bažark, the rat called běšmašk, which eats dealdy roots called *biš* from which antidotes are made ; and large ants in the places where gold-dust is found. Here is an animal [called the] *sawarsan* which can kill an elephant with its tongue and then carry it on a kind of hook which it has on its back, and when it hears any animal cry out, it ejects blood. The unicorn is also found and griffons, which come from the Sinae, are raised here in iron cages. They say that the *p'grē* attacks the griffon and, carried away by fury, both throw themselves into the sea and drown. They say that there are savage peoples here with hard, arrow-proof skins and *Gndandiark'* who are half, or at least one-third, non-Indian; and seven [other people].

The thirty-sixth country, Taprobane, is a large island of India and the largest island in the entire world. From north to south is 1,100 miles long and from east to west 150 miles wide. It lies beyond India and is surrounded by the Indian Sea. Rice is found there which is [a kind of] millet; ginger; beryl, hyacinth and other precious stones, and also much gold and silver and elephants and tigers. It has two mountains in the center, one called Galiba, which is the source of two rivers, and the other called Malaea, which is the source of three rivers. Here are found imperishable woods, ginger, fine pearls, and the most precious stones. There are two cities, they say, 150 miles apart. One is called Manakor and one called Royan. Between them is a mountain named Gaylase from which flows a river in which the most precious stones are found. There are twelve nations in the north who always dress their hair like that of women. Two of these nations are called the *Hac'acank'* and the *Hac'aink'*.

In the south the plains are used for pasturing elephants. They say that one nation which dwells in this country is made up of women and that at a certain time of the year dogs come among the elephants and have intercourse with the women who give birth to twins, one [male] puppy and the other a [human] girl. The sons cross the river to their fathers while the girls remain with their mothers. But I believe that this is just an allegory for they say the same about the Amazons in the Book of Alexander [the Great]. The allegory means that they are a quick-turning (?) people. Ptolemy says that there are temples of the moon in the southern extremity of the island. There are 1,378 other islands around Taprobane, some inhabited and others uninhabited but of which [only] nineteen names [are known to us]. The Equator crosses the south of this large island."[54]

The description is far richer than the initial text by Claudius Ptolemy, to such an extent that it is impossible to translate a great number of Indian productions because they have not been attested anywhere else. Such movements don't seem to have been totally disrupted by the Islam conquest because a precious Armenian document was copied in the twelfth century and is now kept in the Matenadaran of Yerevan. It contains a review of the distances the routes between Armenia and India represented, and it mentions the names of hundreds of towns. The text is a part of the itineraries compiled between the ancient Christianity times and the modern times; itineraries designed to help prepare journeys to the sub-continent. Besides, and as an example, in the lists of the Eastern cities the Armenians would go to, we can read:

> Nakhebtin is a big city with many Christian inhabitants and several churches. All these cities border the sea. From Nakhebtin we can reach Schabatin, and there, people can go to the holy apostle Thomas's tomb. The name of the city is Malab; it is at the seaside, and some Christians are still living there. From Malab, travellers go to Zouzer, a big rich city with many shops. In Malab, there is the holy apostle Thomas's tomb; in all the fountains there are leeches; only the water from the fountain located next to the saint's tomb is pure, fresh, and free from leeches."[55]

These itineraries have not been compiled, suggested, written, and copied without a purpose. Pilgrimages took place there, between the Armenian Plateau and Saint Thomas's sanctuary in Chennai. We have already mentioned them at the end of the note dedicated to Saint Thomas in the *haysmavouk* (synaxarion).

Thomas Cana, around 345

An important event in the ancient history of Christianity in India provided the first written evidence of such a pilgrimage. Being in Europe did not make it really possible to establish a precise enough analysis of this issue, but the one possible thing is that the Christians from the South of India apparently affirm that they do have some evidence of the visit of a certain Thomas of Jerusalem, an Armenian merchant who would have been there around A.D. 345 and settled down near the apostle's tomb, together with four hundred Christians from seventy-two families.[56] The fact that Armenians came there at a time when Shapour II was reigning and ordered many Christians to be put to death seems to be quite likely. The fact is notably attested in Portuguese sources, the two most ancient sources of which are the following ones:

Padre Alvaro Penteado, between 1515–1518, wrote to the king in Portugal:

> The establishment of these Christians, both from Cranganore and Coulao when they all came following St. Thomas, was brought about in this way: leaving Coulao, about which your Highness must have certain information, there went forth from Cranganore an Armenian merchant of advanced years who had no hope of ever returning to his homeland; he bought a piece of deserted land with its revenues from the ruler of those parts, both of the water and of the land, according to his landmarks which are still in existence; it is said that he married, and having had two

sons, the first became a priest and the heir to those revenues, which upon his death he left to the church, which today bears the name St. Thomas, and likewise he bought native men and women, whom he converted and married and protected and helped. His second son became a Justice of the Peace."[57]

Gaspar Correa, who lived in Goa between from 1512 to his death (between 1561 and 1583), mention named Thomas Chanaan.[58] About the same person Padre Francisco de Sousa, SJ, was written:

> This Armenian had numerous descendants, some from his legitimate wife, one Nayra Christian, others from a concubine: the legitimate descendants peopled Cranganor, Caturte, Cottete, Diamper, and other places: the bastards dispersed over other areas: and all greatly spread the Christianity of the Mountains. And inasmuch as all the other Christians with the exception of those in Travancor and Todamala were allied to these two families through marriage, there resulted two distinct groups which were at such variance in matters of honour that they would not intermarry. [...]
>
> Further adding that numerous Armenians who went to Malabar intermarried.[59]

The name of a man close to Thomas Cana, "Siphir," is an adulteration of the name "Sapor," which takes us back to the Sassanid period, more likely than to the Muslim domination.[60] Anyway, this Armenian merchant, Thomas, who became a pilgrim, would have received from the local king some privilege carved on the copper blades that were kept there until 1603 but were lost when being sent to Portugal. The privilege granted them a right to settle down on a land where they would build the city of Kuramaklur. The migration is supposed to have favored the Christian presence in the area and it created a solid foundation for future relationships with Armenia. I would like to get more information about it.[61]

Gregory of Tallard, around A.D. 380

The second fact I want to evoke is the arrival in the French Alps, in Tallard, near Gap, around 405, of an Armenian bishop who died there. He had been expelled from his country and his bishopric by a Sassanid invasion in 370. The Latin historian Ammianus Marcellinus, a contemporary of the fact, reported the event:

> Šapuh gathered his considerable forces and he largely destroyed Armenia, looting openly whatever was there."[62]

An Armenian source written around 460, the *Buzandaran*, completed this too short evocation. He added that the Sassanid armies first besieged the fortress where the queen, Pharandzêm, was confined:

Fig. 5: Gregory of Tallard setting off on a pilgrimage to India[63]

Then Šapuh the king of Persia sent two of his princes one of whom was called Zik and the other Karēn, with [a lot of] men against the realm of Armenia [...] They ravaged and devastated the entire land."[64]

Then began the systematic invasion of the whole country.[65] Part of the population was massacred and the other part made captive; "As for the prisoners, they were sent either to Assyria or to Khuzestan." Bishop Gregory was apparently taken to Khuzestan (Susian), but he soon left it to continue his exile, which became a real pilgrimage:

Having to flee away, Gregory consulted with the five persons who had shared danger with him about the place where they should go and seek refuge. History has transmitted only the names of four bishops, John, Paul, Mark, and Polycarp. They agreed they would go through India, Gregory's intention being to go and weep on Saint Thomas's tomb, to cry over his Church's woes and to draw on the supernatural force he needed to sustain the terrible assault the infernal spirit has engaged against him."[66]

The rest of his journey through Asia comprises six episodes, the four first ones concerning his journey to Chennai, but making an analysis of that journey is no easy task.

I - *A wreck in Bactria?*

The ship, which was carrying the bishops who had run away, ran aground along a not very hospitable shore, due to a tempest.[67] Having no information about the moment of the year when the voyage began, we cannot suppose what pitfalls they had to face. Navigation on the Persian Gulf being rather easy, it is very unlikely that the tempest may have happened while they were sailing along the Iranian coast. Besides, we are led to suppose that the first stage in their voyage was planned beyond the Sassanid kingdom or at least in its margins that were dominated by vassal sovereigns. So, the action of the run-away bishops must be placed beyond these regions. In Iran, indeed, they were considered as deportees fleeing their exile site. The wreck may rather have occurred along the Mekran coastline (the current Pakistan). In that region, there were actually peoples that Christianity saw as pagans, as they worshipped idols in temples. But the local sources made available to me don't mention any preaching mission in the years 380.

II - *Tolobia, or Northern India*

The second country where the Christian Armenians stopped was called Tobbia.[68] It is not easy to find the name hidden under this heading. In any case, with its poisonous snakes, the area described evokes the abundant vegetation of Northern India. Hinduism being established in the region, it left little room for a Christian preaching, about that not a single word is said anyway.

III - *Nobia, or Southern India*

As they continued their journey, they reached the South of India where, in the current Kerala area, the population had long been Christianized.[69] There, the hospitable attitude of the population was probably due to their Christian character, but also to the religious and business relationships they maintained with the country the bishops came from.

IV - *Arrival in Chennai (Madras)*

The description of their arrival in Madras, now called Chennai, was clearly influenced by what was written in the Portuguese reports.[70] However, the chapel that had been built at the top of Saint Thomas's Mount is a fact. Similarly, in the current church, which incorporates an older building, an ancient cross with an inscription written in Syriac is still above the altar. It may be there as a memorial, or as a representation of the cross that is mentioned in paragraph 39. The tears the bishop shad over the apostle's tomb are only the *cliché* they usually used in such occasions. The recall of the apostle's death is made in terms so general that they can't allow any historical or literary analysis. Yet, they assuredly correspond to the traditional account that was made of the apostle's death.[71]

Fig. 6: Gregory of Tallard baptizing and then marrying an Indian prince[72]

We have to suppose that this pilgrimage was sufficiently frequent to enable a regular transmission of information:

> The new danger Gregory and his companions had just avoided increased their trust in a divine providence watching over them, and it was so obvious to them that they handed their fates and safeguard to it and fearlessly continued their journey. The rumour that Gregory had affected many conversions among the idolaters and of the miracles that proved the holy character of his mission had been spread ahead of him in Annice, boosting the impatience people had to see him again.[73]

After they had achieved their pilgrimage, the Armenian pilgrims regained the Mediterranean region via a road that is not precisely reported. Their intention was to go on a pilgrimage in the Holy Land [§ 54-74]. Afterwards, Gregory headed for the Latin world and walked as far as Tallard, where his life ended after he had preached the Word in the region.

We have carefully studied that *vita* and edited it in French, and we have come to the conclusion that even if it had been progressively magnified, its historical background could not have been invented and that it really corresponded to a journey through the Indian sub-continent. In the documents attached to this communication, there is a visual graph of the whole journey Gregory undertook through Asia.

Beyond these journeys, there were attested relationships at an ecclesial and theological level.

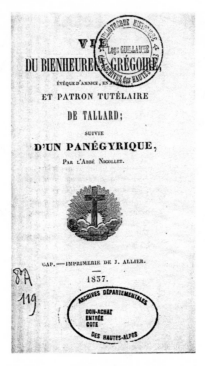

Fig. 7: Edition of the life of Gregory of Tallard by Father Nicollet[74]

THE ARMENIAN CATHOLICOS SAHAK III DSOROPORETSI RECOGNIZES THE INDIANS' ORTHODOXY

Now we must come to a top-class document. Earlier, we have too briefly evoked the foundation of a Christian Church in Armenia, under the leadership of a Catholicos, Saint Gregory the Illuminator, at the end of the third century. The Catholicos of Vagharshapat—a city later called Etchmiadzin—was, and still is, despite the vagaries of history, the supreme guide of the Armenian Apostolic Church. The Catholicos was the leader of the bishops he consecrated, and he also was the supreme legal recourse and the guardian of the Doctrine. The symbol of the unity of all the members of that Church was the consecration of the Holy Chrism, the *Myron*, by the Catholicos, who would do it at regular intervals in the presence of the bishops. Being the guardian of the Doctrine, he would send bishops to the ecumenical councils—cf. the Council of Nicea, in A.D. 325—and bring together national Councils. It is on this basis that the Armenian Catholicos became a reference in the East.

The Catholicos we are interested in is Sahak Dzoraporesti (Սահակ Զորոփորեցի). He was the Bishop of Rotakk before he was elected Catholicos in 667.[75] His Pontificate took place at an essential moment of the Middle-East history, when the Armenian lords had to repel the Khazars' invasion during the seventh year of his pontificate (685) and had also to fight the Muslim invaders.

During the year 691, Caliph Abd al-Malig's armies conquered militarily Armenia. As he was a sharp political leader, the Caliph designated Sembat VI Bagratuni—a man who was not favorable to the Byzantine Greeks—as the crown prince (691–711) responsible for the management of that difficult transitory period and for the integration of the Armenian plateau into the Muslim world.[76] In 695, Sembat VI Bagratuni tried to rebel but the Muslim general Mohamed Ibn Merwan made him a prisoner, together with the Catholicos Sahak III, and sent them both to Damascus as prisoners. After a while, Sembat VI Bagratuni went back to Armenia, but Sahak III was confined in Syria.[77] He probably stayed there until he died (703), but continued to play a spiritual and a political role in the negotiation of the Armenian integration into the Islamic empire.

His theological thought was known through those of his works that came to us. He is the author of liturgical hymns (*charagans*), which are still being used in the Armenian church, and also of a homily that has been saved.[78] Council acts were written under his pontificate and probably drafted under his direction.[79]

His main theological work—one we are most concerned with, as it directly serves our purpose—is a speech by Sabak III, or an *Explanation of the unanimous theology of the holy spiritual fathers, in accordance with the tradition the apostles of Christ's Church have established, with the Armenian's theology of the true orthodox tradition, pronounced against the diophysite Nestorians, given by the saint doctor and great interpreter Sahak, the Catholicos of Armenia.*[80]

The Speech, which is in fact a genuine theological treaty, has been kept in the *Book of Letters*, գիրք Թղթոց, a collection of ninety-eight official letters the Armenian church sent to prelates of the Christian world. We shall note that the first part of the collection was compiled, probably in the seventh century, whereas the letters edited in the second part were written later, during the Cilician period (eleventh and twelfth centuries). The only complete manuscript, copied in the Armenian Cilicia in 1298–1299, is now being kept in the Bzommar convent, in document 431. It has been re-edited three times since it was discovered.[81] We have also examined the text on the basis of defending its authenticity as well as its having been attributed to the Catholicos Sahak III, even though such an important text was used later as a model for several texts of the same kind.[82]

Text analysis

Here is now a more precise presentation of the *Speech* he wrote about 691.[83] The text has been studied and translated into French by Michel van Esbroeck, who sees in it a review of the religious thought of the Armenian church of the period. The Belgian Armenologist rightly detected the "Manifesto of the Armenian Faith"[84] the text stood for. It is long and dense, and begins with a historical introduction stating that there was a special link between Armenia and the Greek culture, which permitted a transmission of faith without risking a suspicion of heresy (1–5). The Trinitarian faith is founded on the teachings of Gregory the Illuminator as they appear in the central part of Agathangelos' history (6–10). Then, Sahak III tackled the Incarnation issue in its various aspects, referring to an important patristic file (11–15) and its characteristics: Natures (16–21), Divine Names (22–24), energy (25–27) and will (28–29), Jesus who is sitting on God's right and will be until the Judgment Day (30–38). After that positive approach, the same themes are taken again to show the groundlessness of the adverse theses, the unique Nature of Christ (39–44), the unique will (45–46), the unique activity (47–48), the incorruptible flesh (49–51), the life-giving Cross (53–58) and the passible and the impassible (59–65). Then, concerning a possible addition of the Trisagion, he develops the historical issue of the Armenian church as a communion (66–70). The next part is again dedicated to reducing the adverse theses (71–83). The end of the text is dedicated to the Eucharistic question of unleavened bread and of pure grape wine (84–89). The way the text is constructed is quite complex, with an alternation of an affirmation of the Armenian church's faith and a criticism of the positions of the opposing side, the conclusion affirming the Eucharistic position of that Church.[85]

The document, therefore, has a real intrinsic value and a great significance.

The orthodoxy of Indian church

The most important point for us is the § 67 from the *Speech*. In that passage, which appears in the last third of the text, after he had shared his thoughts about theology, Sahak III uses an argument that is neither scriptural, nor theological, nor patristic, but is rather linked to the communion of his See with the rest of the Christian world:

Իսկ եթէ Յոյնք ոչ ընդունին զպատմութիւնն Սոկրատեայ եւ զաւանդութիւն երանելոյն Յովհաննու, յայտնապէս վարդապետացն իւրեանց իսին անարգիչք, որպէս եւ հրեայք՝ մարգարէիցն։ Բայց եթէ զայս ոչ ընդունին ցուցցեն յաստուածեղէն գրոց, եթէ ո՞ ի սրբոց հարցն ասաց, Սուրբ Աստուած առանց՝ խաչեցարի, եւ յորո՞ւմ գիրս գրեալ է։ Ապա եթէ ոչ կարեն ցուցանել, ուրեմն ճշմարիտ է պատմութիւնն

248

Սոկրատեայ: Վասն որոյ եւ մեք ընդ սուրբ, եւ ընդ Իգնատիոսի եւ ընդ
Ոսկեբերանին Յովհաննու խոստովանեալ եմք եւ ասեմք ի սկզբանէ
մինչեւ ցայսաւր, " Սուրբ Աստուած հզաւր եւ անմահ, որ խաչեցար
վասն մեր, ողորմեա՝ մեզ:" եւ ոչ միայն մեք, այլ եւ Եգիպտացիք,
եւ Ափրիկեցիք, եւ արեւմտեան Հնդիկք, եւ Եթովպացիք, եւ
Հռովմայեցիք, եւ Սպանիացիք, եւ մեծ ազգն Փռանգաց, եւ արեւելեան
Հնդիկք, եւ Ճենաստանեայք, եւ Ասորիք, եւ ազգ մի ի Հնաց աշխարհին,
եւ Աղուանք, եւ մեք հայաստանեայսս: Այս ազգք երկոտասան միաբան
ամենեքեան ասեմք. "Սուրբ Աստուած հզաւր եւ անմահ, որ խաչեցար
վասն մեր, ողորմեա մեզ":- Now, if the Greeks don't accept Socrates'
speech and the tradition coming from John Chrysostom, it means that
they clearly deny their own doctors, just as the Jews deny their prophets. But the fact they don't accept it is shown in their theological books:
Which one of the Holy Fathers said: 'Saint God, without the *'Ye who wert
crucified for us'*, and in which one of the books has this been written? If
they are unable to show it, then Socrates' history at least is quite true.
That is the reason why, together with the saints, with Ignatius and John
Chrysostom, we have confessed and said, from the origin to this very
day: Saint God, Thou that art strong and immortal, Thou that wast crucified, have mercy on us!

> And not only us, but also the Egyptians, the Africans, the West Indians,
> the Ethiopians, the Romans, the Spanish, the vast nation of the Franks, of
> the East Indians, the Chinese, the Assyrians, and those from a nation of the
> Huns country, the peoples of the Caucasus and we, the Armenians.

We who are from twelve different nations say all in unison: Saint
strong and immortal God, Thou that wast crucified for us, have mercy
on us![86]

The model for that list was obviously the peoples table on Pentecost
Day, in the *Apostles' Acts* (II, 8–11), but this updating of it deserves some
comments. The Caucasian Albania (the Ałuank), constituted a Church
very similar to the Armenian church throughout the Middle-Ages and
until the Touranian tribes' invasion and the decimation of the population.
Similarly, the Assyrians maintained close ties with the Armenian church
because the Catholicos Nerses II consecrated a bishop designated for their
church, in 555, and then again, in 723, another Catholicos, Yovhannes
Ōjnecʻi (John of Odzoun), invited some Syrian bishops to one of the main
Armenian councils of the eighth century, the Manazkert Council.[87] Their
presence at the Council shows that their communion was still consistent
a generation after Sahak III's *Speech*. The mention of the Huns' country
probably refers to the consequences of the bishop Macarius' predication
evoked earlier. The Copts and the Ethiopians (Egyptians, West Indians,
African Ethiopians), well before that period, already maintained close
ties with the Armenians, precisely in Jerusalem, where the Armenian
patriarch was in charge of the Oriental Orthodox (non-Chalcedonian)

Christians. In 1459, at the time when the Ottomans organizedthe Holy Land, the Syrians, and the Copts and those who depended on them were linked to the Armenian Patriarch of Constantinople. Therefore, the Indians and the Ethiopians were also subjected to that patriarch, which explains why Jacome Abuna was sent to India (as we shall explain later).[88]

As for the relationships with the Latin world peoples (the Spanish, the Franks, and the Romans), the fact is not really surprising. Let's remember that, in 649, an Armenian monastery was attested in Rome.[89] It must have been very active, because its prior attended a council of the Roman Church. And in 642 also, an Armenian Prince, Artabasdos, was exiled in Spain by a Byzantine emperor who may have been Heraclius. He was probably not the only one to be thus sent to the Visigoths kingdom, and he married a royal princess there. They had a son who became king of the Visigoths (680–687).[90] A part of his Court may have returned to the East when the Emperor died. Finally, the fact that a few years before, in 591, the bishop Symeon, who fled Persia and servitude, ended his life at the Court of the Merovingian kings, shows clearly that the ties between both nations really existed.[91]

Now, what of the Eastern nations? We have underlined the great importance of the Christian Chinese being mentioned, for it allows us to affirm that after it was established by the apostle Thomas,[92] that Church developed and maintained some ties with the other Christian Churches. Moreover, its being explicitly mentioned in a Christological text bears witness to our point of view concerning the orthodoxy of that Church. After a stele carved in 781 was discovered in Si-n'gan-fou, near Xi'an, the historians were inclined to think that the Chinese Christians, if they ever existed, were all "Nestorians." Yet, the Catholicos Sahak III's testimony makes us temper that position.

And what about the Indians? We must insist that the fact is well established in two manuscripts still preserved.[93] It is a precisely dated attestation of the orthodoxy of the Indian Christianity, after it was founded by the apostle Thomas and had developed in connection with the Middle-East and with Egypt, as attested by the papyrus 413 found in Oxyrhynque, Actually, the fact the Catholicos Sahak III took the Chinese church into account takes much importance in his speech and it will be a landmark and serve as a model in the future relationships of his Church with the Byzantine Church. The mention proves that the relationships between India and Armenia were reasonably usual for the Catholicos to know that a Christian Church existed there and what its theological orientation was. *The Speech* required, for the Catholicos Sahak III, to be fully aware of being in communion with the church of the Indian community, which apparently dated back to Thomas's preaching. His approach would then be the one of a Primate of the church Bartholomew founded, a Primate who would fraternally address the members of the church his mission companion, Thomas, had founded. This indeed is not a meaningless symbol of communion.

This position was solid enough and fairly well accepted to be restated and confirmed by another Catholicos, Khatchik I Arsharouni (973-992). In his answer to a letter the Chalcedonian Metropolitan from Melitene sent to him, he justified at length the doctrinal position of his Church and ended his letter by emphasizing the fact that the Armenians, as many other Eastern nations, don't recognize the Council of Chalcedon, thus including once more the Indians within his Communion:

"ամենայն Հայք, Աղուանք, Լփինք, Կաղքք, Ճիղքք, Ասորեստանեայք որք են Յակոբիկ, ամենայն եգիմպտոս, Եթիովպա մեծ, Արաբինար, եւ ամենայն աշխարհն Հնդկաց:- Armenian, Ałuans, Lepnik, Gałpk, Giłpk, Assyrians who are the Jacobites, the whole of Egypt, Great Ethiopia, Arabia, Arabinar and the whole world of India."[94]

We find again the same affirmation, three times, under the pen of Ananias of Narek (tenth century) who was the founder of the theological school of Narek, especially known through the name of Gregory of Narek (†1001), the thirty-sixth Doctor of the Catholic Church.[95]

The last point we would like to emphasize is that we have found no other affirmation being so clearly expressed of the full orthodoxy of the Indian church (in Kerala and Chennai) corresponding to the patristic or to the medieval period.

These elements mostly represent what we can learn from a review of the Armenian sources dating back to the fifth to the eleventh centuries, or from the volumes 1 to 20 from the *Madenakirk hayotz* collection (Armenian Classical Authors), i.e., about 20,000 pages that bring together all the essential Armenian texts about Thomas for that period. Now we shall examine the historical elements in the Armenian-Indian relationships.

We lack the time to develop how extensive the links the Armenian and the Indian Christians shared, but we shall highlight two events relating to the medieval period, events that will open new research avenues for the future.

On the one hand, the researcher Raphael Liogier, in his book *Jesus, a Western Buddhah*, remarked that the *Lalatavistara*, "one of the oldest texts of the Buddhist canon of the Big Vehicle, comprises some strange similarities with the Armenian version of the Christian apocryphal of the *History of Jesus' Childhood*."[96]

251

On the other hand, the Latin missionaries' testimonies are first-value sources as far as the thirteenth and fourteenth centuries are concerned. Through their letters, we learnt there was an Armenian colony on the Chinese coastline, in Zaiton, in the region of Fujan, Zaiton being a port used for trading exchanges with the Southern seas and with the West. When the Franciscan missionaries arrived, in 1309, a rich Armenian lady funded the first Western Church (a catholic one) in China:

> In the city of Cayton (Zaytun) we have a good church witch an Armenian lady left us, with a house, and she provided the necessities of life for ourselves and for others if they come.[97]

André de Pérouse, the catholic bishop of Zaiton himself, related this fact in a letter he addressed to the Pope.[98] And again, in 1321 or 1322, Odoric de Perdenone, is a witness to the use of the Armenian language in the Indian Ocean, and Armenian was still being used at the beginning of the fourteenth century in the same area.[99] So, it was a language people used when they travelled in Asia.

As a conclusion, Thomas, Bartholomew's companion, and the apostle of India, holds a major place in the Armenian tradition. Furthermore, for ages the Armenian Catholicos have been considering that the Christians who lived in India were of their Communion, and their history was curiously governed by two Armenians of conviction and of high values: Thomas Cana and Jacome Abuna.

BIBLIOGRAPHY

Primary sources

Armenian sources

ACA   *Armenian Classical Autors* (Մատենագիրք Հայոց), Yegavian Zaven (dir.), Antelias, Libanon, Yerevan, Armenia, since 2003, XX vols.

Agathange, éd. Tēr-Mkrtč'ean–Kanayeanc', 1909-1980 = Karapet Tēr-Mkrtč'ean et StepanKanayeanc', Ագաթանգեղայ պատմութիւն –*Agathange, Histoire des Arméniens*, Tiflis, 1909-1980.

Agathange, tr. Thomson, 1976 = Robert W. Thomson, Agathangelos, *History of the Armenians*, Albany, 1976.

Agathange, tr. Thomson, 2001 = Robert W. Thomson, *The Teaching of Saint Gregory*, New York, St. Nersess Armenian Seminary, "Avant," 2001.

Lafontaine, 1973 = Guy Lafontaine, "Une vie grecque abrégée de saint Grégoire l'Illuminateur, cod. Sin. Gr., 376," *LM*, 86, 1973, 125-145.

Muradyan, 1982 = Papoyr Muradyan, Ագաթանգեղոսի Հին վրացերէն խմբագրությունները (*Les vieilles recensions géorgiennes d'Agathange*), Erevan, Académie des Sciences, "Arméno-géorgica 2," 1982, *en armé-nien et géorgien*.

Lives of Saint Gregory, trad. Thomson, 2010 = Robert W. Thomson, *The Lives of Saint Gregory: The Armenian, Greek, Arabic, and Syriac Versions of the History Attributed to Agathangelos, translated with Introduction and Commentary*, Ann Arbor, Caravan Books, 2010.

Anania, ed. Abrahamyan, 1944 = Ašot Abrahamyan, Անանիա Շիրակացու մատենագրությունը (*Ananias of Sirak, Bibliography*), Yerevan, 1944.

Armenian Geographical Notices, ed. Venise, 1882 = "Notices géographiques d'après des manuscrits arméniens ," *P*, Venise, 1882, 40-4, 311–319.

Armenian synaxarion of Ter Israel, ed.tr. Bayan, 1909-1930 = G. Bayan, *Le synax-aire arménien de Ter Israel*, Turnhout, Brepols, *PO*, XII vols., 1909–1930.

Ašxarhac'oyc', tr. Hewsen, 1992 = Robert H. Hewsen, *The geography of Ananias of Sirak, Ašxarhac'oyc', the long and the short recensions*, Wiesbaden, L. Reichert, "Beihefte zum Tübinger Atlas des Vorderen Orients. Reihe B, Geisteswissenschaften," 1992.

Asołik, ed. Malxaseanc', 1885 = Stepan Malxaseanc', Սթեզերական պատմութիւն, Ստեփանոս Ասողիկ Տարոնեցի (*Stephen of Taron, Asołik, Stories*), Saint-Petersbourg, 1885.

Asołik, tr. Dulaurier, 1883 = Édouard Dulaurier, *Açogh'ig de Daron, Étienne, Histoire universelle, première partie*, Paris, E. Leroux, 1883.

Asołik, tr. Macler, 1917 = Frédéric Macler, *Étienne Asoghik de Taron, Histoire uni-verselle, 2ᵉ partie, Livre III*, Paris, Impr. Nationale, 1917.

Book of letters, ed. Izmireanc', 1901 = J. Izmireanc', Գիրք Թղթոց (*Book of letters*), Tiflis, 1901.

Book of letters, ed. Połarean, 1994 = Mgr N. Połarean, Գիրք Թղթոց (*Book of letters*), Jerusalem, 1994.

Buzandaran, ed. Venise, 1933 = Ի չորս դպրութիւնս, Պատմութիւն Հայոց, (*Buzandaran, Histoiry of the Armemians*), Venice, Mekhitarists Press, 1933.

Buzandaran, tr. Garsoïan, 1989 = Nina Garsoïan, *The Epic Histories attribued to Phawstos Buzand, Buzandaran patmoutioun*, Cambridge, Harvard University Press, "Texts and Studies no 8," 1989.

Gregory Magistros, ed. Kostaneanc̕, 1910, = K. Kostaneanc̕, Գրիգոր Մագիստրոս,թղուղթ (*Letters of Gregory Magistros*), Alexandroplis 1910.

Kirakos of Ganjak, ed. Melik-Ohanǰanyan, 1961 = K. Melik-Ohanǰanyan, Կիրակոս Գանձակեցի, Պատմութիւն Հայոց (*Kirakos of Ganjak, Universal history*), Yerevan, Academy of Sciences, 1961.

Komitas, ed. Tēr-Mkrtč̕ean, 1914 = Karapet Tēr-Mkrtč̕ean, Կնիք Հաւատոյ ընդհանուր սուրբ եկեղեցւոյ յուղղափառ եւ Ս. Հոգեկիր Հարցն մերոյ դաւանութեանց յաղագս կոմխտաս կաթողիկոսի ՀամաՀաւաքեալ (*Seal of the faith of the holy universal Church, and inspired our Orthodox holy Fathers, made in the days of Catholicos Komitas*), Etchmiadzin, Catholicossales Press, 1914, cxxviii (anastatic reprint of the edition of 1914 by Peeters Publishing, Louvain 1974).

Łazar P̕arpec̕i, ed. Tēr-Mkrtč̕ean–Malxaseanc̕, 1904 = Karapet Tēr-Mkrtč̕ean et Stepan Malxaseanc̕, Ղազար Փարպեցի, Պատմութիւն Հայոց (*Ghazar Parpetsi, History of Armenia*), Tiflis, 1904.

Łazar P̕arpec̕i, ed. Ouloupapyan, 1982 = Pakrat Ouloupapyan, Ղազար Փարպեցի, Պատմութիւն Հայոց (*Ghazar parpetsi, History of Armenia*), Yerevan, University Press of Yerevan, 1982.

Łazar P̕arpec̕i, tr. Thomson, 1991 = Robert W. Thomson, *The History of Lazar P̕arpec̕i*, Atlanta, Scholars Press, "Columbia University Program in Armenian Studies, Suren D. Fesjian Academic Publication," 1991.

Movsēs Dasxuranc̕i, tr. Dowsett, 1961 = Charles J.F. Dowsett, *Movses Daskhourantsi, The history the Caucasian Albanians*, Paris, Oxford University Press, "London Oriental Series no 8," 1961.

Movsēs Kałankatwac̕i, ed. Arakelyan, 1983 = Arakelyan Varak, Մովսէս Կաղանկատուացի, Պատմութիւն Աղուանից (*Movses Kałankatwac̕i, History of the countries of Albanians*), Yerevan, 1983.

Movses Khorents̕i, tr. Thomson, 1978 = Thomson Robert W., *Movses Khorenats̕i, History of the Armenians*, Londres, Harvard university press, "Harvard Armenian texts and studies no 4," 1978.

Movses Khorents̕i, ed. Abełyan–Harut̕iunyan, 1991 = Abełyan Manouk et Harut̕iunyan Stepan, Մովսէս Խորենացի, Հայոց պատմություն (*Movses Khorenats̕i, History of the Armenians*), Yerevan, 1991.

Movses Khorents̕i, tr. Thomson, 2006 = Thomson Robert W., *Movses Khorenats̕i, History of the Armenians*, Revised edition, Ann Arbor, Caravan Books, 2006.

Mxit'ar, ed. Émine, 1860 = Émine Jean-Baptiste, *Mékhitar d'Aïrivank, Histoire d'Arménie*, Mouscou, 1860.

Mxit'ar, tr. Brosset, 1869 = Marie-Félicité Brosset, *Mékhitar d'Aïrivank, Histoire chronologique*, Mémoire de l'Acad. des Science de Saint-Pétersbourg, t. XIII, 5, Saint-Pétersbourg, 1869.

Sahak III, tr. van Esbroeck, 1995 = Michel Van Esbroeck, "Le discours du catholicos Sahak III en 691 et quelques documents arméniens annexes au Quinisexte," *Kanonika*, Pontificio Istituto Orientale, VI, 1995, 323-463.

Samuēl, tr. Brosset, 1876 = Marie-Félicie Brosset, "*Samuel d'Ani, Tables chronologiques*," in Collections d'historiens arméniens, 2, Saint-Petersbourg, Académie impériale des sciences, 1876, vol. II, 348–483.

Samuēl, ed. Tēr-Mik'aēlean, 1893 = Tēr-Mik'aēlean., *Սամուէլ Անեցի, Հաւաքմունք ի գրոց պատմագրաց* (*Samuel d'Ani, Chronographie*), Etchmiadzin, 1893.

Sebēos, tr. Macler, 1904 = Macler Frédéric, *Histoire d'Héraclius par l'évêque Sebeos*, Paris, E. Leroux, 1904.

Sebēos, ed. Abgaryan, 1979 = Guevork Abgaryan, *Պատմութիւն Սեբէոսի* (*Histoire de Sebēos*), Yerevan, Academy of Sciences, 1979.

Sebēos, tr. Thomson, 1999 = Robert W. Thomson et James Howard-Johnston, *The Armenian History Attributed to Sebeos*, Liverpool, Liverpool University Press 1999.

Socrates, tr. Thomson, 2001 = Robert W. Thomson, The *Armenian Adaptation of the Ecclesiastical History of Socrates Scholasticus: Translation of the Armenian Text and Commentary*, Louvain, Peeters, "Hebrew University Armenian studies 3," 2001.

Step'annos Siwnec'i, ed.-tr. Findikyan, 2004 = Michael Daniel Findikyan, *The commentary on the armenian daily office by bishop Stepanos Siwnetsi (†735), critical edition and translation with textual and liturgical analysis*, Rome, pontificio Instituto Orientale, "Orientalia Christiana Analecta no 270," 2004.

Step'annos Orbēlean, tr. Brosset, 1864-1866 = Marie-Félicité Brosset, *Stepanos Orbelean, Histoire de la Siounie*, Saint-Pétersbourg, Academy of Sciences, 1864-1866, II vols.

T'ouma Arcruni, tr. Thomson, 1985 = Robert W. Thomson, *Thomas Artsruni, History of the House of the Artsrunik*, Detroit, Wayne State University Press, 1985.

Typicon, 1782 = *Typicon de l'Église arménienne*, Venise, 1782.

Uxtanēs, tr. Brosset, 1870 = Marie-Félicité Brosset, "Histoire de l'Arménie par Uxtanēs d'Édesse," *Deux historiens arméniens*, St-Petersbourg, 1870.

Uxtanēs, ed. Etchmiadzin, 1871 = *Հայոց պատմություն* (Uxtanēs*of Edessa, History of Armenia*), Etchmiadzin, 1871.

Uxtanēs, tr. Arzoumanian, 1985 = Zaven Arzoumanian, *Bishop Ukhtanes of Sebastia. History of Armenia, Part II, History of the Severance of the Georgians from the Armenians*, Fort Lauderdale, 1985.

Vardan, ed. Ališan, 1862 = Léonce Alishan (Ališan), *Vardan Arevelt, Histoire de l'Arménie*, texte réédité par Robert Thomson, New York, 1862-1991.

Vardan, ed.-tr. Muyldermans, 1927 = Joseph Muyldermans, *La Domination arabe en Arménie, extrait de l'Histoire universelle de Vardan*, Louvain, 1927.

Vardan, tr. Thomson, 1989 = Robert W Thomson., The *Historical Compilation of Vardan Arewelc'i*, Dumbarton Oaks Papers, 1989, 43, 125–226.

Yovhannēs Drasxanakertc'i, tr. Boisson-Chenorhokian, 2004 = Patricia Boisson-Chenorhokian, *Yovhannēs Drasxanakertc'i, Histoire d'Arménie*, CSCO, vol. 605, sub. 115, 2004.

Apocryphal literature

Thaddeus'Acts, tr. Palmer, 2005 = Andew Palmer, "Actes de Thaddée ," in *Christian apocryphal writings*, II, 2005, 645-660.

Armenians apocryphals, ed. Č'rak'ean, 1904 = Č'rak'ean K'ervpē, (*Non-canonical apostolic writings*), Venise, Mechitarist Press, 1904.

Armenians apocryphals, tr. Leloir, 1986–1992 = Leloir Louis dom, *Écrits apocryphes sur les apôtres, traduction de l'édition arménienne de Venise*, Turnhout, Brepols, CC, series Apocryphorum, 3 et 4, 1986–1992.

Armenian Gospel of the Infancy, trad. Terian, 2008 = Terian Abraham, *The Armenian Gospel of the Infancy, with three early versions of the Protevangelium of James*, Oxford University Press, 2008.

Calzolari, 2011 = Valentina Calzolari, *Les Apôtres Thaddée et Barthélemy, aux origines du christianisme arménien*, Turnhout, Brepols, Collection: "Apocryphes n° 13 ," 2011.

Christian Apocryphal Writings, I, 1997 = Bovon François et Geoltrain Pierre (dir.), *Écrits apocryphes chrétiens, I [sélection d'écrits apocryphes sur Jésus et Marie, sur Jean-Baptiste et les apôtres, et des visions et révélations]*, Paris, Gallimard, "Bibliothèque de la Pléiade n° 442," 1997.

Christian apocryphal writings, II, 2005 = Geoltrain Pierre et Jean-Daniel Kaestli, *Écrits apocryphes chrétiens II, Contient une sélection d'écrits apocryphes sur Jésus et Marie, sur Jean-Baptiste et les apôtres, et des visions et révélations*, Paris, Gallimard, 2005.

Laboubna, ed Phillips, 1876 = George Phillips, The doctrine of Addai, the apostle, 1876, London, Trübner & Co, *in Syriac and English*.

Laboubna, ed. Alishan, 1868 = Leonce Alishan, *Abgar's Letter*, 1868, Venice, *in Armenian*.

Laboubna, tr. Emine, 1869 = Jean-Baptiste Emine, "Histoire d'Abgar et de la prédication de Thaddée," in V. Langlois, *Collection des historiens anciens et modernes de l'Arménie*, Paris, 1869 reprint in 1880 and 2001, vol. I, 313–321.

Lipsius-Bonnet, 1959 = Richard A. Lipsius and Bonnet Maximilien, *Apostolorum Apocrypha*, II volumes in 3 toms, Hildesiem-New York, Georg Olms, 1898-1959 (reedition).

Greek sources

Eusèbe, tr. Bardy, 1952-1960 = Gustave Bardy, *Eusèbe de Césarée, Histoire ecclési-astique*, SC 31, 41, 55 et 73, Paris, Le Cerf, 1952–1960.

Eusèbe, ed. Winkelmann, 1999 = Friedhelm Winkelmann, *Eusebius Werke, Die Kirchengeschichte*, Akademie Verlag, Berlin, 1999, III vols.

Eusèbe, tr. Bardy, 2003 = Gustave Bardy, *Eusèbe de Césarée, Histoire ecclésiastique*, traduction revue par Louis Neyrand, Paris, Cerf, "Sagesses chrétiennes," 2003.

Sozomenos, ed.-tr. Festugière–Grillet 1983-2008 = J. A. Festugière et Bernard Grillet, Grillet Bernard, *Sozomène, Histoire Ecclésiastique*, Paris, Le Seuil, SC no 306, 418, 495 et 516, 1983–2008, IV vols.

Strabo, ed.-tr. Lassère, 1981 = Lassère François, *Strabon, Géographie*, IX (Livre XII), Paris, Les Belles Lettres, "Collection des Universités de France," 1981.

Strabo, ed. Meineke 1895-1898 = Meineke August, *Strabonis Geographica*, Lipsig, B. G. Teubneri, 1877, 3 vols.

Syriac and Aramean sources

Gregorius Barhebraeus, *Chronicon Ecclesiasticum,*Syriac and Latin, éd. J.-B. Abbeloos et T. J. Lamy, Louvain, 1872–1877, 3 vols.

Zacharias Rhetor, ed. Brooks, 1919 = *Historia ecclesiastica Zachariae Rhetori*, ed. Brooks E. W., Paris, J. Gabalda, CSCO 84 et 88, Syr. 39 et 42, 1919-1924.

Latin sources

Ammianus Marcellinus, ed.-tr. Galletier, 1968-1999 = Galletier Édouard et Fontaine Jacques, *Ammien Marcellin, Histoires*, Paris, Belles Lettres, 1968–1999, VI.

Trigault, 1615 = Nicolas Trigault, *De Christiana expeditione apud sinas suscepta ab Societate Jesu. Ex P. Matthaei Riccii eiusdem Societatis commentariis Libri V: Ad S.D.N. Paulum V. In Quibus Sinensis Regni mores, leges, atque instituta, & novae illius Ecclesiae difficillima primordia accurate & summa fide describun-tur.* French transl. *Histoire de l'expédition chrestienne au royaume de la Chine rédigée à l'aide des papiers laissés par Matteo Ricci*, Lyon, 1616, and Modern édition: Matthieu Ricci SJ et Nicolas Trigault SJ: *Histoire de l'expédition chré-tienne du royaume de la Chine, 1582-1610.* Introduction par Joseph Shih SJ, établissement du texte et annotations par Georges Bessière, tables et index par Joseph Dehergne SJ, Paris, Desclée de Brouwer, Bellarmin, 1978. In-80, 744 pages, 8 planches. (Collection Christus, Textes no 45).

Portuguese sources

de Barros–do Couto 1777 – 1778 = João de Barros and Diogo do Couto, *Décadas da Ásia, dos feitos que os feitos que os portuguezes fizeram no descubrimento, e conquista dos mares, e terras do Oriente*, Lisbon, Regia Officina Typografica, 1777–1778, 24 vols.

Sousa, 1710 = Sousa, Francisco de, S.J., *Oriente conquistado a Jesu Christo pelos Padres da Companhia de Jesus da Provincia de Goa*, Lisbon, Officina de Valentim da Costa Deslandes, Impressor de Sua Magestade, 1710, 2 vols.

Studies (selected bibliography)

Bernard, 1935 = Henri Bernard, *La découverte de Nestoriens Mongols aux Ordos et l'histoire ancienne du Christianisme en Extrême-Orient*, Tientsin, 1935.

Boulnois, 2001 = Lucette Boulnois, *La Route de la soie, Dieux, guerriers et marchands*, Genève, Olizane, 2001.

Dauvillier, 1975 = Jean Dauvillier, "Les Arméniens en Chine et en Asie centrale au Moyen-Age," *Mélanges de sinologie offerts à M. Paul Deniéville*, Paris, 1975, t. 2, 1–17.

Farquhar,1972 = J. N. Farquhar, *The Apostle Thomas in India According to the Acts of Thomas*, Kerala, 1972.

Garitte, 1971 = Gérard Garitte, "La passion arménienne de S. Thomas l'apôtre et son modèle grec," *Le Muséon* 84, 1971, 171–195.

Gillman – Klimkeit, 1999 = Ian Gillman, and Hans-Joachim Klimkeit, *Christians In Asia Before 1500*, Ann Arbor, University of Michigan, 1999.

Kollaparampil, 1992 = Jacob Kollaparampil, *The Babylonian origin of the Southists among the St. Thomas Christians*, Roma, OCA, 214, 1992.

Medlycott, 1905 = A.E. Medlycott, *India and the Apostle Thomas*, London, David Nutt, 1905.

Mekkattukulam, 2007 = Jiphy Francis Mekkattukulam, *L'initiation chrétienne selon les actes de Thomas, l'unité liturgique et théologique du don de l' "onction – baptême – eucharistie ,"* Thèse de doctorat en histoire des religions et anthropologie religieuse et théologie, Paris IV-Sorbonne (prof. Monique Alexandre) et l'Institut catholique de Paris, Paris, Octobre 2007, 3 vols.

Menon, 1924 = Padmanabha Menon K.P., *History of Kerala*, 1924, *in malayalam.*

Mingana,1926 = Alphonse Mingana, "The Early Spread of Christianity in India," *Bulletin of the John Rylands Library*, 1926, 10, 2, 435–514.

Mundadan, 1984 = A. Mathias Mundadan, CMI, *History of Christianity in India multi-volume Series, Volume I, From the Beginning up to the Middle of the Sixteenth Century*, Church History Association of India, Bangalore, 1984,

Moule, 1930 = Arthur C. Moule, *Christians in China, Before the Year 1550*, Londres, 1930, 354, reissue Gorgias Press, "Syriac Studies Library 220," 1930 & 2011.

Moule, 1934 = Arthur C. Moule, *Nestorians in China, Some Corrections and Additions*, London, The China Society, 1940.

Nedungatt, 2008 = George Nedungatt, *Quest for the Historical Thomas Apostle of India: A Re-reading of the Evidence*, Bangalore, TPI, 2008, 430 pages.

Neill, 1984 = Neill Stephen, *A History of Christianity in India*, Cambridge University Press, 1984.

Neill, 2004 = Neill Stephen, *A History of Christianity in India, The Beginnings to AD 1707*. Cambridge University Press, 2004.

Perrier, 2011 = Pierre Perrier, *L'apôtre Thomas et le prince Ying à Kong Wang Shan, L'évangélisation de la Chine de 64 à 87*, Paris, Édition du Jubilé, 2011.

Robert, 1993 = Jean-Noël Robert, *De Rome à la Chine, Sur les Routes de la Soie au temps des Césars*, Paris, Les Belles Lettres, 1993 (3e tirage en 2004).

Sansterre, 1983 = Jean-Marie Sansterre, *Les moines Grecs et Orientaux à Rome, aux époques byzantine et carolingienne (milieu du VIe s.–fin du IXe s.)*, 2e série, LXVI,1–1983, Bruxelles, Palais des Académies, "Mémoires de la Classe de Lettres," 1993.

Seth, 1937 = Jacob Mesrob Seth, *Armenians in India—From the Earliest Times to the Present*, Calcutta, 1937.

Settipani, 2006 = Christian Settipani, *Continuité des élites à Byzance durant les siècles obscurs, les princes caucasiens et l'Empire du VIe au IXe siècle*, Paris, De Boccard, "De l'Archéologie à l'Histoire," 2006, 642 pages, 224–231.

Tchouhadjian, 2011 = Armand Tchouhadjian, *Pèlerins d'Arménie, saints d'Occident*, Lyon, Sources d'Arménie, "Armenia Christiana, 5," 2011.

Upadhyaya, 1996 = Padmanabha Upadhyaya, *Coastal Karnataka, Rashtrakavi Govind Pai Samshodhana Kendra*, 1996.

Yevadian, 2006 = Maxime Yevadian, *Dentelles de pierre, d'étoffe, de parchemin et de métal, Les arts des chrétiens d'Arménie du Moyen Age, la grammaire ornementale arménienne*, Lyon, Sources d'Arménie, 2006.

Yevadian, 2007 = Maxime Yevadian, *Christianisation de l'Arménie, Retour aux sources, La genèse de l'Église d'Arménie, I (des origines au milieu du IIIᵉ siècle)*, Lyon, Sources d'Arménie, Armenia Christiana, 1.

Yevadian, 2008 = Maxime Yevadian, *Christianisation de l'Arménie, Retour aux sources, L'œuvre de saint Grégoire, II (du milieu du IIIᵉ siècle aux années 330)* Lyon, Sources d'Arménie, *Armenia Christiana*, 2.

Yevadian, 2011 = Maxime Yevadian, *Saint Grégoire d'Arménie Patron de Tallard*, Lyon, Sources d'Arménie, "Armenia Christiana, 6*," 2011.

Yevadian, 2013 = Maxime Yevadian, "Le Catholicos arménien Sahak III Dzoroporetsi et l'Église de Chine," *Actes du Colloque de Paris des 30 novembre et 1ᵉʳ décembre 2012*, Paris, 2013, 123–166.

Yevadian, 2017 = Maxime Yevadan, "Les rapports entre Aganthange et les Vies et leurs conséquences sur l'étude de la catéchèse attribuée à saint Grégoire l'Illuminateur», *Oriens Christianis*, 2017, 100, 104-128.

Yevadian, 2018 = Maxime Yevadian, *Arménie un atlas historique*, Lyon, Sources d'Arménie, 2016¹, 2017,²⁻³, 2018.⁴⁻⁵

Yevadian–Khayiguian, 2014 = Maxime Yevadian and Georges Khayiguian, *Saint Servatius Patron de Maastricht*, Lyon, Sources d'Arménie, "Armenia Christiana, 7," 2012.

LIFE OF GREGORY OF TALLARD

In Yevadian, 2011, 65–70.

Chapitre troisième:

Voyage de Grégoire aux Indes

24. La paix dont jouissait l'église d'Amnice sous le gouvernement de Grégoire fut troublée par une violente irruption de barbares qui, voulant rétablir le culte des idoles, mirent tout à feu et à sang, à cause de la résistance qu'ils trouvèrent dans les chrétiens d'Amnice. **25.** Le saint patron ne craignit point d'affronter le péril pour confirmer son peuple dans la foi, et l'encourager à verser son sang pour la gloire de Dieu, qui le premier versa le sien pour notre salut. **26.** Le ciel bénit ses [22] efforts, car aucun de ceux qu'il avait évangélisés ne renia sa foi. **27.** Contraint de fuir, Grégoire se concerta avec les cinq personnes qui avaient partagé avec lui le danger, sur le lieu où ils iraient chercher un asile. **28.** L'histoire ne nous a transmis que le nom de quatre évêques, Jean, Paul, Marc et Polycarpe. **29.** Ils convinrent de passer aux Indes, car l'intention de Grégoire était d'aller pleurer, sur le tombeau de l'apôtre saint Thomas, les maux de son Église, et d'y puiser la force de soutenir le terrible assaut que lui livrait l'esprit infernal. **30.** Le ciel voulant faire subir une nouvelle épreuve à la vertu de ses serviteurs, permet que la tempéte leur ferme le passage de la mer, et les oblige à jeter l'ancre dans un lieu opposé à leur dessein.

I–**31.** [23] Voyant leur vie en danger, nos pèlerins, tout en bénissant la providence cèdent à l'orage et s'acheminent à travers un sentier raboteux dont ils ignorent l'issue. Contre leur attente, ils arrivent bientôt dans une province idolâtre, non éloignée du lieu où ils avaient débarqué. **32.** Grégoire se rappelant ces paroles du Sauveur: que son évangile doit être prêché dans tout l'univers, "cette bonne nouvelle du royaume sera prêchée dans le monde entier," se hâte de l'annoncer, convaincu que le Seigneur l'a détourné de sa course pour procurer à ces infortunés, le bonheur de connaître leur créateur. **33.** Pratiquant [Grégoire] le premier les vertus qu'il annonce, ces idolâtres abjurent bientôt leurs erreurs. La douceur, le calme peint sur tous ses traits au milieu des [24] revers dont il est la proie depuis longtemps, lui gagnent les coeurs et les portent à l'imiter. **34.** Se voyant entouré de nombreux prosélytes, Grégoire dédie au Seigneur les temples que le démon occupait il n'y a qu'un instant, et il a la joie de pouvoir offrir à Dieu la seule victime qui lui soit agréable dans un lieu où le culte qui lui est dû, était rendu à des dieux étrangers. [25]

Chapitre quatrième:
Grégoire continue, par terre, son voyage aux Indes

II–35. Après un séjour de trois mois dans ce pays idolâtre, ayant confirmé dans la foi les nouveaux convertis, Grégoire suivi de ses compagnons d'infortune, continua son pèlerinage. Ils s'engagèrent alors dans un chemin beaucoup plus difficile encore que celui qui les avait conduits dans ce lieu. Ils traversèrent des endroits tout-à-fait stériles; les sentiers étaient frayés au milieu de sablières, d'où l'on ne pouvait se tirer qu'avec beaucoup de peine. 36. Après [26] des efforts presque incroyables, ils arrivèrent à Tholobie, pays plus mauvais encore, occupé par des serpens et autres animaux venimeux qui les eussent infailliblement dévorés, si le Seigneur, pour l'amour duquel ils souffraient tant de maux, ne les eût délivrés en ralentissant la faim de ces monstres, et en amortissant leur venin.

III–37. Nos voyageurs éprouvèrent à Nobie, d'une manière bien sensible, l'effet de cette promesse du Sauveur, qui dit que son joug est léger pour celui qui le porte avec courage: là ils rencontrèrent un peuple chrétien qui les reçut avec une charité vraiment hospitalière et qui compatit, autant qu'il le put, au triste récit de leur malheur.

IV–38. Remis des peines de leur long et pénible voyage, ils continuent [27] leur route avec une nouvelle ardeur, espérant que le Seigneur, qui vient de leur accorder tant de consolations, leur donnera encore celle de vénérer l'objet de leurs voeux. 39. Leur confiance n'est point trompée, car sous peu ils arrivent à *Meliapour* ou *Coeloemines*15, elle [la route qu'il empruntait] joint le golfe de Bengale ou Coromandel. C'est dans cette ville, que l'apôtre saint Thomas dédia une église au Seigneur, en mémoire des prodiges qu'il y avait opérés pour sa gloire et par sa puissance; il est même dit dans la légende du bienheureux Grégoire, qu'il trouva dans cette église une croix en pierre érigée par l'apôtre saint Thomas, portant cette inscription:

> *Quand par permission divine les vagues de la mer viendront mouiller cette pierre, de nouveaux apôtres [28] d'une terre étrangère confirmerons la doctrine que je vous prêche.*

40. Cette prophétie eut son accomplissement à l'époque où les Portugais firent la conquête de ce pays. 41. Fidèle gardien du temple qu'il avait voué au Seigneur, saint Thomas mourut d'un coup de lance, que lui porta un des sacrificateurs des idoles qui voulait profaner le lieu saint. 42. Les chrétiens de Meliapour, en proie à la douleur la plus cuisante à la vue du massacre du saint apôtre, lui prouvèrent leur attachement en exposant leur vie pour ravir son corps à ses meurtriers; le ciel ayant secondé leurs efforts, ils l'ensevelirent dans le caveau de l'enceinte sacrée où il avait remporté la palme du martyre. 43. L'aspect du tombeau du saint apôtre pénétra Grégoire [29] et ses compagnons de la plus vive émotion. Ils l'arrosèrent de leurs larmes et, après avoir imploré

son secours avec une ferveur vraiment digne du crédit dont il jouit auprès du Dieu tout-puissant, enflammés d'un courage tout nouveau, ils pensèrent à regagner leur chère patrie dont ils espéraient adoucir les maux, en annonçant à leurs concitoyens qu'ils venaient de leur conquérir un puissant secours dans la protection de l'apôtre saint Thomas.

V–**44.** Les souffrances et les tribulations étant la voie ordinaire par laquelle Dieu conduit ses saints à la gloire, il permit qu'au sortir de Meliapour, nos pèlerins tombassent au pouvoir des émissaires d'un roi barbare. **45.** Ceux-ci les chargèrent de fers comme s'ils [30] eussent été de grands criminels, les conduisirent à leur maître, qui les fit jeter dans un obscur cachot, [où il leur] fit souffrir toutes sortes de tortures et finit par les condamner à mort. **46.** Tous ces tourmens, ni la vue d'une mort prochaine, n'ébranlent point le courage des glorieux captifs, ils savent que le royaume du ciel souffre violence et qu'à ce prix seul, on peut le conquérir, témoin le divin Sauveur qui nous dit à tous dans la personne de ses disciples: il me fallait endurer tous ces maux pour entrer en possession de ma gloire17. **47.** Cette pieuse pensée les rend tout rayonnans de joie dans les fers, et leur fait espérer que, comme saint Thomas, ils verseront leur sang pour le Seigneur; ils le prient continuellement et ne lui demandent d'autre faveur. [31] **48.** Dieu les exauce et, content du sacrifice de leurs coeurs, il ne veut voir en eux que des martyrs de la charité. Aussi les délivre-t-il de la mort, et les glorifie-t-il en présence de celui qui, aux yeux du monde, les avait couverts d'opprobre. **49.** Le fils du roi barbare tombe subitement malade, sa mort paraît inévitable, **50.** son épouse voit que le ciel punit dans la personne de son fils la cruauté du père. Elle le conjure de rétracter ses ordres sanguinaires elle court elle-même dans le cachot pour annoncer aux innocents captifs leur délivrance, et prie Grégoire de demander à Dieu la guérison de son fils, son unique consolation. **51.** Grégoire, plus jaloux de leur procurer la vie de la grâce que celle du corps demande à Dieu le prodige [32] l'ayant obtenu, il fait connaître à la mère et au fils celui qui tient entre ses mains la vie et la mort des hommes les ayant instruits de sa doctrine, il les régénéra tous deux dans les eaux du baptême, et ils furent fidèles à en observer les obligations. [33]

APPENDIX 2

ANANIAS OF SHIRAK, *GEOGRAPHY* (Ašxarhacʻoycʻ)

Ed. Hewsen, 1992, 74A–75A.

35. The thirty-fifth country of Asia is India, east of Ariana and Scythia by the Imaeus Mountains. [It extends] from there as far as the Aemodae Mountains and the border of China, and divided into two parts east and west of the River Ganges. Ptolemy shows seven rivers here, each with its own name, which, uniting near the Gymnosophists, are called the Phison. There are three rivers rising among the Gymnosophists: first, the Diamunas River, then Ganges and then the Sarabus, witch, uniting is called the Imoyn. To the right of the River Indus ara fifty-seven nations. Here are found *heašir, dahanak* and excellent tin. The Gymnosophists feed only on fruit, rice, and sugar; they are called the Shaman and Brahmin nation by the Persians. They abstain from women and meat and in the morning, they worship the sun saying: "We believe you [to be God], but if there is any other superior to you, to him do we render our work-ship." Here are found animals witch the Persians call *šarpašank*. There are sev-enty-two nations east to Granges River [extending] as far as the land of Sinae. Here are other districts called the "Golden" and the "Silver." In their capital are found crows, white parrots, and bearded roosters. Two other districts are also called the "Golden" and the "Silver" and another, the "Copper" district. Here are found elephants and tigers which they say are subdued by magic and are as fast as the wind. Here are found peper, and aromatics [such as] *boačaṙs, axiri-boyek, goziboyek, agisboyeak, cassia, dwałak, šahaworar, kʻakołak,* witch eats camphor, sandal, nayiboyeak, several medicines and bažark, the rat called bēšmašk, which eats dealdy roots called *biš* from which antidotes are made ; and large ants in the places where gold-dust is found. Here is an animal [called the] *sawarsan* which can kill an elephant with its tongue and then carry it on a kind of hook which it has on its back, and when it hears any animal cry out, it ejects blood. The unicorn is also found and griffons, which come from the Sinae, are raised here in iron cages. They say that the *pʻgrē* attacks the griffon and, carried away by fury, both throw themselves into the sea and drown. They say that there are savage peoples here with hard, arrow-proof skins and *Gndandiarkʻ* who are half, or at least one-third, non-Indian; and seven [other people]. The *Dēpuxkʻ* [are found here] and the *Spahlabalora*, i.e., red water hyacinths; then *Čʻngłibalos* where *grtapoz* is found and the musk ox resem-bling, in form and size, a four-month old goat except for the teeth which they say, are like those of a fox, [and which] eats mice. Some say, wrongly, that [the musk sack] is the testicles, while others say that the musk [sack] is in front of the testicles. There is another province called *Kalah* where the horned ass is found. Another province is *Hakʻer* where there is teakwood, which is an imperishable wood, and ginger. There are several islands here: [those of] the warrior peoples and the cannibals near the island of [*Ia*] *batiu* whose capital

city abounds in gold and silver [and which is located in] the Green Sea, where, according to the Greeks, three kinds of aloes are found: one is called *ningre* which is black in color and [sometimes] yellow and resembles a sharp and porous comb. It costs five, six and even seven *dahekan* per liter. The second, called [aloes] of Camtʿ is black, and [which smells?] like resinous pine, 96 and [which being] heavy, costs four *dahekan*. The third is called [aloes] of Kalah. Yellowish and lightweight, a liter costs three *dahekan*.

[36] The thirty-sixth country, Taprobane, is a large island of India and the largest island in the entire world. From north to south is 1,100 miles long and from east to west 150 miles wide. It lies beyond India and is surrounded by the Indian Sea. Rice is found there which is [a kind of] millet; ginger; beryl, hyacinth and other precious stones, and also much gold and silver and elephants and tigers. It has two mountains in the center, one called Galiba, 106 which is the source of two rivers, and the other called Malaea, which is the source of three rivers. Here are found imperishable woods, ginger, fine pearls, and the most precious stones. There are two cities, they say, 150 miles apart. One is called Manakor and one called Royan. 108 Between them is a mountain named Gaylase from which flows a river in which the most precious stones are found. There are twelve nations in the north who always dress their hair like that of women. Two of these nations are called the *Hacʿacankʿ* and the *Hacʿainkʿ*.

In the south the plains are used for pasturing elephants. They say that one nation which dwells in this country is made up of women and that at a certain time of the year dogs come among the elephants and have intercourse with the women who give birth to twins, one [male] puppy and the other a [human] girl. The sons cross the river to their fathers while the girls remain with their mothers. But I believe that this is just an allegory for they say the same about the Amazons in the Book of Alexander [the Great]. The allegory means that they are a quick-turning (?) people. Ptolemy says that there are temples of the moon in the southern extremity of the island. There are 1,378 other islands around Taprobane, some inhabited and others uninhabited but of which [only] nineteen names [are known to us]. The Equator crosses the south of this large island.[100]

ENDNOTES

1   Alexis de Menezes, *La Messe des anciens chrestiens dicts de S. Thomas... repur-gée des erreurs et blasphèmes du nestorianisme*, y premise une Remonstrance catholique aux peuples du Pays-bas, Anvers, de H. Verdussen, 1609, 139 pages ; *Synodo Diocesano da Igreia e Bispado de Angamale. dos antigos chris-taos de Sam Thome das Serras do Malauar das partes da India Oriental ce-lebrado pello Reuerendissimo Senhor Dom Frey Aleixo de Menezes Arcebispo Metropolitano de Goa, Primaz da India et partes Orientaes*, Coimbra, Officina de Diogo Gomez Loureyro, impressor da Universidade, 1606, 124 pages; *Historia ecclesiae Malabaricae cum Diamperitana synodo apud Indos Nestorianos, S. Thomae Christianos nuncupatos*, Roma, Ex Typographya Hieronymi Mainardi, 1745.

2   Laboubna, tr. Destrumeaux, 1997, *in Christian Apocryphal Writings*, I, 1485–1525 for a French translation.

3   Laboubna, ed. Alishan, 1868, 45, l. 3-5.

4   Laboubna, ed. Phillips, 1876, 96, l. 8-9 = tr. Destrumeaux, 1997, 1521.

5   Laboubna, ed. Alishan, 1868, 45, l. 3-5 = tr. Emine, 1867, 318.

6   Laboubna, ed Phillips, 1876, 56 = tr. Destrumeaux, 1997, 1489.

7   *Thaddeus'Acts*, ed. Lipsius, 1891, 273-278 = tr. Palmer, 2005, 651–660.

8   *Life of Mesrop Machtot's*, VII, 1.

9   *Life of Mesrop Machtot's*, VII, 2.

10 *Book of Letters*, ed. Bogharian (Połarean), 1994, 51: *Letter of Acacius of Melitena to the Catholicos Sahak I*; 142: *Treaty of the Catholicos Yovhannes Mandakouni*; 360: *Letter of the Catholicos Abraham I Ałbat'anec'i*; 383: *Answer by Vrtanēs Kertoł to (lords) Albanians*; 447 and 509: *Letters of Step'anos Siwnec'i*; 328: *Letter of the vardapet Sahak Merut to Armeniens lords*; 589 (= ACA, X, 2009, § 61, 670): *Answer of the Metropolit of Sebastia to the Catholicos Khatchik I (Xač'ik Ier Aršaruni)*; 646: *Answer of the vartapet Georg to John the Patriarch of the Syrians*.

11 Komitas, ed. ACA, IV, 2005, § 56-57, 91; § 170, 115 (cf. Գիրք Հարցնոյց / Rule ≠ ed. Uluhogian, 1993); § 180, 323; § 226, 326 (Thomas and Barthelemy).

12 Gregory Magistros, *Poetry*, ՊԿ, ACA XVI, 2012, 177 and *Letters* no 9, ACA XVI, 2012, 235, § 264 (after Jn X, 26-27). With mention of the mission to the Indians, § 100, 38 (same volume) and Grigor of Narek, commentary of "ով է դա," ACA, XII, 2008, § 115, 894. See too Hovsēp Anapadakan, (memorial) § 21, 585, ACA, IV, 2005 ; Step'anos Siwnec'i, § 214, 6-10 (on Jn 20, 24-25), ACA, VII, 2007; Zakaria Jagec'i, § 174 (17), ACA IX, 2008, 294 ; T 'ovma Arc'rouni, *Histories*, chap. 6, § 49, ACA, XI, 2010, 90.

13 Cf. Yevadian, 2008, 357-370.

14 Agathange, ed. Tēr-Mkrtč'ean – Kanayeanc', 1909–1980, 355; tr. Thomson, 2001, 221.

15 ACA, VII, 2007, § 82, 227.

16 Socrates Scholasticus, tr. Thomson, 9–11.

17 Socrates Scholasticus, tr. Thomson, 12–26.

18 Socrates Scholasticus, tr. Thomson, 111.

19 Movses Khorenac'i, tr. Thomson, 2006, II, 27-34, 162-173.

20   Stepanos Asołik, ed. Malxaseanc', 1885, 45; tr. Dulaurier, 1883, 38.
21   Stepanos Asołik, ed. Malxaseanc', 1885, 46; ACA, XV, 2012, § 116, 667; tr. Dulaurier, 1883, 39.
22   Stepanos Asołik, ed. Malxaseanc', 1885, 20; tr. Dulaurier, 1883, 28.
23   Stepanos Asołik, ed. Malxaseanc', 1885, 213; tr. Dulaurier, 1883, 90.
24   Book I, chap. 5 (6), ed. Tarminian–Melikian, 2006, 55; ACA, XI, 2010, chap. 6, 90; tr. Brosset, 1874, 40.
25   ACA, XI, 2010, chap. 6, § 12, 376, tr. Boisson-Chenorhokian, 2004, chap. VI, 88.
26   *Armenians apocryphals*, ed. Tcherakian (Č'rak'ean), 1896 and 1904.
27   *Armenians apocryphals,* tr. Leloir, 1986-1992.
28   *Armenians apocryphals,* tr. Leloir, II, 1992, 531-646.
29   Garitte, 1971, 151-195.
30   *Armenians apocryphals,* tr. Leloir II, 1992, 539-541.
31   The text we are interested in was printed on 91b to 94a of the Constantinople edition and in the booklet *PO* 5, 3 (1910), 420-426
32   *Armenian synaxarion of Ter Israel*, ed.-tr. Bayan, 1910, V, 3, (29) 421, *cf.* Yevadian, 2011, 101–106.
33   *Armenian synaxarion of Ter Israel*, ed.-trad. Bayan, 1910, V, 3, (29) 421 [77].
34   *Synaxarion,* ed. Petrosyan, 2008-2010.
35   *Synaxarion,* ed. Petrosyan, 2010; 17 Hori, 62–71.
36   *Cf.* Herodotus, *Histories,* v. 52-54, viii, 98 and *The Persian Royal Road System,* 1994.
37   Strabon, *Geography,* XIV, 2, 29, ed. Meineke, III, 1913, 930.
38   Boulnois, 2001, 48–49.
39   Credit: Yevadian, 2018, 13.
40   Boulnois, 2001, 129–136.
41   Boulnois, 2001, 251.
42   Credit: Yevadian, 2018, 19.
43   Credit: Sources d'Arménie, 2018.
44   Strabon, *Geography,* XI, XIV, 4, ed.-tr. Lassère, 1981, 122.
45   Yevadian, 2007, 142–147.
46   *Acta Andrae,* cap. 2, ed.-tr. Prieur, 1989, 685.
47   The question of Bartholomew's itinerary should be considered if the current reassessment of Thomas's Acts was confirmed. This point remains open.
48   Credit: Yevadian, 2018, 19.
49   Sozomenus, II, 8, 2, tr. Festugière, 1983, 264–265.
50   For the western world, see Tchouhadjian, 2011.
51   *Zachary the Rhetor,* ed. Brooks, 1919, 217 of the Syriac text.
52   Bar Hebraeus, *Chroniques ecclésiastiques,* III, 280-282, *cf.* Grousset, 1965, 244–246.
53   Dauvillier, 1975, 5.
54   *Ašxarhac'oyc',*tr. Hewsen, 1992, § 35–36, 74A-75A.
55   *Armenian Geographical Notices,* § 20, ed. Venise, 1882, 312.
56   Seth, (1937) 2005, 612: "Fully seven centuries prior to the landing of Vasco de Gama on the Malabar Coast on that memorable day, the 20th of May 1498

A.D. an enterprising Armenian merchant, Mar Thomas by name, had landed on the same coast in the year A.D. 780 when one Sheo Ram was the native ruler of Cranganore, and in whose eyes he found great favor, which resulted in his amassing considerable riches by trading in muslins and spices, his main object in seeking the Indian shores." The date given by Mesrop Seth, is false but the factual elements are interesting.

57 In Silva Rego, III, 1950, doc. 112, 547.

58 João de Barros and Diogo do Couto, 1777, chap. 5, 282–283.

59 De Sousa, II, 1710, 113 and 115, several others mentions to Armenians.

60 The Muslims rarely moved populations that did not belong to their religion. They'd rather found military colonies, so as to control the territories. Similarly, they had itinerant Muslim tribes settle down in Christian countries in order to increase their control over these territories.

61 I think Jacob Kollaparambil's, Kollaparambil, 1992, recent analysis is questionable for several reasons. On one side, the Southern Babylonia place-names he identifies in the names of Thomas Cana and in those of his relatives do not give any precision concerning the ethnic origin of these Christians. On the contrary, mixing peoples was for the Sassanid governments an efficient way to control the population, as was the case during the war against Armenia in 370. Finally, Babylonia was one of the primary centers for rabbinic Judaism, so that the establishment of a Christian community in the early period of Christianity would have been a cause for problems.

62 Ammianus Marcellinus, ed. and tr. Galletier, 1984, V, XXVII, XII, 11, 142.

63 Credit: Yevadian, 2011, 67.

64 *Buzandaran*, IV, 55, trad. Émine, 1869, 273 et trad. Garsoïan, 1989, 173–174.

65 *Buzandaran*, IV, 55, tr. Émine, 1869, 275 and tr. Garsoïan, 1989, 176.

66 Yevadian, 2011, *Life of Gregory of Tallard*, § 27-29, 102.

67 Yevadian, 2011, *Life of Gregory of Tallard*, § 31-34.

68 Yevadian, 2011, *Life of Gregory of Tallard*, § 35-36.

69 Yevadian, 2011, *Life of Gregory of Tallard*, § 37.

70 Yevadian, 2011, *Life of Gregory of Tallard*, § 38 and 34.

71 Yevadian, 2011, 104-105.

72 Credit: Yevadian, 2011, 71.

73 Yevadian, 2011, *Life of Gregory of Tallard*, § 52, 70 and 102, for analysis.

74 Credit: Yevadian, 2011, 60.

75 Yovhannes Drasxanakertci, trad. Boisson-Chenorhokian, 2003, chap. XX, 153.

76 Yovhannes Drasxanakertci, trad. Boisson-Chenorhokian, 2003, chap. XX, 154-155.

77 *Idem*, 155-156.

78 *ACA* V, 2005, 1287-1292.

79 The so-called posthumous canons are published in *ACA*, V, 2005, 1293-1300 and about Théodosiopolis' canons, see Sahak III, tr. van Esbroeck, 1995, 439-444.

80 "Բացայայտութիւն համաձայն աստուածաբանութեան հոգելից Հարցն սրբոց ըստ առաքելասահման աւանդիցն եկեղեցւոյ Քրիստոսի,

հանդերձ հաւատարանութեամբն ճշմարիտ ուղղափառ դաւանութեան Հայաստանեայց, աստացեալ սրբոյ վարդապետին Սահակայ հայոց կաթուղիկոսի եւ մէջի թարգմանչի ընդդէմ երկաբնակաց նեստորականացն," *ACA*, IX, 2008, 373.

81 *Letter's book*, ed. Izmireantz, 1901 ; ed. Połarean (Bogharian), 1994 and Léon Melikset-Bek, "Un essai de correction des erreurs de copie dans quelques parties du Livre des Lettres», *Sion*, 1961, 35, pp. 46–49, *In Armenien*; Michel Van Esbroeck, "Le discours de Catholicos Sahak III en 6914 et quelques documents arméniens annexes au Quinisexte, *Kanonika, Pontificio Istituto Orientale*, VI, 1995, 323-463.

About the discussion on the attribution ot this texte Mᵍʳ Norayr Połarean (Bogharian), *La démonstration du Vartapet Sahak*, Presses du patriarcat arménien de Jérusalem, 1993, 110 pages, cf. *ACA*, IX, 2008, pp. 373–423; Igor Dorfmann-Lazarev, *Arméniens et Byzantins à l'époque de Phostius: deux débats théologiques après le triomphe de l'orthodoxie*, Louvain, Peeters, CSCO, 609, Subsidia, 117, 2004, 90, n. 209; Jean-Pierre Mahé, *REArm*, NS, 1994-1995, 25, 472–475 [Review of Sahak III, trad. van Esbroeck, 1995]; van Esbroeck, 2003, *Armenology today and Prospects for its developpement, (15-20 septembre 2003), Abstracts of papers*, Erevan 2003, 226; Garsoïan Nina, *Interregnum, introduction to a Study on the Formation of Armenia Identity*, Louvain, Peeters, CSCO, 640, *Subsidia*, 127, XVIII-195 pages, pp. 86–87 and 135.

About the patristics quotations: Yervantz Ter-Minassiants, *Die armenische Kirche in ihren Beziehungen zu den Syrischen Kirchen bis zum Ende des 13. Jahrhunderts*, Leipzig, Hinrichs, 1904, 12–212 pages, pp. 136–141; Jordan Hermann, "Armenische Irenäus-Fragmente," *Texte und Untersuchungen*, 1913, XXXVI, fasc. 3, 222 pages; Nerses Akinian, "Denys d'Alexandrie, Lettre sur la pénitence à Merouzan évêque des Arméniens.," *Handes Amsoya*, 1949, 36, 59–78; Bernard Outtier, "La version arménienne du commentaire des Psaumes de Théodoret," *Revue des études arméniennes*, N.S., XII, 1977, 169–180 ; Michel Van Esbroeck, "Citations apollinaristes conservées en arménien dans la Lettre de Sahak III, Dzoroporetsi (691)," *OCP*, 1994, 60, 41–67.

82 Yevadian, 2013, pp. 157–159.

83 *Letter's book*, ed. Izmireantz J., Tiflis, 1901, 234–240; Sahak III, tr. van Esbroeck, 1995, 367–354 and ACA, IX, 2008, 373–423.

84 Sahak III, tr. van Esbroeck, 1995, 347.

85 Sahak III, tr. van Esbroeck, 1995, 347-348.

86 Sahak III, *Speech*, § 67, ACA, IX, 2008, 411-412 and tr. van Esbroeck, 1995, § 67, 411–412.

87 Asołik, ed. Malxassianc', 1885, 102-103; tr. Dulaurier, 1883, 131-132 *cf.* Yevadian, 2008, 226–227 for an overview.

88 Fortescure, 1913, 418 and Gulbenkian, 1995, 105.

89 "Thalassus priest and abbot of the venerable monastery of the Armenians," Mansi, X, 904, cf. Sansterre, 1983, 10.

90 Settipani, 2006, 224–231.

[91] Gregory of Tours, *History of Francs*, X, 24, = *Libri historiarum X, MGH, SS rer. Merov.* I, 1, ed. Krusch Bruno, 515-516; Grégoire de Tours, *Histoire des Francs*, tr. Latouche, 1975, 302-303.

[92] Perrier, 2011.

[93] ACA, IX, 2008, 412.

[94] *Book of Letters*, ed. Połarean, 1994, 321-322.

[95] "Եթովպիա մեծ եւ փոքր մինչեւ ցծովն Հնդկաց ի նոյն Հաստատեալ Հաստ", ACA, X, 2009, § 1075–1077, 558; § 1093, 559 (with the mention of Thomas); 1099, 560; to complete with Timotʻēos vardapet (10th century), ACA, X, 2009, § 262, 919.

[96] Liogier Raphael, *Jésus Bouddha d'Occident*, Paris, Calmann-Lévy, 1999, 273.

[97] Letter of Andrew of Perugia: "*Est quaedam magna ciuitas iuxta mare Occeanum, que uocatur lingua persica Zayton, in qua ciuitate una diues domina Armena ecclesia erexit pulcram satis et grandem.*" ed. A. Van den Wyngaert, *Sinica franciscana*, 1929, I, 374 and Dauvillier, 1975, 9.

[98] *Relatio*, ed. A. Van den Wyngaert, *Sinica franciscana*, 1929, I, 437.

[99] Bernard, 1935, 29.

[100] *Ašxarhacʻoycʻ*, trad. Hewsen, 1992, 74A–75A.

INDEX

A

Acta Thomae 15, 21, 30, 53, 66, 83, 86, 147

Acts of Judas Thomas (AJT) 8, 9, 10, 20, 22, 42, 50, 86, 149, 158, 159, 161, 170

Acts of Thomas v, vi, 8, 24, 31, 36, 37, 38, 39, 40, 42, 43, 44, 45, 49, 52, 56, 57, 66, 70, 78, 79, 80, 84, 89, 90, 94, 95, 116, 131, 132, 133, 134, 135, 136, 140, 142, 143, 145, 146, 147, 159, 161, 164, 167, 169, 176, 177, 178, 180, 183, 188, 193, 195, 196, 200, 201, 206, 209, 218, 258

Adam 102

Adolf von Harnack 69

Afghanistan 11, 55, 57, 65, 70, 84, 116, 179

Afras 62, 63

Alaha Nayan 96

Alexander the Great 5, 74, 75

Alexandria 4, 5, 6, 7, 10, 12, 13, 16, 25, 28, 34, 55, 67, 77, 136, 152, 178, 183, 192, 193, 206, 234, 236

Alexandria of Egypt 206

Amman Koil 103

Ananias de Shirak 239

ancient folk songs 89, 91

ancient songs 89, 90, 91, 92, 99, 101, 115, 118, 119, 120

Ancient Songs of the Syrian Christians of Malabar 90

Andrew 8, 134, 162, 163, 189, 197, 230, 237, 269

Andrew' Acts 237

Anpan Misiha 96

Anpattukal 95

anthamcharth 101, 102

Antioch 41, 91, 97, 98, 105, 106, 180, 182, 189, 192, 228, 234

Antiochean Rite 123

Apocryphal vi, 31, 146, 161, 171, 218, 219, 225, 226, 256, 265

Apostle v, vi, 14, 15, 20, 21, 22, 24, 25, 27, 28, 29, 30, 31, 32, 33, 35, 37, 39, 41, 44, 46, 48, 49, 50, 52, 53, 54, 55, 60, 65, 66, 67, 69, 70, 75, 77, 78, 79, 80, 81, 82, 83, 84, 85, 86, 87, 104, 107, 109, 114, 116, 117, 120, 121, 125, 132, 133, 135, 137, 140, 143, 144, 147, 159, 160, 162, 163, 164, 165, 168, 170, 172, 185, 188, 197, 207, 209, 225, 226, 227, 229, 233, 258

Apostle Thomas vi, 14, 15, 20, 21, 22, 24, 25, 27, 28, 29, 30, 31, 33, 37, 39, 41, 44, 46, 48, 49, 50, 53, 54, 55, 65, 66, 67, 69, 70, 75, 77, 78, 81, 82, 83, 84, 86, 116, 121, 132, 133, 135,

137, 140, 144, 147, 160, 162, 163, 164, 168, 170, 172, 233, 258

Apostolate of St. Thomas v, vi, 9, 11, 12, 16, 25, 29, 38, 53, 96, 100

apostolic mission 40, 69, 77, 161, 209

AR/ Aramaic 3, 11, 30, 135, 146, 177, 178, 180, 181, 182, 183, 191, 194, 195, 197, 199, 200, 203, 205, 206, 207, 208, 209, 210, 211, 214, 223, 224, 226, 230

Archaeological evidence 10, 18

archives viii, 120

Arivan paraven 138

Armenian Thaddeus' martyrdom 227

arrival of Knaithomma 97

arrival of St. Thomas 10, 41

ARSI, Goa 101, 128

B

Babylonian Origin of the Southists among St. Thomas Christians 91

baptism 46, 105, 106, 109, 114, 135, 144, 165, 166, 186, 194, 197, 228

Baron Textor of Ravisi 60

Barthelomew 171, 197

Bar Thoma 13

Barygaza 6, 9, 13, 14, 16, 31

Beas River 4

Bharuch 29, 55, 65, 67

biblical stories 98

bishop 18, 21, 101, 117, 118, 119, 121, 122, 123, 135, 136, 137, 144, 164, 221, 238, 239, 242, 244, 249, 250, 252, 255

bishop Mar Youseph 101

blessing 106, 107, 202

Brahmin 23, 62, 93, 103, 107, 134, 136, 139, 143, 157, 161, 239, 263

Brahmins 23, 24, 40, 62, 94, 95, 107, 111, 136, 139, 141, 157, 158, 161, 163

Brief History of the Suriani Church of Kerala Vanchippattu 98

Burthey 60, 67

C

Caliph Abd al-Malig 247

Carmelite missionaries 46

catechesis 60, 98

Catholicos 97, 106, 112, 117, 118, 119, 228, 229, 246, 247, 249, 250, 251, 252, 254, 259, 265, 268

Catholicos and historian Yovhannēs Drasxanakertc'i (899–929) 229

Catholicos, Khatchik I Arsharouni (973-992) 251

Catholicos Komitas (618-628) 228, 254

Catholicos of Bagdad 97, 106

Catholicos Sahak III Dzoraporesti (667-703) Bishop of Rotakk 247

Catholicos Yovhannēs Awjnec'i 229

Chaldean prelate 97

Chandragupta Maurya 4, 67

Chang'an (Xi'an) 233

Chanthamcharth 92, 101, 102

chantham charthatte 102

Chanthamcharth song 102

Chathurvethimangalam 103

Chayal 91, 107, 114, 138

Chera Kingdom 134, 150

Cherakon 110
Cheraman Perumal 96, 104
China 17, 55, 56, 63, 64, 106, 134,
        135, 152, 153, 161, 179, 186,
        188, 193, 197, 199, 200, 202,
        203, 204, 205, 206, 207, 209,
        212, 213, 214, 215, 223, 224,
        226, 232, 234, 237, 239, 252,
        258, 263
Chinam 97, 99, 109
Chinnamalai 103, 104
Christ vii, ix, 1, 2, 3, 4, 7, 14, 25, 26,
        28, 46, 47, 57, 60, 62, 63, 66,
        76, 92, 93, 96, 97, 107, 109,
        112, 136, 143, 149, 162, 163,
        164, 165, 169, 180, 182, 190,
        195, 199, 203, 204, 209, 212,
        218, 227, 228, 232, 247, 248
Christian ancient folk songs 89, 91
Christian church 162
Christian community 12, 22, 24,
        26, 42, 46, 83, 84, 96, 117,
        119, 120, 124, 145, 153, 155,
        156, 158, 159, 185, 267
Christian faith 8, 22, 43, 84, 93, 222
Christianity 8, 9, 12, 13, 14, 15, 23,
        24, 25, 29, 31, 32, 35, 37, 40,
        41, 42, 44, 45, 46, 47, 48, 49,
        50, 51, 52, 53, 54, 56, 65, 69,
        71, 76, 78, 81, 84, 85, 86, 87,
        89, 96, 112, 116, 117, 119,
        122, 125, 126, 134, 146, 147,
        153, 157, 158, 208, 216, 224,
        238, 241, 242, 244, 250, 258,
        267
Christianity in India 25, 29, 31, 32,
        37, 40, 41, 42, 44, 47, 48, 50,
        51, 52, 53, 54, 85, 86, 87, 89,
        126, 146, 241, 258
Christian settlements 150
Christians of Kerala ix, 22, 23, 24,
        89
Chunkom church 98

Churches of the Law of Thomas 99
Church in Kerala 86, 98, 214
church of Edessa 169
colony of Jewish Christians 101
colophon 95, 229
copper plates 96, 119, 126
Coromandal coast 150
C.P.T. Winkworth 62, 63
Cranganore 5, 23, 43, 46, 93, 101,
        116, 120, 121, 153, 241, 267
Cross of Chunkom 98
Cross of Persian style 103
Cunningham 10, 11, 12, 30, 59, 65,
        66, 67

D

Darius I 4, 30, 74, 223, 233, 234
Dawson 59
death of St. Thomas 97, 103
Diamper 126, 127, 133, 146, 242
Discovery and Transfer to Armenia
        of Thomas's mortal remains
        (BHO 1224) 232
Documenta Indica 101, 127, 128
Dravidians 170
Dr. Jacob Kollaparambil 91, 94,
        100, 101, 104, 126, 267
Dr. Jacob Vellian 94, 101
Dr. P.J. Thomas 36, 46, 94, 96, 146
Dr. Scaria Zacharia 91
Dr. Sr. Deepa SJC 91
Dr. Thomas Koonammakkal v, 95,
        131
Dukrana 81, 87, 98, 107

E

East Syriac Church 78, 81, 135
Edakkattu church 99
Edessa 3, 8, 9, 18, 20, 21, 22, 26, 37,
        39, 40, 41, 44, 45, 49, 50, 78,

79, 86, 87, 117, 143, 145, 147, 164, 165, 167, 168, 169, 201, 204, 206, 215, 223, 224, 226, 227, 229, 230, 233, 255

Edessa and the merchant 165

Empire 4, 5, 6, 16, 17, 20, 23, 27, 28, 32, 50, 56, 72, 76, 85, 116, 117, 119, 163, 177, 197, 207, 214, 215, 222, 259

Ends of the Earth 2, 3, 72, 73, 74, 76

Ephrem vi, 9, 18, 20, 26, 32, 39, 77, 78, 146, 161, 163, 164, 165, 167, 168, 169, 170, 172

episcopal activities of St. Thomas 99

Ettuthira Vattakkali 99

Eucharist 135, 198

Europe 6, 8, 28, 31, 47, 72, 84, 89, 238, 241

Eve 102

F

Fathers of the church 35, 36, 45, 161, 170

feast of Dukrana of St. Thomas 98

five Chaldean bishops in Kerala 98

folkloristic 91

folk songs v, 89

Fr. Antonio Gouvea 89

Fr. Bernard Thoma (Alencheril) 23, 33, 52, 91, 92, 95, 100

French 40, 49, 50, 60, 66, 158, 183, 215, 216, 217, 218, 223, 226, 230, 232, 242, 245, 248, 257, 265

Fr. Francis Dionisio, SJ 89, 101

Fr. Mathew Vattakkalathil 90

Fr. Thomas J. Mundackal 104

Fr. Wicki, SJ 36, 101, 127, 128

G

garden of jasmine 98, 107

Gaspar Correa 19, 34, 242

GK/ Greek 3, 4, 7, 8, 9, 11, 13, 15, 16, 17, 28, 29, 30, 45, 56, 57, 65, 74, 93, 134, 141, 142, 143, 144, 145, 147, 150, 152, 161, 163, 177, 182, 183, 194, 201, 204, 205, 208, 209, 210, 215, 220, 221, 224, 226, 228, 229, 230, 232, 233, 236, 238, 239, 248, 253, 257

goddess Amman 103

Gondophares 9, 11, 12, 13, 14, 15, 16, 56, 57, 58, 59, 65, 66, 84, 184, 186, 207, 214

Gondophernes 70, 79, 84, 85

Goriun 228

granite sheet 96

Greco-Roman 5, 7, 176, 183

Greek mythology 93

Gregory of Narek 251

Gregory of Tallard 242, 243, 245, 246, 260, 267

Gudnaphar 9, 10, 12, 131, 142, 143

H

Haugue 62

Havan 93

haymavouk (synaxarion) 232

head churches 107

Hebrew 3, 7, 15, 25, 111, 153, 162, 171, 177, 179, 181, 183, 184, 194, 196, 200, 207, 208, 211, 220, 223, 224, 255

Helioforum 131, 133, 143

Hellenistic 5

historians 7, 8, 16, 18, 26, 45, 55, 61, 69, 70, 96, 156, 195, 250

historical and linguistic auxilium 91

Historical songs 90, 97

Historical Sources on the Knanites 91, 101, 127, 128

Historiography v, 35, 52, 53, 69

History vii, 4, 27, 28, 31, 32, 37, 38, 41, 42, 47, 48, 49, 50, 52, 53, 54, 70, 74, 85, 86, 87, 98, 125, 126, 128, 154, 159, 171, 228, 229, 243, 251, 253, 254, 255, 258, 269

Holy book 97

Holy See of Etchmiadzin 233

Holy Spirit 3, 4, 62, 73, 97, 135, 176, 194, 196, 197

Hydaspes river 4

I

iconographical 93

Ilakka 99, 109

immigration 97, 118

immortality 93

inculturization 92

Indian Apostolate 11, 12, 29, 38, 53, 89

Indian Church History 41, 53, 54, 86, 171

Indian Vedic representations 93

Indo-Parthians 56, 58

Indus river 74

Innu nee njangale kaivitto Marone 97

inscription 10, 11, 12, 14, 21, 56, 57, 58, 59, 60, 61, 62, 63, 67, 85, 244, 261

invocatory hymn 92, 93, 99, 103

Islamabad 13

J

Jacobite 41, 101, 116

Jacob of Serugh 77, 148, 163, 164, 169, 170

Jerusalem 1, 3, 7, 14, 16, 56, 65, 72, 73, 97, 105, 115, 119, 155, 162, 176, 179, 182, 184, 187, 188, 189, 190, 191, 192, 193, 194, 196, 197, 198, 205, 211, 212, 214, 215, 218, 220, 221, 222, 230, 241, 249, 254

Jesus and Abgar 226

Jesus Christ 1, 2, 3, 4, 7, 66, 76, 93, 97, 109, 112, 143, 195, 199, 203

Jewish Diaspora 117

Jornada 46, 54, 159

Joseph iii, vii, ix, x, 9, 15, 29, 36, 43, 53, 63, 67, 72, 93, 118, 125, 127, 146, 165, 222, 232, 256, 257

Judas Iscariot 4, 93

K

Kadapur 133, 137

Kaipuzha church 99

Kalakanchi 94

Kali, the Hindu goddess 23, 39, 44, 66, 94, 95

Kaliyamman temple 103

Kaliyar 103

Kallucherry 98

Kalyanapadangal 99

Karoshti script 11, 15

kavyas 95

Kepa 134, 135, 136, 137

Keralathile Kristheeya Sahityam 96

Khazars 247

Kingdom of Parthia 234

King of Chozha Mandala 93

Knaithomman 92, 96, 101

Knanaya community 23, 92, 101, 118, 119, 120, 122, 123, 124

Knanaya Jacobite Bhadrasanam of Chingavanam 101

Knanites 91, 92, 97, 101, 102, 120, 121, 122, 123, 124, 127, 128
Kodungalloor/ Kodungallur 14, 17, 22, 24, 41, 43, 91, 96, 97, 101, 104, 105, 106, 107, 117, 118, 120, 125, 150, 151, 152, 153, 155, 157, 158
Kokkamangalam 22, 91, 107, 108, 150, 158
Kollam 91, 95, 107, 134, 137, 138, 141, 150, 151, 153, 154, 157, 158, 159
kolvilakku 102
kosmos 72, 73
Kottakkayal 91, 107, 108
Kottayam Cheriya Pally 98
Kottayam Edakkattu 99
Kuravilangad 133, 137, 140, 157
Kushans 12, 16, 31, 56, 184, 185, 186

L

Laboubna 226, 227, 256, 265
Law of Thomas 62, 97, 98, 99
literary work 10, 94, 95
Lord Srikrishna 93
lotus 61

M

Madrashe 165
Mahodayapuram 93, 151
Mahosa 13, 93
Mailanchippattu 102
Mailanchiyiteel 92, 102
Makkam 97, 99, 106, 109
Makothevar Pattanam 95
Malabar vii, 5, 6, 15, 16, 18, 21, 22, 24, 33, 38, 39, 40, 41, 42, 43, 44, 46, 47, 49, 50, 52, 59, 63, 67, 84, 86, 89, 90, 91, 101, 104, 116, 118, 119, 121, 122, 123, 125, 126, 127, 150, 151, 152, 153, 157, 158, 159, 161, 195, 242, 266
Malabar Church 38, 41, 50, 86, 89, 101, 116, 157
Malabar Coast vii, 22, 42, 49, 116, 118, 266
Malacca 18, 99, 106, 206
Malanadu 99, 106, 109, 110, 111, 138
Malankara 101, 112, 116, 123, 135, 138, 145, 151
malayalamizing 92
Malayalam language 92
Malayalam Literature and Christians 94
Malayala Sahithyavum Kristianikalum 94
Malayalathe Suriyani Kristianikalute Purathanappattukal 90
Malyamkara 131, 141
manavala chekkanu 102
Manorama Press 101
Mar 20, 33, 39, 52, 63, 82, 92, 97, 101, 116, 118, 122, 123, 124, 125, 126, 127, 129, 140, 155, 157, 172, 215, 222, 267
Mar Abraham 97, 122
Margam 39, 44, 92
Margamkali 92, 94, 120, 126
Margam Kali 39, 44
Margamkali Attaprakaram 94, 126
Margamkalippattu 23, 90, 92, 93, 94, 95, 103
Marthoma 23, 42, 53, 95, 116, 122
Mar Thoma 33, 39, 52, 82, 129, 140, 155
Marthoma Christians 122
Marthomaparvam 94, 95
Marthomasleeha 89
Marthomasleeva 103

Marthommakristhyanikal 91

Marthomman 90, 91, 92, 97, 102, 103, 104, 105, 106, 108, 109, 110

marthommanvazhi 91

martyrdom 9, 20, 21, 22, 43, 65, 74, 79, 86, 91, 93, 104, 131, 135, 136, 142, 143, 144, 150, 162, 168, 179, 189, 191, 197, 200, 202, 203, 205, 208, 209, 213, 214, 215, 223, 227, 231, 237

Mary 3, 31, 67, 72, 98, 127, 155, 189, 190, 191, 192, 193, 205, 208, 211, 216, 222

Masson 11, 56

Mathura 9, 13, 56, 61, 67, 135

Maues 58

Maurya Empire 4

Mayilapur/ Mylapore 18, 19, 20, 21, 25, 26, 32, 33, 37, 38, 39, 40, 41, 43, 44, 45, 46, 53, 56, 61, 62, 63, 64, 78, 79, 80, 81, 83, 87, 91, 95, 97, 99, 103, 104, 105, 109, 120, 150, 156, 157, 158, 161, 167, 185, 200, 201, 202, 203, 204, 206, 209, 210, 214, 222, 223, 224

Mazdai 66, 86, 131, 135, 142, 143, 144, 162, 167, 172

Mediterranean 7, 16, 17, 28, 41, 64, 72, 73, 75, 76, 77, 151, 152, 207, 234, 245

Middle East 120, 124, 153

migration 41, 47, 115, 117, 118, 119, 124, 126, 140, 144, 150, 155, 156, 242

missionary activity of Knaithomma 97

missionary works of St. Peter 98

missionary works of St. Thomas 93

mosaic 93

Mount St. Thomas 103

Movses Khorents'i 229, 254

Munnam Malankara 101

mural 31, 56, 93

Muruga 93

Muziris 5, 6, 7, 14, 16, 17, 28, 29, 31, 32, 39, 45, 56, 101, 115, 125, 150, 151, 152, 153, 154, 155, 157, 188, 192, 197, 200, 201, 206, 222, 223, 226

Myalaporepattanam 104

N

Nallororossilam thannil Nagariyil 97

Nambudiri 23

Nanda Empire 4

Narayana Panan 96

Naredra Gumpasnon 95

Nayars 99

Nazrani 38, 45

Nedungatt 14, 18, 19, 20, 25, 30, 31, 32, 33, 34, 35, 36, 52, 60, 67, 85, 126, 127, 258

Nestorian 41, 50, 116, 126

Nilackal/ Nilakkel 22, 82, 138, 155, 156, 160

Niranam 22, 91, 107, 133, 137, 138, 140, 150, 151, 154, 155, 159, 160

Nisibis 18, 145, 164

Nobia 244

northern gate of Kodungallur temple 96

Numismatic Evidences v, 55

O

Octavian 5, 16, 27

oral tradition 45, 89, 91, 92, 95, 104, 131, 132, 146, 176, 177, 178, 183, 184, 195, 196, 202, 214, 216, 223

Oriental Research Institute and
    Manuscripts Library 104
Ormis 97, 106

P

Padre Alvaro Penteado 241
Padre Francisco de Sousa 242
Pahlavi 21, 61, 62
Paingolam 98
Pakalomattam 24, 131, 133, 157
Pakistan 8, 9, 10, 13, 26, 30, 41, 53,
    55, 57, 84, 244
Pala 98
Palayoor 150, 151, 157
Palestine 72, 176, 210, 220
Pallippattukal 95, 98
palm leaf texts 90
Palur 91, 107, 150, 157
Pamir 180, 201, 233, 234
Panan 96
Pananpattu 23, 90, 92, 96, 101, 116,
    120
Pananpattukal 96
Pandi 135, 138
Parangimalai 103
Paravur 140, 141, 150, 157
parayipetta panthirukula aithihyam
    96
Parichamuttukali 90, 99
Parthia 35, 49, 84, 116, 147, 149,
    159, 162, 163, 164, 169, 170,
    234, 237
Parvam 39
Pattala 10, 187, 188, 192, 198, 211
Pattanam 17, 64, 95
Pattanam excavations 64
Paul 8, 71, 72, 77, 91, 97, 105, 133,
    137, 163, 171, 213, 219, 230,
    243, 258, 260
pavata 102

peacock 93, 103, 105
Penpattukal 95
penquita 164, 169
performing art form 92, 95
Persian church 115, 116, 117, 119,
    121, 124
Peshwar 58
Placid Podipara 36, 38, 44
poetic fictional narration 93
previous studies 91
Prof. Babu Thomas 91
Ptolemaic Kingdom 5
P.U. Lukas 90, 98, 101, 103, 126,
    127
Punjab 4, 9, 11, 15, 30, 56, 57, 58,
    66, 74
Punnathura church 99
Purathanapattukal 120, 126, 127
Puthuppally 98, 99, 110

Q

qurbana 184, 194, 197, 209, 212

R

Raman Panan of Piravom 96
Rambanpattu 92, 94, 95, 144, 146
Ramban Pattu v, 44, 131, 154
Ramban Song 132
Rangapooja 99
Reinaud 11, 30, 56, 65
rite of puberty 101, 102
ritual bathe 102
River Periyar 17, 150
royal documents 96

S

Sagar 12, 59
Saint-Thomas monastery, Řešouni
    232
Sakas 58, 65, 66